THE TEXT OF THE APOSTOLOS IN
EPIPHANIUS OF SALAMIS

Society of Biblical Literature

The New Testament in the Greek Fathers

Edited by
Michael W. Holmes

Number 6

THE TEXT OF THE APOSTOLOS IN
EPIPHANIUS OF SALAMIS

Carroll D. Osburn

THE TEXT OF THE APOSTOLOS IN
EPIPHANIUS OF SALAMIS

Carroll D. Osburn

Society of Biblical Literature
Atlanta

THE TEXT OF THE APOSTOLOS IN EPIPHANIUS OF SALAMIS

Copyright © 2004 by the Society of Biblical Literature

All rights reserved. No part of this work may be reproduced or transmitted in any form or by any means, electronic or mechanical, including photocopying and recording, or by means of any information storage or retrieval system, except as may be expressly permitted by the 1976 Copyright Act or in writing from the publisher. Requests for permission should be addressed in writing to the Rights and Permissions Office, Society of Biblical Literature, 825 Houston Mill Road, Atlanta, GA 30329, USA.

Library of Congress Cataloging-in-Publication Data

Osburn, Carroll D.
  The text of the Apostolos in Epiphanius of Salamis / by Carroll D. Osburn.
     p. cm. — (New Testament in the Greek fathers ; no. 6)
  Includes bibliographical references (p.   ).
  ISBN 1-58983-139-X (paper binding : alk. paper)
  1. Epiphanius, Saint, Bp. of Constantia in Cyprus. 2. Bible. N.T.--Criticism, Textual. 3. Bible. N.T.—Quotations, Early. I. Title. II. Series.

BS1938.O73 2004
225.4'86—dc22
                                              2004020824

Printed in the United States of America
on acid-free paper

In honorem

MATTHEW BLACK

CONTENTS

Editor's Preface ix

Acknowledgements xi

Abbreviations xiii

Chapter 1: Epiphanius and the Text of the New Testament 1

Chapter 2: Epiphanius' Text and Apparatus 23

Chapter 3: Methodology of Textual Analysis 169

Chapter 4: Epiphanius' Text of Acts 185

Chapter 5: Epiphanius' Text of the Catholic Epistles 207

Chapter 6: Epiphanius' Text of the Pauline Epistles 213

Chapter 7: Conclusion 255

Appendix I: Epiphanius in the Apparatus of NA^{27} 259

Appendix II: Epiphanius in the Apparatus of UBS^4 269

Bibliography 273

EDITOR'S PREFACE

Properly interpreted, patristic evidence for the text of the New Testament offers a major resource of primary importance for establishing the text of the NT as well as for writing the history of its transmission. In contrast to the earliest NT MSS, which can often be dated only rather generally and about whose geographical provenance nothing is known, citations of the NT by Christian writers of Late Antiquity can be located, often with some degree of precision, with respect to both time and space. It is this feature of patristic citations that makes them particularly important for the task of writing the history of the transmission and development of the text of the documents that now comprise the NT. The ability of patristic evidence to document the existence of a variant reading or textual tradition at a particular time in a specific geographical location renders this category of testimony invaluable for the historian of early Christianity.

The Society of Biblical Literature's monograph series, *The New Testament in the Greek Fathers*, is devoted to explorations of patristic texts and authors that will contribute to a better understanding of the history of the transmission of the NT text. Each volume investigates the text of the NT (or parts thereof) as preserved in the writings of a significant Christian author. While the series does not impose a specific format, each volume provides an exhaustive presentation of the relevant data, an apparatus that indicates the alignment (or lack thereof) of this data with carefully selected representative textual witnesses, and a statistical analysis of these data and alignments—typically both a quantitative assessment of their affinities with leading representatives of known textual traditions and a profile analysis that nuances the quantitative findings. Finally, since the goal is not only to gather and assess the evidence, but to interpret its significance, conclusions or observations are offered regarding the implications of the findings for the history of the text and its transmission.

Dr. Osburn's contribution to the series takes the form of a comprehensive and substantial investigation of the text of the *Apostolos* (that is, Acts, Catholic epistles, and Pauline letters) in the writings of Epiphanius of Salamis (*ca.* A.D. 315-403). A native of Palestine, where he founded a monastery in his early twenties, Epiphanius was an ardent supporter of the Nicene form of Christianity. Deeply intolerant of any whiff of heresy, he participated in the Apollinarian and Melitan controversies and attacks on Origenism, and did much to contribute to the enduring legacy of the Council of Nicaea. A colleague of Jerome and a contemporary of Chrysostom, his travels took him to Egypt, Rome,

Jerusalem, and Constantinople; he spent much of his later life on Cyprus, after being named Bishop of Salamis in 367. A prolific (though somewhat unskilled) writer, Epiphanius made extensive use of Scripture in his writings, the most well known of which is probably his *Panarion*, or "Refutation of All Heresies." In all, he was a leading figure during the turbulent second half of the fourth century—a critical time for the history of the NT text. Dr. Osburn's careful study reveals that Epiphanius probably used a Byzantine form of the Catholic letters, but a Late Egyptian form of Acts and the Pauline writings. In short, this volume is a substantial contribution to the series that will be of interest to NT and Patristic scholars alike.

Finally, for the sake of bibliographers and others who may be curious as to why volume 6 appears several years after volume 7, a word of explanation. At an earlier time in the history of the series, a proposal was accepted for inclusion and volume numbers 5 and 6 were reserved for it; subsequently the next proposal accepted was designated volume 7. But whereas the latter proposal came to fruition relatively quickly and was published in 1997, the former proposal has never materialized as planned. The reserved volume numbers have therefore been re-assigned, number 5 to the volume by J.-F. Racine (*The Text of Matthew in the Writings of Basil of Caesarea* [Atlanta: Society of Biblical Literature, 2004]) and number 6 to the present volume, both of which thus appear some years after volume number 7.

Michael W. Holmes

Editor, *The New Testament in the Greek Fathers*

ACKNOWLEDEGMENTS

Three decades have passed since Matthew Black involved me in the fascinating world of textual criticism in the attractive setting of St. Mary's quadrangle at St. Andrews, concentrating on the text of the Pauline epistles in Epiphanius of Salamis. The present volume, several years in the making, is vastly different from the earlier study. The text critical enterprise has advanced considerably during the intervening three decades. Epiphanius' citations of Acts, the Catholic Epistles, and Revelation have been included with the Pauline Epistles. In this study, attention has been given to ascertaining which of Epiphanius' citations are likely to be representative of a biblical exemplar. Care has been taken to select control manuscripts that have claim to be representative of the different textual traditions. Citations are analyzed not only in terms of traditional statistical analysis but in terms of a profile analysis common to volumes in this series.

It is pleasant to recall conversations over the years in shaping the present work along these lines with Kurt Aland, Bruce Metzger, George Kilpatrick, Jean Duplacy, Ian Moir, J. Harold Greenlee, Gordon Fee, Thomas C. Geer, Jr., Keith Elliott and Barbara Aland.

I am grateful to the staff of the Institut für neutestamentliche Textforschung in Münster for their collegiality over the years, and especially during my sabbatical in 2001. The Ancient Biblical Manuscript Center at Claremont made available several NT manuscripts on microfilm, and the Dumbarton Oaks Centre for Byzantine Studies in Washington, D.C., permitted access to their collection of resources on the early Byzantine era. The staffs at the Bodleian Library in Oxford, the University of St. Andrews, and Vanderbilt University have been most helpful.

To my research assistants, Duane McCrory and Alex Kyrycherko, must be expressed special gratitude. Michael Holmes' and Leigh Andersen's editorial work in helping to bring the volume into print is greatly appreciated.

Carroll D. Osburn
The Carmichael-Walling Distinguished Professor of New Testament
   Language and Literature
Abilene, Texas
1 March 2004

ABBREVIATIONS

AB	Anchor Bible
ACW	Ancient Christian Writers
AnBib	Analecta biblica
ANTF	Arbeiten zur neutestamentlichen Textforschung
ATR	*Anglican Theological Review*
AUSS	*Andrews University Seminary Studies*
BETL	Bibliotheca ephemeridum theologicarum lovaniensium
Bib	*Biblica*
BibB	Biblische Beiträge
BJRL	Bulletin of the John Rylands Library
BZ	*Biblische Zeitschrift*
ByzZ	*Byzantinische Zeitschrift*
BZNW	*Beihefte zur Zeitschrift für die neutestamentliche Wissenschaft*
CBQ	*Catholic Biblical Quarterly*
CCG	Corpus Christianorum, Series Graeca
CCL	Corpus Christianorum, Series Latina
CNRS	Centre National de la Recherche Scientifique
ConB	Coniectanea biblica
ConNT	Coniectanea neotestamentica
CSEL	Corpus scriptorum ecclesiasticorum latinorum
DHGE	*Dictionnaire d'histoire et de géographie ecclésiastique*
ETL	*Ephemerides theologicae lovanienses*
GCS	Die griechischen christlichen Schriftsteller der ersten drei Jahrhunderte
GRBS	*Greek, Roman, and Byzantine Studies*
HKNT	Handkommentar zum Neuen Testament
HNT	Handbuch zum Neuen Testament
HTR	*Harvard Theological Review*
HTS	Harvard Theological Studies
ICC	International Critical Commentary
JBL	*Journal of Biblical Literature*
JEH	*Journal of Ecclesiastical History*
JHS	*Journal of Hellenic Studies*
JSNT	*Journal for the Study of the New Testament*
JTS	*Journal of Theological Studies*
LCC	Library of Christian Classics
MeyerK	Meyer's Kritischer-Exegetiker Kommentar

ABBREVIATIONS

NedTTs	*Nederlands theologisch tijdschrift*
Neot	*Neotestamentica*
NA	Nestle-Aland Greek New Testament
NTS	*New Testament Studies*
NTTS	New Testament Tools and Studies
NAPSPMS	North American Patristic Society Patristic Monograph Series
NovT	*Novum Testamentum*
NovTSupp	Novum Testamentum Supplement
OrChr	*Oriens christianus*
PG	J.-P. Migne, *Patrologia Graeca*
PL	J.-P. Migne, *Patrologia Latina*
PO	Patrologia Orientalis
PNF	Post-Nicene Fathers
RAC	*Reallexikon für Antike und Christentum*
RechBib	Recherches bibliques
RSR	*Recherches de science religieuse*
RB	*Revue biblique*
RHPR	*Revue d'histoire et de philosophie religieuses*
SBLDS	SBL Dissertation Series
SBLMS	SBL Monograph Series
SBLNTGF	SBL New Testament in the Greek Fathers
SC	Sources chrétiennes
SD	Studies and Documents
SecCent	*Second Century*
SNTSMS	SNTS Monograph Series
SP	Studia Patristica
TextsS	Texts and Studies
TR	Textus receptus
ThPh	*Theologie und Philosophie*
TQ	*Theologische Quartalschrift*
TU	Texte und Untersuchungen
UBS	United Bible Societies Greek New Testament
VC	*Vigiliae Christianae*
WTJ	*Westminster Journal*
ZNW	*Zeitschrift für die neutestamentliche Wissenschaft*
ZTK	*Zeitschrift für Theologie und Kirche*

CHAPTER 1

EPIPHANIUS OF SALAMIS AND THE TEXT OF THE NEW TESTAMENT

Epiphanius of Salamis achieved fame as a fourth-century bishop mainly due to his intense zeal for orthodoxy. In playing a major role in the events that shaped both Byzantine history and the history of Christian thought, Epiphanius wrote several theological treatises that were at the heart of fourth-century religious controversy. His frequent use of scripture in these writings makes him an important patristic witness to the text of the NT in the Eastern Mediterranean.

Major questions exist concerning the text of the NT during this era. Was a major recension of the text undertaken during the third or fourth century? How widespread was the so-called "Western" text? What is the relationship of the so-called "Western" text to the Alexandrian text? Were there two forms of text dating from an early period in Alexandria? Was there a Caesarean text? How is one to understand the origins of the Byzantine text? This study will analyze the quotations of the Apostolos[1] in Epiphanius to ascertain the type of text he used and its value for understanding the developing textual tradition of the NT.

1. THE LIFE AND TIMES OF EPIPHANIUS[2]

A. EPIPHANIUS' EARLY LIFE

Epiphanius was born between A.D. 315 and 320 near Eleutheropolis, southwest of Jerusalem on the road to Ashkelon.[3] At this time, the Roman world was transitioning from Rome to Constantinople, the Empire faced a variety of external as well as internal problems, and pagan religions were locked into a battle with Christianity.[4]

---

[1] "Apostolos" is used here as in Basil of Caesarea, *On the Holy Spirit* 27, "We do not content ourselves with what was reported in the Apostolos and in the Gospels, but, both before and after reading them, we add other doctrines, received from oral teaching and carrying much weight in the mystery."

[2] See Jon F. Dechow, *Dogma and Mysticism in Early Christianity: Epiphanius of Cyprus and the Legacy of Origen* (NAPSPMS 13; Macon, Ga.: Mercer University Press, 1988), 25–124, for sources.

[3] Karl Holl, *Epiphanius* (GCS, 25, 31, 37; Leipzig: Hinrichs, 1915, 1922, 1933), esp. 3.13.

[4] See among others, Cyril Mango, *Byzantium: The Empire of New Rome* (New York: C. Scribner's Sons, 1980).

During Epiphanius' childhood, problems arose in the East when Licinius banned Christian synods, expelled various bishops and priests and instituted a reign of terror against Christians. After he was killed in 323, confiscated properties were returned to Christians; however, pagans were permitted to continue in the old faith if they chose.[5] While paganism was largely tolerated, heresy among Christians was not.

For viewing the Son as subordinate to the Father, Arius was excommunicated in 320. After moving to Syria, however, he achieved both patristic and synodal approval and returned to Egypt demanding to be re-instated. When Archbishop Alexander refused, rioting ensued. By the time Constantine assumed control of the Empire in 323, the initial matter of Arius' theological divergence had become an inflammatory issue all around the eastern Mediterranean.[6] The Council of Nicea in 325, with approximately 220 Eastern bishops in attendance, but only a handful of Western "observers" present, nullified Arianism, at least for the time being. Christianity was divided. Among church leaders, Athanasius, a strong opponent of Arius, became archbishop of Alexandria in 328. On the imperial side, however, Eusebius of Nicomedia took advantage of his proximity to the Imperial court to attack Athanasius relentlessly. At a synod of pro-Arian bishops at Tyre in 335, Athanasius was deposed and later banished by Constantine to Trier.

Epiphanius states that during this period he followed the Nicean faith of his parents.[7] Epiphanius was sent as a young man to Egypt, where he was instructed by the most celebrated monks from ca. 330–335. Although he could have known both Anthony and Pachomius,[8] it was Hilarion who became Epiphanius' spiritual mentor. A well-known teacher and ascetic who had been mentored by Anthony, Hilarion influenced not only Epiphanius' earlier life in Egypt but also his later

---

[5] See Aline Pourkier, *L'hérésiologie chez Épiphane de Salamine* (CA 4; Paris: Beauchesne, 1992). The sometimes useful work of John Julius Norwich, *Byzantium: The Early Centuries* (New York: Knopf, 1989), should be used with care.

[6] John Meyendorff, *Byzantine Theology: Historical Trends and Doctrinal Themes* (New York: Fordham University Press, 1974).

[7] See Karl Holl, "Die Schriften des Epiphanius gegen die Bilderverehrung," *Gesammelte Aufsätze zur Kirchengeschichte II* (Tübingen: Mohr, 1928), 360. The text is preserved in Nicephorus, *Adversus Epiphanius* 15.61, in J. B. Pitra, *Analecta sacra spicilegio solesmensi parata* (Paris: Roger et Chernowitz, 1852–58), 340.

[8] Sozomen, *Historia ecclesiastica* 6.32.3. Dechow, *Dogma and Mysticism in Early Christianity*, 32–34, argues against the possibility that Epiphanius was trained in a Pachomian monastery or that his anti-Origenism is attributable to Pachomius.

monastic life in Palestine.[9] Epiphanius' training involved both formal studies in Alexandria[10] and monastic practice in the Egyptian desert.[11] As part of his monastic training, Epiphanius studied Greek, Hebrew, Latin, Syriac and Coptic.[12]

During these years in Egypt, Epiphanius' Nicene orientation was challenged by ideas that he viewed later as "poisonous snakes." One important threat came from a sexually oriented group that he later termed "Gnostics."[13] In his response to this threat, Epiphanius demonstrated the zeal for unmasking error that became characteristic of his later life.[14]

> With impudent boldness moreover, they tried to seduce me themselves . . . I was pitied and rescued by my groaning to God. . . . Now the women who taught this trivial myth were very lovely to look at, but in their wicked minds they had all the devil's ugliness. . . . I lost no time reporting them to the bishops there, and finding out which ones were hidden in the church. They were expelled from the city, about eighty of them.

Athanasius returned to Egypt after the Council of Nicea and had a good reception in pro-Nicene monastic circles that were loyal to himself and Alexander, his anti-Arian predecessor.[15] In this pro-Nicene monastic environment, Epiphanius' anti-Arian views were strengthened.

---

[9] Jerome, *Vita Hilarionis eremitae* 1–3. See also Pierre Nautin, "Épiphane de Salamine," *DHGE* 15.617–31, and W. Schneemelcher, "Epiphanius von Salamis," *RAC* 5.909–27.

[10] Jerome, *Vita Hilarionis eremitae* 2 [PL 23:30C].

[11] *Ibid.* [PL 23:31 A-C].

[12] Jerome, *Adversus Rufinum* 2.22 [PL 23:466C]. Jürgen Dummer, "Die Sprachkenntnisse des Epiphanius," in *Die Araber in der alten Welt* (ed. F. Altheim and R. Stiehl; Berlin: de Gruyter, 1968), 434–35, argues that Jerome may have been inclined to overstate the linguistic prowess of Epiphanius in order to enhance his own polemic against Rufinus.

[13] See Pourkier, *L'hérésiologie chez Épiphane de Salamine*, 30–32; and Bentley Layton, "The Riddle of the Thunder," in *Nag Hammadi, Gnosticism, and Early Christianity* (ed. C. Hedrick and R. Hodgson; Peabody, Mass.: Hendrickson, 1986), 52.

[14] Epiphanius, *Panarion haereses* 26.17.4–9.

[15] Epiphanius' awareness of Alexander's anti-Arian correspondence dates from this period, and it is possible that an acquaintance with Peter's, *On the Soul* and *On the Resurrection*, may have influenced him in an anti-Origenist direction (*Pan* 69.4.3). See also Dechow, *Dogma and Mysticism*, 35–36.

B. EPIPHANIUS, ABBOT OF A PALESTINIAN MONASTERY

About the age of twenty (c. 335), Epiphanius returned to Palestine, where he founded a monastery near Eleutheropolis, some thirty miles inland from Gaza.[16] Hilarion had founded a monastery near Gaza some years earlier, and Epiphanius' friendship with Hilarion continued long after his move from Egypt to Palestine.[17]

Although abbot of the monastery until 367,[18] Epiphanius was also busy keeping the wider community free of heresy. For example, he mentions the "unmasking" of an elderly ex-priest and monk at a village "in the district of Eleutheropolis [and] Jerusalem, three mile-stones beyond Hebron." The old man had been deposed earlier for being a Gnostic, but later returned and, having distributed his possessions to the poor, lived in a cave with only a sheep's fleece for clothing. For this, Peter was quite popular among the villagers. Upon learning that a certain Eutactus, who was returning to Armenia, had stayed with Peter and learned Peter's Archontic teaching, Epiphanius says,

> from things he had whispered to certain persons, I unmasked him and he was anathematized and refuted by my poor self. And after that he sat in a cave, abhorred by all and deserted by the brotherhood, and by most who were attending to their salvation (*Pan* 40.1.1-8).

Constantine died in 337, and was succeeded by Constantius, during whose reign (337–61) there was considerable political and ecclesiastical confusion. By 355, his cousin, Julian, was selected as Caesar in the West. A student of philosophy and rhetoric, Julian was influenced by the anti-Christian philosopher and self-confessed pagan, Libanius.[19] By 351, Julian renounced Christianity. By 356, he had established control throughout Europe, and by 361 he avowed pagan gods. When Constantius died, Julian became sole Emperor of the Empire and pagan hopes revived. When news of Constantine's death reached Alexandria, the Arian bishop, George, was murdered by a mob of enraged pagans.

---

[16] Epiphanius, *Ancoratus*, preface. See P. C. de Labriolle, "The Origins of Monasticism," *The Church in the Christian Roman Empire* (ed. J. R. Palanque, G. Bardy, and P. de Labriolle; trans. E. C. Messenger; New York: Macmillan, 1956), 2.448, for the date of A.D. 335, and Mango, *Byzantium*, 109, on monasticism.

[17] At Hilarion's death in 371, Epiphanius wrote a brief notice that was widely circulated. See Jerome, *Vita Hilarionis eremitae* 1 [PL 23:29C].

[18] Jerome, *Contra Joannem Hierosolymitanum* 4 [PL 23:374D].

[19] A. F. Norman, "Libanius, the Teacher in an Age of Violence," *Libanius* (ed. G. Fatouros and T. Krischer; Wege der Forschung 621; Darmstadt: Wissenschaftliche Buchgesellschaft, 1983), 150–69.

Traveling to Constantinople early in his reign, Julian found various forms of corruption and a thoroughgoing purge dismissed thousands of people from Constantius' government. Julian thought Christianity to be largely responsible for the degradation of the military and the corruption of traditional Roman morals. Instead of the old virtues of reason, duty and honor, Christians emphasized feminine qualities of gentleness, meekness and offering the other cheek. So, Julian framed laws detrimental to Christianity and worked to re-establish the old pagan cults throughout the Empire. By re-opening pagan temples and granting amnesty to pro-Arian exiles, he apparently hoped to stimulate friction between Christian groups.[20]

In this context, Epiphanius' zeal against heresy put him into heated conflict with Eutychius, bishop of nearby Eleutheropolis, who vacillated on Arianism. About 359-60, Arianism was widespread.[21] Nicene emphasis was reversed at the Council of Seleucia in 359.[22] Eunomius became bishop of Cyzicus, and Cyril was deposed in Jerusalem and replaced by the Arian, Arrenius. In spite of these reversals, Jerome mentions Epiphanius' courage to voice at this time his pro-Nicene beliefs in a note to John of Jerusalem.[23]

> At the very time when the whole East (except pope Athanasius and Paulinus) was controlled by the heresies of the Arians and the Eunomians, . . . he [Epiphanius] not only, as a monastery abbot, gained a hearing with Eutychius, but also, later, as bishop of Cyprus, was untouched by [the Emperor] Valens.

In 362, Julian[24] moved to Antioch in preparation for war against the Persians. Appalled that pagan cults were not noticeably involved in charity, Julian's exhortations for pagans to establish hospitals and orphanages, and even monasteries and convents as had Christians, were largely futile. So, in June 362, an edict was issued that all teachers must be approved by local city councils, and an explanatory circular stipulated that Christians should not be approved to teach classical authors because they did not, in fact, believe in them.[25] Christians protested, but in October 362 the Great Church of Antioch was closed and numerous

---

[20] Henry Chadwick, *The Church in Ancient Society: From Galilee to Gregory the Great* (Oxford: Oxford University Press, 2001), 231.

[21] Jerome, *Altercatio Luciferiani et orthodoxi* 19 [PL 23:181C].

[22] Chadwick, *The Church in Ancient Society*, 287–88.

[23] Jerome, *Contral Joannem Hierosolymitanum* 4 [PL 23:374D].

[24] See A. Lippold, "Julian," *Reallexikon für Antike und Christentum* 19 (1999): 442–88.

[25] See Mango, *Byzantium*, 125–34.

incidents followed. In March 363, Julian left for the East with his army, and although several victories came their way, Julian was killed.

Jovian succeeded Julian. Undaunted, Epiphanius was involved with a synodal letter composed at Antioch in 363 that was sent to the Emperor Jovian in support of the Nicene Creed.[26] In 364, Jovian issued an edict of religious toleration that restored rights to Christians. However, his influence was short-lived, for he died on 16 February 364.

Valentinian was installed as Jovian's successor and reigned A.D. 364-75. He refused to depose Arian bishops and even appointed his brother, the pro-Arian Valens, as co-emperor to rule the East. Apparently, his wife influenced him in favor of the Arian, Eudoxius, Bishop of Constantinople until A.D. 370, and then in favor of his successor, Bishop Demophilus.

C. EPIPHANIUS, BISHOP OF SALAMIS

It is generally agreed that Epiphanius left Eleutheropolis sometime after 363 while controversy was swirling in the Eastern Mediterranean. Apparently, he traveled to Cyprus, and it is possible that this is related to the devastating effects of Julian's religious policy in Syria and Palestine. In fact, Hilarion's monastery was destroyed, and he had already fled to Cyprus due to the severity of Julian's persecution. It is not known whether Epiphanius' monastery at Eleutheropolis was affected by Julian's policy at this same time.[27]

In 367, Epiphanius was appointed Bishop of Salamis, the principal port city of ancient Cyprus near the modern town of Famagusta. It had been damaged during the Jewish revolt of A.D. 116-117 and by several earthquakes, but was rebuilt by Constantius during the years 337-361, and renamed Constantia.[28] Very little is known of his episcopal administration in Salamis, but his monastic emphasis attracted novices there from all over the world.[29] Although Cyprus was considered part of the

---

[26] See Frank Williams, *The Panarion of Epiphanius of Salamis* (Leiden: Brill, 1987), 1.xii.

[27] See Dechow, *Dogma and Mysticism*, 42, n. 69–71.

[28] For the archaeological report, see the dated but useful work of J. A. R. Munro and H. A. Tubbs, "Excavations in Cyprus, 1890: The Third Season's Work. Salamis," *JHS* 12 (1891): 59–198.

[29] Epiphanius, *Pan* 28.6.6, mentions travels to Galatia and Asia Minor that would have resulted in recruitment and fund raising. Jerome, *Epistulae* 108.7.3, tells of his ascetic friend Paula, who gave funds for monasteries on Cyprus in 383. Palladius, *Dialogus de vita Joannis Chrysostomi* 17, tells of Olympias, a wealthy deaconess from Constantinople, who gave Epiphanius both money and land.

diocese of the East, whose capital was Antioch,[30] Epiphanius was willing to consult with its bishop, Athanasius, but staunchly maintained Cypriot independence and conservatism. In fact, Jerome states that Epiphanius was so respected as Bishop of Salamis that even the pro-Arian emperor Valens (364-78) would not persecute him.[31]

Epiphanius was instrumental in establishing Nicene thought on Cyprus and in helping Christianity to emerge as the dominant power on the island. The island retained pagan traditions,[32] as well as a variety of Christian groups, and this infuriated Epiphanius.[33] Ps.-Polybius says that Epiphanius obtained an order from Theodosius I (379-395) to expel all heresies from Cyprus.[34] Epiphanius considered that all such heresies were either related to or exceeded by the heresy of Origen.[35]

The church on Cyprus held to the Antiochian tradition of celebrating Easter on the Sunday after the Jewish Passover, although the Council of Nicea tried to make universal the Alexandrian practice of celebrating Easter after the vernal equinox. At the council in 370, Epiphanius favored the Syrian minority (about one-fourth of the bishops in attendance) in opposition to the Alexandrian practice. In the interest of uniformity, the Syrians acquiesced. Epiphanius' view was based upon his calculations of chronology and his interpretation of the *Didaskalia*.[36] The earliest datable extant work of Epiphanius is a fragment of a *Letter to Eusebius, Marcellus, Bibianus and Carpus*,[37] preserved on pages 238-239 of Codex Ambrosianus 515, and written between 367 and 373, that contains a chronology of the Passion Week and argument in favor of the Sunday after Nisan 14. Athanasius' request that Epiphanius cease pressing the issue had no effect upon Epiphanius' theological inflexibility.

---

[30] A. H. M. Jones, *The Later Roman Empire, 284–602: A Social, Economic and Administrative Survey* (Oxford: Blackwell, 1964), 1.373; 3.381.

[31] Jerome, *Contra Ioannem Hierosolymitanum* 4 [PL 23:374D].

[32] C. G. Bennett, "The Cults of the Ancient Greek Cypriotes" (Ph.D. dissertation, University of Pennsylvania, 1980). See also Henry Chadwick, *The Early Church* (rev. ed.; London: Penguin, 1993), 152–59.

[33] Epiphanius, *Pan* 30.18.1; 42.1.2. John Chrysostom, *Epistulae* 221 [PG 52: 733] mentions that at one point Marcionites had nearly taken over Salamis. Pseudo-Polybius, *Vita Epiphanii* 59 [PG 41:99AB] is not altogether trustworthy, but mentions also the presence of Valentinians, Ophites, Nicolaitans, Simonians, Carpocratians and Sabellians.

[34] Ps.-Polybius, *Vita Epipharii* 59 [PG 41:99BC].

[35] Epiphanius, *Pan* 64.4.1; Jerome, *Epistulae* 51.3.3.

[36] See Annie Jaubert, *The Date of the Last Supper: The Biblical Calendar and Christian Liturgy* (Staten Island, NY: Alba House, 1965), 76–78, 160–61.

[37] See Karl Holl, "Ein Bruchstück aus einem bisher unbekannten Brief des Epiphanius," *Gesammelte Aufsätze II*, 204–224.

D. EPIPHANIUS AND THE FOURTH CENTURY ECCLESIASTICAL CRISIS

In 374, Epiphanius wrote the *Ancoratus* (' Αγκυρωτός)[38] while the pro-Arian Valens was emperor in the East and the pro-Nicene Valentinian ruled the West. In the form of a letter to the church of Syedra in Pamphylia, Epiphanius stressed that the church's "boat" cannot enter the harbor because of contrary winds of bad doctrine. He argued that the church should become "anchored" in the face of these winds, especially regarding the Trinity, the Incarnation, the Resurrection, Origen's treatment of Genesis, and pagan gods. *Ancoratus* 12.7-13.8 gives an outline of what, three years later, was to become the *Panarion haereses*.

A conflict was raging in Antioch regarding the interpretation of the Nicene Creed and church politics.[39] The church in Antioch had split into four factions, headed by Euzoeus (an ardent Arian), Melitius (appointed under Arian auspices, but in exile), Apollinarius (who denied a human mind to Christ), and Paulinus. From at least 370, Epiphanius had been dealing with disciples of Apollinarius who apparently were teaching a distorted version of Apollinarius' views.[40] In fact, a synod was convened to deal with these individuals.[41] Accumulating controversies led Epiphanius began work on his *Panarion haereses* (Πανάριον) in A.D. 375 while on Cyprus. It was intended as a comprehensive refutation of everything heretical. In A.D. 376, he went to Antioch with aspirations of reconciling that situation, but found Vitalis, whom Apollinarius had appointed bishop of Antioch, to be teaching an incorrect Christology. So, Epiphanius cast his lot with Paulinus and the controversy continued.

In 376, during this Christological controversy in Antioch, the Empire was threatened by the Huns. Gothic refugees fled southward in sizeable numbers to avoid their cruelty. In spite of Imperial orders to provide food and shelter to these refugees, local authorities exploited them and many of the fleeing Goths faced starvation. By the summer of 377, these frustrated Goths began active resistance. The Romans sent an army to subdue them, but the Goths were victorious and were soon joined by the

---

[38] Holl, *Ancoratus*, GCS 25 (1915), 1–149.

[39] See Stuart Hall, *Doctrine and Practice in the Early Church* (London: SPCK, 2000), 121–36.

[40] Epiphanius, *Pan* 77.2.2-4. See Pourkier, *L'hérésiologie chez Épiphane de Salamine*, 42–45.

[41] Epiphanius, *Pan* 77.2.5. Athanasius, *Epistula ad Epictetum* 30 [PG 26: 1069A] says the individuals recanted and left Cyprus in peace. Later, Apollinarius, *Fragmenta* 159–60, himself disowns the erroneous views expressed by these individuals.

Huns in a full-scale attack on the Empire. It was during this major crisis that Epiphanius wrote much of the *Panarion* while in Antioch.[42]

Returning to Cyprus from Antioch, Epiphanius sought Basil's support in reconciling the factions in Antioch.[43] However, his proposal for unity involved alterations in the language concerning the incarnation in the Nicene Creed that Basil rejected in his answer.[44] Basil's response is replete with church diplomacy, since he had been involved in 358 in the preparation of a tribute to Origen—a fact that might raise Epiphanius' suspicions. Epiphanius was unable to interest Basil in the Christological question.[45] His efforts to heal the schism in Antioch failed, and Apollinarius gained the reputation of being a heretic.

While working on *Panarion* 64, Epiphanius was preoccupied with christological problems related to Origen. Epiphanius' inability to understand Origen's metaphysical thinking led to hatred for him.[46] In light of work on the *Panarion* and the ecclesiastical problems he faced in 376, Epiphanius concluded that Origen was responsible for Arianism. Various Christological issues, such as those surfaced by Apollinarius, are treated in his essay against Origen. Epiphanius considered Origen and Apollinarius as the most significant and damaging of all heretics. By A.D. 377, Apollinarius no longer worked collegially with Epiphanius and appointed his own bishops. However, when Epiphanius wrote *Panarion* 77 against Apollinarius early in 377, he did not wish Apollinarius excommunicated but only to see him renounce his views.[47] Apollinarius' appeal to churches in Egypt for assistance was rejected primarily because he was not in communion with Epiphanius.[48]

Basil then wrote to Damasus and the Western bishops, asking them to denounce Apollinarius.[49] At the same time, Apollinarius had sent a delegate to a Roman synod in late 377, asking them to anathematize Basil. The result was the rejection of Apollinarius by Rome. The anathema against Apollinarius was supported by synods at Alexandria in 378 and Antioch in 379. Three years after Valens was killed and the pro-Nicene Theodosius took the reigns, a council held at Constantinople

---

[42] Dechow, *Dogma and Mysticism*, 66–70.

[43] Epiphanius, *Pan* 77.14.2–3.

[44] Basil, *Epistulae* 258.2.12–27. These are the anti-Apollinarian expressions that by 374 included an expansion of the Nicene Creed. See *Anc* 119.3–12.

[45] See Chadwick, *The Church in Ancient Society*, 331–47.

[46] See A. Louth, *The Origins of the Christian Mystical Tradition: From Plato to Denys* (Oxford: Oxford University Press, 1981).

[47] Epiphanius, *Pan* 77.18.16

[48] Facundus, *Pro defensione trium capitulorum*, 4.2 [PL 67:619B].

[49] Basil, *Epistulae* 265.2.5–11.

condemned Arianism.⁵⁰ Epiphanius is not listed among the bishops in attendance at Constantinople in 381,⁵¹ but there is a strong similarity between the creedal formula issuing from the council and Epiphanius' own creed in *Anc* 118.9-12.⁵² Then in 382, Epiphanius, along with Paulinus and Jerome, attended a synod at Rome convened by Damasus to deal with tensions between East and West.

In 388, the army of Theodosius and Valentinian wintered in Milan, which was seething with unrest due to barbarian troops being billeted there. When a mob killed the Gothic captain, Ambrose, bishop of Milan, appealed for restraint, but the soldiers killed seven thousand. Ambrose held Theodosius responsible and withheld communion from him until he repented. Theodosius complied and went to Milan to seek forgiveness. In 391, Theodosius forbade all non-Christian religious ceremonies in Rome and in Egypt, and in 392 outlawed pagan worship throughout the Empire.⁵³ In Theodosius' reign, however, there was no official persecution or forceful attempt to change peoples' convictions.

In 392, Epiphanius published *De Mensuris et Ponderibus* (Περὶ μέτρων καὶ σταθμῶν),⁵⁴ a manual for students of scripture. The next year, Epiphanius went to Jerusalem. On the way, he ripped down a curtain in the small church at Anablatha because of an image painted on it. Jerusalem was home to many of Origen's admirers, but in the Church of the Holy Sepulchre, Epiphanius delivered a vehement sermon against

---

⁵⁰ See P. Karlin-Hayter, "Activity of the Bishop of Constantinople Outside his *Paroikia* Between 381 and 451," ΚΑΘΗΓΗΤΡΙΑ: Essays presented to Joan Hussey," (ed. J. Chrysostomides; Camberley, Surrey: Porphyrogenitus, 1988), 179–88.

⁵¹ W. Schneemelcher, "Epiphanius von Salamis," *RAC* 5 (1962): 911, argues that the completeness of the list is questionable, and Gustav Bardy, "Épiphane," *CHAD* 4 (1953): 320, argues that Epiphanius was present. Dechow, *Dogma and Mysticism*, 87–88, observes that Epiphanius' authority would have been substantial even if he were not in attendance.

⁵² Holl, *Epiphanius*, GCS 25(1915), 146, holds the creed in *Anc* to be Epiphanius' own, but B. M. Weischer, "Die ursprüngliche nikänische Form des ersten Glaubenssymbols im *Ancyrotos* des Epiphanios von Salamis: ein Beitrag zur Diskussion um die Entstehung des konstantino-politanischen Glaubenssymbols im Lichte neuester äthiopischen Forschungen," *ThPh* 53 (1978): 407–14, views it as an interpolation.

⁵³ See Hall, *Doctrine and Practice in the Early Church*, 171–72.

⁵⁴ A Syriac version preserves the entire treatise, but the extant Greek text contains only a small portion of the text. Fragments exist in Armenian and Sahidic. See J. E. Dean, *Epiphanius' Treatise on Weights and Measures* (SAOC, 11; Chicago: University of Chicago Press, 1935), for the Syriac translation, and E. Moutsoulas, "La tradition manuscrite de l'oeuvre d'Epiphane de Salamine *De mensuris et ponderibus*," *Texte und Textkritik* (ed. J. Dummer; Berlin: Akademie-Verlag, 1987), 429–40.

Origen. A quarrel resulted in Jerome ceasing support of Origen and attempting to pressure the bishop into condemning Origen. When the bishop refused, Epiphanius broke off communion with him.[55] As a result of criticism from the Anablatha incident, Epiphanius wrote a stinging *Pamphlet Against the Images*,[56] viewing as idolatry the manufacture of images of Christ, the Mother of God, martyrs, angels or prophets.[57] He also wrote a *Letter to Emperor Theodosius I*, on the problem of images.[58] Finally, he wrote a *Last Will and Testament*,[59] encouraging Christians to retain the image of God in their hearts rather than in their churches.

Epiphanius' anti-Origenist literature had a significant influence on fourth-century Christian thought.[60] Although noted earlier in *Anc* 54–63, 87–92, Origen's teachings receive extensive critique in *Pan* 64. His later *Letter to John*[61] is essentially an anti-Origenist tract. In the context of Theodosius' aggressive anti-pagan policies, opposition to images was important to Epiphanius. In *Pan*, he attacks pagan images for the most part, although 27.6.9-10 treats specifically Christian images. About 394 or 395, Epiphanius wrote *De XII Gemmis* (Περὶ τῶν δώδεκα λίθων), an allegorical treatise on the symbolism of the stones on the high priest's breastplate, representing medicinal usages for the twelve tribes of Israel.

At the death of Theodosius, his ten-year old son, Honorius, became Emperor of the West, and Theodosius' older son, Arcadius, ruled in the East, influenced by Rufinus, a corrupt and ambitious man who coveted the throne, and by the unscrupulous and ambitious Eutropius. Alaric and the Goths invaded Greece and the Eastern government fell into serious corruption. In the spring of 399, anti-Gothic locals attacked the Goths in Constantinople and killed seven thousand. In the summer of 401, Alaric and the Goths invaded Italy.

---

[55] See Johannes Quasten, *Patrology* (Utrecht: Spectrum, 1966), 3.384.

[56] The pamphlet must be reconstructed from portions surviving in the Acts of the Councils of 754 and 787, in the works of John of Damascus (De imaginibus Oratio I.25), and in a tract that Nicephorus (*Apologia Minor* [PG 100:837B]) wrote against Epiphanius in 815. See Holl, *Gesammelte Aufsätze zur Kirchengeschichte II*, 356–59, on the pamphlet.

[57] Epiphanius, *De imaginibus fragmenta*.

[58] Epiphanius, *Epistulae ad Theodosium fragmenta*. See Holl, *Gesammelte Aufsätze zur Kirchengeschichte II*, 360–62, on the letter.

[59] See Holl, *Gesammelte Aufsätze zur Kirchengeschichte II*, 363, on the "last will and testament."

[60] See Dechow, *Dogma and Mysticism*, 376–378.

[61] In 395, Jerome translated Epiphanius' *Letter to John* into Latin in order to give wider circulation to an already well-known document. Jerome, *Epistulae* 51, incurred severe criticism. Jerome defended his translation in his Letter to Pammachius *On the Best Method of Translating* (*Epistulae* 57), in which he insisted that his intention was "to give sense for sense and not word for word" (57.5).

In the midst of these tremendous upheavals in the Empire, Epiphanius' spent the last years of his life concentrating on the Origenist controversy. Theophilus, patriarch of Alexandria, ordered several of the leading monks to be expelled from the monasteries of Nitria and from the monasteries in the desert. Rioting and chaos ensued.[62] In 400, a synod in Alexandria condemned the reading and/or possession of the works of Origen, followed by an appeal to the secular authority in Alexandria to expel all Origenists from Nitria. Theophilus then appealed to Pope Anastasius I of Rome, who subsequently issued a condemnation of Origen's writings.[63] The cells and libraries of many Origenists were burned and about three hundred were forced to leave the country. His appeal to Epiphanius for support of this severe policy led Epiphanius to call a similar synod on Cyprus that likewise condemned the reading of Origen's works, a move that had significant effect in curtailing Origenism as a major option for the orthodox Christian faith.[64]

About eighty of these exiled monks from Nitria fled to Constantinople where they appealed for help from the bishop, John Chrysostom. Chrysostom had considerable sympathy for these exiles and wrote to Theophilus in Alexandria, strongly urging a reversal of his anti-Origenist stance and a return of these exiles to communion.[65] This infuriated Epiphanius, who set out immediately for Constantinople with the intent of discrediting Chrysostom and all Origenists living there.

Chrysostom, bishop of Constantinople from 398, denounced Empress Eudoxia in blistering sermons, and in the process created no little tension between the court and the Church.[66] Cameron[67] notes,

> We should, therefore, see the fourth century, after the death of Constantine, as a time of ferment and competition between pagans and Christians, when despite imperial support for Christianity the final outcome was still by no means certain . . . despite advances that had been made, Christianity was by no means evenly spread in the cities of the East at the end of the fourth century, and much of the countryside remained pagan for far longer.

---

[62] See H. G. Evelyn White, *The Monasteries of the Wâdi'n Natrun, 2: The History of the Monasteries of Nitria and of Scetis* (ed. W. Hanser; New York: Metropolitan Museum of Art, 1932), 128.

[63] Jerome, *Epistula* 95.2.

[64] Jerome, *Epistula* 91.

[65] In his Festal Letter of 402, Theophilus referred to Origen as the "Hydra of heresies." See Quasten, *Patrology*, 3.384.

[66] Mango, *Byzantium*, 63.

[67] Averil Cameron, *The Mediterranean World in Late Antiquity (A.D. 395–600)* (London: Routledge, 1993), 13.

In 403, the dispute between Chrysostom and Theophilus of Alexandria gave Eudoxia an opportunity to have Chrysostom deposed and exiled to Bithyria. However, riots broke out in the streets between local citizens and people who had come from Alexandria. The Empress recalled and reinstated Chrysostom as bishop. Even so, the distance between the Church and the imperial family remained irreconcilable.

Epiphanius arrived in Constantinople in the spring of 403, intending to oust Chrysostom as bishop and remove the Origenists in that city from his protection. He refused Chrysostom's offer of hospitality and communion. Instead, he held a service at St. Johns Church, outside the city, and flouted Chrysostom's authority by ordaining a deacon. On the way to a debate in the Church of the Holy Apostles in Constantinople, Chrysostom's emissary, Serapion, confronted Epiphanius, accusing him of not following canonical procedure and of possibly precipitating a riot.[68] Curiously, Epiphanius turned around and left Constantinople. He died on 12 May 403 aboard ship on the return to Cyprus. He played a prominent role in the turbulent era that marked the end of the ancient world and the beginning of the Christian middle ages, not the least of which was his significant contribution to Nicene orthodoxy becoming widely accepted.

2. EPIPHANIUS' USE OF THE NT

In the fourth century, the institutionalizing Christian church was of great importance for the institutionalizing Empire. In this connection, a monolithic image for the Church was considered important if Christianity was to triumph over the old institutions and play a significant role in the Empire. Epiphanius himself had a major role in these developments. As Dechow[69] put it,

> the triumph of Athanasian over Arian Christianity would have been hard put to endure without the recalcitrant steadfastness of Epiphanius and the fourth-century Christian right.

Ancient characterizations tend to present a more positive view of Epiphanius than do modern studies. For instance, Jerome calls him "highly venerated" and "the holy father."[70] Sozomen even says that he is "the most revered man under the whole heaven," and "the most

---

[68] Socrates, *History* 6.10–14. Sozomen, *History* 8.14–15, says that Epiphanius was convinced of his own unfairness due to a conversation with Ammonius.

[69] Dechow, *Dogma and Mysticism*, 463.

[70] Jerome, *Contra Joannem Hierosolymitanum* 4 [PL 23:374C; 379B].

distinguished of his contemporaries."[71] On the other hand, Murphy[72] says that Epiphanius is "of considerable but ill-digested erudition, joining a certain narrowness of outlook and singleness of purpose to an indisputable piety." Dean[73] characterizes him as a dogmatic reactionary who had a far-reaching influence, noting,

> His quarrels and his writings show Epiphanius to have had a crabbed old single-track mind, and the track he covers is usually a sidetrack. He clearly knew too much for his limited understanding. His style is discursive; his thought is poorly organized. Good and bad information, important and unimportant matters, stand side by side and form a rather unsavory mess.

Schmidtke[74] holds that Epiphanius shows a "completely uncritical arbitrariness in the utilization of previously known material," and detects several incongruencies. Thomas[75] holds that he is simply given to too much invective when dealing with heresy. Quasten[76] says, "Most of his treatises are hasty, superficial and disorderly compilations of the fruits of his extensive reading."

More recently, Williams[77] has observed that Epiphanius was essentially a heresiologist[78] and that,

> An author such as Epiphanius should be seen against the background of his century. It was a time of intellectual ferment when the church, newly recognized by the state, needed to define its identity more clearly; when the man on the street was deeply involved in ecclesiastical affairs. In such an atmosphere the appearance of heresiology is understandable, and surprised no one. The tradition of Christian

---

[71] Sozomen, *Historia ecclesiastica* 6.32.3–4; 8.14.1–4.

[72] Francis X. Murphy, *Rufinus of Aquileia: His Life and Works* (Washington, D.C.: Catholic University of America, 1945), 66.

[73] Dean, *Epiphanius' Treatise on Weights and Measures: The Syriac Version*, 1.

[74] A. Schmidtke, *Neue Fragmente und Untersuchungen zu den Judenchristlichen Evangelien: Ein Beitrag zur Literatur und Geschichte des Judenchristen* (TU 37.1; Leipzig: Hinrichs, 1911), 96. See also Gustav Hönnecke, *Das Judenchristentum in Ersten und Zweiten Jahrhundert* (Berlin: Twowitzsch, 1908), 230.

[75] Joseph Thomas, *Le Mouvement Baptiste en Palestine et Syrie (150 av. J.-C. - 300 ap. J.-C.)* (Gembloux: Duculot, 1935), 264.

[76] Quasten, *Patrology*, 3.385.

[77] Williams, *Epiphanius*, 1.xvi–xvii.

[78] See Walter Bauer, *Orthodoxy and Heresy in Earliest Christianity* (trans. R. Kraft and G. Krodel; London: SCM, 1971); Hans Dieter Betz, "Orthodoxy and Heresy in Primitive Christianity," *Interpretation* 19 (1965): 299–311; and H. Paulsen, "Schisma und Häresie, Untersuchungen zu 1 Kor. 11,18.19," *ZTK* 79 (1982): 180–83.

> heresiology was already ancient when Epiphanius wrote. . . . Epiphanius was merely trying to do, systematically and comprehensively, a work which others before him had done, and for which a demand existed.
>
> Despite the criticisms to which he is open, Epiphanius should not be viewed as essentially negative. . . . Epiphanius writes not so much to attack heresy as to defend an ideal.

Epiphanius' writings were significant in the developing dichotomy between orthodoxy and heresy. The widespread diffusion of Epiphanius' writings, not only in Greek and Latin but in Armenian, Coptic, Syriac and Georgian, testifies to his popularity. According to Jerome,[79] Epiphanius' works were "eagerly read by the learned on account of their subject matter, and also by the plain people on account of their language."[80] Holl[81] observes Epiphanius' language to be an "elevated Koine." Of his works, Quasten[82] notes, "Their style is careless, verbose and according to Photius (*Bibl. cod.* 122) 'like that of one who is unfamiliar with Attic elegance.'" This is not surprising, in that Epiphanius was suspicious of all Hellenistic learning and considered the Greek philosophical schools to be heretical.

It cannot be assumed tacitly that Epiphanius used only one biblical text in his lifetime or at any given time or place. With reference to the geographical provenance of Epiphanius' text, Kenyon[83] posed that "previous to his appointment to the See of Salamis, his home was in Palestine, so that his evidence with regard to the Scriptural text is probably to be credited to that locality." This view was followed by Eldridge,[84] who argued 1) that most of Epiphanius' quotations appear to be from memory and exhibit a type of text with which he had been familiar for many years, and 2) that most quotations appear in works written too soon after his move from Palestine to Cyprus to permit extensive changes in the textual character of his memorized quotations.

---

[79] Jerome, *De viris illustribus* 114.

[80] See Karl Holl, *Die handschriftliche Überlieferung des Epiphanius* (TU 36; Leipzig: Hinrich's, 1910): 1–98, for discussion of the manuscripts of Epiphanius' works. See Manlo Simonett, "Some Observations on the Theological Interpretation of Scripture in the Patristic Period," *Biblical Interpretation in the Early Church* (Edinburgh: T&T Clark, 1994), for discussion of the use of Scripture in these controversies.

[81] Holl, *Epiphanius* (GCS 25): vii.

[82] Quasten, *Patrology*, 3.385.

[83] F. G. Kenyon, *Handbook to the Textual Criticism of the New Testament* (London: Macmillan, 1901), 221.

[84] Lawrence A. Eldridge, *The Gospel Text of Epiphanius of Salamis* (SD 41; Salt Lake City: University of Utah Press, 1969), 6.

While this is possible, the decade or more after Epiphanius' relocation in Cyprus is certainly ample to permit the use of texts that he may have acquired from Caesarea, Antioch or even Alexandria. Longer citations probably reflect a text or texts that he used on Cyprus and/or while writing in Antioch. Shorter quotations could reflect texts memorized earlier, but could also have been memorized during the heated disputes while he was in Salamis. While his quotations are an important witness to the text in the Eastern Mediterranean, they cannot be assumed to reflect a Palestinian text form.

Epiphanius has been noted as "notoriously slovenly" in his habits of quotation.[85] In many instances, this is true; however, in many other instances, his work reflects *verbatim* the Greek text of the NT, and at times even in extensive portions of several verses cited as a block of text. His citation of 1 Cor 15:12–15 is given with remarkable fidelity. Only in the last verse did he substitute a term for a phrase that was not necessary for his purpose. Similarly, Heb 6:4–8 is given precisely, with the exception that Epiphanius omits the last part of v. 4. Only a few lines later, Epiphanius quotes Heb 6:9–10 in an exact form. Thus, in *Pan* 59 seven verses of Hebrews reflect a biblical exemplar. In many instances, however, only that part of a verse is cited that is required for his immediate purpose, with merely the gist given of the remainder. At times, Epiphanius gives only the essence of a text, including wording from the text important for his argument. An example is Rom 13:1–4 in *Pan* 40.4.3–4. The citation begins with a fairly accurate quotation of the last clause of 13:1. Following v. 1 is a formula of citation, ὡς λέγει ὁ ἀπόστολος, indicating clearly his intent to cite the text rather than to allude to it. The second verse is then quoted with precision, with the exception that he omits the second part of the verse and substitutes a synonym for ἀντιτασσόμενος. Then Epiphanius lapses into a very loose quotation of v. 3, displaying several omissions, additions and variations in word order and syntax not found in any other known NT MSS. He omits the first part of v. 4, gives a very accurate clause, and follows with a loose rendering of the final clause. It is not uncommon for him to adjust the beginning and/or ending of an otherwise verbally precise citation so as to make the reference fit his sentence structure. Occasionally, he transposed words or phrases, and in a few instances he even altered the order of verses. Simple allusions are commonplace in his writings.

---

[85] Fee, "Use of the Greek Fathers," *Text of the NT in Contemporary Research*, 192–93.

Epiphanius' quotations present special problems. While verbal inexactitude exists in many of his references, numerous instances of accurate citation also occur.[86] In fact, of 132 quotations of Acts, sixty-four (48.5%) exhibit verbal precision. Of forty-eight quotations of the Catholic Epistles, thirty-one are verbally precise (64.6%). And of 789 quotations of the Pauline Epistles, 431 are verbally exact (54.6%). Obviously, care must be taken to include only quotations that have substantial claim to be representative of an exemplar. When such care is taken, there are sufficient texts, both in quantity and quality, to permit serious inquiry into the textual affinities of Epiphanius' quotations of the Apostolos.

3. PREVIOUS EXAMINATIONS OF EPIPHANIUS' QUOTATIONS

No significant attempt has been published regarding the textual characteristics of Epiphanius' text of Acts, the Catholic or the Pauline Epistles. Using only minute evidence, von Soden[87] concluded that the I-text[88] could be discerned in Epiphanius' quotations of Acts[89] and the Pauline Epistles,[90] and he noted that among fourth-century Palestinian Fathers Epiphanius attests the most K readings.[91] Given the fragmentary basis of his observations, von Soden's statements are inconclusive.

Hutton[92] included Epiphanius among witnesses attesting "triple readings," assigning Epiphanius' quotations of Matt 8:28, Luke 8:26, John 15:26, Acts 15:1, Rom 15:8, 1 Cor 15:47, and Rev 3:7 to the Alexandrian text, John 2:17, Acts 2:28, and 1 Cor 7:8 to the "Western" text, and 1 Cor 7:32 and 9:7 to the Syrian text. Of twelve readings, only two are from Acts and five are from the Pauline Epistles, which is hardly sufficient to constitute a significant contribution to Epiphanius' text.

---

[86] See James A. Brooks, *The New Testament Text of Gregory of Nyssa* (SBLNTGF 2; Atlanta: Scholars Press, 1991), 25–26, on exactitude in patristic quotations. More will be said on this below, pp. 26–36.

[87] Hermann von Soden, *Die Schriften des Neuen Testaments in ihrer ältesten erreichbaren Textgestalt* (Göttingen: Vandenhoeck und Ruprecht, 1913).

[88] I-text contains a variety of manuscripts with diverse textual peculiarities, resulting in several sub-groups. See *cp cit.*, 2.xiv–xv.

[89] von Soden, *op cit.*, 1.3.1739.

[90] von Soden, *op cit.*, 1.3.1953. von Soden did not present specific evidence pertaining to the textual character of Epiphanius' quotations of the Gospels and considered the infrequent quotations from the Catholic Epistles to be relatively unimportant (see *op cit.*, 1.3.1873).

[91] von Soden, *op cit.*, 2.xix. The Byzantine text is also referred to as the Koine text, and earlier was known as the Syrian, Antiochian, or Ecclesiastical text.

[92] E. A. Hutton, *An Atlas of Textual Criticism* (Cambridge: Cambridge University Press, 1911), see the charts inside the back cover.

Eldridge[93] addressed Epiphanius' textual affinities in the gospels. The study is in two parts: 1) a list of two hundred and seventy variation units from quotations of the gospels, and 2) an examination of textual relationships. His analysis consists of determining the percentages of agreement with NT witnesses representing the respective text-types following the quantitative method advocated by Colwell and Tune.[94] Eldridge found Matt 1:18-11:18 to be predominantly Alexandrian, and 11:19-26:50 textually mixed, but somewhat Byzantine. On the basis of twenty-two readings, Mark was determined to be "Western," exhibiting frequent agreement with the African Old Latin. Luke and John were concluded to have primary agreement with the Alexandrian text, with some Byzantine influence. He also concluded that Epiphanius' frequent agreement with the Alexandrian text likely reflects his use of a fourth century Palestinian text that still preserved many pre-Byzantine readings that were subsequently lost through Byzantine revision and are thus absent from most late Caesarean manuscripts. Eldridge also noted that Epiphanius' text of Luke and John witnesses to a stage in the development of the Caesarean text intermediate between the pre-Byzantine text current in Caesarea during the third century and the thoroughly revised text that occurs in later Caesarean manuscripts.

Because of verbal inexactitude in many of Epiphanius' quotations, Eldridge concluded that Epiphanius probably quoted from memory and likely from a text that he had known and used for many years. Eldridge thought Epiphanius' quotations to reflect a type of text that he had used in southern Palestine during the earlier part of his life. His use of a Caesarean type of text leads Eldridge to conclude that this text-type cannot be localized only in Caesarea during the fourth century.

Unfortunately, Eldridge's work on John was criticized strongly.[95] Fee notes that the presentation of textual data is incomplete. Eldridge should have included 211 variants for John, whereas he only has ninety-two. Fee notes that instead of simply presenting lists of variants, Eldridge should have presented the full gospel text. Fee also concludes that Eldridge's analysis includes too many textual trivia. In view of the fact that eleven references are from one loose and conflated quotation, one must also question whether the twenty-two variants used in Mark are adequate to justify the conclusion that Epiphanius used a "Western" text of Mark.

---

[93] Lawrence A. Eldridge, *The Gospel Text of Epiphanius of Salamis* (SD 41; Salt Lake City: University of Utah Press, 1969).

[94] E. C. Colwell and E. W. Tune, "Variant Readings: Classification and Use," *JBL* 83 (1964): 253–61.

[95] See Gordon D. Fee, review of Eldridge, *The Gospel Text of Epiphanius of Salamis*, *JBL* 90 (1971): 368, 370.

Fee concludes, "The textual affinities of Epiphanius still await definition." In addition, Mullen[96] criticizes Eldridge for working with incorrect control groups, i.e., using the Armenian and Georgian versions as "Caesarean" witnesses, although neither of these versions exists in a critical edition, as well as using large numbers of Old Latin witnesses whose relationships to one another have not been clarified.

In 1980, Thomas C. Geer, Jr., completed an M.Th. thesis on "The Text of Acts in Epiphanius of Salamis" at Harding Graduate School of Religion.[97] Geer found problems with Eldridge's work on Epiphanius' quotations of Luke.[98] For instance, thirty-six quotations of Luke (encompassing twenty-five different verses) were not included in Eldridge's list of Epiphanius' quotations of Luke. Also, variants, which according to Eldridge's own criteria should have been included, were omitted from the apparatus. Geer provided two illustrations.

1) Luke 2:40 (*Anc* 31.7; *Anc* 38.1)

    a. τῷ πνεύματι Epiph TR A E F G H X 036 037 039 041
    b *om* ℵ B D L W

Epiphanius refers to this passage twice, once including τῷ πνεύματι, and once omitting it. Epiphanius obviously knew the longer text, but the omission cannot be used in support of Epiphanius' awareness of a shorter text as the omission occurs at the end of a quotation.

2) Luke 22:43–44 (*Anc* 31.5; *Anc* 37.1; *Anc* 37.3–4; *Pan haer* 69.19.4; *Pan haer* 69.61.1)

    ὤφθη δὲ αὐτῷ ἄγγελος ἀπ' οὐρανοῦ ἐνισχύων αὐτόν. καὶ γενόμενος ἐν ἀγωνίᾳ ἐκτενέστερον προσηύχετο· καὶ ἐγένετο ὁ ἱδρὼς αὐτοῦ ὡσεὶ θρόμβοι αἵματος καταβαίνοντος ἐπὶ τὴν γῆν

    a. Epiph ℵ*β D K L X 036* Θ 041 Ψ *f*¹ 565 700 892* 1241 1242 1253 1365 1546 2148 2174 *Byz* it^{d.e} vg Diatessaron Iren
    b. *om* 𝔓⁷⁵ ℵ^c A B T W it^f syr^s cop^{sa.bo} Clem Or Cyr
    c. include with asterisks 036 041^c 892^c 1079 1195 1216

---

[96] Roderic L. Mullen, *The New Testament Text of Cyril of Jerusalem* (SBLNTGF, 7; Atlanta: Scholars Press, 1997), 49–51.

[97] Thomas C. Geer, Jr., "The Text of Acts in Epiphanius of Salamis" (M.Th. thesis, Harding Graduate School of Religion, 1980).

[98] Geer presented a communication entitled "The Text of Luke-Acts in Epiphanius of Salamis" at the Seventh International Conference on Patristic Studies, Oxford, 9 September 1975.

Geer noted that by introducing at least two of his quotations with ἐν τῷ κατὰ Λουκᾶν εὐαγγελίῳ φησι, Epiphanius clearly indicates the passage to be Lukan. Geer concluded that while Eldridge set out a commendable method, his lack of thoroughness in following that method raises questions regarding the textual affinities of Epiphanius in Luke.

Geer presented the full text of the quotations of Acts in Epiphanius (seventy-seven verses), followed by a critical apparatus of one hundred genetically-significant variation units. He collated the text of Epiphanius fully against fifty-eight MSS selected as representative of the major textual traditions. Since Epiphanius' quotations are often free, Geer examined all verbally-precise citations in Acts that are introduced by formulas. This examination adapted a profile from Fee's[99] analysis of the text of John in Origen and Cyril of Alexandria. Geer concluded that Epiphanius' primary agreement is with the later "Western" cursives which have a definite Byzantine influence, and Epiphanius appears to have some relationship with 1739.

Geer's dissertation at Boston University was "An Investigation of a Select Group of So-Called Western Cursives in Acts." Several MSS of Acts dating from the ninth to the fourteenth centuries have been classified as "Western" cursives, implying that they have been influenced by the "Western" textual tradition. However, the precise extent of that influence has never been specified. Geer examines the text of 181 383 614 913 945 1175 1518 1611 1739 1891, addressing 1) their relationship to each other, 2) their connection to the "Western" tradition, and 3) their value for the history of the text of Acts. Comparing thirty-five MSS and fourteen fragments against each other, Geer presents a preliminary statistical analysis, followed by a detailed examination of genetically-significant variations in eight sample chapters of Acts. Geer found that five of the MSS (181 945 1175 1739 1891) are Egyptian witnesses, influenced significantly by the Byzantine textual tradition, but only in a minor way by the "Western" text. Within these five, a family relationship was discovered among three (945 1739 1891), a triad he termed "Family 1739." The other five MSS (383 614 913 1518 1611) are basically Byzantine, yet influenced by the "Western" tradition. None of the MSS consistently maintains a text similar to that of Codex Bezae, and none merits the designation "Western." These MSS indicate that certain MSS in the Egyptian and Byzantine traditions, between the ninth and fourteenth centuries, included certain "Western" readings.

---

[99] Gordon D. Fee, "The Text of John in Origen and Cyril of Alexandria: A Contribution to Methodology in the Recovery and Analysis of Patristic Citations," *Bib* 52 (1971): 357–94.

Given Epiphanius' probable relationship with 1739, Geer followed with an examination of Family 1739 in Acts.[100] Geer's study is valuable in that his quantitative conclusions are based upon 2838 places of variation in Acts, rather than upon selected data in a sampling method. More precisely, he limited his qualitative analysis to 147 genetically-significant units of variation in eight chapters of Acts that permitted specific profiles to emerge. Already aware that 945 1739 and 1891 were primary members of the family, Geer was able to add 1704 to the family, and to recognize 630 and 2200 as secondary members. He concluded that all members of Family 1739 belong to the Egyptian textual tradition of Acts. Further, 206 429 and 522 are related significantly to the family, but comprise their own special relationship, especially 429 and 522. Although sharing certain readings with Family 1739, these three MSS are essentially Byzantine in character. Family 1739, then, has become a recognized group of MSS that is especially important for the examination of Epiphanius' textual affinities.

In 1974, Osburn[101] completed a Ph.D. dissertation at St. Andrews on "The Text of the Pauline Epistles in Epiphanius of Salamis." The full text of Epiphanius' quotations is presented, with a critical apparatus of variations in the MS tradition of Epiphanius as well as in the NT text with only minimal textual support. This is followed by a list of 319 variation units, including data from fourteen papyri, sixteen uncials and thirty-six cursives collated in full against the text of Epiphanius. Osburn first provides a quantitative analysis based upon all variation units. Although Epiphanius' quotations are often brief and probably from memory, Osburn included in his study all instances of textual agreement in Epiphanius. Knowing that Epiphanius' quotations are often adapted, Osburn followed with a profile adapted from Fee's above mentioned (see n. 100) profile that permitted a closer examination of all significant readings found in the seven longer citations of Epiphanius in the Pauline Epistles, which have legitimate claim to reflect an actual biblical exemplar. Osburn concluded his study with attention to places in which Epiphanius comments specifically on various readings known to him in the manuscript tradition or in other patristic writings, concentrating upon two: 1 Cor 10:9 (κύριον, Χριστόν, θεόν) and 2 Tim 4:10 (Γαλλίαν, Γαλατίαν, Γαλιλαίαν). Osburn concluded that Epiphanius' text demonstrates little affinity with the "Western" text or with the older

---

[100] Thomas C. Geer, Jr., *Family 1739 in Acts* (SBLMS 48; Atlanta: Scholars Press, 1994).

[101] Carroll D. Osburn, "The Text of the Pauline Epistles in Epiphanius of Salamis" (Ph.D. dissertation, University of St. Andrews, Scotland, 1974).

Egyptian MSS, but is primarily "later Alexandrian" with some influence from the earlier form of the developing Byzantine tradition.

However, since these studies were completed, considerably more has been learned of groupings of manuscripts selected as representative of the various textual groups. Too, more has been learned about selecting quotations for use in textual analysis. Also, while Fee's profile represented the best available procedure for analyzing the readings in a patristic writer, major advances have been made in methodology in analyzing the quotations of a patristic writer,[102] all of which make it necessary for the text of the Apostolos to be investigated afresh. Finally, while Revelation is not properly a part of the Apostolos, as defined by Basil, quotations from Revelation are included in this study, but due to insufficient evidence are not analyzed.

---

[102] See Bart D. Ehrman, "The Use of Group Profiles for the Classification of New Testament Documentary Evidence," *JBL* 106 (1987): 465–86, and Gordon D. Fee, "The Use of Greek Patristic Citations in New Testament Textual Criticism: The State of the Question," in *Studies in the Theory and Method of New Testament Textual Criticism* (SD 45; ed. E. Epp and G. Fee; Grand Rapids: Eerdmans, 1993).

CHAPTER 2

EPIPHANIUS' TEXT AND APPARATUS

1. THE TEXT OF THE APOSTOLOS IN PALESTINE

Ropes[1] held that Origen's citations reflect an Old Egyptian type of text that is also reflected in Eusebius' citations.[2] He did not think that a distinctive type of text in Acts was to be found in Palestine.[3] Von Soden, however, thought that Epiphanius and Cyril of Jerusalem reflect Western influence.[4] Lake[5] thought that 1739 might represent an Origenian-Caesarean text of the epistles, and held, "it is natural to presume that the same may be true of Acts, but here the evidence fails." Haenchen[6] followed Lake's lead and thought 1739 might evidence a Caesarean text-type in Acts, but did not continue this line of thinking in his commentary.[7] Boismard and Lamouille found some readings in 1739 to be useful in reconstructing the "Western" text but found no distinctive Caesarean type of text for Acts.[8] However, Geer[9] found that 1739 reflects a "later Alexandrian" type of text in Acts, with some Western and Byzantine influence." Apparently a specific type of text of Acts did not

---

[1] James Hardy Ropes, "The Text of Acts," *The Beginnings of Christianity, Part I, The Acts of the Apostles* (ed. F. J. Foakes-Jackson and Kirsopp Lake; London: Macmillan, 1926), clxxxix, ccxci.

[2] See M. Jack Suggs, "The New Testament Text of Eusebius of Caesarea" (Ph.D. dissertation, Duke University, 1954).

[3] Ropes, *Beginnings of Christianity*, 1.cxc–cxci.

[4] Hermann von Soden, *Die Schriften des Neuen Testaments in ihrer ältesten erreichbaren Textgestalt* (Göttingen: Vandenhoeck und Ruprecht, 1911), 1.2, 1759.

[5] Kirsopp Lake, J. de Zwaan, and Morton S. Enslin, "Codex 1739," in *Six Collations of New Testament Manuscripts* (HTS 17; ed. K. Lake and S. New; Cambridge: Harvard University Press, 1932), 145.

[6] Ernst Haenchen, "Zum Text der Apostelgeschichte," *ZTK* 54 (1957): 54–55.

[7] Ernst Haenchen, *The Acts of the Apostles* (Philadelphia: Westminster, 1971).

[8] M.-É. Boismard and A. Lamouille, *Le Texte Occidental des Actes Apôtres: Reconstitution et Réhabilitation*, Tome 1, *Introduction et Textes* (Paris: Editions Recherche sur les Civilisations, 1984), 25, 27.

[9] Thomas C. Geer, Jr., "Codex 1739 in Acts and Its Relationship to Manuscripts 945 and 1891," *Bib* 69 (1988): 31, 41–42.

exist in Roman Palestine and 1739, while related to the region, is to be viewed as later Egyptian in character rather than as a "Caesarean" text.

Suggs[10] posited that Eusebius' text of the Catholic Epistles has some relationship with Family 2412, without claiming that 2412 represented a type of text actually used in Palestine. Carder[11] proposed that 1243 does represent a Caesarean text-type in the Catholic Epistles, to which Aland[12] responded that one could only term a text "Caesarean" when Origen and Eusebius confirm its presence in Caesarea, and that according to Carder's method most Byzantine manuscripts would have to be considered "Western." In Richard's[13] study of the Johannine Epistles, 1243 and 2412 were found to be Alexandrian rather than Caesarean. No text-type has been demonstrated in the Catholic Epistles with reference to Palestine.

Regarding the Pauline Epistles, Zuntz[14] found that 1739 has close affinity with the Egyptian text reflected in Origen and thought the so-called "Caesarean" manuscripts to be a sub-group of the Egyptian text. Murphy[15] suggested that Eusebius reflects an Egyptian text in Romans and 1 Corinthians, and suggested that the so-called "Euthalian" manuscripts used by Zuntz[16] have diverse text-types. MS 015, for instance, reflects an Old Egyptian text-form, while 88 is Byzantine. On the basis of this analysis, Willard[17] decided that colophons have no actual bearing on the text-type of manuscripts and that manuscripts with the "Euthalian apparatus" do not necessarily reflect a Caesarean text-type. So, analysis of the manuscripts that have been used to suggest a Caesarean text-type in the Pauline epistles shows that only 1739 has any clear link to that region. The patristic data in Origen and Eusebius do not evidence any distinctive text-type. The textual affinities of the Pauline corpus in Caesarea were more Egyptian in character.

---

[10] Suggs, "The New Testament Text of Eusebius," 149, 285–88.

[11] Muriel Carder, "A Caesarean Text in the Catholic Epistles," *NTS* 16 (1969): 252–70.

[12] Kurt Aland, "Bemerkungen zu den gegenwärtigen möglichkeiten textkritischer Arbeit aus Anlass einer Untersuchung zum Cäesarea-Text der Katholischen Briefe," *NTS* 17 (1970): 4.

[13] W. Larry Richards, *The Classification of the Greek Manuscripts of the Johannine Epistles* (SGLDS 35; Missoula, MT; Scholars Press, 1977), 68–69, 195–98.

[14] Günther Zuntz, *The Text of the Epistles: A Disquisition upon the Corpus Paulinum* (London: Oxford University Press, 1953), 66, 80, 153–55.

[15] Harold Murphy, "Eusebius' New Testament Text in the *Demonstratio Evangelica*," *JBL* 78 (1954): 162–68.

[16] Zuntz, *Text of the Epistles*, 13–14, 20–24, 78.

[17] L. Charles Willard, "A Critical Study of the Euthalian Apparatus" (Ph.D. dissertation, Yale University, 1970), 1.

Hannah[18] concluded that Origen's text of 1 Corinthians is decidedly Egyptian in character. His move from Alexandria to Caesarea evidences no separate text. The "Western" text is notably absent from Origen's text of 1 Corinthians, raising the question of just how widespread was its presence in Egypt in the third and fourth centuries. Interestingly, Mees[19] concluded that Clement of Alexandria's citations of the Pauline Corpus evidence little affinity with the "Western" text. This might suggest that "Western" influence in Egypt during the second century was restricted to some copies of the Gospels ($\mathfrak{P}^{69}$; ℵ in John) and Acts ($\mathfrak{P}^{29}$ $\mathfrak{P}^{38}$ $\mathfrak{P}^{48}$). Hannah concluded that the Byzantine text is nonexistent in Egypt during the third century, and the Byzantine influence that is detected in Origen occurs when the Egyptian and Byzantine witnesses share the same reading.

Recently, Mullen[20] found a dearth of "Western" influence in Cyril of Jerusalem's NT citations. He also found that Cyril's text of Acts was certainly Egyptian in character, and from what little is known of the text of Acts in Origen and Eusebius, it appears that the dominant text of Acts used by patristic writers in the eastern Mediterranean was Egyptian. Due to the paucity of evidence, no conclusion can be made regarding the text of Cyril's Catholic Epistles, but more is available for analysis of his citations of the Pauline Epistles. Varying from book to book, Cyril's text of Romans, Ephesians, as well as 1 Thessalonians-Titus is close to the Egyptian text-form, while Hebrews, and possibly 2 Corinthians, Galatians, and Colossians is Byzantine. Cyril's text of 1 Corinthians was determined to be basically Egyptian, with some Byzantine influence. This suggests to Mullen that the dominant text in Roman Palestine was Egyptian, but the presence of Byzantine readings indicates that forces that would later produce the Byzantine text were already at work in Cyril's day.

It appears, then, that the text of the Apostolos in use in fourth-century Palestine was essentially Egyptian in character, with some Byzantine influence at certain places, and that the so-called "Western" text was not a textual factor. However, the link of 1739 to Caesarea does have implications for the study of the Apostolos in Epiphanius.

---

[18] Darrell D. Hannah, *The Text of 1 Corinthians in the Writings of Origen* (SBLNTGF 4; Atlanta: Scholars Press, 1997), 291–93.

[19] Michael Mees, *Die Zitate aus dem Neuen Testament bei Clemens von Alexandrien* (Bari: Istituto de Letteratura Cristiana Antica dell'Universita, 1970).

[20] Roderic L. Mullen, *The New Testament Text of Cyril of Jerusalem* (SBLNTGF 7; Atlanta: Scholars Press, 1997), 398–400.

2. RECONSTRUCTION OF A PATRISTIC TEXT: PROBLEMS OF METHOD

The suggestion was proposed by Jack Suggs[21] years ago that rather than merely presenting all data, scholars should aim at publishing "'critically reconstructed' texts" of the patristic witnesses to the text of the New Testament. Although reconstructed texts or presentations of the full textual data are currently available for most of the important Latin fathers,[22] the full NT text of most of the Greek fathers does not exist. Numerous earlier studies of the texts of Greek fathers often presented only variants from the TR or merely statistics based upon those variants.

The presentation of a Father's text should attempt, as far as possible, to reconstruct the text which the father used, either in his lifetime or in a given period or locale, or in a given work or part of a work. In this connection, a critical evaluation of the data presented is essential.

A. THE RECOVERY OF PATRISTIC DATA

Fee[23] argues that the presentation of a father's citations must be complete, including all known quotations and adaptations, although not all allusions. His categories and definitions in 1971 were:

Allusion: Reference to the *content* of a biblical passage in which *verbal* correspondence to the NT Greek text is so remote as to offer no value for the reconstruction of that text.

Adaptation: Reference to a biblical passage, which has clear *verbal* correspondence to the Greek NT, but which has been adapted to fit the Father's discussion and/or syntax.

Citation: Those places where a Father is consciously trying to cite, either from memory or by copying, the very words of the biblical text. Anyone who works closely with a given Father's text will probably make a further distinction in this category by noting citations at times to be "genuine" or "loose".

---

[21] M. Jack Suggs, "The Use of Patristic Evidence in the Search for a Primitive New Testament Text," *NTS* (1958): 147.

[22] See Gordon D. Fee, "The Text of John in Origen and Cyril of Alexandria: A Contribution to Methodology in the Recovery and Analysis of Patristic Citations," *Bib* (1971): 358, n. 2.

[23] Fee, "Text of John in Origin and Cyril," *Bib* (1971): 362.

However, locating usable data in Epiphanius' citations and excluding data that should not be incorporated is not a simple matter. It is widely assumed that simple verbal precision amounts to a usable citation. Using simple verbal correspondence and not examining citations in their patristic contexts, Geer used 100 units of variation in Acts and concluded, "his agreement is with the later 'Western' cursives which have a definite Byzantine influence."[24] When it was decided to add Acts to this study, a complete reexamination was undertaken. Using the criteria discussed below, only thirty-four usable units of variation are found in Acts in the present investigation. Using only one-third of the variations in Geer's thesis, the "Western" cursives do not figure prominently and are not included in this study. In fact, Epiphanius does not agree with the so-called "Western" cursives, but with Family 1739 and the Later Egyptians.

Similarly, in Osburn's dissertation,[25] 319 units of variation were included for Paul, but following the criteria below only 127 units remain usable. After excluding 60% of the earlier data, a more accurate understanding emerges. Epiphanius' text of the Pauline Epistles does not reflect "an early stage of the Koine text," but a Later Egyptian affinity.

Duplacy[26] asks, "S'agit-il d'une réminiscence, d'une allusion, d'une citation accommodée aux besoins d'un contexte ou d'une véritable citation?" Fee's categorizations are useful, especially when treating the text of Fathers, such as Hippolytus, Methodius and Origen, whose habits of citation are relatively good. However, with a Father such as Epiphanius, the three-fold classification leaves unclear the "loose citations" that Fee found enigmatic.[27] Needed are criteria to differentiate loose citations from adaptations and adaptations from allusions and allusions from reminiscences.

This approach was later used by Fee, along with Ehrman and Holmes,[28] but with revised definitions. While "citation" still refers to "a

---

[24] Thomas C. Geer, "The Text of Acts in Epiphanius" (M.Th. thesis, Harding Graduate School of Religion, 1980), 90.

[25] Carroll D. Osburn, "The Text of the Pauline Epistles in Epiphanius of Salamis" (Ph.D. dissertation, University of St. Andrews, 1974).

[26] Jean Duplacy, "Citations patristiques et critique textuelle du Nouveau Testament," *RSR* 47 (1959): 393.

[27] Gordon D. Fee, "The Text of John in *The Jerusalem Bible*: A Critique of the Use of Patristic Citations in New Testament Textual Criticism, *JBL* 90 (1971): 169.

[28] Ehrman, Fee and Holmes, *The Text of the Fourth Gospel in the Writings of Origen*. This approach is followed by Mullen, *The New Testament Text of Cyril of Jerusalem*; John J. Brogan, "The Text of the Gospels in the Writings of Athanasius" (Ph.D. dissertation, University of North Carolina, 1997), and Annewies van den

verbally-exact quotation of the biblical text," "adaptation" now refers to "a quotation that has been modified (syntactically or materially) in light of the context," and "allusion" signifies "a clear echo of a passage which nonetheless lacks a sustained verbal agreement." They note, "we will use the term 'quotations' to refer to all lemmata, citations, and adaptations; the term 'references' will signify all quotations and allusions."[29] Ernest[30] observes, "Some grade deflation is evident between the first and second sets of definitions: what would have qualified as a loose citation in the 1971 schema would be an adaptation under the newer definitions; and some adaptations under the older schema would be demoted to allusions under the new." Even with revised definitions, however, it is not easy to decide when an adaptation is usable for establishing a father's text, nor is it easy to determine when an allusion is to be included in the assessment.

While uniformity concerning terminology used in assessing the exactitude of patristic citations is lacking, the following appears to reflect Fee's revisions, as well as suggestions by others working on the topic:

Citation. A verbally exact quotation, whether it corresponds entirely (for very brief instances) or largely (for longer instances) and whether made from a text or from memory, often having an introductory formula and always having an explicit or implicit que to the reader that it is intended as a deliberate citation.

Adaptation. A quotation from a recognizable text, without an introductory formula, in which much of the lexical and syntactical structure of the text is preserved and woven unobtrusively into the patristic context, reflecting intent to cite, but which is adapted to the patristic context and/or syntax.

Allusion. A reference to the content of a certain biblical passage in which some ostensive verbal or motif correspondence is present, but reflecting intent to give only the gist of the text rather than to cite.

Reminiscence. A clear reference to a biblical text, but lacking significant verbal content and reflecting no intent to cite; a faint echo of a biblical text that has little or no verbal correspondence to the text.

Hoek, *Clement of Alexandria and His Use of Philo in the Stromateis: An Early Christian Reshaping of a Jewish Model* (Leiden: Brill, 1988), 20.

[29] Ehrman, Fee, and Holmes, *The Text of the Fourth Gospel*, 22.

[30] James D. Ernest, "Uses of Scripture in the Writings of Athanasius" (Ph.D. dissertation, Boston University, 2000), 31, n. 88.

The following criteria were used in gauging the accuracy of Epiphanius' citations and determining their usefulness.

1. ACCURATE CITATIONS.

Accurate citations are addressed by Fee[31] and Barbara Aland[32] and need not be discussed at length here. One might only add that sometimes a citation will have accurate terminology, yet evidence incidental transposition of a phrase or term that does not affect the meaning of the text. For instance, in Acts 15:29, cited in *Pan* 29.8.6, Epiphanius follows v. 28 with ἀπέχεσθαι αἵματος καὶ πνικτοῦ καὶ πορνείας καὶ εἰδωλοθύτου of v. 29. While εἰδωλοθύτου is transposed to the end of the list, Epiphanius clearly knows both πνικτοῦ and εἰδωλοθύτου as singular, with Family 1739, rather than plural with ℵ A B C 81 1175. Also, note the incidental transposition of terms in both citations of Acts 21:4 that does not affect the usefulness of the citations.

οἵτινες φησίν, ἔλεγον τῷ Παύλῳ διὰ τοῦ πνεύματος μὴ ἀναβαίνειν εἰς Ἰερουσαλήμ (*Anc* 68.7; *Pan* 74.5.7; from *Anc*)

The transposition of ἔλεγον prior to τῷ Παύλῳ does not affect the remainder of the citation, which is verbally precise. In this case, Epiphanius reads ἀναβαίνειν with 𝔐 against ἐπιβαίνειν in 𝔓[74] ℵ A B.

2. ADAPTATION TO PATRISTIC CONTEXT OR SENTENCE STRUCTURE.

A biblical citation may be adapted to the patristic context and/or sentence structure, yet retain much of the lexical and syntactical structure of the text. Adaptations often involve grammatical alterations in order to accommodate the patristic discussion, but may involve significant alterations to the text as well. The choice of whether to cite accurately or to adapt appears to be based primarily upon how well the language of the biblical text coincided with with the patristic point being made. The adjustment of citations was a commonly accepted practice in the Greco-Roman world that continued into the patristic era.[33]

---

[31] Gordon D. Fee, "The Use of Greek Patristic Citations in New Testament Textual Criticism," *ANRW* 26.1 (1992): 256–62.

[32] Barbara Aland, "Die Rezeption des neutestamentlichen Textes in den ersten Jahrhunderten," in *The New Testament in Early Christianity* (ed. J.-M. Sevrin; BETL 86; Leuven: Leuven University Press, 1989), 1–38.

[33] Christopher Stanley, *Paul and the Language of Scripture: Citation Technique in the Pauline Epistles and Contemporary Literature* (SNTSMS 69; Cambridge:

Adaptations vary in type. On one hand, the subtlety of an adaptation could render it undetectable by a reader, but it also possible that an obvious reworking of a text would be immediately recognizable as such. Common is the omission of words, phrases, or even whole clauses that a writer considered irrelevant for the immediate purpose. Of course, stylistic considerations could account for many such omissions; however, the conscious removal of extraneous material could result in a wording that conveyed the sense in which a reader would be expected to understand the text, especially if the deleted material contained wording inimical to the patristic intent in using the quotation. A quotation that in its original context might evoke problematic understandings could be extracted from that context and assigned new meaning in a different context. Alterations could involve grammatical or ideological changes. A word or phrase could be replaced by another more in line with a writer's intended point. Similarly, words or phrases could be added to emphasize a particular word or phrase that was crucial to the writer's use of the text. Changes could be made to clarify or change a vague referent. For various reasons, a writer could adapt a text in order to insert the text into the patristic discussion, or to ensure that a reader would understand the point that the writer wanted to make in mentioning the text. Obviously, while adaptations can, under certain circumstances, be understood as representative of a Father's text, they do not have the same degree of certainty in establishing the text of the NT as do citations. Even so, by using caution and careful analysis, certain adaptations can be included in the analysis of patristic quotations.

a. *Accurate Citation with Conscious Adaptation, Giving Only the Gist of Non-Essential Text*. At times, a text may be cited accurately in the necessary part, but only the gist given in the remainder. In such instances, the unadapted portion may be understood to represent a biblical exemplar. For instance, in *Pan* 66.81.3, Epiphanius cites Acts 3:6, precisely except for the very end.

ὅτι·
ἀργύριον καὶ χρυσίον οὐχ ὑπάρχει μοι, ὃ δὲ ἔχω, τοῦτό σοι δίδωμι,
ἐν τῷ ὀνόματι Ἰησοῦ Χριστοῦ ἀνάστα καὶ περιπάτει

Cambridge University Press, 1992), 275–91, 334–37, notes that Paul does not differ from Philo or the Greco-Roman writers in viewing as normal the tendency to alter biblical citations in order to advance arguments, and that this practice continued as part of the cultural and literary ethos of the patristic era as well. Clement of Alexandria, *Stromata*, and Rufinus, at the beginning of his translation of Origen's *Peri Archon*, both mention the common tendency to modify texts.

However, the citation is imprecise following Χριστοῦ, eliminating τοῦ Ναζωραίου and using common Christian terminology. Therefore, one cannot be certain that Epiphanius' exemplar read ἔγειρε καὶ περιπάτει with A C E P 049, rather than just περιπάτει with ℵ B D.

As a general rule, only units of variation that occur in the unaffected portions of a citation should be included; however, on rare occasions an argument can be made that even the affected portion could still evidence the reading of an exemplar. For instance, Epiphanius cites Gal 2:9 in *Pan* 30.25.5.

πάλιν δὲ ὁ ἅγιος Παῦλος μαρτυρεῖ καὶ αὐτὸς τοῖς περὶ Πέτρον λέγων·
Ἰάκωβος καὶ Ἰωάννης καὶ Κηφᾶς, οἱ δοκοῦντες στῦλοι εἶναι, δεξιὰς ἔδωκαν ἐμοί τε καὶ Βαρναβᾷ κοινωνίας

Here Κηφᾶς is transposed after Ἰωάννης, probably due inadvertently to the preceding discussion in 30.22–25, but the remainder is accurate. In the discussion Πέτρος is used of Peter, but Κηφᾶς is retained in this citation and likely represents the biblical exemplar. This means that Epiphanius can be cited in favor of Ἰάκωβος καὶ Κηφᾶς καὶ Ἰωάννης (Epiph 1.3.2) with 𝔐 ℵ B C K L P 1739, rather than Πέτρος καὶ Ἰάκωβος καὶ Ἰωάννης in ($\mathfrak{P}^{46}$ 2.1.3) D F G it$^{d.f.g}$ Or, or Ἰάκωβος καὶ Ἰωάννης in A.

b. *Adaptation to Patristic Context.* Epiphanius, *Pan* 38.8.4, cites, ἀφ᾽ οὗ παρέβη Ἰούδας ἀπελθεῖν εἰς τὸν τόπον τὸν ἴδιον from Acts 1:25 against the Cainites. Of the ten words, eight are precise, with nothing added, omitted or transposed. Two words are adjusted, involving an alteration and a substitution. Epiphanius evidently has Acts 1:18–25 open before him. Beginning this section, he says (8.2), "I know that I am giving a bulky list of texts," and gives two precise citations of Acts 1:18, 20 against Judas, whom he links with the Cainites. He then (8.3) continues his castigation of Judas by stressing his abandonment of his salvation, and in 8.4 says, "Thus the apostles made Matthias one of their number in his place, saying, ἀφ᾽ οὗ παρέβη Ἰούδας ἀπελθεῖν εἰς τὸν τόπον τὸν ἴδιον." With reference to the text of Acts 1 open before him, he makes two conscious alterations to this verse in order to drive home his point that Judas did not simply "go away" as the text says, but in fact *abandoned* "his whole salvation"(8.3) and went "to perdition" (8.5). In the first instance, οὗ is still genitive, but now masculine because of its new patristic antecedent, ἀριθμόν, instead of the biblical τῆς διακονίας ταύτης καὶ ἀποστολῆς. Secondly, Luke's πορευθῆναι (to depart) was consciously strengthened by the substitution of ἀπελθεῖν (to abandon association with someone; see Danker, *BDAG*, 102). In so doing, Epiphanius makes explicit what Luke leaves implicit. This being the case, Epiphanius can be understood to read ἀφ' with ℵ A B C D 81 945 1175 1704 1739 rather than ἐξ with TR 𝔐 E H 049 630 1073 1352.

Theological adaptations may involve add/omit, substitution, or transposition. With regard to add/omit and/or transposition in which all of the text is biblical, adaptation that consists of patristic alteration of the meaning of the biblical text raises the question of what is useable as text-critical data. Epiphanius, *Pan* 79.3.5 cites Acts 2:17 using accurate terminology, but transposing the phrase ἐνυπνίοις ἐνυπνιασθήσονται from the πρεσβύτεροι to the θυγατέρες because he is dealing with young women in the context, and he deletes the phrase dealing with the presbyters because he is addressing the topic of participation of women in public worship. Immediately after, Epiphanius says, "The word of God does not allow a woman 'to speak' in church either, or 'bear rule over a man.'" With this conscious alteration, then, women are no longer "prophesying," but silently "dreaming dreams." In this theologically-motivated alteration in which all of the text is biblical, Epiphanius clearly knows the dative ἐνυπνίοις rather than the accusative plural ἐνύπνια with 𝔐 (LXX).

c. *Conflation* is a form of adaptation that involves inserting a text within another text, more or less accurately. At times, Epiphanius conflates two passages into a single citation. This could reflect either poor quoting habits or poor memory, but could also be understood as very intentional if the reworked text is understood as central to his developing argument. For instance, 1 Cor 11:7 and 14:15 are conflated in *Pan* 70.3.7 and 80.6.6. Also 1 Cor 2:4 and 13 are conflated in *Pan* 74.7.8. Since in *Anc* 70.8 he cites the text accurately, he knew the correct text. Even so, while conflations should not be rejected *a priori*, they must be subjected to intense scrutiny before their data are usable in reconstructing a Father's text.

3. ALLUSION

Allusion involves reference to the *content* of a biblical passage in which some *verbal* correspondence is present, but with clear intent to give only the gist of the text rather than to cite. For instance, in *Pan* 9.4.9, Epiphanius uses Acts 2:38:

καὶ κατανυγεῖσι τὴν καρδίαν εἶπε·
μετανοήσατε, ἄνδρες ἀδελφοί, καὶ βαπτισθήτω ἕκαστος ἐν τῷ ὀνόματι Ἰησοῦ Χριστοῦ τοῦ κυρίου ὑμῶν καὶ ἀφεθήσονται ὑμῖν αἱ ἁμαρτίαι καὶ λήψεσθε τὴν δωρεὰν τοῦ ἁγίου πνεύματος.

The introduction is not overtly an intention to cite, but merely to give the gist of a well-known text in support of his argument. Accordingly, Epiphanius cannot be said to read ἐν with B C D 945 1739 1891 rather than ἐπὶ with TR 𝔐 ℵ A E H P 049 81 1073 1175 1352, nor τοῦ κυρίου Ἰησοῦ Χριστοῦ with D E 945 1739 1891 rather than Ἰησοῦ Χριστοῦ with TR 𝔐 𝔓⁷⁴ ℵ A B C H P 049 81 1073 1175 1352.

In *Pan* 44.6.1, Epiphanius cites Acts 7:56: ἀπεκρίναντο λέγων· ἰδού, ὁρῶ τὸν οὐρανὸν ἠνεῳγμένον καὶ τὸν υἱὸν τοῦ ἀνθρώπου ἑστῶτα ἐκ δεξιῶν τοῦ πατρός. However, in this allusion, Epiphanius substitutes words, changes plural to singular, and alters word order, and thus cannot be said to agree either with ἀνεῳγμένους in TR 𝔐 𝔓⁷⁴ D⁽*⁾ E H P 049 1073 1352 rather than διηνοιγμένους in ℵ A B C 81 945 1175 1739 1891, nor can he be taken to agree with ἑστῶτα ἐκ δεξιῶν in ℵ* A C E 1175 rather than ἐκ δεξιῶν ἑστῶτα in TR 𝔐 𝔓⁷⁴ ℵᶜ B D H P 049 81 945 1073 1352 1739 1891. That he is alluding to Acts 7:56 is clear, but verbal consistency is lacking.

One might also note Acts 10:12 in *Pan* 48.7.4: 11: καὶ πάντα τὰ τετράποδα καὶ ἑρπετὰ καὶ τοῦ οὐρανοῦ τὰ πετεινὰ ἐν αὐτῇ. It could be argued that while Epiphanius omits τῆς γῆς and changes the order of τοῦ οὐρανοῦ, he does keep the list in the same order, with three groups instead of four, as in 𝔓⁷⁴ ℵ A B and Family 1739. However, this two-verse citation is clearly only an allusion giving the gist of the verse and it is not at all certain whether Epiphanius' exemplar read τετράποδα καὶ ἑρπετὰ τῆς γῆς καὶ πετεινὰ τοῦ οὐρανοῦ with 𝔓⁷⁴ ℵ A B Cᶜ 81 (945 τὰ ἑρπετά) 1175 (1739 1891 τὰ ἑρπετά) rather than τετράποδα τῆς γῆς καὶ τὰ θηρία καὶ τὰ ἑρπετὰ καὶ τὰ πετεινὰ τοῦ οὐρανοῦ with TR 𝔐 H L P 049 1073 1352, or τετράποδα καὶ ἑρπετὰ τῆς γῆς καὶ τὰ θηρία καὶ τὰ πετεινὰ τοῦ οὐρανοῦ with E itᵉ, or τετράποδα καὶ τὰ θηρία καὶ τὰ ἑρπετὰ τῆς γῆς καὶ πετεινὰ τοῦ οὐρανοῦ with C*ᵛⁱᵈ.

In *Pan* 28.4.5, Epiphanius cites Acts 15:1: λέγοντας ὅτι· ἐὰν μὴ περιτμηθῆτε καὶ φυλάξητε τὸν νόμον, οὐ δύνασθε σωθῆναι. In this allusion, Epiphanius adds καὶ φυλάξητε and alters τῷ ἔθει to τὸν νόμον. Although he gives the gist of the text, there is no compelling reason to think that he is quoting a text at this point. So, one does not know whether his exemplar read περιτμηθῆτε with 𝔓⁷⁴ ℵ A B C D 81 1175, or περιτεμνῆσθε with 𝔐 E H L P 049 630 945 1073 1352 1704 1739 1891 Chr CyrJer.

Epiphanius' lengthy allusion to Rom 13:1–4 in *Pan* 40.4.3–4 includes several precise phrases, but is too loose to permit the conclusion that his exemplar read οὖσαι ἐξουσίαι with TR 𝔐 Dᶜ L P 049 33 104 699 1739 rather than οὖσαι with ℵ A B D* F G 81 1594 itᵈ·ᵉ·ᶠ·ᵍ in v. 1, or that it read θεοῦˢᵉᶜ with ℵ* A B D F G P 81 104 1739 rather than τοῦ θεοῦ TR 𝔐 ℵᶜ L 049 33 699 1594 Or.

One might note Mullen's[34] argument that, "at Luke 23:45, Cyril's several allusions make it clear that his text reads 'ἐκλίποντος'." Mullin lists also Rom 8:26, where Cyril's allusion reads τῆς ἀσθενείας for τῆς ἀσθενεία with B ℵ against ταῖς ἀσθενείαις of 𝔐 and τῆς δεήσεως of F G. Even so, one must exercise great caution, because the uncritical use of allusion in establishing the text of a Father could destroy the very exactitude desired in the process.

4. REMINISCENCE

Reminiscence may involve some verbal inaccuracy with clear reference to a biblical text, or it may be simply a brief reference to a biblical text. Reminiscences are not included in this study.[35]

5. OTHER CONSIDERATIONS

a. *Common Patristic Terminology.* Locution accounts for several instances of verbal correspondence with biblical texts, but with no intent to cite. In *Pan* 69.77.5, Epiphanius cites Acts 1:11: καί· οὕτως ὄψεσθε αὐτόν, ὃν τρόπον εἴδετε αὐτὸν ἀναλαμβανόμενον. Here, Epiphanius' imprecision and use of common Christian phraseology means that one cannot be certain of the reading of his biblical exemplar from this reference. Epiphanius' common patristic terminology is not included in this volume.

b. *Citations in Multiple Text-Forms.* Fee[36] draws attention to instances in which a Father presents quotations reflecting two or more text forms, and suggests the following guidelines:

1. At times, careful analysis indicates that the Father knew and used only one text form, and that the second quotation reflects either (a) faulty memory, or (2) inconsequential omissions or adaptations to the new context. In most such cases, Fee suggests, the long form reflects the Father's text and the short form is a Father's abbreviated version.
2. At other times, it appears that the Father knew and used two or more different forms of the text, e.g., Origen's citations of Mark in his "Commentary on John."

---

[34] Mullen, *New Testament Text of Cyril of Jerusalem*, 22, n. 85.
[35] See Robert Grant, "Citation of Patristic Evidence," in *New Testament Manuscript Studies* (ed. M. Parvis and A. Wikgren; Chicago: University of Chicago Press, 1950), 118.
[36] Fee, "Greek Patristic Citations," *ANRW* 26.1, 260.

3. When one cannot decide in this regard, Fee suggests that it is less likely that a Father knew and used two different texts than either that he is careless or that an error has made its way into his own textual tradition. This being the case, one cannot know the reading of the Father's text.

c. *Old Testament Citations* are sometimes adapted to the NT context, and patristic comments on citations often place them either within the OT or NT. At Pan 61.2.2, Epiphanius cites Acts 1:20 (Ps 68:26) with reference to Judas:

ὡς λέγει πάλιν ἄλλος προφήτης·
γενέσθω ἡ ἔπαυλις αὐτοῦ ἔρημος καὶ τὴν ἐπισκοπὴν αὐτοῦ λαβέτω
ἕτερος, σημαίνων ὅτι ἀπέθανεν κακῷ θανατῷ ὁ Ἰούδας

While the introduction might suggest the citation is from the OT, the context makes clear that the reference is to Acts rather than to Psalms. In the previous section, Epiphanius was working from Matt 27, stressing the fulfillment of prophecy regarding Judas' downfall. There, he cites Matthew's citation of Zech 11:12–13, making reference not to Zechariah but saying only, "As it was written of him in the prophets." So, although Zech 11:12–13 is in view, Epiphanius evidently had the text of Matt 27 open before him. Then, he turns to Acts 1 to continue his castigation of Judas, saying, "Let his habitation be desolate (Ps 68.26 LXX) and his bishopric another take (Ps 108:8 LXX)," which here is clearly from Acts 1:20 and which is followed immediately by citations from Acts 1:18 and 1:25. So, while the OT is very much in focus with Epiphanius' stated intent to prove from Scripture that Judas' actions and fate were foretold by "the prophets," he utilized the references to those texts in Matt 27 and Acts 1 to make his point. Accordingly, in Acts 1:20 Epiphanius should be cited in support of λαβέτω with ℵ A B C D rather than λαβοί with 𝔐.

d. *Readings in Lemmata and Commentary.* Fee[37] discusses the problems of assigning priority to readings in *lemmata* and commentary, using Origen and Cyril of Alexandria as examples. With regard to Origen, highest priority is given to readings found in the commentary, particularly *ad loc.* citations and adaptations. Readings in *lemmata* are taken second. Third, citations other than *ad loc.* are considered, supposing Origen would be likely to "look up" a passage in such instances. On the other hand, Cyril of Alexandria, whose habits of citing are less exact than those of Origen, gives the impression that he rarely consulted his biblical text when

---

[37] Fee, "The Text of John in Origen and Cyril," *Bib* (1971): 363–4.

citing, often conflating references to the text. Accordingly, Fee assigns first priority to the text of Cyril's commentary, the *lemmata* second, and variants from elsewhere in the commentary and all other works a distant third.

Admittedly, the reconstruction of the text of the Apostolos in Epiphanius of Salamis poses problems. Epiphanius may have used several biblical texts during his writing over the years. His own manner of citation may vary from work to work or even section to section. Further, each of his works has undergone its own textual modifications through the centuries. In view of these difficulties, one may wonder whether it is possible to reconstruct his text of the Apostolos. If so, certainly judgments must be made that are based upon a thorough working knowledge of the father's habits of citation as well as the nature of the data available in his extant works. This amounts to a reduction of approximately 66% of the data having verbal correspondence with the biblical text, but which clearly cannot be understood as representative of Epiphanius' exemplar.

B. PRESENTATION OF PATRISTIC DATA

Two methods of presentation of data are suitable for the presentation of the text of the Pauline epistles in Epiphanius. One is followed by G. M. Rolando and T. Caragliano[38] in their edition of the text of Luke and John in Ambrose, and advocated by Fee[39] in his discussion of methodology in the recovery and analysis of patristic citations. A running text of the father is given, to the extent that it can be reconstructed from the available sources. Along with this text are two or three sections of apparatus. The first apparatus consists of a list and full text of citations or adaptations presently available only in translation. These are not used in the reconstruction of the text because they are not sufficiently reliable representations of the father's Greek text, and consequently they require to be evaluated separately.[40] A second

---

[38] Giovanni M. Rolando and Tyndarus Caragliano, "Ricostruzione Teologico-Critica del Testo Latino del Vangelo di S. Luca Usato da S. Ambrogio," *Bib*, 26 (1945): 238–276; 27 (1946): 3–17, 30–64, and 210–240. A comparison of this presentation with that of R. W. Muncey, *The New Testament Text of St. Ambrose* (Cambridge: Cambridge University Press, 1959), illustrates what should and should not be done in the presentation of the biblical text of a father. See Metzger's review of Muncey's work in *JBL* 80 (1961): 187–188.

[39] Fee, *Bib* (1971): 357–394.

[40] See G. Bardy, "Le texte de l'epître aux Romains dans le commentaire d'Origène-Rufin," *RB* 29 (1920): 229–241, who arrived at the same conclusion regarding the text of Origen.

apparatus includes the references to all citations, the extent of text of each citation, and the complete text of all adaptations that have verbal significance. A third apparatus lists, and discusses as need arises, all of the variations, whether biblical or patristic.

An alternative format, and the one chosen for the present investigation, is found in Mees' analysis of the text of the NT in Clement of Alexandria.[41] Fee suggests this approach for patristic writers who cite freely.[42] Each citation or adaptation is listed separately by verse number. Critical evaluations appear in a separate discussions of the text itself or in footnotes to the text. A separate critical apparatus presents textual data, including agreements or disagreements with the biblical manuscript tradition. In this work, the critical apparatus is included within the text itself for ease of reference.

The format of presentation is that followed by the SBLNTGF series. Following the verse number, formulas of introduction are reproduced when they occur within the text of Epiphanius. Such formulas are concluded with a Greek semi-colon and the text of the citation itself begins on the next full line. When the formula occurs within or following the citation, the cited portion of the biblical text is underlined and the introductory material is not underlined. At times the patristic context is presented to the extent to which it is in relation with the text of the citation, in which case biblical words are underlined. All variant forms of Epiphanius' text are noted in the footnotes using patristic sigla, with the exception of the significant variants in the biblical portions that are set out in the critical apparatus following the text.

In the event a citation may belong to any of several biblical passages, those passages are mentioned in the footnotes. When several biblical passages are conflated or mixed by Epiphanius and presented as one passage, the text is presented in full for each biblical passage involved, and those words which are from the verse under consideration are underlined. Given in parentheses after each patristic citation is its location in the works of Epiphanius, given not by volume, page, and line of the printed edition, but by patristic chapter and section.

---

[41] M. Mees, *Die Zitate aus dem Neuen Testament bei Clemens von Alexandrien* (Bari: Istituto de Letteratura Cristiana Antica dell' Universita, 1970).

[42] Gordon D. Fee, "The Use of the Greek Fathers for New Testament Textual Criticism," in *The Text of the New Testament in Contemporary Research: Essays on the "Status Quaestionis,"* (SD 46; ed. B. Ehrman and M. Holmes; Grand Rapids: Eerdmans, 1995), 199.

For the NT, chapters and verses are numbered after the twenty-seventh edition of *Novum Testamentum Graece*[43] and for the OT the numeration of Rahlfs is followed.[44] The Gregory system is followed for NT MSS, except for major uncials.[45] Epiphanius' manuscripts are designated by the sigla used by Holl. When both Gregory and Holl use the same siglum, the manuscript of Epiphanius is indicated by a superscript ^{epiph}. For example, G refers to codex Boernerianus, whereas G^{epiph} refers to codex Vaticanus 503; and P refers to biblical codex Porphyrianus, but P^{epiph} refers to codex Paris gr. 833.

3. THE TEXTUAL APPARATUS FOR NT WITNESSES

A method based upon direct comparison of MSS is essential. The text of Epiphanius was collated in its entirety against NT manuscripts selected as representative of the various textual traditions.[46] The commonly accepted textual groups and their witnesses are:

A. ACTS

Egyptian:
    Old Egyptian – $\mathfrak{P}^{74}$ ℵ B
    Later Egyptian –
        A C 81 1175
        Family 1739 – 945 1704 1739 1891
"Western" uncials – D E + old Latin or vulgate
Byzantine – 𝔐 H L P 049 1073 1352

---

[43] Barbara Aland, *et al.*, eds. *Novum Testamentum Graece* (27th ed.; Stuttgart: Deutsche Bibelgesellschaft, 1993).

[44] Alfred Rahlfs, ed., *Septuaginta* (8th ed.; Stuttgart: Württembergische Bibelanstalt, 1965).

[45] See Kurt Aland, *Kurzgefasste Liste der griechischen Handschriften des Neuen Testaments* (*ANTF*, 1; Berlin: de Gruyter, 1963).

[46] Classification of witnesses according to text-type follows essentially the standard classification found in Bruce M. Metzger, *A Textual Commentary on the Greek New Testament* (2nd ed.; New York: United Bible Societies, 1994): 15*-16*; Kurt Aland and Barbara Aland, *The Text of the New Testament* (2nd ed.; trans. E. Rhodes; Grand Rapids: Eerdmans, 1989), 83–163; and J. Harold Greenlee, *Introduction to New Testament Textual Criticism* (rev. ed.; Peabody, Mass.: Hendrickson, 1995), 117–18.

B. CATHOLIC EPISTLES

Egyptian – $\mathfrak{P}^{72}$ ℵ A B C Ψ 33 323 1739
Byzantine – 𝔐 L 049 105 201 325 1022

C. PAULINE EPISTLES

Egyptian:
  Old Egyptian – $\mathfrak{P}^{46}$ ℵ B 1739
  Later Egyptian – A C P 33 81 104
"Western" uncials – D F G
Byzantine – 𝔐 K L 049 599 1594

D. REVELATION The seven verses from Revelation cited by Epiphanius are insufficient basis for analyzing his text of the Apocalypse, but brief observations are based upon: Older Primary (A C Oecumenius), Older Secondary (ℵ), Later Andreas (P Andreas), and Later Koine (𝔐 TR 046).

In 1980, Geer[47] concluded that the text of Epiphanius in Acts was closely related to 1739. He pursued this line of investigation further in his doctoral work at Boston University,[48] and in his analysis of Family 1739 in Acts.[49] Because of Geer's conclusion that the text of Epiphanius in Acts is closely related to 1739, selected MSS from Family 1739 are included in this study as a special group: 945 1704 1739 1891; however, Epiphanius has no special relationship with these MSS in the Catholic or Pauline Epistles.

Duplacy[50] gave some credence to the possibility of a "Western" text in the Catholic Epistles, but provided little evidence, and was followed in this assessment by C.-B. Amphoux.[51] This study of Epiphanius does not assume a "Western" text in the Catholic Epistles. Bover[52] discusses

---

[47] Geer, "The Text of Acts in Epiphanius of Salamis," (1980).

[48] Geer, "An Investigation of a Select Group of So-called Western Cursives in Acts" (Ph.D. dissertation, Boston University, 1985).

[49] Geer, *Family 1739 in Acts* (SBLMS 48; Atlanta: Scholars Press, 1994), esp. p. 113.

[50] Jean Duplacy, "Le texte occidental des épîtres catholiques," *NTS* 16 (1970): 397–99.

[51] C.-B. Amphoux, "Le Texte des épîtres catholiques. Essais de classement des états de texte, préparatoires à une histoire du texte de ces épîtres" (Ph.D. dissertation, Paris-Sorbonne, 1931).

[52] J. M. Bover, *Novi Testamenti Biblia Graeca et Latina* (5th ed.; Madrid: Gráficas Cóndor, 1968), xlvi–xlvii.

the possibility of finding a Caesarean text in the Pauline Epistles, but efforts to identify such a text-type there have been unsuccessful.[53]

The groupings selected above assume a constant textual affinity throughout the Pauline corpus. However, individual books may have divergent textual affinities. Some manuscripts evidence a different text type even within a given book.[54] In an M.A. thesis, Morrill[55] concluded that in 1 Corinthians five of the so-called "Western" cursives (181, 917, 1836, 1874, 1875),

> are very good representatives of the Alexandrian text-type for over half of the book, up to about 1 Cor 12:6, after which they switch to supporting a Byzantine type of text. . . . [All] are significantly closer to the Byzantine and Alexandrian texts than to the 'Western.' (112)

He also concluded that in 1 Corinthians 326 is a very mixed text, that Ψ and 6 have mixed texts much closer to the Byzantine tradition, and that 1908, often said to be a later Alexandrian MS in Paul, is strictly a Byzantine text in 1 Corinthians (113). P and 104 are called "borderline" Egyptians, but display mixed texts in 1 Corinthians (112). He observes concerning the Egyptian text in Corinthians,[56]

> The nucleus of the group is formed by manuscripts ℵ A B 33 81 and 1739, as well as C where it is extant. $\mathfrak{P}^{46}$ generally has a greater disparity to all other groups than does the "nucleus" of manuscripts, except that it normally is slightly closer than others to the "Western" group.

Although commonly considered as Egyptian witnesses, it is important to exclude Ψ 6 326 1908 from the analysis lest they skew the data.

Further, Metzger[57] lists Ψ 33 104 and 326 as Later Alexandrians in Acts. It is clear from Geer's[58] study that 33 is Byzantine in the first eleven

---

[53] See Kurt Aland, "The Significance of the Papyri for N.T. Research," in *The Bible in Modern Scholarship* (ed. J. P. Hyatt; London: Carey Kingsgate, 1966), 336–37; and *idem*, "Bemerkungen zu den gegenwärtigen Möglichkeiten textkritischer Arbeit aus Anlass einer Untersuchung zum Cäsarea-Text der katholischen Briefe," *NTS* 17 (1970): 1–9.

[54] See Thomas C. Geer, Jr., "The Two Faces of Codex 33 in Acts," *NovT* 31 (1989): 39–47, who concluded that 33 is basically Byzantine in Acts 1:1–11:25 and an excellent Egyptian witness in Acts 11:26–28:31."

[55] Bruce Morrill, "The Classification of the Greek Manuscripts of 1 Corinthians" (M.A. thesis, Harding Graduate School of Religion, 1981).

[56] See also Zuntz, *The Text of the Epistles*, 96–107.

[57] Metzger, *Text of the NT*, 216.

chapters, and Egyptian thereafter. The Alands[59] note that 33 has twenty-one Byzantine readings, twenty shared Byzantine and original text readings, thirty-four original text readings and twelve singular readings (24%; 23%; 39%; 14%). Given this mixture, 33 is not included in the Egyptian group in Acts. The Alands[60] also note (p. 118) that Ψ has forty-two Byzantine, twenty-five shared, twenty-three original and fifteen singular readings (40%; 24%; 22%; 14%), and assign it to Category III in Acts. MSS 104 and 326, although Late Egyptians in Paul, clearly are not so in Acts. The Alands list 104 as Category V in Acts, while 326 is only Category III. The higher category for 326 is misleading, for 104 has sixty-one Byzantine, twenty-six shared, nine original and eight singular readings (59%; 25%; 9%; 8%), while 326 has sixty-three Byzantine, twenty-seven shared, eight original and seven singular readings (60%; 26%; 8%; 7%). From the Alands' test readings, 326 is just as Byzantine in Acts as 104 and should be in Category V rather than Category III. For this reason, 104 and 326 are also excluded from this study of Acts.

All significant variants are included in the apparatus in which the reading of Epiphanius and at least one other reading have valid support from at least three Greek manuscripts used as control witnesses.[61] Other readings are relegated to footnotes. The reading of Epiphanius in the passage under consideration is always given first. Witnesses are cited in support of a reading in the following order: a) TR 𝔐, b) papyri, c) uncials, d) minuscules, and when appropriate, e) lectionaries, f) versions, and g) Fathers. Absence of a Greek witness in the apparatus indicates a lacuna or unreadable text. Parentheses denote differences in readings that do not affect the main point of the variant, as well as to denote a minor deviation from the reading being cited but which does not affect the principal point of the reading. When a word in a reading occurs more than once in a quotation, it is cited with *pr*, *sec*, or *tert* in parentheses to indicate which occurrence of the word is under consideration.

---

[58] Thomas C. Geer, Jr., "The Two Faces of Codex 33 in Acts," *NovT* 31 (1989): 39–47.

[59] Kurt Aland and Barbara Aland, *The Text of the New Testament*, 129.

[60] See Kurt Aland, *Text und Textwert der griechischen Handschriften des Neuen Testaments. III Die Apostelgeschichte* (ANTT 20; Berlin: de Gruyter, 1993), 684–709, esp. 692.

[61] As Hort, *The New Testament in the Original Greek: Introduction*, 46, noted, with three MSS in agreement, the statistical probability of independent scribal error decreases radically in comparison with agreement of only two witnesses. See also W. Larry Richards, *The Classification of the Greek Manuscripts of the Johannine Epistles* (SBLDS 35; Missoula: Scholars Press, 1977), 35ff., who suggests that no less than four witnesses are vital for statistical research. The "Western" triad of D F G, however, necessitates our use of three witnesses.

Insignificant variations are not included in the apparatus: obvious itacism, orthographical variation in proper names and place names, moveable ν, variable ς, ουτω/ουτως interchanges, and abbreviations such as ἀλλ' for ἀλλά. Particularly at the beginning, but also at the ending, of patristic citations, the text is often modified to fit patristic syntax and variants in those places are not included, nor are instances in which Epiphanius has a shorter ending of a text that is known to be longer elsewhere. In instances of minor variation, parentheses are placed around the siglum to indicate insignificant variation.

While scribal changes in MSS are often reflected in the apparatus, they are not included in the analysis. Versional and patristic data are included in the apparatus from printed editions of the NT, and patristic data from volumes in the SBLNTGF series.

4. TEXTUAL ABBREVIATIONS AND SIGLA

Symbols, abbreviations, and Latin terms are those commonly used in printed editions of the NT, such as NA^{27} and UBS^{4}.

5. ACTS AND EPISTLES IN EPIPHANIUS OF SALAMIS

Acts 1:4
ἤ·
περιμένειν τὴν ἐπαγγελίαν τοῦ πατρὸς ἣν ἠκούσατε (*Anc* 69.8)

καὶ πάλιν ἔλεγει·
ἀπὸ Ἱεροσολύμων μὴ χωρίζεσθε, ἀπεκδεχόμενοι τὴν ἐπαγγελίαν τοῦ πνεύματος ἣν ἠκούσατε (*Pan* 66.61.5)

ἤ·
περιμένειν τὴν επαγγελίαν τοῦ πατρὸς ἣν ἠκούσατε (*Pan* 74.6.8; from *Anc*)

Acts 1:7–8
καὶ ἔλεγεν αὐτοῖς·
7) οὐχ ὑμῶν ἐστι γνῶναι χρόνους καὶ καιρούς, οὓς ὁ πατὴρ ἔθετο ἐν τῇ ἰδίᾳ ἐξουσίᾳ, 8) ἀλλὰ λήψεσθε δύναμιν ἐπελθόντος τοῦ ἁγίου πνεύματος ἐφ' ὑμᾶς (*Pan* 66.61.4)

8) οὐδὲ οὐκέτι τὸ παρὰ τοῦ σωτῆρος εἰρημένον στήσεται τό·
ἔσεσθέ μοι μάρτυρες ἄχρι ἐσχάτου τῆς γῆς (*Pan* 61.2.2)[62]

---

a. μοι Epiph TR 𝔐 E H 049 81 630 945 1073 1352 1704 1739 1891
b. μου ℵ A B C D 1175

Acts 1:11
ὡς λέγουσιν·
ἄνδρες Γαλιλαῖοι, τί ἑστήκατε ἀτενίζοντες εἰς τὸν οὐρανόν; οὗτος ὁ[63] Ἰησοῦς ὁ ἀφ' ὑμῶν ἀναληφθεὶς οὕτως ἐλεύσεται ὃν τρόπον ἐθεάσασθε αὐτὸν ἀναλαμβανόμενον (*Pan* 44.5.12)

---

[62] Epiphanius adapts this text by omitting the portion not needed for his argument, replacing it with ἄχρι and retaining with verbal accuracy the beginning and ending of the citation. Holl cites the reference as "Ps 18:5 (Röm 10:18)," but the patristic context clearly refers to the Romans passage.
[63] ὁ] *om* 33 105.

Acts 1:11 cont.

ἀλλὰ ἤκουν ἐρρωμένῃ τῇ διανοίᾳ ὅτι·
<u>ἄνδρες Γαλιλαῖοι, τί ἑστήκατε εἰς τὸν οὐρανὸν ἀτενίζοντες; οὗτος ὁ Ἰησοῦς ὁ ἀφ' ὑμῶν εἰς τὸν οὐρανὸν ἀναληφθεὶς οὕτως ἐλεύσεται</u> (Pan 48.8.2)

εἰπόντες·
<u>ἄνδρες Γαλιλαῖοι, τί ἑστήκατε εἰς τὸν οὐρανὸν ἀτενίζοντες; οὗτος ὁ Ἰησοῦς ὁ ἀφ' ὑμῶν εἰς τὸν οὐρανὸν</u>[64] <u>ἀναληφθεὶς οὕτως ἐλεύσεται</u>[65] ὡς αὐτὸν εἴδετε ἀναλαμβανόμενον (Pan 62.6.8)

καὶ λέγοντας ὅτι·
τοῦτον τὸν Ἰησοῦν ὃν ἑωράκατε ἀφ' ὑμῶν ἀναλαμβανόμενον, <u>οὕτως ἐλεύσεται ὃν τρόπον</u> εἴδετε αὐτὸν ἀναλαμβανόμενον (Pan 66.87.8)

καί·
οὕτως ὄψεσθε αὐτόν, ὃν τρόπον εἴδετε αὐτὸν ἀναλαμβανόμενον (Pan 69.77.5)

καὶ εἶπον δύο ἄνδρες·
τί ἑστήκατε, ἄνδρες Γαλιλαῖοι; οὗτος ὁ ἀφ' ὑμῶν ἀναληφθείς (Pan 77.19.3)

Acts 1:18
ὅς·
πρηνὴς γενόμενος ἐλάκησε μέσος, καὶ ἐξεχύθη πάντα[66] τὰ σπλάγχνα αὐτοῦ (Pan 38.8.3)

Acts 1:20
ὡς λέγει πάλιν ἄλλος προφήτης·
<u>γενέσθω ἡ ἔπαυλις αὐτοῦ</u>[67] <u>ἔρημος</u>[68] <u>καὶ τὴν ἐπισκοπὴν αὐτοῦ λαβέτω ἕτερος</u>, σημαίνων ὅτι ἀπέθανεν κακῷ θανατῷ ὁ Ἰούδας[69] (Pan 38.8.2)

---

[64] εἰς τὸν οὐρανόν] om D it^d.
[65] οὕτως ἐλεύσεται] οὗτος ἐλεύσεται 1073; οὕτως ἐλεύσεται πάλιν 104.
[66] πάντα] om A.
[67] αὐτοῦ 1704] αὐτῶν 049* 81 it^{d*} vg.
[68] ἔρημος] ἠρημωμένη 81.
[69] Holl (2.71, n. 2). The patristic context makes clear that the passage is from Acts 1:20, rather than Ps 68:26. Acts 1:18 follows immediately.

Acts 1:20,cont.

a. λαβέτω Epiph ℵ A B C D 81 1175 it^e Chr
b. λαβοί^{70} TR 𝔐 E H 049 630 945 1073 1352 1704 it^d Or

Acts 1:25
λέγοντες·
ἀφ'^{71} οὗ παρέβη Ἰούδας ἀπελθεῖν εἰς τὸν τόπον τὸν ἴδιον^{72} (*Pan* 38.8.4)

a. ἀφ' Epiph ℵ A B C D 81 945 1175 1704 1739 it^d
b. ἐξ TR 𝔐 E H 049 630 1073 1352 it^e

Acts 2:17
ἔδει γὰρ πληροῦσθαι τό·
προφητεύσουσιν οἱ υἱοὶ ὑμῶν καὶ αἱ^{73} θυγατέρες ὑμῶν^{74} ἐνυπνίοις ἐνυπνιασθήσονται,^{75} καὶ οἱ νεανίσκοι ὑμῶν^{76} ὁράσεις ὄψονται (*Pan* 79.3.5)

a. ἐνυπνίοις Epiph 𝔓^{74} ℵ A B C 049 81 630 945 1175 1704 1739
b. ἐνύπνια TR 𝔐 E H P 1073 1352 it$^{d.e}$
c. *om* D*

---

^{70} MS 1739 is not included with this reading because 1:1–2:5 is by a later hand. MS 1891 is missing this folio.

^{71} See discussion of this citation on pp. 31–32 above.

^{72} *om* τὸν ἴδιον 𝔓^{74}; ἴδιον τόπον C; τόπον τὸν δίκαιον A.

^{73} *om* αἱ C* D.

^{74} ὑμῶν . . . ὑμῶν] αὐτῶν . . . αὐτῶν D.

^{75} Epiphanius transposes ἐνυπνίοις ἐνυπνιασθήσονται to the phrase dealing with young women and deletes the phrase dealing with the πρεσβύτεροι because he is addressing the topic of the participation of women in public worship. Immediately after, Epiphanius says, "The word of God does not allow a woman 'to speak' in church either, or 'bear rule over a man.'" With this conscious alteration, women are no longer "prophesying" but silent. In this adaptation, Epiphanius clearly knows the dative ἐνυπνίοις rather than ἐνύπνια with 𝔐 (LXX).

^{76} ὑμῶν] *om* ὑμῶν D it^d; *om* οἱ νεανίσκοι ὑμῶν 049.

Acts 2:22

ὡς καὶ οἱ ἀπόστολοί φασιν·
<u>Ἰησοῦν τὸν Ναζωραῖον, ἄνδρα ἀποδεδειγμένον</u> ἔν τε σημείοις καὶ τέρασι (*Pan* 29.5.6)

ὡς καὶ οἱ ἀπόστολοί φασιν, . . .·
Ἰησοῦν <u>ἄνδρα ἀποδεδειγμένον εἰς ἡμᾶς</u> σημείοις καὶ τέρασι (*Pan* 35.2.8)

ὑπὸ Πέτρου εἰρημένων ὅτι·
Ἰησοῦν τὸν Ναζωραῖον, ἄνδρα ἀποδεδειγμένον εἰς ὑμᾶς[77] τέρασι καὶ σημείοις (*Pan* 77.31.6)

Acts 2:24

φησὶ δὲ ὁ Πέτρος·
καθότι οὐκ ἦν δυνατὸν κρατεῖσθαι αὐτὸν ὑπ' αὐτοῦ (*Anc* 34.2)

ἵνα πληρώσῃ τὸ εἰρημένον παρὰ τῶν ἀποστόλων, ἀδύνατον γὰρ <u>ἦν κρατεῖσθαι αὐτὸν ὑπὸ τοῦ</u> ῞Αιδου[78] (*Pan* 69.66.2)

Acts 2:27

καὶ Πέτρος τῷ Δαυὶδ συνῳδά·
<u>οὐκ ἐάσεις[79] τὴν ψυχήν μου εἰς ῞Αιδην οὐδὲ δώσεις τὸν ὅσιόν σου ἰδεῖν διαφθοράν</u> (*Anc* 34.1)

---

a. ῞Αιδην Epiph ℵ A B C D 81 630 945 1175 1704 1739 1891
b. ῞Αιδου TR 𝔐 E H P 049 1073 1352

Acts 2:33

ἐὰν δὲ ἀκούσῃς ὅτι·
τῇ δεξιᾷ τοῦ θεοῦ ὑψωθεὶς τήν τε ἐπαγγελίαν τοῦ πνεύματος λαβὼν[80] παρὰ τοῦ πατρός (*Anc* 69.8)

---

[77] ὑμᾶς] ἡμᾶς D.
[78] NA²⁷ notes that D it^(d.e) have ῞Αιδου instead of θανάτου at the end of the preceding phrase, which Epiphanius inserts here, not in the preceding phrase. It is clear from *Anc* 34.2 that he knows αὐτοῦ here as his text and understands it to mean ῞Αιδου.
[79] ἐάσεις] ἐνκαταλείψεις B* D E; ἐγκαταλείψεις *rell*. Although possibly citing from memory, Epiphanius clearly evidences the accusative, εἰς ῞Αιδην, in this otherwise precise citation.

Acts 2:33, cont.

ἐὰν δὲ ἀκούσῃς ὅτι·
τῇ δεξιᾷ τοῦ θεοῦ ὑψωθεὶς τήν τε ἐπαγγελίαν τοῦ πνεύματος λαβὼν παρὰ τοῦ πατρός (*Pan* 74.6.8; from *Anc*)

Acts 2:36

καὶ γνωστὸν ὑμῖν ἔστω <u>πᾶς οἶκος Ἰσραήλ, ὅτι τοῦτον τὸν Ἰησοῦν, ὃν ὑμεῖς ἐσταυρώσατε, κύριον καὶ Χριστὸν αὐτὸν ὁ θεὸς ἐποίησε</u> (*Anc* 41.1)

καὶ διὰ τοῦτο ὁ Πέτρος σαφῶς διαγορεύει λέγων·
τοῦτον τὸν Ἰησοῦν, ὃν ὑμεῖς ἐσταυρώσατε (*Anc* 44.2)

διὰ τὸ εἰρηκέναι αὐτὸν αὐτοῖς ὅτι·
τοῦτον τὸν Ἰησοῦν, ὃν ὑμεῖς ἐσταυρώσατε (*Pan* 9.4.9)

καὶ τὸ ἐν ταῖς Πράξεσι γεγραμμένον ὅτι·
γνωστὸν ὑμῖν ἔστω <u>πᾶς οἶκος Ἰσραήλ, ὅτι τοῦτον τὸν Ἰησοῦν ὃν ἐσταυρώσατε, καὶ κύριον καὶ Χριστὸν αὐτὸν ὁ θεὸς ἐποίησε</u> (*Pan* 69.14.2)[81]

τὴν ὑπὸ τοῦ ἁγίου Πέτρου ἐν ταῖς Πράξεσιν εἰρημένην ὅτι·
φανερὸν ἔστω ὑμῖν <u>πᾶς οἶκος Ἰσραήλ, ὅτι τοῦτον τὸν Ἰησοῦν ὃν ἐσταυρώσατε καὶ[82] κύριον καὶ Χριστὸν αὐτὸν ὁ θεὸς ἐποίησε</u> (*Pan* 69.42.1)

τοῦτον οὖν τὸν Ἰησοῦν ὃν ἐσταυρώσατε (*Pan* 69.42.5)

διὰ τοῦτο <u>καὶ κύριον καὶ Χριστὸν ὁ θεὸς ἐποίησε</u> (*Pan* 69.42.6)

---

[80] τοῦ πνεύματος λαβών J *Pan*] λαβὼν τοῦ πνεύματος L^{epiph}.

[81] In presenting the Arian argument, Epiphanius notes Arius' reliance upon such texts as Prov 8:22, Heb 3:1–2, Jn 1:15 and Acts 2:36, in each instance placing emphasis upon the Arian idea of Jesus having been "created." In his discussion of the meaning of Acts 2:36 in *Pan* 69.42.1, Epiphanius changes the Arian emphasis upon the phrase "God made him" to "this Jesus whom you crucified," stressing that the writer's emphasis is upon the human nature rather than the divine nature of Jesus at this point in the text. In all three of his longer citations of this verse, Epiphanius intentionally transposes "this Jesus whom you crucified" to place emphasis upon it. The remainder of the verse is cited accurately in all instances in *Pan*.

[82] καί] om TR 049.

Acts 2:36, cont.

---

a. οἶκος   Epiph TR 𝔐 $\mathfrak{P}^{74}$ ℵ A B E H P 049 81 630 945 1175 1352 1704 1739 1891 Chr
b. ὁ οἶκος   C D 1073

---

a. κύριον καὶ Χριστὸν αὐτὸν   Epiph TR 𝔐 E H P 049 81 1073 1352 it^e
b. κύριον αὐτὸν καὶ Χριστόν $\mathfrak{P}^{74}$ ℵ A B C D^c 630 945 1175 1704 1739 1891 vg Chr
c. κύριον καὶ Χριστόν   D* it^d

---

a. ὁ θεὸς ἐποίησε   Epiph TR 𝔐 $\mathfrak{P}^{74}$ A C D E H P 049 630 945 1175 1352 1704 1739 1891 it$^{d.e}$ Chr
b. ἐποίησε ὁ θεός   ℵ B 81 1073 vg

Acts 2:37
λέγουσιν αὐτῷ·
τί^{83} ποιήσωμεν, ἄνδρες ἀδελφοί; (*Pan* 9.4.9)

---

a. ποιήσωμεν   Epiph 𝔐 $\mathfrak{P}^{74}$ ℵ A B C E P 049 81 1175 1704 1891 CyrJer Chr
b. ποιήσομεν   TR D H 630 945 1073 1352 1739 it$^{d.e}$

Acts 2:38
καὶ κατανυγεῖσι τὴν καρδίαν εἶπε·
μετανοήσατε, ἄνδρες ἀδελφοί, καὶ βαπτισθήτω ἕκαστος ἐν^{84} τῷ ὀνόματι Ἰησοῦ Χριστοῦ τοῦ κυρίου ὑμῶν καὶ ἀφεθήσονται ὑμῖν αἱ ἁμαρτίαι καὶ λήψεσθε τὴν δωρεὰν τοῦ ἁγίου πνεύματος (*Pan* 9.4.9)

---

[83] τί] τί οὖν D it^g Iren Aug.

[84] The introduction is not overtly an intention to cite, but merely to give the gist of a well-known text in support of his argument. Accordingly, Epiphanius cannot be said to read ἐν with B C D 945 1739 1891 rather than ἐπὶ with TR 𝔐 ℵ A E H P 049 81 1073 1175 1352, nor τοῦ κυρίου Ἰησοῦ Χριστοῦ with D E 945 1739 1891 rather than Ἰησοῦ Χριστοῦ with TR 𝔐 $\mathfrak{P}^{74}$ ℵ A B C H P 049 81 1073 1175 1352.

Acts 3:6
ὅτι·
ἀργύριον καὶ χρυσίον οὐχ ὑπάρχει μοι, ὃ δὲ ἔχω, τοῦτό σοι δίδωμι, ἐν τῷ ὀνόματι Ἰησοῦ Χριστοῦ ἀνάστα καὶ[85] περιπάτει (Pan 66.81.3)

Acts 4:35
καὶ τὸ ἐπώλού τὰ ὑπάρχοντα αὐτῶν καὶ ἐτίθουν παρὰ τοὺς πόδας τῶν ἀποστόλων (Anc Intro.)

Acts 4:36
καὶ γὰρ καὶ[86] Βερνάβαν λέγει, Ἰωσήφ ποτε καλούμενον Βαρνάβαν δὲ μετακληθέντα, υἱὸν παρακλήσεως ἑρμηνευόμενον, Λευίτην Κύπριον[87] τῷ γένει (Pan 30.25.6)

Acts 5:3–4
φησὶν οὖν ὁ μακάριος Πέτρος τοῖς περὶ Ἀνανίαν·
3) τί ὅτι ἐπείρασεν[88] ὑμᾶς ὁ σατανᾶς ψεύσασθαι τῷ πνεύματι τῷ ἁγίῳ;
4) καί φησιν· οὐκ ἐψεύσω ἀνθρώποις,[89] ἀλλὰ τῷ θεῷ (Anc 9.2)

3) ἢ· διὰ τί ἐπλήρωσε[90] τὴν καρδίαν σου ὁ Σατανᾶς (τῷ Ἀνανίᾳ Πέτρος) ψεύσασθαί σε τὸ πνεῦμα τὸ ἅγιον;[91] 4) καὶ μετὰ ταῦτα· οὐκ ἀνθρώποις ἐψεύσω, ἀλλὰ τῷ θεῷ (Anc 69.8)

λέγων τοῖς περὶ Ἀνανίαν·
3) τί ὅτι ἐπείρασεν ὑμᾶς ὁ σατανᾶς ψεύσασθαι[92] τὸ ἅγιον πνεῦμα; 4) οὐκ ἀνθρώπῳ ἐψεύσασθε, ἀλλὰ θεῷ (Pan 59.8.1)

3) ἢ διὰ τί ἐπλήρωσε τὴν καρδίαν σου ὁ Σατανᾶς (τῷ Ἀνανίᾳ Πέτρος) ψεύσασθαί σε τὸ πνεῦμα τὸ ἅγιον; 4) καὶ μετὰ ταῦτα· οὐκ ἀνθρώποις ἐψεύσω, ἀλλὰ θεῷ (Pan 74.6.8; from Anc)

---

[85] Because Epiphanius is imprecise following Χριστοῦ, eliminating τοῦ Ναζωραίου and using common Christian phraseology, one cannot be certain that his biblical exemplar read ἔγειρε καὶ περιπάτει with A C E P 049 81 945 1739 rather than περιπάτει with ℵ B D.

[86] καί V] om M

[87] Λευίτην Κύπριον] Κύπριος Λευίτην D.

[88] ἐπείρασεν $\mathfrak{P}^{74}$ vg Did] ἐπήρωσεν ℵ*; ἐπλήρωσε rell.

[89] ἀνθρώποις J] ἀνθρώπῳ L^{epiph}.

[90] In citations of 5:3, Epiphanius reads both ἐπλήρωσεν and ἐπείρασεν, but Pan 74.6.8 (quoting Anc 69.8) is the most verbally precise, and reads the former.

[91] τὸ πνεῦμα τὸ ἅγιον] τὸ ἅγιον πνεῦμα D.

[92] Text: U] add ὑμᾶς M.

Acts 5:3-4, cont.
4) καί φησιν·
οὐκ ἐψεύσασθε ἀνθρώπῳ, ἀλλὰ τῷ θεῷ (*Anc* 118.2)

Acts 7:2
ὅτι·
ὤφθη ὁ θεὸς τῷ Ἀβραὰμ ὄντι ἐν τῇ Μεσοποταμίᾳ (*Pan* 70.7.2)

Acts 7:14
ἐν ψυχαῖς ἑβδομήκοντα πέντε (*Anc* 59.2)

κάτεισι τοίνυν ὡς προεῖπον ὁ Ἰακὼβ εἰς Αἴγυπτον καὶ οἱ αὐτοῦ υἱοὶ καὶ γυναῖκες·
καὶ ἔκγονοι <u>ἐν ἑβδομήκοντα πέντε ψυχαῖς</u> ἀριθμηθέντες[93] (*Pan* 8.4.5)

a. ἐν ψυχαῖς ἑβδομήκοντα πέντε Epiph TR 𝔐 𝔓[74] ℵ A B C E P 049 1073 1175 1352 it[e] vg
b. ἐν ἑβδομήκοντα πέντε ψυχαῖς H 630 945 1704 1739 1891 it[d]
c. ἐν ἑβδομήκοντα καὶ πέντε ψυχαῖς D

Acts 7:15
<u>κατέβη</u>, γάρ φησιν ἡ γραφή, <u>Ἰακὼβ εἰς Αἴγυπτον</u>[94] (*Anc* 59. 2)

Acts 7:56
ἀπεκρίναντο λέγων·
ἰδού, ὁρῶ τὸν οὐρανὸν ἠνεῳγμένον καὶ τὸν υἱὸν τοῦ ἀνθρώπου ἑστῶτα ἐκ δεξιῶν τοῦ πατρός (*Pan* 44.6.1)[95]

ὡς ὁ μακάριος Στέφανος φησιν·
ἰδού, ὁρῶ τὸν οὐρανὸν ἀνεῳγμένον καὶ τὸν υἱὸν τοῦ ἀνθρώπου[96] ἑστῶτα ἐκ δεξιῶν[97] τοῦ θεοῦ (*Pan* 54.5.10)

---

[93] The *Pan* 8.4.5 allusion has significant patristic adjustments to the text, while *Anc* 59.2, is precise, including that portion of v. 15 which prefaces v. 14.

[94] εἰς Αἴγυπτον] *om* B.

[95] In these allusions, Epiphanius substitutes words, changes number, and alters word order, and thus cannot be said to agree either with ἀνεῳγμένους in TR 𝔐 𝔓[74] D* E H P 049 1073 1352 rather than διηνοιγμένους in ℵ A B C 81 945 1175 1739 1891, nor does he agree with ἑστῶτα ἐκ δεξιῶν in ℵ* A C E 1175 rather than ἐκ δεξιῶν ἑστῶτα TR 𝔐 𝔓[74] ℵ[c] B D H P 049 81 945 1073 1352 1739 1891.

[96] ἀνθρώπου] θεοῦ 𝔓[74] 614.

Acts 7:56, cont.
τίνα δὲ ἔβλεπεν ὁ μακάριος Στέφανος ὅτε ἔλεγεν·
ἰδού, ὁρῶ τὸν οὐρανὸν ἀνεῳγμένον καὶ τὸν υἱὸν τοῦ ἀνθρώπου ἑστῶτα
ἐκ δεξιῶν τοῦ θεοῦ (*Pan* 62.6.9)

φησὶ γὰρ ὁ ἅγιος Στέφανος ὁ πρωτομάρτυς·
ἰδού, ὁρῶ τὸν οὐρανὸν ἀνεῳγμένον, καὶ τὸν υἱὸν τοῦ ἀνθρώπου ἐκ δεξιῶν
ἑστῶτα τοῦ θεοῦ καὶ πατρός (*Pan* 70.6.3)

Acts 9:4
τοῦ ἀκούσαντος ἀπ' οὐρανῶν·
Σαοὺλ Σαούλ, τί με διώκεις (*Anc* 11.4)

Acts 9:6
ὅμοιον τῷ λέγειν, ὁ δὲ κύριος εἶπεν·
εἴσελθε εἰς τὴν πόλιν κἀκεῖ[98] λαληθήσεταί σοι τί σε δεῖ ποιεῖν (*Anc* 68.3)

ὅμοιον τῷ λέγειν, ὁ δὲ κύριος εἶπεν·
εἴσελθε[99] εἰς τὴν πόλιν κἀκεῖ λαληθήσεταί σοι τί σε δεῖ ποιεῖν (*Pan* 74.5.3; from *Anc*)

---

a. τί σε δεῖ Epiph TR 𝔐 H L P 049 1073 1352
b. ὅ τι σε δεῖ 𝔓⁷⁴ ℵ A B C 81 630 1175 (1704 *om* σε) 1739 1891
c. τί δεῖ σε E
d. ὅ δεῖ 945

Acts 10:11–12
11) εἶδε γὰρ ὀθόνην καθιεμένην τέσσαρσιν ἀρχαῖς δεδεμένην[100] 12) καὶ
πάντα τὰ τετράποδα καὶ ἑρπετὰ καὶ τοῦ οὐρανοῦ τὰ πετεινὰ ἐν αὐτῇ[101]
(*Pan* 48.7.4)

---

[97] ἐκ δεξιῶν M] ἐν δεξίᾳ U.
[98] κἀκεῖ with 326, but probably a sub-singular reading] καί *rell*.
[99] εἴσελθε Holl, *Anc*] εἰσέλθετε J.
[100] δεδεμένην 1505 *l*611] δεδεμένον *rell*. Although it could be argued that the inclusion of δεδεμένην indicates awareness of that term in this allusion, the total lack of accuracy in this part of the citation means that one cannot be certain that

Acts 10:13
τό·
ἀναστὰς¹⁰² θῦσον καὶ φάγε (*Pan* 48.7.5)

Acts 10:14
ἀποκρινόμενος καὶ λέγων·
μηδαμῶς, κύριε (*Pan* 48.8.4)

Acts 10:38
καὶ Ἰησοῦν τὸν ἀπὸ Ναζαρέτ, ὃν¹⁰³ ἔχρισεν πνεύματι ἁγίῳ (*Anc* 69.6)

ἔχρισε τὸν Χριστὸν ἐν πνεύματι ἁγίῳ (*Pan* 69.18.7)

<u>ἔχρισε</u> γὰρ <u>αὐτὸν πνεύματι ἁγίω</u>, φησὶν ἡ γραφή (*Pan* 69.56.10)

καὶ·
Ἰησοῦν τὸν ἀπὸ Ναζαρέτ, ὃν¹⁰⁴ ἔχρισεν ὁ θεὸς πνεύματι ἁγίῳ¹⁰⁵ (*Pan* 74.6.6; from *Anc*)

ὃν ἔχρισεν ὁ θεὸς πνεύματι ἁγίῳ (*Pan* 77.31.6)

Acts 10:42
ὁ <u>κριτὴς ζώντων καὶ νεκρῶν</u> (*Anc* 19.1)

Acts 11:3
λέγων ὅτι·
εἰσῆλθε πρὸς ἄνδρας ἀκροβυστίαν ἔχοντας (*Pan* 28.2.5)

Epiphanius' exemplar read ἀρχαῖς δεδεμένον with TR 𝔐 C* H L P 049 81 945 1073 1352 1739 1891 it^d rather than simply ἀρχαῖς with 𝔓⁷⁴ ℵ A B E 1175 it^e.

[101] It could be argued that while Epiphanius omits τῆς γῆς and changes the order of τοῦ οὐρανοῦ, he does keep the list in the same order, with three groups instead of four, as in 𝔓⁷⁴ ℵ A B and Family 1739. However, this two-verse citation is clearly only an allusion giving the gist of the verse and it is not at all certain whether Epiphanius' exemplar read τετράποδα καὶ ἑρπετὰ τῆς γῆς καὶ πετεινὰ τοῦ οὐρανου with 𝔓⁷⁴ ℵ A B C^c 81 (945 τὰ ἑρπετά) 1175 (1739 1891 τὰ ἑρπετά), rather than τετράποδα τῆς γῆς καὶ τὰ θηρία καὶ τὰ ἑρπετὰ καὶ τὰ πετεινὰ τοῦ οὐρανοῦ TR 𝔐 H L P 049 1073 1352, or τετράποδα καὶ ἑρπετὰ τῆς γῆς καὶ τὰ θηρία καὶ τὰ πετεινὰ τοῦ οὐρανοῦ E it^e, or τετράποδα καὶ τὰ θηρία καὶ τὰ ἑρπετὰ τῆς γῆς καὶ πετεινὰ τοῦ οὐρανοῦ C*^vid.

[102] ἀναστάς] ἀναστά 104 181.

[103] ὃν D] ὅς 498 614; ὡς *rell*.

[104] ὃν D] ὅς 498; ὡς *rell*.

[105] πνεύματι ἁγίῳ] ἐν πνεύματι ἁγίῳ E L; ἁγίῳ πνεύματι D.

Acts 11:3, cont.

a. εἰσῆλθε *ante* πρὸς ἄνδρας Epiph B 81 1175
b. εἰσῆλθε *post* ἀκροβυστίαν ἔχοντας L
c. εἰσῆλθες *ante* πρὸς ἄνδρας $\mathfrak{P}^{74}$ ℵ A D 630 945 1704 1739 1891
d. εἰσῆλθες *post* ἀκροβυστίαν ἔχοντας TR 𝔐 E H P 049 1073 1352

Acts 11:5–9,1–12
φησὶ γὰρ ὁ ἅγιος Πέτρος·
5) ἐγὼ ἤμην ἐν πόλει[106] Ἰόππῃ καὶ εἶδον ἐν μέσῃ τῇ ἡμέρᾳ περὶ ὥραν ἕκτην ὀθόνην καθιεμένην, δεδεμένην ἐν τέτρασιν ἀρχαῖς 6) ἐν ᾗ ἦν πάντα τὰ[107] τετράποδα καὶ ἑρπετὰ 7) καὶ εἶπεν μοι θῦσον καὶ φάγε 8) ἐγὼ δὲ εἶπον[108] κύριε μηδαμῶς, ὅτι οὐδέποτε κοινὸν ἢ ἀκάθαρτον εἰσῆλθεν εἰς τὸ στόμα μου 9) ἀπεκρίθη δέ μοι ἐκ δευτέρου φωνὴ ἐκ τοῦ οὐρανοῦ·[109] ἃ ὁ θεὸς ἐκαθάρισε, σὺ μὴ κοίνου 11) καὶ ἐξαυτῆς ἰδοὺ δύο ἄνδρες εἱστήκεισαν εἰς τὴν οἰκίαν 12) καὶ εἶπέν μοι τὸ πνεῦμα· πορεύου σὺν αὐτοῖς μηδὲν διακρινόμενον[110] (*Pan* 28.3.2)

7) καὶ φωνῆς κυρίου λεγούσης·
ἀναστὰς θῦσον καὶ φάγε 8) καὶ τοῦ Πέτρου λέγοντος· μηδαμῶς, κύριε· οὐδὲν κοινὸν ἢ ἀκάθαρτον εἰσῆλθεν εἰς τὸ στόμα μου 9) ἃ ὁ θεὸς ἐκαθάρισε, σὺ μὴ κοίνου (*Pan* 30.22.6)

Acts 11:8
ἔλεγε·
μηδαμῶς, κύριε· οὐδέποτε[111] κοινὸν ἢ[112] ἀκάθαρτον εἰσῆλθεν εἰς τὸ στόμα μου (*Pan* 48.3.7)

---

[106] ἐν πόλει Ἰόππῃ] ἐν Ἰόππῃ πόλει D.
[107] τὰ] *om* D*.
[108] εἶπον] εἶπα D; εἶπεν 81.
[109] ἀπεκρίθη δέ μοι ἐκ δευτέρου φωνὴ ἐκ τοῦ οὐρανοῦ Epiph E it^e] ἀπεκρίθη δέ μοι φωνὴ ἐκ δευτέρου ἐκ τοῦ οὐρανοῦ TR 𝔐 H L P 049 1073; ἀπεκρίθη δὲ φωνὴ ἐκ δευτέρου ἐκ τοῦ οὐρανοῦ $\mathfrak{P}^{74}$ ℵ A 81 945 1175 1739 1891; ἀπεκρίθη δὲ ἐκ δευτέρου φωνὴ ἐκ τοῦ οὐρανοῦ B; ἐγένετο φωνὴ ἐκ τοῦ οὐρανοῦ πρός με D*.
[110] In this allusion, Epiphanius gives the gist of the text, but not with enough exactitude to know whether he read μοι τὸ πνεῦμα with 𝔐 E H L P 049 630 945 1073 1352 1704 1739 1891, or τὸ πνεῦμα μοι with $\mathfrak{P}^{74}$ ℵ A B D 81 1175; nor whether he read διακρινόμενον with 𝔐 H L P 049 1073 1352, διακρίναντα with ($\mathfrak{P}^{74}$ ανακρ—) ℵ^c A B 81 630 945 1704 1739 1891, διακρίνοντα ℵ* E 1175, or *om* $\mathfrak{P}^{45}$ D it^d.
[111] Epiphanius has οὐδέποτε prior to κοινόν with 614 1611 2138.

Acts 11:8, cont.
ἀλλά φησι πρὸς τὸν κύριον·
<u>μηδαμῶς κύριε· οὐδέποτε</u> γὰρ <u>κοινὸν ἢ ἀκάθαρτον εἰσῆλθεν εἰς τὸ στόμα μου</u> (*Pan* 48.7.5)

---

a. κοινόν   Epiph 𝔓⁷⁴ ℵ A B D E 049 81 1175 it^{d.e} vg Chr
b. πᾶν κοινόν   TR 𝔐 H L P 945 1073 1352 1704
c. κοινόν τι   630 1739 1891

Acts 11:27–28
ἀλλὰ καὶ πάλιν·
27) ἐν Ἀντιοχείᾳ κατῆλθον προφῆται καὶ 28) κατήγγελλον λιμὸν ἔσεσθαι καθ' ὅλης τῆς οἰκουμένης (*Pan* 48.8.5)

καὶ ὅτι·
προφῆται ἀπὸ Ἱεροσολύμων κατέβησαν (*Pan* 66.61.7)

28) λέγουσα·
ἥτις ἐγένετο ἐπὶ Κλαυδίου Καίσαρος (*Pan* 48.8.5)

ὡς λέγει ὅτι·
Ἄγαβος ἐπροφήτευσε περὶ λιμοῦ ἐσομένου (*Pan* 66.61.7)

---

a. ἥτις   Epiph 𝔓⁷⁴ ℵ A B D 81 1175 1739 1891 it^d vg
b. ἥτις καί   E it^e
c. ὅστις καί   TR 𝔐 H L P 049 630 945 1073 1352 1704

---

a. Κλαυδίου Καίσαρος   Epiph TR 𝔐 E H L P 049 630 945 1073 1175 1352 1704 1739 1891 it^e Chr
b. Κλαυδίου   𝔓⁷⁴ ℵ A B D 81 it^d vg

Acts 13:2
<u>λειτουργούντων</u>[113] <u>δὲ αὐτῶν</u>, φησί, <u>τῷ κυρίῳ· καὶ νηστευόντων εἶπε τὸ πνεῦμα τὸ ἅγιον· ἀφορίσατε δή</u>[114] <u>μοι Βαρνάβαν καὶ Σαῦλον εἰς τὸ ἔργον ὃ προσκέκλημαι αὐτούς</u> (*Anc* 68.3)

---

[112] ἢ M] καί U 945.
[113] λειτουργούντων] λειτουργώντων C.

Acts 13:2, cont.
λειτουργούντων δὲ αὐτῶν, φησί, κυρίῳ καὶ νηστευόντων εἶπε τὸ πνεῦμα τὸ ἅγιον, ἀφορίσατε δή μοι Βαρνάβαν καὶ Σαῦλον εἰς τὸ ἔργον ὃ προσκέκλημαι αὐτούς (*Pan* 74.5.3 from *Anc*)

φασί·
καὶ εἶπε τὸ πνεῦμα τὸ ἅγιον· ἀφορίσατέ μοι Βαρνάβαν καὶ Σαῦλον εἰς τὸ ἔργον ὃ προσκέκλημαι αὐτούς (*Pan* 74.13.5)

---

a. Σαῦλον Epiph 𝔓^{74} ℵ^c A B C D E 81 630 945 1175 1704 1739 1891 Chr
b. τὸν Σαῦλον TR 𝔐 ℵ* H L P 049 1073 1352

Acts 13:4
αὐτοὶ μὲν οὖν ἐκπεμφθέντες ὑπὸ τοῦ ἁγίου πνεύματος κατῆλθον^{115} εἰς Σελεύκειαν (*Anc* 68.4)

αὐτοὶ μὲν οὖν ἐκπεμφθέντες ὑπὸ τοῦ ἁγίου πνεύματος κατῆλθον εἰς Σελεύκειαν (*Pan* 74.5.4; from *Anc*)

---

a. αὐτοὶ μὲν οὖν Epiph 𝔓^{74} ℵ A B C 630 945 1175 1704 1739 1891 it$^{d.e}$
b. οὗτοι μὲν οὖν TR 𝔐 E H L P 1073 1352 Chr
c. οἱ μὲν οὖν 049 D
d. αὐτοὶ μέν 81

---

a. τοῦ ἁγίου πνεύματος Epiph 𝔓^{74} ℵ A B C^c 81 630 945 1175 1704 1739 1891 CyrJer
b. τοῦ πνεύματος τοῦ ἁγίου TR 𝔐 (D *om* τοῦ^{sec}) E H L P 049 1073 1352 it$^{d.e}$ vg Chr

---

a. εἰς Σελεύκειαν Epiph 𝔓^{74} ℵ B C^c D 81 630 945 1175 1704 1739 1891 Did
b. εἰς τὴν Σελεύκειαν TR 𝔐 A C* E H L P 049 1073 1352

---

^{114} δή *Pan* Holl] *om* L^{epiph} ʃ 33 it^d.
^{115} κατῆλθον] ἀπῆθον 𝔓^{74} A; καταβάντες D; κατῆλθεν 88.

Acts 15:1
λέγοντας ὅτι·
ἐὰν μὴ περιτμηθῆτε[116] καὶ φυλάξητε τὸν νόμον, οὐ δύνασθε σωθῆναι (*Pan* 28.4.5)

Acts 15:24
λέγοντες ὅτι·
ἔγνωμέν τινας ἐξ ἡμῶν[117] πρὸς ὑμᾶς ἐλθόντας[118] καὶ ταράξαντας ὑμᾶς λόγοις, οἷς οὐ διεστειλάμεθα (*Pan* 28.2.3)

Acts 15:28–29
28) ἔδοξε γὰρ τῷ πνεύματι τῷ ἁγίῳ μηδὲν ἄλλο ἐπιτίθεσθαι βάρος, πλὴν τῶν ἐπάναγκες[119] (*Anc* 68.5)

εἰρηκότι τοῖς ἐξ ἐθνῶν πεπιστευκόσι·
28) μὴ βάρος, ἐπιτίθεσθαι πλὴν τῶν ἐπάναγκες 29) ἀπέχεσθαι αἵματος καὶ πνικτοῦ καὶ πορνείας καὶ εἰδωλοθύτου;[120] (*Pan* 29.8.6)

28) ἔδοξε γὰρ τῷ πνεύματι τῷ ἁγίῳ[121] μηδὲν ἄλλο ἐπιτίθεσθαι βάρος πλὴν τῶν ἐπάναγκες (*Pan* 74.5.5; from *Anc*)

---

[116] In this allusion, Epiphanius adds καὶ φυλάξητε and alters τῷ ἔθει to τὸν νόμον. Although he gives the gist of the text, there is no compelling reason to think that he is quoting a text at this point. So, one does not know whether his exemplar read περιτμηθῆτε with 𝔓⁷⁴ ℵ A B C D 81 1175, or περιτεμνῆσθε with 𝔐 E H L P 049 630 945 1073 1352 1704 1739 1891 Chr CyrJer.

[117] While clearly referring to 15:24, it is also clear that Epiphanius is not citing the text with exactitude; therefore, it is unclear that his text read ἐξ ἡμῶν with 𝔐 𝔓⁷⁴ ℵᶜ A B C D E L P 049 81 630 945 1073 1175 1704 1739 1891 rather than ἐξ ὑμῶν with ℵ* H 1352.

[118] ἐλθόντας] ἐλθόντες H L; om ℵ* B 88 1175; ἐξελθόντες rell.

[119] τῶν ἐπάναγκες (𝔓⁷⁴ ἐξάναγκες) A] τούτων ἐπάναγκες ℵ* D*; τούτων τῶν ἐπάναγκες ℵᶜ B C Dᶜ H 049 81 498 630 945 1175 1704 1739 1891; τῶν ἐπάναγκες τούτων TR 𝔐 E L P 1073.

[120] The terminology of the citation is accurate and, although εἰδωλοθύτου is transposed to the end of the list, Epiphanius clearly knows πνικτοῦ and εἰδωλοθύτου as singular rather than plural. The transposition is incidental and does not affect the meaning of the text.

[121] In the context of emphasizing the role of the Holy Spirit, Epiphanius cites accurately the portion of text dealing with the Holy Spirit, but adapts the remainder of the verse by omitting the authoritative statements of the apostles that would detract from his argument.

Acts 15:28–29, cont.

28)_____

    a. τῷ πνεύματι τῷ ἁγίῳ Epiph 𝔓⁷⁴ ℵ A B 81 vg
    b. τῷ ἁγίῳ πνεύματι TR 𝔐 C D E H L P 049 630 945 1073 1175 1352
       1704 1739 1891 it^{d.e} O~ CyrJer Chr

29)_____

    a. καὶ πνικτοῦ Epiph TR 𝔐 𝔓⁷⁴ ℵ^c A^c E H L P 049 630 945 1073 1352
       1704 1739 1891 it^e vg CyrJer
    b. καὶ πνικτῶν ℵ* A* B C 31 1175 Or
    c. om D it^d

---

    a. εἰδωλοθύτου Epiph 630 945 1704 1739 1891
    b. εἰδωλοθύτων TR 𝔐 𝔓⁷⁴ ℵ A B C D E H L P 049 81 1073 1175 1352
       CyrJer

Acts 16:6–7

    6) διῆλθον δὲ[122] τὴν Φρυγίαν καὶ τὴν Γαλατικὴν χώραν, κωλιθέντες ὑπὸ τοῦ πνεύματος τοῦ ἁγίου λαλῆσαι[123] τὸν λόγον[124] ἐν τῇ Ἀσίᾳ 7) ἐλθόντες δὲ εἰς τὴν Μυσίαν ἐπείραζον[125] εἰς τὴν Βιθυνίαν πορεύεσθαι καὶ οὐκ εἴασεν αὐτοὺς τὸ πνεῦμα (Anc 68.6)

    6) διῆλθον δὲ τὴν Φρυγίαν καὶ τὴν Γαλατικὴν χώραν, κωλιθέντες ὑπὸ τοῦ πνεύματος τοῦ ἁγίου λαλῆσαι τὸν λόγον ἐν τῇ Ἀσίᾳ 7) ἐλθόντες δὲ εἰς τὴν Μυσίαν ἐπείραζον εἰς τὴν Βιθυνίαν πορεύεσθαι καὶ οὐκ εἴασεν αὐτοὺς τὸ πνεῦμα (Pan 74.5.6; from Anc)

6)_____

    a. διῆλθον Epiph 𝔓⁷⁴ ℵ A B C D E 81 630 945 1175 1352 1704 1739
       1891 it^{d.e}
    b. διελθόντες TR 𝔐 H L P 049 1073

---

[122] δέ] τε 498.
[123] λαλῆσαι] μηδὲν λαλῆσαι D.
[124] τὸν λόγον] τὸν λόγον τοῦ θεοῦ D vg.
[125] ἐπείραζον] ἤθελαν D.

Acts 16:6–7, cont.

6)

    a. τὴν Γαλατικήν   Epiph TR 𝔐 E H L P 049 630 945 1073 1352 1704 1739 1891

    b. Γαλατικήν $\mathfrak{P}^{74}$ ℵ A B C D 81 1175

7)

    a. ἐλθόντες δέ   Epiph $\mathfrak{P}^{74}$ ℵ A B C D E 81 630 945 1175 1704 1739 1891 it$^{d.e}$

    b. ἐλθόντες   TR 𝔐 H L P 049 1073 1352 Chr

---

    a. εἰς τὴν Βιθυνίαν   Epiph $\mathfrak{P}^{74}$ ℵ A B C E 81 630 945 1175 1352 1704 1739 1891 Chr

    b. κατὰ τὴν Βιθυνίαν   TR 𝔐 H L P 049 1073

    c. εἰς Βιθυνίαν   D

---

    a. πορεύεσθαι   Epiph TR 𝔐 $\mathfrak{P}^{74}$ C D H L P 049 630 945 1073 1352 1704 1739 1891 Chr

    b. πορευθῆναι   ℵ A B E 81 1175

Acts 16:13

ὅτι, φησίν·
ἐδόκει τόπος προσευχῆς εἶναι (*Pan* 80.1.5)

Acts 16:17

ὡς ἡ παιδίσκη ἡ ἔχουσα πνεῦμα Πύθωνος ἔλεγεν·
οὗτοι οἱ ἄνθρωποι[126] τοῦ θεοῦ δοῦλοι[127] τοῦ ὑψίστου εἰσί (*Pan* 48.12.7)

Acts 16:31–32,34

31) <u>πίστευσον</u>, φησίν, <u>εἰς[128] τὸν κύριον Ἰησοῦν καὶ σωθήσῃ</u> 32) <u>καὶ ἐλάλησε</u>, φησίν, <u>αὐτοῖς τὸν λόγον τοῦ κυρίου</u>,[129] 34) ἀναγαγών τε αὐτοὺς εἰς τὸν οἶκον παρέθηκεν αὐτοῖς[130] τράπεζαν καὶ ἠγαλλιάσατο πανοικὶ πεπιστευκὼς τῷ θεῷ (*Anc* 69.9)

---

[126] ἄνθρωποι] *om* D it^d.
[127] δοῦλοι U] *om* M.
[128] εἰς with E] ἐπί *rell.*
[129] τοῦ κυρίου] τοῦ θεοῦ ℵ B; *om* τοῦ D.
[130] αὐτοῖς E] *om* αὐτοῖς *rell.*

Acts 16:31–32,34, cont.
31) <u>πίστευσον</u>, φησί, <u>εἰς τὸν κύριον Ἰησοῦν καὶ σωθήσῃ</u> 32) <u>καὶ ἐλάλησε</u>, φησίν, <u>αὐτοῖς τὸν λόγον τοῦ κυρίου</u> 34) ἀναγαγών τε αὐτοὺς εἰς τὸν οἶκον παρέθηκεν αὐτοῖς τράπεζαν, καὶ ἠγαλλιάσατο πανοικὶ[131] πεπιστευκὼς τῷ θεῷ[132] (*Pan* 74.6.9; from *Anc*)

31) _____

    a. κύριον Ἰησοῦν Epiph $\mathfrak{P}^{74}$ ℵ A B 81
    b. κύριον Ἰησοῦν Χριστόν TR 𝔐 C D E H L P 049 630 945 1175 1073 1352 1704 1739 1891 it$^{d.e}$ Chr

34) _____

    a. εἰς τὸν οἶκον Epiph B C P 81 945 1352 1704* 1739 1891 Chr
    b. εἰς τὸν οἶκον αὐτοῦ TR 𝔐 $\mathfrak{P}^{74}$ ℵ A D E H L 049 630 1073 1175 1704^c it$^{d.e}$

    a. ἠγαλλιάσατο Epiph TR $\mathfrak{P}^{74}$ ℵ A B C^c E H L 049 81 630 945 1175 1704 1739 1891 vg
    b. ἠγαλλίατο 𝔐 C*^{vid} D P 1073 1352 it$^{d.e}$

Acts 20:16
    ἔσπευδεν ὅπως ποιήσῃ τὴν Πεντηκοστὴν εἰς Ἱερουσαλήμ (*Pan* 75.6.1)

Acts 20:22
    καὶ νῦν ἰδοὺ ἐγὼ δεδεμένος τῷ πνεύματι πορεύομαι (*Anc* 68.8)

    καὶ νῦν ἰδοὺ ἐγὼ δεδεμένος τῷ πνεύματι πορεύομαι (*Pan* 74.5.8; from *Anc*)

    a. ἐγὼ δεδεμένος Epiph TR 𝔐 D H L P 049 1073 1352 it^d
    b. δεδεμένος ἐγώ $\mathfrak{P}^{74}$ ℵ A B C E 630 945 1175 1704 1739 1891 it^e

---

[131] πανοικί] σὺν τῷ οἴκῳ αὐτοῦ D.
[132] τῷ θεῷ] ἐπὶ τὸν θεόν D it^d; τῷ κυρίῳ 049.

Acts 20:23
πλὴν τὸ πνεῦμά μοι διαμαρτύρεται κατὰ πόλιν[133] λέγον (*Anc* 68.9)

πλὴν τὸ πνεῦμά μοι διαμαρτύρεται κατὰ πόλιν λέγον[134] (*Pan* 74.5.9; from *Anc*)

Acts 20:28
ἡ αὐτὴ δὲ ἡ διακονία τοῦ πνεύματος καὶ τοῦ λόγου·
<u>προσέχετε, φησίν, ἑαυτοῖς καὶ παντὶ τῷ ποιμνίῳ, ἐν ᾧ ὑμᾶς ἔθετο τὸ πνεῦμα τὸ ἅγιον</u>[135] <u>ἐπισκόπους ποιμαίνειν τὴν ἐκκλησίαν τοῦ θεοῦ</u> (*Anc* 69.10)

ἡ αὐτὴ δὲ ἡ διακονία τοῦ πνεύματος καὶ τοῦ λόγου·
<u>προσέχετε</u>, φησίν,[136] <u>ἑαυτοῖς καὶ παντὶ τῷ ποιμνίῳ, ἐν ᾧ ὑμᾶς ἔθετο τὸ πνεῦμα τὸ ἅγιον ἐπισκόπους ποιμαίνειν τὴν ἐκκλησίαν τοῦ θεοῦ</u> (*Pan* 74.6.10; from *Anc*)

---

a. τοῦ θεοῦ Epiph TR ℵ B 1175 1704ᶜ vg
b. τοῦ κυρίου 𝔓⁷⁴ A C* D E 630 945 1704* 1739 1891 it^{d.e}
c. τοῦ κυρίου καὶ θεοῦ 𝔐 Cᶜ H L P 049 1073 1352

Acts 20:34
τῷ·
αἱ χεῖρες αὗται ἐπήρκεσαν οὐ μόνον ἐμοί, ἀλλὰ <u>καὶ τοῖς σὺν ἐμοί</u> (*Pan* 26.11.2)

---

[133] κατὰ πόλιν] κατὰ πᾶσαν πόλιν D; *om* E.

[134] In this brief allusion involving several adjustments, one cannot be certain that Epiphanius' exemplar read διαμαρτύρεται μοι λέγον with ℵ* B C 630 945 1352 1704 1739 1891 rather than διαμαρτύρεται λέγον with 𝔐 049 1073, διαμαρτύρεται μοι λέγων D L P 1175, διαμαρτύρεται λέγων H, διεμαρτύρατο μοι λέγον 𝔓⁷⁴ ℵᶜ A, or διεμαρτύρατο μοι λέγων E.

[135] τὸ πνεῦμα τὸ ἅγιον] τὸ ἅγιον πνεῦμα D 915.

[136] The presence of φησίν precludes knowing whether Epiphanius read προσέχετε with 𝔓⁷⁴ ℵ A B D 1175 itᵈ vg rather than προσέχετε οὖν with 𝔐 C E H L P 049 630 945 1073 1352 1704 1739 1891 itᵉ.

Acts 20:35
ἤ·
μνημονεύετε τῶν λόγων[137] κυρίου, ὅτι αὐτὸς[138] εἶπεν, ἀγαθὸν διδόναι μᾶλλον[139] ἢ λαμβάνειν (*Anc* 68.7)

μνημονεύετε τῶν λόγων κυρίου, ὅτι αὐτὸς εἶπεν, ἀγαθὸν διδόναι μᾶλλον ἢ λαμβάνειν (*Pan* 74.5.7; from *Anc*)

Acts 21:4
οἵτινες, φησίν, ἔλεγον τῷ Παύλῳ διὰ τοῦ πνεύματος μὴ ἀναβαίνειν εἰς Ἰερουσαλήμ (*Anc* 68.7)

οἵτινες, φησίν, ἔλεγον τῷ Παύλῳ διὰ τοῦ πνεύματος μὴ ἀναβαίνειν εἰς Ἰερουσαλήμ (*Pan* 74.5.7; from *Anc*)

---

a. ἀναβαίνειν Epiph TR 𝔐 E H L P 049 630 945 1073 1352 1704 1739 1891
b. ἐπιβαίνειν 𝔓⁷⁴ ℵ A B C 1175

Acts 21:9
καὶ ὅτι·
ἦσαν τέσσαρες θυγατέρες τῷ Φιλίππῳ προφητεύουσαι (*Pan* 66.61.7)

ἦσαν δέ, φησί, τέσσαρες θυγατέρες Φιλίππῳ τῷ εὐαγγελιστῇ προφητεύουσαι (*Pan* 79.3.5)

Acts 21:11
ἢ Ἄγαβος·
τάδε λέγει τὸ πνεῦμα τὸ ἅγιον, τὸν ἄνδρα οὗ ἐστιν ἡ ζώνη αὕτη (*Anc* 68.7)

φησίν·
οὗτος οὗ ἐστιν ἡ ζώνη αὕτη, δήσουσιν αὐτὸν καὶ ἀποίσουσιν εἰς Ἰερουσαλήμ[140] (*Pan* 48.8.4)

---

[137] μνημονεύετε τῶν λόγων Epiph A] μνημονεύειν τῶν λόγων D; μνημονεύειν τε τὸν λόγον L P 049 630 1073 1704 1891; μνημονεύειν τε τῶν λόγων TR 𝔐 𝔓⁷⁴ ℵ B E H 498 945 1175 1739.

[138] αὐτός] οὗτος D.

[139] διδόναι μᾶλλον TR 630 1891; μᾶλλον διδόναι *rell*.

Acts 21:11, cont.
ἢ Ἄγαβος·
τάδε λέγει τὸ πνεῦμα τὸ ἅγιον, τὸν ἄνδρα οὗ ἐστιν ἡ ζώνη αὕτη (*Pan* 74.5.7; from *Anc*)

Acts 21:39
ὅτι·
Ταρσεύς εἰμί, οὐκ ἀσήμου πόλεως πολίτης (*Pan* 30.16.8)

Acts 22:3
καὶ φησι·
περιτομῇ ὀκταήμερος καὶ ἀνατεθραμμένος[141] παρὰ τοὺς πόδας Γαμαλιὴλ καὶ Ἑβραῖος ἐξ Ἑβραίων (*Pan* 30.25.3)

Acts 24:5
ὡς λέγουσι κατηγοροῦντες Παύλου τοῦ ἀποστόλου·
τοῦτον τὸν ἄνθρωπον ηὕρομεν λοιμὸν καὶ διαστρέφοντα τὸν λαόν, πρωτοστάτην τε[142] ὄντα τῆς τῶν Ναζωραίων αἱρέσεως (*Pan* 29.6.1)

Acts 24:12–14
φησὶ γὰρ ἐπὶ τοῦ βήματος·
12) <u>οὔτε ἐν τῷ ἱερῷ ηὗρόν με πρός τινα[143] διαλεγόμενον ἢ ἐπίστασιν</u>[144] τινα ὄχλου ποιοῦντα 13) οὐδὲ ὧν μου κατηγοροῦσιν οὐδὲν πεποίηκα 14) ὁμολογῶ δέ σοι τοῦτο, ὅτι κατὰ τὴν ὁδὸν ἣν αἵρεσιν οὗτοι φάσκουσιν οὕτω λατρεύω, πιστεύων πᾶσι τοῖς ἐν τῷ νόμῳ καὶ ἐν τοῖς προφήταις (*Pan* 29.6.4)

12)_____

a. ἐπίστασιν Epiph 𝔓[74] ℵ A B E 1739 1891
b. ἐπισύστασιν TR 𝔐 H L P 049 630 945 1073 1352 1704
c. ἐπιστασίαν 81[145] 1175

---

[140] εἰς Ἱερουσαλήμ Epiph 𝔓[74] D] ἐν Ἱερουσαλήμ TR 𝔐 ℵ A B C E H L P 049 630 945 1073 1175 1704 1739 1891.
[141] ἀνατεθραμμένος] ἀναθρέμμενος 33.
[142] τε] δέ E 33 it^e.
[143] τινα] τινας E.
[144] ἐπίστασίν V Holl] ἐπισύστασιν M.
[145] ἐπιστασίαν in 81 is misspelled ἐποστασίαν in J. H. Ropes, *The Beginnings of Christianity*. Part I *The Acts of the Apostles* (London: Macmillan, 1926): 3.224, and cited erroneously as ἐπίστασιν in NA[27].

Acts 26:14
   τί μάχῃ τῷ ἀκαταμαχήτῳ
   σκληρόν σοι πρὸς κέντρα λακτίζειν (*Anc* 14.6)

Acts 27:37
   καί·
   ἦμεν ἐν τῷ πλοίῳ ὡς ὀγδοήκοντα ψυχαί (*Anc* 59.2)

   ἦσαν γὰρ, φησίν, <u>ἐν τῷ πλοίῳ ἑβδομήκοντα ψυχαί</u> (*Anc* 78.1)

James 1:13-15
  13) <u>ἀπείραστος</u> γὰρ <u>ἐστιν ὁ θεὸς κακῶν, πειράζει δὲ αὐτὸς οὐδένα</u>, οὐδὲ οἱ αὐτοῦ δοῦλοι, πρὸς ἀπάτην 14) ἕκαστος δὲ πειράζεται ἐκ τῆς ἰδίας ἐπιθυμίας ἐξελκόμενος καὶ δελεαζόμενος 15) εἶτα ἡ ἐπιθυμία τίκτει ἁμαρτίαν, ἡ δὲ ἁμαρτία ἀποτελεσθεῖσα ἀποκύει[146] θάνατον (*Pan* 79.9.4)

James 1:27
  ὅτι·
  θρησκεία δὲ[147] καθαρὰ[148] τῷ θεῷ καὶ πατρὶ[149] αὕτη ἐστίν, ἐπισκέπτεσθαι ὀρθανοὺς καὶ χήρας ἐν τῇ θλίψει αὐτῶν, ἄσπιλον ἑαυτὸν[150] τηρεῖν[151] ἀπο τοῦ κόσμου (*Pan* 77.27.7)[152]

---

a. τῷ θεῷ Epiph TR ℵᶜ A B C* Ψ 33 325 1739
b. θεῷ 𝔐 ℵ* Cᶜ L 049 105 201 323 1022

James 2:23
  καὶ τῷ μὲν Ἀβραὰμ προσετέθη τὸ <u>φίλος θεοῦ</u> καὶ οὐ διαλυθήσεται (*Pan* 78.6.2)

James 3:8-10
  8) Ἰάκωβος φάσκει λέγων περὶ τῆς γλώσσης ὅτι·
  ἀκατάσχετον κακόν,[153] μεστὴ ἰοῦ θανατηφόρου 9) ἐν αὐτῇ εὐλογοῦμεν τὸν θεὸν καὶ πατέρα, καὶ ἐν αὐτῇ καταρώμεθα τοὺς ἀνθρώπους, τοὺς κατ᾽ εἰκόνα θεοῦ γεγονότας 10) οὐ χρὴ ταῦτα οὕτως γίνεσθαι, ἀδελφοί μου[154] (*Pan* 70.3.8)[155]

---

[146] As Epiphanius would have written ΑΠΟΚΥΕΙ without accent, as do ℵ A B C, there is no way to tell whether he intended ἀποκύει with TR 𝔐 049 105 201 325 1022 or ἀποκυεῖ L Ψ 33 323 1739.
[147] Epiph *add* δέ with 43 330 *l*422 *l*1441 it syʰ* copˢᵃ.
[148] Epiph *om* καὶ ἀμίαντος with 623.
[149] πατρί] τῷ πατρί A.
[150] ἑαυτόν] σεαυτόν A.
[151] ἄσπιλον ἑαυτὸν τηρεῖν] ὑπερασπίζειν αὐτούς 𝔓⁷⁴.
[152] As only παρά before τῷ θεῷ is missing and the remainder of the citation is accurate or represented in the manuscript tradition, Epiphanius' exemplar is understood to have read τῷ θεῷ.
[153] κακόν] τὸ κακόν 1891 2805; κακῶν 181 1243 1874.
[154] ἀδελφοὶ μου] ἀδελφοὶ μου ἀγαπητοί 1022 1352.
[155] Vv. 8–9 reflect Epiphanius' exemplar; v. 10 is an adaptation.

James 3:8–10, cont.

(8)_____

    a. ἀκατάσχετον Epiph TR 𝔐 C L Ψ 049 105 201 323 325 1022 1739^c
    b. ἀκατάστατον ℵ A B 1739*

(9)_____

    a. θεόν Epiph TR 𝔐 L 049 105 201 323 325 1022
    b. κύριον ℵ A B C Y 33 1739

James 3:15, 17

καὶ πάλιν ὁ ἅγιος Ἰάκωβος λέγων περὶ τῆς τοιαύτης διδασκαλίας ὅτι
15) οὐκ ἔστιν ἄνωθεν αὕτη ἡ σοφία^{156} κατερχομένη, ἀλλὰ ἐπίγειος
ψυχικὴ δαιμονιώδης 17) ἡ δὲ ἄνωθεν σοφία πρῶτον μὲν ἁγνή ἐστιν,
ἔπειτα εἰρηνική,^{157} εὐπειθής, ἀδιάκριτος, μεστὴ^{158} ἐλέους καὶ καρπῶν
ἀγαθῶν (*Pan* 31.34.6)^{159}

16) γάρ·
ἀκαταστασία καὶ πᾶν παρανομον πρᾶγμα (*Pan* 31.34.7)

17)_____

    a. ἀγαθῶν Epiph TR 𝔐 ℵ A B L Y 049 33 105 201 325 1022
    b. ἔργων ἀγαθῶν C 323 1739

James 5:12

λέγοντος·
μὴ ὀμνύναι μήτε τὸν οὐρανὸν μήτε τὴν γῆν μήτε ἕτερόν τινα ὅρκον,
ἀλλ' ἤτω ὑμῶν τὸ ναὶ ναὶ καὶ τὸ οὒ οὒ (*Pan* 19.6.2)

---

[156] αὕτη ἡ σοφία] ἡ σοφία αὕτη C 1739.
[157] Epiph *om* ἐπιεικής with 049.
[158] μεστή *post* ἐλέους 𝔓^{74}.
[159] Because of his concluding emphasis that the Valentinians have no discernible "good works," he cites the verse accurately, excepting the inconsequential transposition of ἀδιάκριτος and omission of ἐπιεικής.

1 Peter 1:19
    τιμίῳ αἵματι[160] ἀμνοῦ ἀμώμου καὶ ἀσπίλου Χριστοῦ (*Pan* 66.79.3)

1 Peter 2:22
    ἁμαρτίαν γὰρ οὐκ ἐποίησεν, οὐδὲ εὑρέθη δόλος ἐν τῷ στόματι αὐτοῦ (*Anc* 80.1)[161]

    ἁμαρτίαν γὰρ οὐκ ἐποίησεν, οὐδὲ εὑρέθη δόλος ἐν τῷ στόματι αὐτοῦ (*Pan* 77.14.5; from *Anc*)

1 Peter 2:24
    ἐλθὼν δὲ αὐτὸς <u>τὰς ἁμαρτίας ἡμῶν[162] ἀνήνεγκεν ἐπὶ ξύλου</u> (*Pan* 66.79.9)

1 Peter 3:10
    χείλη μὴ λαλήσαντα δόλον (*De fide* 15.2)

1 Peter 3:18
    τῶν ἀποστόλων Πέτρος . . . λέγων·
    θανατωθεὶς[163] σαρκί, ζωοποιηθεὶς δὲ πνεύματι[164] (*Anc* 34.9)

    ὥς φησι Πέτρος·
    θανατωθεὶς σαρκί, ζωοποιηθεὶς δὲ πνεύματι (*Anc* 44.3)

    ὥς φησιν ὁ ἅγιος Πέτρος·
    θανατωθεὶς σαρκί, ζωοποιηθεὶς δὲ πνεύματι (*Anc* 93.6)

    ὡς καὶ ὁ ἀπόστολος Πέτρος λέγει·
    θανατωθεὶς σαρκί, ζωοποιηθεὶς δὲ πνεύματι (*Pan* 24.9.4)

    καὶ πάλιν·
    θανατωθεὶς σαρκί, ζωοποιηθεὶς δὲ πνεύματι (*Pan Chr* 2.7)

    ὡς λέγει Πέτρος·
    θανατωθεὶς σαρκί, ζωογονεθεὶς δὲ τῷ πνεύματι (*Pan* 51.25.8)

---

[160] Epiph *om* ὡς with P.
[161] Epiphanius is citing 1 Peter 2:22, rather than Isaiah 53:9, because he reads ἁμαρτίαν instead of ἀνομίαν.
[162] ἡμῶν] ὑμῶν 𝔓^{72} B.
[163] Epiph *om* μέν with 𝔓^{72} Ψ.
[164] πνεύματι] ἐν πνεύματι 𝔓^{72}; τῷ πνεύματι TR; τῷ χριστῷ 325.

1 Peter 3:18 cont.

καὶ πάλιν·
ἀποθανὼν ἐν σαρκί, ζωογονηθεὶς δὲ τῷ πνεύματι (*Pan* 69.42.5)

κατὰ τὸ εἰρημένον·
θανατωθεὶς σαρκί, ζωοποιηθεὶς δὲ τῷ πνεύματι (*Pan* 77.32.5)

1 Peter 4:1

καὶ πάλιν·
Χριστοῦ οὖν ὑπὲρ ἡμῶν παθόντος σαρκί (*Anc* 44.3)

καὶ πάλιν·
Χριστοῦ οὖν παθόντος ὑπὲρ ἡμῶν σαρκί, καὶ ὑμεῖς τὴν αὐτὴν ἔννοιαν ὁπλίσασθε (*Anc* 93.6)

<u>Χριστοῦ</u> γὰρ <u>παθόντος ὑπὲρ ἡμῶν σαρκί</u>, φησὶν ἡ θεία γράφη (*Pan Chr* 2.7)

ἀλλὰ τὸ μὲν παθεῖν ἐν σαρκί, καθὼς εἶπε Πέτρος ὅτι·
Χριστοῦ παθόντος ὑπὲρ ἡμῶν σαρκί (*Pan* 69.42.5)

καὶ πάλιν·
Χριστοῦ παθόντος ὑπέρ ἡμῶν σαρκί (*Pan* 77.32.5)

Χριστοῦ πάσχοντος ὑπέρ ἡμῶν σαρκί (*De fide* 17.1)

---

a. παθόντος ὑπὲρ ἡμῶν σαρκί   Epiph TR 𝔐 ℵ^c A L 33 105 201 325 1022
b. παθόντος σαρκί 𝔓⁷² B C Ψ 323 1739
c. ἀποπαθόντος ὑπὲρ ὑμῶν σαρκί ℵ*
d. παθόντος ἐν σαρκί 049*
e. παθόντος ἐν σαρκὶ ὑπὲρ ἡμῶν 049^c

---

2 Peter 1:19
ὥς φησιν Πέτρος ἐν τῇ ἐπιστολῇ·
προσέχοντες τῷ προφητικῷ λόγῳ ὡς λύχνῳ φαίνοντι ἐν αὐχμηρῷ τόπῳ, ἕως φωσφόρος ἀνατείλῃ καὶ ἡμέρα[165] καταυγάσῃ[166] ἐν ταῖς καρδίαις ὑμῶν (*Pan* 66.64.5)

2 Peter 2:19
ἔλεγεν τοῖς Ἰουδαίοις·
ᾧ γάρ τις ἥττηται, τούτῳ καὶ δεδούλωται (*Pan* 38.4.9)

ᾧ γὰρ ἥττηταί τις, τούτῳ καὶ δεδούλωται (*Pan* 40.6.6)

---

a. καί Epiph TR 𝔐 ℵ^c A C L Ψ 049 33 105 201 323 325 1022 1739
b. *om* 𝔓⁷² ℵ* B

---

[165] In this allusion, Epiphanius' imprecision precludes knowing whether his exemplar read ἡμέρα with TR 𝔐 𝔓⁷² ℵ A B C L 049 105 201 323 325 1022 or ἡ ἡμέρα with Ψ 33 1739.

[166] καταυγάσῃ] διαυγάσει 33 323 1891*; διαφαύσῃ 1352; διαυγάσῃ *rell*.

1 John 1:1
καὶ Ἰωάννης μαρτυρεῖ λέγων·
ὃ ἦν ἀπ' ἀρχῆς, ὃ ἠκούσαμεν καὶ τοῖς ὀφθαλμοῖς ἑωράκαμεν, καὶ αἱ χεῖρες ἡμῶν ἐψηλάφησαν (Pan 57.9.3)

ὡς καὶ Ἰωάννης μαρτυρεῖ·
ὃ ἀκηκόαμεν ἀπ' ἀρχῆς (Pan 69.40.7)

1 John 1:5
αἱ γραφαί φασι περὶ τοῦ θεοῦ ὅτι <u>φῶς ὁ θεός</u> (Pan 69.32.3)

1 John 2:18–19
λέγοντος ὅτι·
18) ἠκούσατε ὅτι Ἀντίχριστος ἔρχεται καὶ νῦν Ἀντίχριστοι πολλοὶ γεγόνασιν 19) <u>ἐξ ἡμῶν ἐξῆλθον, ἀλλ' οὐκ ἦσαν ἐξ ἡμῶν· εἰ γὰρ ἦσαν ἐξ ἡμῶν, μεμενήκεισαν[167] ἂν μεθ' ἡμῶν</u>· ἀλλ' ἵνα γνωσθῶσιν ὅτι οὐκ ἦσαν ἐξ ἡμῶν.[168] τούτου χάριν γράφω ὑμῖν, τεκνία (Pan 48.1.6)

19) εἰ γὰρ ἦσαν ἐξ αὐτῶν, μεμενήκεσαν ἂν μετ' αὐτῶν (Anc 116.7)

(18)_____

a. ὅτι Epiph ℵ* B C Ψ 1739
b. ὅτι ὁ TR 𝔐 ℵc 049 33 105 201 323 325 1022
c. ὁ A L

(19)_____

a. ἦσαν ἐξ ἡμῶν^sec Epiph TR 𝔐 ℵ A L 049 33 105 201 323 325 1022 1739
b. ἐξ ἡμῶν ἦσαν B C Ψ

1 John 4:1
φάσκοντος τοῦ ἀποστόλου Ἰωάννου ἐν τῇ ἐπιστολῇ ὅτι·
δοκιμάζετε τὰ[169] πνεύματα, εἰ ἔστιν ἐκ τοῦ θεοῦ (Pan 48.1.6)

1 John 4:12
λέγειν·
θεὸν οὐδεὶς πώποτε τεθέαται (Anc 53.8)

---

[167] μεμενήκεισαν] μεμενήκασιν 33 630.
[168] ἡμῶν] ὑμῶν Ψ.
[169] τά] πᾶν Ψ.

1 John 5:19
ὁ ἀπόστολος γάρ φησιν·
ὅλος ὁ κόσμος ἐν τῷ πονηρῷ κεῖται (*Pan* 66.66.3)

ἀλλὰ ὡς λέγει·
πᾶς ὁ κόσμος ἐν τῷ πονηρῷ κεῖται (*Pan* 66.67.5)

2 John 10
Ἰωάννης γὰρ λέγει <u>εἴ τις ἔρχεται</u>, φησι, <u>πρὸς ὑμᾶς, καὶ οὐ φέρει τὴν διδαχὴν ταύτην</u>[170] (*Pan* 26.15.4)

2 John 11
<u>ὁ γὰρ λέγων αὐτοῖς</u>,[171] φησι, <u>χαίρειν κοινωνεῖ τοῖς ἔργοις αὐτῶν τοῖς πονηροῖς</u> (*Pan* 34.13.3)

---

a. ὁ γὰρ λέγων Epiph TR 𝔐 L Ψ 049 105 201 325 1022
b. ὁ λέγων γάρ ℵ A B 33 323 1739

---

[170] οὐ φέρει τὴν διδαχὴν ταύτην M] ταύτην τὴν διδαχὴν οὐ φέρει V *rell*.
[171] αὐτοῖς] om 049 105 221 945 1022 1891; αὐτῷ *rell*. The citation is exact with two exceptions, both being adaptations due to Epiphanius' argument: αὐτοῖς rather than αὐτῷ and consequently αὐτῶν rather than αὐτοῦ.

Jude 8–10

8) ἐνυπνιαζόμενοι σάρκα μὲν[172] μιαίνουσι, κυριότητα[173] δὲ ἀθετοῦσι, δόξας δὲ βλασφημοῦσι· 9) Μιχαὴλ δὲ ὁ ἀρχάγγελος διαλεγόμενος τῷ διαβόλῳ περὶ τοῦ Μωυσέως σώματος οὐκ ἤνεγκε λόγον βλασφημίας, ἀλλὰ εἶπεν, ἐπιτιμήσαι σοι[174] κύριος.[175] 10) οὗτοι δὲ[176] ὅσα οὐκ οἴδασι φυσικῶς βλασφημοῦσιν (Pan 26.11.5)

8) ἀπὸ τῆς ἐπιστολῆς τοῦ Ἰούδα ... λέγειν·
καὶ οἱ μὲν ἐνυπνιαζόμενοι σάρκα μὲν μιαίνουσι, κυριότητα δὲ ἀθετοῦσι, δόξας δὲ βλασφημοῦσιν (Pan 26.13.7)

10) ὡς λέγει ὅτι·
ὅσα μὲν οὐκ οἴδασιν, ἀγνοοῦντες ἁλίσκονται, ὅσα δὲ οἴδασιν, ὡς τὰ ἄλογα ζῷα φθείρονται (Pan 26.11.3)

(9)_____

a. σοι κύριος Epiph TR 𝔐 𝔓⁷² ℵᶜ A B C L Ψ 049 33 105 201 325 1022
b. σοι ὁ θεός ℵ* 323 1739

_____

---

[172] μέν M] om V 𝔓⁷².
[173] κυριότητα] κυριότητας ℵ Ψ.
[174] Text M] add ὁ V.
[175] In this allusion, Epiphanius clearly knows Michael's response to the Devil as ἐπιτιμήσαι σοι κύριος.
[176] δέ] μέν 630.

Romans 1:4
ἐν δυνάμει κατὰ πνεῦμα ἁγιωσύνης (*Anc* 68.10)

λέγων·
προορισθέντος[177] υἱοῦ θεοῦ ἐν δυνάμει κατὰ πνεῦμα[178] ἁγιωσύνης ἐξ ἀναστάσεως νεκρῶν, τοῦ κυρίου ἡμῶν Ἰησοῦ Χριστοῦ[179] (*Pan* 54.6.2)

ἐν δυνάμει κατὰ πνεῦμα ἁγιωσύνης (*Pan* 74.5.10; from *Anc*)

ὥς φησι·
κατὰ πνεῦμα ἁγιωσύνης ἐξ ἀναστάσεως νεκρῶν τοῦ κυρίου ἡμῶν Ἰησοῦ Χριστοῦ (*Pan, De fide* 17.11)

Romans 1:14
πάλιν ἐν ἑτέρῳ τόπῳ λέγει οὕτως·
ὀφειλέτης εἰμὶ Ἕλλησίν τε καὶ βαρβάροις, σοφοῖς τε καὶ ἀνοήτοις, ἵνα δείξῃ σοφοὺς μὲν τοὺς Ἰουδαίους, ἀνοήτους δὲ τοὺς Σκύθας. καὶ φησιν ὀφειλέτης εἰμί (*Pan* 8.3.4)

Ἕλλησί τε καὶ βαρβάροις, σοφοῖς τε καὶ ἀνοήτοις (*Pan* 26.1.1)

Romans 1:18
ὡς λέγει ὁ ἀπόστολος ἐπὶ τούτοις καὶ τοῖς ὁμοίοις αὐτῶν·
ἀποκαλύπτεσθαι ὀργὴν θεοῦ καὶ δικαιοκρισίαν ἐπὶ τοὺς τὴν ἀλήθειαν ἐν ἀδικίᾳ κατέχοντας[180] (*Pan* 24.3.8)

Romans 1:25
ἐλάτρευσαν γὰρ τῇ κτίσει[181] παρὰ τὸν κτίσαντα (*Anc* 70.3)

μάλιστα τοῦ ἀποστόλου λέγοντος·
καὶ ἐλάτρευσαν τῇ κτίσει παρὰ τὸν κτίσαντα (*Pan* 69.36.2)

ἐλάτρευσαν γὰρ τῇ κτίσει παρὰ τὸν κτίσαντα (*Pan* 74.7.3)

καὶ ὁ ἀπόστολός φησιν·
ἐλάτρευσαν τῇ κτίσει παρὰ τὸν κτίσαντα (*Pan* 76.8.8)

---

[177] προορισθέντος it[d.e.g] Euseb; ὁρισθέντος *rell*.
[178] κατὰ πνεῦμα] καὶ πνεύματι eth syr[p] (syr[h] *om*. καί) Chr[txt].
[179] τοῦ κυρίου ἡμῶν Ἰησοῦ Χριστοῦ M; Ἰησοῦ Χριστοῦ τοῦ κυρίου ἡμῶν U.
[180] καὶ δικαιοκρισίαν ἐπὶ τοὺς is an allusion to 2:5.
[181] τῇ κτίσει] τὴν κτίσιν P*.

Romans 1:25 cont.
κτίσιν παρὰ τὸν κτίσαντα, ὅς ἐστιν εὐλογημένος εἰς τοὺς αἰῶνας ἀμήν (*Pan* 76.16.1)

Romans 1:26
λέγων·
αἵ τε γὰρ θήλειαι[182] αὐτῶν μετήλλαξαν τὴν φυσικὴν χρῆσιν[183] εἰς τὴν παρὰ φύσιν (*Pan* 26.16.2)

Romans 1:27
κατὰ τὸ γεγραμμένον·
τὴν ἀντιμισθίαν τῆς πλάνης ἐν ἑαυτοῖς[184] ἀπολαμβάνοντες[185] (*Pan* 26.11.8)

ὅτι·
ἄρρενες ἐν ἄρρεσι τὴν ἀσχημοσύνην κατεργαζόμενοι (*Pan* 26.16.2)

ὡς καὶ ὁ ἀπόστολός φησι·
τὴν γὰρ ἀντιμισθίαν ἣν ἔδει τῆς πλάνης αὐτῶν ἐν ἑαυτοῖς[186] ἀπολαμβάνοντες (*Pan* 26.19.3)

Romans 2:6
ὁ ἑκάστῳ ἀποδιδοὺς κατὰ τὰ ἔργα αὐτοῦ (*Pan* 66 24.8)

Romans 2:11
προσωποληψία παρὰ τῷ[187] θεῷ (*Anc* 98.2)

προσωποληψία ἐστὶ παρὰ θεῷ (*Pan* 76.8.3)

Romans 2:25
ἡ περιτομὴ ἀκροβυστία αὐτοῖς γίνεται (*Pan* 42.12.3, *refut.* 8)

Romans 2:29
καὶ περιτομὴ καρδίας ἐν πνεύματι[188] (*Anc* 68.11)

---

[182] θήλειαι] θήλει L.
[183] χρῆσιν] κτίσιν D*.
[184] ἐν ἑαυτοῖς] ἐν αὐτοῖς B K.
[185] ἀπολαμβάνοντες] ἀντειλαμβάνοντες G.
[186] ἐν ἑαυτοῖς] ἐν αὐτοῖς B K.
[187] τῷ] *om* D*.

Romans 2:29 cont.
καὶ περιτομὴ καρδίας ἐν[189] πνεύματι (*Pan* 74.5.11, from *Anc*)

Romans 3:5–6
ἀλλ᾽·
5) ἀδίκως ἐπιφέρει τὴν ὀργήν[190] ὁ θεὸς κατὰ τῶν ἀνθρώπων 6) μὴ γένοιτο (*Anc* 87.6)

Romans 3:8
ὡς καὶ ὁ μακάριος Παῦλός φησιν·
ὥστε τινὰς τολμᾶν <u>ἡμᾶς λέγειν</u>[191] <u>ὅτι</u>[192] <u>ποιήσωμέν τα</u>[193] <u>κακά, ἵνα ἔλθῃ ἐφ᾽ ἡμᾶς</u>[194] <u>τὰ ἀγαθά, ὧν τὸ κρίμα ἔνδικόν ἐστι</u> (*Pan* 26.11.7)

<u>τὸ δὲ κρίμα τούτων</u> κατὰ τὸ γεγραμμένον <u>ἔνδικόν ἐστιν</u>, ὡς ὁ ἅγιος ἀπόστολος Παῦλος ἔφη (*Pan* 27.4.2)

Romans 3:23–24
23) πάντες ἥμαρτον καὶ ὑστεροῦνται τῆς δόξης τοῦ θεοῦ 24) δικαιούμενοι[195] δωρεὰν τῇ χάριτι (*Pan* 61.4.10)

Romans 3:26
διάστασις δὲ ἦν καὶ ἔχθρα <u>ἐν τῇ ἀνοχῇ τοῦ θεοῦ</u> (*Anc* 65.8)

διάστασις δὲ ἦν καὶ ἔχθρα <u>ἐν τῇ ἀνοχῇ τοῦ θεοῦ</u> (*Pan* 74.2.8, from *Anc*)

Romans 3:28
ἐκ πίστεως ἡ δικαιοσύνη <u>χωρὶς ἔργων</u>[196] <u>νόμου</u> (*Anc* 67.3)

ἐκ πίστεως ἡ δικαιοσύνη <u>χωρὶς ἔργων νόμου</u> (*Pan* 74.4.2, from *Anc*)

---

[188] The citation is omitted in L^{epiph} and J, but included in *Pan,* and is thus inserted by Holl into the text of *Ancoratus*. Καί is included as part of the quotation in *Panarion*, but is the introduction to the citation in *Ancoratus*.
[189] ὅς G it$^{d.e.g}$.
[190] *add* αὐτοῦ ℵ*
[191] ἡμᾶς τινες λέγειν 1739; τινες ἡμᾶς λέγειν *rell*.
[192] ὅτι M Holl; *om* V with G it^g vg Or.
[193] τά] *om* D*.
[194] ἐφ᾽ ἡμᾶς V Holl with 81 cop^{bo}; *om* ἐφ᾽ ἡμᾶς M with *rell*.
[195] δικαιούμενοι U; *add* δέ M.
[196] ἔργων *Pan*. Holl; *om* L^{epiph} J.

Romans 4:19
Ἀβραὰμ γηραλέος λαμβάνει παῖδα <u>νενεκρωμένου ἤδη</u>[197] <u>τοῦ σώματος</u> καὶ ἐκ νεκρῶν ὁ θεὸς τὴν ἐλπίδα κεχάρισται, νεκρωθείσης μάλιστα <u>τῆς μήτρας Σάρρας</u> (*Anc* 94.5)

Romans 5:1
ὅμοιον τῷ εἰπεῖν·
δικαιωθέντες δὲ ἐκ πίστεως εἰρήνην ἔχομεν πρὸς τὸν θεὸν διὰ τοῦ κυρίου ἡμῶν Ἰησοῦ Χριστοῦ (*Anc* 69.1)

ὅμοιον τῷ εἰπεῖν·
δικαιωθέντες δὲ ἐκ πίστεως εἰρήνην ἔχομεν πρὸς τὸν θεὸν διὰ τοῦ κυρίου ἡμῶν Ἰησοῦ Χριστοῦ (*Pan* 74.6.1; from *Anc*).

---

a. ἔχομεν Epiph TR 𝔐 ℵ^c B^c F G P 104 1594 1739
b. ἔχωμεν ℵ* A B* C D K L 049 33 81 699 it$^{d.e.f.g}$

Romans 5:6
<u>ἔτι γὰρ Χριστὸς ὄντων ἡμῶν ἀσθενῶν ἔτι κατὰ καιρὸν ὑπὲρ ἀσεβῶν ἀπέθανεν</u>. τὸ <u>ἔτι</u> καὶ <u>ἀπέθανεν</u> οὐ δοκήσεως ἀλλὰ ἀλτθείας ἐστὶ σημαντικόν. εἰ γὰρ δόκησις ἦν, τίς χρεία τοῦ <u>ἔτι</u> λέγεσθαι, δυναμένου τοῦ Χριστοῦ πάντοτε καὶ τότε καὶ νῦν δοκήσει φαίνεσθαι καὶ μὴ λέγεσθαι <u>ἔτι ὄντων ἡμῶν ἀσθενῶν;</u>[198] (*Pan* 42.12.3, *refut.* 31)

---

a. ἔτι γὰρ...ἔτι Epiph ℵ A C D* 81 104 Marcion
b. ἔτι γὰρ...*om* TR 𝔐 D^c [K (L δέ for γάρ) P] 049 33 699 1594 1739 Chr
c. εἴ γε...ἔτι B
d. εἰς τί γάρ...ἔτι F G t$^{d.f.g}$

Romans 5:14
φησιν·
ἐβασίλευσεν ὁ θάνατος ἀπὸ Ἀδὰμ μέχρι Μωϋσέως (*Pan* 66.78.3)

---

[197] From this loose allusion, one cannot be certain that Epiphanius' exemplar read ἤδη with TR 𝔐 ℵ A C D K L P 049 33 81 104 699 1594 rather than *om* with B F G 1739 it$^{d.e.f.g}$ Meth.

[198] In the preceding paragraph, Epiphanius states that several of Marcion's citations of the Pauline epistles are accurate, but conflict with his theology. Here, his argument is based upon the second clause.

Romans 6:9
    <u>οὐκέτι ἀποθνῄσκει, θάνατος αὐτοῦ οὐκέτι κυριεύει</u> κατὰ τὸ γεγραμμένον (*Anc* 92.5)

    <u>οὐκέτι γὰρ κύριος ἀποθνῄσκει, θάνατος αὐτοῦ οὐκέτι κυριεύει</u> κατὰ τὸ γεγραμμένον (*Pan* 51.31.9)

    <u>θάνατος[199] αὐτοῦ οὐκέτι κυριεύει</u>, φησιν ὁ ἀπόστολος (*Pan* 62.7.6)

    οὐκέτι[200] ἀποθνῄσκει, θάνατος αὐτοῦ οὐκέτι κυριεύει (*Pan* 64.64.10)

    οὐκέτι γὰρ ἀποθνῄσκει, φησί, θάνατος αὐτοῦ οὐκέτι κυριεύει[201] (*Pan* 69.42.9)

    ὡς εἶπε περὶ αὐτοῦ ὁ ἀπόστολος·
    ἀνέστη, οὐκέτι ἀποθνῄσκει, θάνατος αὐτοῦ οὐκέτι κυριεύει (*Pan* 69.67.1)

    τοῦ ἁγιωτάτου ἀποστόλου τῆς φωνῆς, τό·
    οὐκέτι ἀποθνῄσκει, θάνατος αὐτοῦ οὐκέτι κυριεύει (*Pan* 77.33.4)

    ὥς φησιν ὁ ἅγιος ἀπόστολος·
    ἀνέστη Χριστός, οὐκέτι ἀποθνῄσκει, θάνατος αὐτοῦ οὐκέτι κυριεύει (*Pan, De fide* 17.8)

    ὥς φησιν ὁ ἀπόστολος·
    θάνατος αὐτοῦ οὐκέτι κυριεύει (*Pan, Christentum* 2.8)

Romans 7:12
    καὶ εἰ ὁ <u>ἅγιος νόμος</u> (*Pan* 77.38.2)

Romans 7:18
    οἶδα γάρ φησιν ὁ ἀπόστολος <u>ὅτι οὐκ οἰκεῖ ἐν ἐμοὶ οὐδὲν ἀγαθόν, τοῦτ' ἔστιν ἐν τῇ σαρκί μου</u> (*Anc* 79.1)

    ὡς ἔφη ὁ ἀπόστολος·
    οἶδα γὰρ ὅτι οὐκ οἰκεῖ ἐν ἐμοί, τοῦτ' ἔστιν ἐν τῇ σαρκί μου,[202] ἀγαθόν (*Pan* 77.27.5)

---

[199] θάνατος U; ὁ θανατος M; γὰρ θάνατος Holl.
[200] οὐκέτι M U; *add* ἀναστὰς δὲ *ante* οὐκέτι Holl.
[201] κυριεύει] κυριεύσει 81 it[d.e.f.g] Euseb.
[202] ἀγαθόν] *add* τό F G Meth[epiph] Cyr.

Romans 7:22
διὸ·
συνείδομεν τὸν νόμον τοῦ θεοῦ κατὰ τὸν ἔσω ἄνθρωπον (*Anc* 65.4)

διὸ·
συνήδομαι τῷ νόμῳ τοῦ θεοῦ²⁰³ κατὰ τὸν ἔσω ἄνθρωπον (*Pan* 74.2.4; from *Anc*)

Romans 7:23
λέγει ἡ γραφή·
ὁρῶ νόμον ἕτερον ἀντιστρατευόμενον ἐν τοῖς μέλεσί μου²⁰⁴ καὶ αἰχμαλωτίζοντά με²⁰⁵ ἐν τῷ νοΐ μου²⁰⁶ τῷ νόμῳ²⁰⁷ τῆς ἁμαρτίας²⁰⁸ τῷ ὄντι ἐν τοῖς μέλεσί μου (*Anc* 56.3)

Romans 7:25
ἐλεύθερος ἐκ <u>νόμου σαρκὸς ἁμαρτίας</u> (*Anc* 65.3)

ἐλεύθερος ἐκ <u>νόμου σαρκὸς ἁμαρτίας</u> (*Pan* 74.2.3; from *Anc*)

Romans 8:3
τοίνυν·
<u>ἐν ᾧ ἐγὼ ἠσθένουν διὰ τῆς σαρκός</u> ἀπεστάλη μοι σωτὴρ <u>ἐν ὁμοιώματι σαρκὸς ἁμαρτίας</u> (*Anc* 65.9)

κατέκρινε τὴν ἁμαρτίαν (*Pan* 66.73.6)

ἵνα·
ἐν τῇ σαρκὶ κατακρίνῃ τὴν ἁμαρτίαν (*Pan* 69.52.8)

τοίνυν·
<u>ἐν ᾧ ἐγὼ ἠσθένουν διὰ τῆς σαρκός</u> ἀπεστάλη μοι σωτὴρ <u>ἐν ὁμοιώματι σαρκὸς ἁμαρτίας</u> (*Pan* 74.2.9; from *Anc*)

---

[203] θεοῦ] νοός B.
[204] μοι F G.
[205] με] om A.
[206] ἐν τῷ νοΐ μου] om. A; τῷ νόμῳ τοῦ νοός μου *rell* with Or Meth^epiph.
[207] In this imprecise allusion, it is unclear whether Epiphanius' text read τῷ νόμῳ with TR 𝔐 A C L 81 104 699 1739 or ἐν τῷ νόμῳ with ℵ B D F G K P 049 33 1594.
[208] *add* τοῦ νοός μου A.

Romans 8:4
καὶ·
τὸ δικαίωμα τοῦ νόμου (*Anc* 65.3)

καὶ·
τὸ δικαίωμα τοῦ νόμου (*Pan* 74.2.3; from *Anc*)

Romans 8:8
καὶ·
οἱ ἐν σαρκὶ δὲ ὄντες θεῷ[209] ἀρέσαι οὐ δύνανται (*Anc* 76.5)

Romans 8:9
καὶ <u>πνεῦμα θεοῦ</u> καὶ <u>πνεῦμα Χριστοῦ</u> (*Anc* 72.6)

Romans 8:11
εἰ τοίνυν τὸ πνεῦμα αὐτοῦ ἐν ἡμῖν, ὁ ἐγείρας αὐτὸν ἐκ νεκρῶν ζωοποιήσει τὰ θνητὰ σώματα ἡμῶν διὰ τοῦ ἐνοικοῦντος πνεύματος ἐν ἡμῖν (*Anc* 66.12)

ὡς λέγει ὁ ἅγιος ἀπόστολος φάσκων·
εἰ δὲ τὸ πνεῦμα τοῦ ἐγείραντος Χριστὸν ἐκ νεκρῶν[210] οἰκεῖ ἐν ὑμῖν, ὁ ἐγείρας Χριστὸν ἐκ νεκρῶν[211] ζωοποιήσει καὶ τὰ θνητὰ σώματα ὑμῶν, διὰ τοῦ ἐνοικοῦντος πνεύματος αὐτοῦ ἐν ὑμῖν (*Pan* 57.7.6)

εἰ τοίνυν τὸ πνεῦμα αὐτοῦ ἐν ἡμῖν, ὁ ἐγείρας αὐτὸν ἐκ νεκρῶν ζωοποιήσει τὰ θνητὰ σώματα ἡμῶν διὰ τοῦ ἐνοικοῦντος πνεύματος αὐτοῦ[212] ἐν ἡμῖν (*Pan* 74.3.12; from *Anc*)

---

a. Χριστὸν ἐκ νεκρῶν Epiph B D^c F G
b. τὸν Χριστὸν ἐκ νεκρῶν TR 𝔐 ℵ^c K L P (049 *add* τῶν) 33 699 1594
c. Χριστὸν Ἰησοῦν ἐκ νεκρῶν D* it^{d.e}
d. Ἰησοῦν Χριστὸν ἐκ νεκρῶν 104
e. ἐκ νεκρῶν Χριστὸν Ἰησοῦν ℵ* A 1739
f. ἐκ νεκρῶν Ἰησοῦν Χριστόν C 81

---

[209] θεῷ] τῷ θεῷ D E.
[210] *om* ἐκ νεκρῶν 1739.
[211] οἰκεῖ ... νεκρῶν] U; *om* οἰκεῖ ἐν ὑμῖν, ὁ ἐγείρας Χριστὸν ἐκ νεκρῶν M, due to haplography as in 426.
[212] πνεύματος αὐτοῦ J; αὐτοῦ πνεύματος Holl. Since *Pan* 57.7.6 is a verbally-exact citation and *Pan* 74.3.12 and *Anc* 66.12 are both adaptations, *Pan* 57.7.6 is accepted as reflecting Epiphanius' exemplar.

Romans 8:11 cont.

---

a. καί Epiph TR 𝔐 B C D F G K L P 049 33 81 104 699 1594 CyrJer
b. *om* ℵ A 1739 Meth^epiph

---

a. τοῦ ἐνοικοῦντος αὐτοῦ πνεύματος (Epiph) ℵ A C P^c 81 104 1594 it^t syr^{h.pal} cop^{sa} Clem Meth CyrJer
b. τὸ ἐνοικοῦν αὐτοῦ πνεῦμα TR 𝔐 B D F G K L P* 049 33 699 1739 it^{d.g} Or

---

Romans 8:13
τὰς πράξεις τοῦ σώματος θανατοῦντες ζήσωμεν[213] (*Pan* 64.63.16)

Romans 8:14
ὅσοι οὖν πνεύματι αὐτοῦ ἄγονται, οὗτοι (*Anc* 66.10)

ὅσοι γοῦν πνεύματι αὐτοῦ ἄγονται, αὐτοί (*Pan* 74.3.10; from *Anc*)

Romans 8:23
καὶ· τὴν ἀπαρχὴν τοῦ πνεύματος ἔχοντες (*Anc* 68.13)

καὶ· τὴν ἀπαρχὴν τοῦ πνεύματος ἔχοντες (*Pan* 74.5.13; from *Anc*)

Romans 8:26
ἀλλ' αὐτὸ τὸ πνεῦμα ὑπερεντυγχάνει ὑπὲρ ἡμῶν (*Anc* 68.14)

ἧς εἶπεν ὁ ἅγιος ἀπόστολος·
τὸ δὲ πνεῦμα ὑπερεντυγχάνει ὑπὲρ ἡμῶν[214] στεναγμοῖς ἀλαλήτοις (*Pan* 55.5.3)

ἀλλ' αὐτὸ τὸ πνεῦμα ὑπερεντυγχάνει ὑπὲρ ἡμῶν (*Pan* 74.5.14; from *Anc*)

---

[213] In this conflation with Gal 5:25, and its adaptation to the patristic sentence structure, it is uncertain whether Epiphanius read τοῦ σώματος with TR 𝔐 ℵ A B C K L P 049 33 81 104 699 1594 1739 or τῆς σαρκός with D F G.

[214] Constantine Tischendorf, *Novum Testamentum* (8th ed.; Leipzig: Giesecke & Devrient, 1872): 2.405, following Petavius' edition, cites Epiphanius incorrectly as supporting the omission of ὑπὲρ ἡμῶν.

Romans 8:26 cont.

---

a. ὑπερεντυγχάνει ὑπὲρ ἡμῶν Epiph TR 𝔐 ℵ^c C K L P 049 33 104 699 1594 it^{ar.dem} Euseb
b. ὑπερεντυγχάνει ℵ* A B D F G 81 1739 it^{d*.g}

Romans 8:33
<u>τίς</u>, γάρ φησιν, <u>ἐγκαλέσει κατὰ ἐκλεκτῶν θεοῦ;</u> (*Pan* 42.12.3 refut. 6)

Romans 8:34
ὅμοιον τῷ εἰπεῖν·
ὅς ἐστιν ἐν δεξιᾷ τοῦ θεοῦ, ὅς καὶ ἐντυγχάνει ὑπὲρ ἡμῶν (*Anc* 68.14)

ὅμοιον τῷ εἰπεῖν·
ὅς ἐστιν ἐν δεξιᾷ τοῦ θεοῦ, ὅς ἐντυγχάνει ὑπὲρ ἡμῶν (*Pan* 74.5.14; from *Anc*)

---

a. ὅς ἐστιν Epiph ℵ* A C 81 it^{d*} Or Chr
b. ὅς καί ἐστιν TR 𝔐 𝔓⁴⁶ ℵ^c B D F G K L 049 33 104 699 1594 it^{d.e.f.g} CyrJer
c. *om* 1739

Romans 9:4–5
4) ὧν φησιν ἡ λατρεία καὶ αἱ διαθῆκαι 5) καὶ ὧν οἱ πατέρες, ἐξ ὧν ὁ Χριστὸς τὸ κατὰ σάρκα,[215] ὁ ὢν ἐπὶ πάντων θεὸς εὐλογητὸς εἰς τοὺς αἰῶνας, ἀμήν (*Pan* 76.47.5)[216]

5) καὶ πάλιν·
<u>ἐξ ὧν ὁ Χριστὸς τὸ κατὰ σάρκα</u>, ὥς φησι Παῦλος (*Anc* 44.3)

<u>5) ἐξ ὧν φησίν ὁ Χριστὸς τὸ κατὰ σάρκα, ὁ ὢν ἐπὶ πάντων θεός</u> (*Anc* 69.9)

---

[215] τὸ κατὰ σάρκα] κατὰ σάρκα F G; τὰ κατὰ σάρκα C*; ὁ κατὰ σάρκα 𝔓⁴⁶.
[216] The gist of 9:4 that prefaces v. 5 is too loose to know whether Epiphanius read αἱ διαθῆκαι with TR 𝔐 ℵ C K 049 33 81 104 699 1594 1739 rather than ἡ διαθήκη with 𝔓⁴⁶ B D F G, or *om* with A L.

Romans 9:5 cont.
καὶ ὁ ἀπόστολος τούτοις μαρτυρεῖ τοῖς λόγοις φάσκων·
ὧν οἱ²¹⁷ πατέρες, ἐξ ὧν²¹⁸ ὁ Χριστὸς τὸ κατὰ σάρκα, ὁ ὢν ἐπὶ πάντων θεὸς εὐλογητὸς εἰς τοὺς αἰῶνας, ἀμήν (*Pan* 57.2.8)

ὡς καὶ ὁ ἀπόστολος διαβεβαιοῦται λέγων·
ὧν οἱ πατέρες καὶ ἐξ ὧν ὁ Χριστὸς τὸ κατὰ σάρκα, ὁ ὢν ἐπὶ πάντων θεός (*Pan* 57.9.1)

<u>ἐξ ὧν φησίν ὁ Χριστὸς κατὰ σάρκα, ὁ ὢν ἐπὶ πάντων θεός</u> (*Pan* 74.6.9; from *Anc*)

Romans 9:20
μενοῦν γε, ²¹⁹ σὺ τίς εἶ ὁ ἀντιλογιζόμενος τῷ θεῷ; (*Anc* 71.1)

μενοῦν γε, σὺ τίς εἶ ὁ ἀντιλογιζόμενος τῷ θεῷ; (*Pan* 74.8.1; from *Anc*)

ἐρεῖ τὸ πλάσμα τῷ πλάσαντι, τί με οὕτως ἐποίησας;²²⁰ (*Pan* 76.53.3)

---

a. μενοῦν γε Epiph TR 𝔐 ℵ (A *om* γε) B Dᶜ K L P 049 33 81 104 699 1594 1739 Chr
b. *om* 𝔓⁴⁶ D* F G it^{d.e.f.g}

Romans 9:32
<u>προσέκοψαν γὰρ τῷ λίθῳ τοῦ προσκόμματος</u> (*Anc* 27.3)

---

a. γάρ Epiph TR 𝔐 ℵᶜ Dᶠ K L P 049 33 104 699 1594 1739 Chr
b. *om* 𝔓⁴⁶ ℵ* A D* F G 81 it^{d.e.f.g}

Romans 10:4
πλήρωμα γὰρ νόμου Χριστὸς κατὰ τὸ γεγραμμένον (*Anc* 94.4)

---

[217] οἱ] *om* F G.
[218] ἐξ ὧν F G it^{f.g}] καὶ ἐξ ὧν *rell*.
[219] In this citation, Epiphanius strengthens his argument by altering the participle to ἀντιλογιζόμενος, but retains the exact wording elsewhere, indicating an awareness of μενοῦν γε.
[220] ἐπλάσας D E syrᵖ.

Romans 10:4 cont.
κατὰ τὸ παρὰ τῷ ἀποστόλῳ εἰρημένον ὅτι·
πλήρωμα <u>νόμου Χριστὸς εἰς δικαιοσύνην</u> (*Pan* 42.12.3 *refut.* 28)

Romans 10:6–7
ὡς κατὰ τὸ εἰρημένον·
μὴ εἴπῃς ἐν τῇ καρδίᾳ σοῦ, τίς ἀναβήσεται εἰς τὸν οὐρανόν; τουτέστι Χριστὸν καταγαγεῖν· ἢ τίς καταβήσεται εἰς τὴν ἄβυσσον; τουτέστι Χριστὸν ἀναγαγεῖν ἐκ νεκρῶν (*Pan* 77.31.5)

Romans 10:9
εἶτά φησιν ὁ ἀπόστολος·
ὁ θεὸς ἤγειρεν αὐτὸν[221] ἐκ νεκρῶν (*Pan* 69.19.4)

Romans 10:10
ὅτι·
καρδίᾳ πιστεύεται εἰς δικαιοσύνην, στόματα δὲ ὁμολογεῖται εἰς σωτηρίαν (*Pan* 19.3.3)

Romans 10:18
εἰς πᾶσαν τὴν γῆν ἐξῆλθεν ὁ φθόγγος αὐτῶν καὶ εἰς τὰ πέρατα τῆς οἰκουμένης τὰ ῥήματα αὐτῶν[222] (*Pan* 61.2.2)

Romans 11:33
<u>ὦ βάθος πλούτου καὶ σοφίας καὶ γνώσεως θεοῦ</u> κατὰ τὸ γεγραμμένον (*Anc* 94.1)

ἀνεξερεύνητα γὰρ τὰ κρίματα αὐτοῦ καὶ ἀνεκδιήγητοι αἱ ὁδοὶ αὐτοῦ (*Pan* 59.5.6)

διὰ τοῦτο γὰρ καὶ ὁ ἀπόστολος ἔφη·
ὦ βάθος πλούτου καὶ σοφίας καὶ γνώσεως θεοῦ (*Pan* 69.60.2)

ὦ βάθος πλούτου καὶ σοφίας καὶ γνώσεως θεοῦ (*Pan* 76.39.16)

---

a. θεοῦ   Epiph TR 𝔐 ℵ A B D L 049 81 104 699 1594 1739

b. τοῦ θεοῦ   F G 33

---

[221] ἤγειρεν αὐτὸν A P] αὐτὸν ἤγειρεν *rell.*
[222] The citation, verbally precise from both Rom 10:18 and Ps 18:5 (LXX), is applied to the church and presumably comes from Romans.

Romans 12:3

μὴ ὑπερφρονεῖν παρ' ὃ δεῖ φρονεῖν, ἀλλὰ φρονεῖν εἰς τὸ σωφρονεῖν (Pan 76.48.10)

ἀπὸ τοῦ ἁγιωτάτου ἀποστόλου τοῦ φήσαντος·
μὴ ὑπερφρονεῖν παρ' ὃ δεῖ φρονεῖν[223] (Pan 77.30.5)

Romans 13:1–4

<u>αἱ γὰρ οὖσαι ἐξουσίαι ἐκ θεοῦ τεταγμέναι εἰσίν,</u> ὡς λέγει ὁ ἀπόστολος· ὥστε οὖν ὁ ἀνθιστάμενος τῇ ἐξουσίᾳ τῇ τοῦ θεοῦ διαταγῇ ἀνθέστηκεν. <u>οἱ γὰρ ἄρχοντες οὐκ εἰσὶ</u> κατὰ τοῦ ἀγαθοῦ, ἀλλὰ ὑπὲρ τοῦ ἀγαθοῦ, καὶ οὐκ εἰσὶ κατὰ τῆς ἀληθείας, ἀλλὰ ὑπὲρ τῆς ἀληθείας. <u>θέλεις δέ, φησί, τὴν ἐξουσίαν μὴ φοβεῖσθαι; τὸ καλὸν ποίει, καὶ ἕξεις ἔπαινον ἐξ αὐτῆς· οὐ γὰρ εἰκῇ τὴν μάχαιραν φορεῖ·</u> διάκονος γάρ ἐστιν[224] εἰς αὐτὸ τοῦτο ἐκ θεοῦ τεταγμένοις <u>τῷ τὸ κακὸν πράττοντι</u> (Pan 40.4.3–4)

Romans 14:3

ὁ γὰρ ἐσθίων τὸν μὴ ἐσθίοντα μὴ ἐξουθενείτω,[225] καὶ ὁ μὴ ἐσθίων τὸν ἐσθίοντα μὴ κρινέτω (Pan 61.3.2)[226]

---

a. καί ὁ μὴ Epiph TR 𝔐 ℵ^c D^c L P 049 33 81 104 699 1594 1739 it$^{d(c)}$
b. ὁ δὲ μὴ 𝔓^{46} ℵ* A B C D* it^d
c. οὐδὲ ὁ μη; F G it$^{f.g}$

Romans 14:7

ἑαυτῷ ζῇ, οὐδὲ ἑαυτῷ ἀποθνῄσκει (Pan 76.29.7)

Romans 14:9

ἵνα καὶ νεκρῶν καὶ ζώντων[227] κυριεύσῃ (Pan 46.3.9)

---

[223] *om* παρ' ὃ δεῖ φρονεῖν F G it$^{f.g}$

[224] The loose nature of this quotation renders it inadvisable to conclude that Epiphanius' exemplar omitted καί at this place with G.

[225] ἐξουθενείτω] κρινέτω A.

[226] This allusion to Rom 13:1–4 has several precise phrases, but is too loose to know whether Epiphanius read οὖσαι ἐξουσίαι with TR 𝔐 D^c L P 049 33 104 699 1739 rather than οὖσαι ℵ A B D* F G 81 1594 it$^{d.e.f.g}$ in v. 1, or that he read θεοῦ^{sec} Epiph ℵ* A B D F G P 81 104 1739 rather than τοῦ θεοῦ TR 𝔐 ℵ^c L 049 33 699 1594 Or.

[227] *add* καὶ νεκρῶν 1739 Clem.

Romans 15:8
λέγω οὖν Χριστὸν διάκονον γεγενῆσθαι περιτομῆς ὑπὲρ ἀληθείας θεοῦ, εἰς τὸ πληρῶσαι τὰς ἐπαγγελίας (*Anc* 68.1)

λέγω οὖν Χριστὸν διάκονον γεγενῆσθαι περιτομῆς ὑπὲρ ἀληθείας θεοῦ, εἰς τὸ πληρῶσαι τὰς ἐπαγγελίας (*Pan* 74.5.1; from *Anc*)

---

a. Χριστόν Epiph ℵ A B C 81 1739 Or
b. Χριστὸν Ἰησοῦν 𝔐 L P 049 33 699 1594 Chr
c. Ἰησοῦν Χριστόν TR D F G 104 it$^{d.e.f.g}$

---

a. διάκονον γεγενῆσθαι Epiph TR 𝔐 ℵ A C^c D^c L P 33 81 104 699 1594 Chr
b. διάκονον γένεσθαι B C* D* F G 049 1739

Romans 15:16
ἵνα γένηται ἡ προσφορὰ τῶν ἐθνῶν εὐπρόσδεκτος, ἁγιασθεῖσα ἐν πνεύματι ἁγίῳ (*Anc* 68.15)

ἵνα γένηται[228] ἡ προσφορὰ τῶν ἐθνῶν εὐπρόσδεκτος,[229] ἁγιασθεῖσα ἐν πνεύματι ἁγίῳ (*Pan* 74.5.15; from *Anc*)

ἱερουργοῦντες τὸ εὐαγγέλιον (*Pan* 79.3.3)

Romans 16:19
εἰς τὸ ἀγαθόν, ἀκεραίους δὲ εἰς τὸ κακόν (*Pan* 37.8.9)

---

[228] γενήθη B.
[229] *om* εὐπρόσδεκτος F G it$^{f.g}$.

1 Corinthians 1:19
λέγων ὅτι·
τὴν σύνεσιν τῶν συνετῶν²³⁰ ἀθετήσω²³¹ (*Pan* 76.33.4)

1 Corinthians 1:20
καὶ· ἐμώρανεν ὁ θεὸς τὴν σοφίαν τοῦ κόσμου²³² (*Anc* 42.7)

καὶ· ἐμώρανεν ὁ θεὸς τὴν σοφίαν τοῦ κόσμου τούτου; (*Pan* 69.20.4)

1 Corinthians 1:21
οἶδεν οὖν ὁ ἀπόστολος λέγειν·
οὐκ ἔγνω ὁ κόσμος διὰ τῆς σοφίας τοῦ θεοῦ τὸν θεόν (*Anc* 42.7)

καὶ·
ἐπειδὴ²³³ ἐν τῇ σοφίᾳ τοῦ θεοῦ²³⁴ οὐκ ἔγνω ὁ κόσμος τὸν θεόν, ηὐδόκησε διὰ τῆς μωρίας τοῦ εὐαγγελίου σῶσαι τοὺς πιστεύοντας²³⁵ (*Pan* 69.20.4)

1 Corinthians 1:23–25
Ἰουδαίοις μὲν σκάνδαλον, Ἕλλησι δὲ μωρία, ἡμῖν δὲ τοῖς²³⁶ κλητοῖς, Ἰουδαίοις τε καὶ Ἕλλησι, Χριστὸς θεοῦ δύναμις καὶ θεοῦ σοφία,²³⁷ ὅτι τὸ μωρὸν τοῦ θεοῦ σοφώτερον τῶν ἀνθρώπων ἐστὶ καὶ τὸ²³⁸ ἀσθενὲς τοῦ θεοῦ ἰσχυρότερον τῶν ἀνθρώπων ἐστί (*Pan* 76.35.4 *refut*)

24) ὁ δύναμις ὢν θεοῦ καὶ σοφία κατὰ τὸ γεγραμμένον ἡμῖν δὲ <u>Χριστὸς δύναμις θεοῦ καὶ θεοῦ σοφια</u> (*Pan* 69.20.4)
(23)_____

    a. Ἕλλησι Epiph TR 𝔐 C² D² 049 699 1594 1739 Chr
    b. ἔθνεσι 𝔓⁴⁶ ℵ A B C* D* F G L P 33 81 104 it^{d.e.f.g} Or CyrJer

---

²³⁰ ἀσυνετῶν (F ἀσινετῶν) G
²³¹ ἀθετήσω indicates 1 Cor 1:19. Isa 29:14 reads κρύψω.
²³² Epiph reads τοῦ κόσμου τούτου with 𝔐 and τοῦ κόσμου with 𝔓⁴⁶ ℵ* A B C* D* P, but as the variation occurs at the end of one citation, it is not possible to determine whether τούτου was omitted.
²³³ ἐπειδή with F G; ἐπειδὴ γάρ *rell*.
²³⁴ θεοῦ] κοσμοῦ 𝔓⁴⁶.
²³⁵ πιστεύσαντας L.
²³⁶ *om* τοῖς F G.
²³⁷ Epiph 𝔓⁴⁶; δύναμιν ... σοφίαν *rell*.
²³⁸ τό] ὁ F G; *om phrase* 𝔓⁴⁶

1 Corinthians 1:23–25 cont.
(24)_____

    a. τε   Epiph TR 𝔐 $\mathfrak{P}^{46}$ ℵ A B C D L P 049 33 81 699 1594 1739 Or
    b. *om* F G 104

(25)_____

    a. σοφώτερον τῶν ἀνθρώπων ἐστι Epiph TR 𝔐 ℵ A B C L P 049 33 81
       104 699 1594 (1739) Or
    b. σοφώτερον ἐστι τῶν ἀνθρώπων D F G it$^{d.e.f.g}$
    c. σοφώτερον τῶν ἀνθρώπων $\mathfrak{P}^{46}$

    a. ἰσχυρότερον τῶν ἀνθρώπων ἐστιν Epiph TR 𝔐 ℵ^c A C L P 049 104
       699 1594 Or Chr
    b. ἰσχυρότερον ἐστιν τῶν ἀνθρώπων D F G it$^{d.e.f.g}$
    c. ἰσχυρότερον τῶν ἀνθρώπων ℵ* B 33 81 1739 Euseb
    d. *om* $\mathfrak{P}^{46}$

1 Corinthians 1:30
καὶ ἐγένετό μοι·
δικαιοσύνη καὶ ἁγιασμὸς καὶ ἀπολύτρωσις (*Anc* 65.9)

καὶ ἐγένετό μοι·
δικαιοσύνη καὶ ἁγιασμὸς καὶ ἀπολύτρωσις (*Pan* 74.2.9; from *Anc*)

1 Corinthians 2:4
ἅ καὶ λαλοῦμεν, <u>οὐκ ἐν πειθοῖ σοφίας λόγοις, ἀλλ' ἐν ἀποδείξει</u>[239]
<u>πνεύματος</u> θεοῦ, πνευματικοῖς πνευματικὰ συγκρίνοντες (*Anc* 70.8)[240]

---

[239] ἀποδείξει] ἀποκαλύψει D* and c

[240] In this allusion, which begins with an imprecise rendering of 2:12 and follows with a conflation of 2:4 and 13, Epiphanius gives the gist of the larger context with significant, but unnecessary, adjustments. One cannot be certain that Epiphanius read πειθοῖς σοφίας λόγοις with (ℵ*) B D 33 1739 rather than πειθοῖς ἀνθρωπίνης σοφίας λόγοις with 𝔐 ℵ^c A C L P 049 81 104 699 1594, or πειθοῖς σοφίας $\mathfrak{P}^{46}$ F G.

1 Corinthians 2:4 cont.
ἃ καὶ λαλοῦμεν, <u>οὐκ ἐν πειθοῖ σοφίας λόγοις, ἀλλ</u>'[241] <u>ἐν ἀποδείξει πνεύματος</u> θεοῦ, πνευματικοῖς πνευματικὰ συγκρίνοντες (*Pan* 74.7.8; from *Anc*)

1 Corinthians 2:8
ἵνα πληρωθῇ ἡ λέγουσα γραφή·
εἰ γὰρ ἔγνωσαν, οὐκ ἂν τὸν κύριον τῆς δόξης ἐσταύρωσαν (*Anc* 93.8)

εἰ γὰρ ἔγνωσαν, οὐκ ἂν τὸν κύριον τῆς δόξης ἐσταύρωσαν (*Pan* 77.32.1)

1 Corinthians 2:9
ἃ ὀφθαλμὸς οὐχ εἶδεν καὶ οὖς οὐκ ἤκουσε καὶ ἐπὶ καρδίαν ἀνθρώπου οὐκ ἀνέβη, ἃ ἡτοίμασεν ὁ θεὸς τοῖς ἀγαπῶσιν αὐτόν (*Pan* 64.69.10)

ἐπειδὴ· ἃ ὀφθαλμὸς οὐκ εἶδε καὶ οὖς οὐκ ἤκουσεν, οὔτε ἐπὶ καρδίαν ἀνθρώπου ἀνέβη ὅσα ἡτοίμασεν ὁ θεὸς τοῖς ἀγαπῶσιν αὐτόν (*Pan* 66.38–39.4)

περὶ ὧν εἴρηται ὅτι·
ἃ ὀφθαλμὸς οὐκ εἶδε καὶ οὖς οὐκ ἤκουσε, καὶ ἐπὶ καρδίαν ἀνθρώπου οὐκ ἀνέβη, ἃ ἡτοίμασεν ὁ θεὸς τοῖς ἀγαπῶσιν αὐτόν (*Pan* 77.37.7)

---

a. εἶδεν Epiph TR 𝔐 $\mathfrak{P}^{46}$ ℵ A B D F G L 81^{vid} 104 699 1739 Or CyrJer
b. ἴδεν C P 049 33
c. οἶδεν 1594

---

a. ἃ ἡτοίμασεν Epiph TR 𝔐 $\mathfrak{P}^{46}$ ℵ D F G L P 049 33 81 104 699 1594 1739 Or
b. ὅσα ἡτοίμασεν A B C^{vid} CyrJer

---

1 Corinthians 2:10
ἐρευνῶν τὰ βάθη τοῦ θεοῦ (*Anc* 7.1)

---

[241] In this conflation of material from 2:4 and 2:13, Epiphanius reads ἀλλ' with 𝔐 against ἀλλά of $\mathfrak{P}^{46}$ B.

1 Corinthians 2:10 cont.

τὸ γὰρ πνεῦμα τοῦ θεοῦ πάντα ἐρευνᾷ, καὶ τὰ βάθη τοῦ θεοῦ (*Anc* 12.3)

ἐρευνᾷ τὰ βάθη τοῦ θεοῦ (*Anc* 15.1)

ἡμῖν δὲ ἀπεκάλυψεν ὁ θεὸς διὰ τοῦ[242] πνεύματος αὐτοῦ (*Anc* 68.16)

ἐρευνᾷ καὶ τὰ βάθη τοῦ θεοῦ (*Anc* 118.2)

ἐρευνῶν καὶ τὰ βάθη τοῦ θεοῦ (*Pan* 74.1.4)

ἡμῖν δὲ ἀπεκάλυψεν ὁ θεὸς διὰ τοῦ πνεύματος αὐτοῦ (*Pan* 74.5.16; from *Anc*)

ἐρευνῶν τὰ βάθη τοῦ θεοῦ (*Pan* 74.11.7)

τὰ βάθη τοῦ θεοῦ ἐρευνῶν; (*Pan* 74.13.7)

ἐρευνῶντός τε καὶ τὰ βάθη τοῦ θεοῦ (*Pan* 76.46.8)

---

a. δέ Epiph TR 𝔐 ℵ A C D F G L P 049 33 81 104 699 1594 it$^{d.f.g}$
b. γάρ $\mathfrak{P}^{46}$ B 1739 it^m

---

a. ἀπεκάλυψεν ὁ θεός Epiph $\mathfrak{P}^{46}$ ℵ A B C D F G P 33 81 1739 it$^{d.e.f.g}$
b. ὁ θεὸς ἀπεκάλυψεν TR 𝔐 L 049 104 699 1594 Or Chr

---

a. διὰ τοῦ πνεύματος αὐτοῦ Epiph TR 𝔐 ℵ^c D F G L P 049 81 104 699 1594 it$^{d.e.f.g}$
b. διὰ τοῦ πνεύματος $\mathfrak{P}^{46}$ ℵ* A B C 33^{vid} 1739

---

1 Corinthians 2:11

οὐδεὶς οἶδε τὰ τοῦ ἀνθρώπου εἰ μὴ τὸ πνεῦμα τοῦ ἀνθρώπου[243] τὸ κατοικοῦν ἐν αὐτῷ (*Anc* 11.5)

---

[242] *Pan.* Holl; *om* τοῦ L^{epiph} J.
[243] τοῦ ἀνθρώπου] *om* F G it$^{f.g}$.

1 Corinthians 2:11 cont.
ὁ αὐτὸς ἅγιος ἀπόστολος <u>οὐδείς</u> φησιν <u>οἶδεν ἄνθρωπος τὸ τοῦ ἀνθρώπου, εἰ μὴ τὸ πνεῦμα τοῦ ἀνθρώπου τὸ κατοικοῦν ἐν αὐτῷ· οὕτω καὶ τὰ τοῦ θεοῦ</u>²⁴⁴ <u>οὐδεὶς ἔγνω</u>²⁴⁵ (*Anc* 12.1–3)

τίς γὰρ οἶδεν ἀνθρώπων²⁴⁶ τὰ τοῦ ἀνθρώπου, εἰ μὴ τὸ πνεῦμα τοῦ ἀνθρώπου; (*Anc* 72.3)

τίς γὰρ οἶδεν²⁴⁷ τὰ τοῦ ἀνθρώπου εἰ μή τὸ πνεῦμα τὸ ἐν τῷ ἀνθρώπῳ²⁴⁸ (*Pan* 74.9.3; from *Anc*)

1 Corinthians 2:12–13
φησὶ δὲ ὁ αὐτὸς ἅγιος ἀπόστολος . . .·
12) ἡμεῖς δὲ τὸ πνεῦμα τοῦ θεοῦ ἐλάβομεν, ὅπως γνῶμεν τὰ ἐκ θεοῦ χαρισθέντα ἡμῖν 13) ἃ καὶ²⁴⁹ λαλοῦμεν, οὐκ ἐν διδακτοῖς σοφίας λόγοις, ἀλλ' ἐν διδακτοῖς²⁵⁰ πνεύματος ἁγίου, πνευματικοῖς²⁵¹ πνευματικὰ συγκρίνοντες²⁵² (*Anc* 14.5)

12) ἡμεῖς δὲ οὐ τὸ πνεῦμα τοῦ κόσμου ἐλάβομεν, ἀλλὰ τὸ πνεῦμα τὸ ἐκ θεοῦ (*Anc* 68.17)

12) <u>ἀλλ' ἐλάβομεν</u> φησί <u>πνεῦμα θεοῦ, ἵδωμεν τὰ χαρισθέντα ἡμῖν ὑπὸ θεοῦ</u> 13) <u>ἃ καὶ λαλοῦμεν</u>, οὐκ ἐν πειθοῖ σοφίας λόγοις, ἀλλ' ἐν ἀποδείξει πνεύματος θεοῦ, <u>πνευματικοῖς πνευματικὰ συγκρίνοντες</u> (*Anc* 70.8)

12) ἡμεῖς δὲ οὐ τὸ πνεῦμα τοῦ κόσμου ἐλάβομεν (*Anc* 72.3)

ὥς φησιν ὁ ἅγιος ἀπόστολος·
12) καὶ ἡμεῖς πνεῦμα θεοῦ ἔχομεν, ἵνα γνῶμεν²⁵³ τὰ ὑπὸ θεοῦ χαρισθέντα ἡμῖν 13) ἃ καὶ λαλοῦμεν (*Pan* 69.28.3)

---

²⁴⁴ τὰ τοῦ θεοῦ] τὸ τοῦ θεοῦ **D***; τὰ ἐν τῷ θεῷ F G it^g.
²⁴⁵ ἔγνω F G; ἔγνωκεν 𝔓⁴⁶ ℵ A B D Ψ *et al*; οἶδεν L 049 *et al*.
²⁴⁶ L^{epiph} J; *om* ἀνθρώπων *Pan* with A 33.
²⁴⁷ οἶδεν J] *add* ἀνθρώπων *Anc* Holl; εἶδεν 6 917.
²⁴⁸ Text J; τοῦ ἀνθρώπου *Anc* Holl.
²⁴⁹ ἃ καί] καί F G; ὅ καί 1912.
²⁵⁰ διδακτικοῖς C.
²⁵¹ πνευματικῶς B 33.
²⁵² συνκρίνομεν F G Clem; συγκρίνοντος P.
²⁵³ Here and in *Anc* 14.5, Epiphanius appears to support 1875 against εἰδῶμεν / ἴδωμεν *rell.*, but these allusions provide no such agreement.

1 Corinthians 2:12–13 cont.
   12) ἡμεῖς δὲ οὐ τὸ πνεῦμα τοῦ κόσμου ἐλάβομεν, ἀλλὰ τὸ πνεῦμα τοῦ[254] θεοῦ (*Pan* 74.5.17; from *Anc* 68.17)

   12) ἀλλ' ἐλάβομεν φησί <u>πνεῦμα θεοῦ, ἵνα ἴδωμεν</u>[255] <u>τὰ χαρισθέντα ἡμῖν ὑπὸ θεοῦ</u> 13) <u>ἃ καὶ λαλοῦμεν</u>, οὐκ ἐν πειθοῖ σοφίας λόγοις, ἀλλ' ἐν ἀποδείξει πνεύματος θεοῦ, <u>πνευματικοῖς πνευματικὰ συγκρίνοντες</u>[256] (*Pan* 74.7.8; from *Anc* 70.8)

   12) <u>ἡμεῖς δὲ οὐ τὸ πνεῦμα τοῦ κόσμου ἐλάβομεν</u> φησί (*Pan* 74.9.3; from *Anc*)
   (12)_____

   a. τὸ πνεῦμα τοῦ κόσμου Epiph TR 𝔐 𝔓^{46} ℵ A B C L P 33 81 104 699 1594 1739 Or Euseb
   b. τὸ πνεύμα τοῦ κόσμου τούτου D F G it$^{f.g}$
   c. τὸ πνεῦμα τό τοῦ κόσμου 049
   (13)_____

   a. πνεύματος ἁγίου Epiph TR 𝔐 D^c L P 049 104 699 1594
   b. πνεύματος 𝔓^{46} ℵ A B C D* F G 33 81 1739 it$^{d.e.f.g}$ Or CyrJer

1 Corinthians 2:14
   <u>ὁ γὰρ ψυχικὸς ἄνθρωπος</u> φησιν <u>οὐ δέχεται</u>[257] <u>τὰ τοῦ πνεύματος· μωρία γὰρ αὐτῷ</u>[258] <u>ἐστιν, ὅτι πνευματικῶς ἀνακρίνεται</u> (*Pan* 64.65.6)

   ὁ γὰρ σαρκικὸς οὐ δέχεται τὰ τοῦ πνεύματος· μωρία γὰρ αὐτῷ ἐστιν (*Pan* 69.76.2)

1 Corinthians 2:16
   ἡμεῖς δὲ νοῦν Χριστοῦ ἔχομεν (*Anc* 76.1)

   φησίν·
   ἡμεῖς δὲ νοῦν Χριστοῦ ἔχομεν (*Pan* 77.31.1)

---

[254] τοῦ J 88 915; τό ἐκ *Anc*. Holl 489; τὸ ἐκ τοῦ *rell*.
[255] In two allusions having ἴδωμεν [with 𝔓^{46} D F G L P 049 33 699] rather than εἰδῶμεν [TR 𝔐 ℵ A B C 81 104 1594 1739], the imprecise citation precludes deciding which is Epiphanius' exemplar.
[256] This is a conflation of 2:4 and 13.
[257] δύναται 81.
[258] *om* αὐτῷ A*.

1 Corinthiains 2:16 cont.
ἡμεῖς, γάρ φησι, νοῦν Χριστοῦ ἔχομεν (*Pan* 77.31.3)

ἡμεῖς δὲ νοῦν Χριστοῦ ἔχομεν (*Pan* 77.33.5)

ὅταν δὲ εἴπῃ ὁ ἀπόστολος·
ἡμεῖς δὲ νοῦν Χριστοῦ ἔχομεν (*Pan* 77.34.3)

---

a. Χριστοῦ Epiph TR 𝔐 $\mathfrak{P}^{46}$ ℵ A C D^c L P 049 33 81 104 699 1594 1739 it$^{d.e}$ Or
b. κυρίου B D* F G it$^{f.g}$

---

1 Corinthians 3:2
ὁ δὲ Παῦλος·
οὔπω γάρ,[259] ἠδύνασθε ἀλλ᾽ οὐδὲ ἔτι[260] δύνασθε (*Pan* 33.11.5)

---

a. οὐδέ Epiph $\mathfrak{P}^{45}$ ℵ A B C D F G P 33 81 104 1739 Or
b. οὔτε TR 𝔐 L 699 1594
c. *om* phrase 049

---

1 Corinthians 3:8
ὅτι·
ἕκαστος κατὰ τὸν ἴδιον κάματον μισθὸν λήψεται (*Pan De fide* 23.4)

1 Corinthians 3:11
θεμέλιον γὰρ ἄλλον οὐδεὶς δύναται θεῖναι[261] παρὰ τὸν κείμενον, ὅς ἐστιν Ἰησοῦς Χριστός[262] (*Anc* 26.5)

1 Corinthians 3:12
εἴ τις γὰρ ἐποικοδομεῖ ἐπὶ τὸν θεμέλιον τοῦτον χρυσίον, ἄργυρον,[263] λίθους, τιμίους, ξύλα, χόρτον, καλάμην (*Anc* 26.5)

---

[259] *om* γάρ 81.
[260] ἔτι with Ψ] *om* ἔτι $\mathfrak{P}^{46}$ B; νῦν δύνασθε *rell*.
[261] θεῖναι *post* κείμενον 33 81.
[262] Ἰησοῦς Χριστός 𝔐] Χριστὸς Ἰησοῦς C^c D E it$^{d.e.f}$ vg Or; Ἰησοῦς ὁ Χριστός TR; Χριστός C*.
[263] J; ἀργύριον L^{epiph}.

1 Cor 3:12 cont.

---

    a. ἐπὶ τὸν θεμέλιον τοῦτον[264]   Epiph TR 𝔐 ℵ^c C^c D L P 049 33 104 699 1594 1739 it^{d.e.f} Or CyrJer Chr
    b. ἐπὶ τὸν θεμέλιον 𝔓^{46} ℵ* A B C* 81

---

1 Corinthians 3:13
    ἡ γὰρ ἡμέρα[265] δηλώσει ὅτι ἐν πυρὶ ἀποκαλύπτεται (*Pan* 59.5.7)

1 Corinthians 3:16
    ὡς καὶ ὁ Παῦλος συνᾴδει τῷ λόγῳ τούτῳ λέγων·
    ὑμεῖς δὲ ναὸς τοῦ θεοῦ ἐστε καὶ τὸ πνεῦμα τοῦ θεοῦ οἰκεῖ ἐν ὑμῖν (*Anc* 9.3)

    εἴπερ πνεῦμα θεοῦ οἰκεῖ ἐν ὑμῖν (*Anc* 68.12)

    ναὸς τοῦ θεοῦ ἐστι[266] καὶ τὸ πνεῦμα τοῦ θεοῦ οἰκεῖ ἐν ὑμῖν (*Anc* 68.18)

    καθὼς εἶπεν ὁ ἅγιος τοῦ θεοῦ ἀπόστολος ὅτι·
    ὑμεῖς <u>ναὸς θεοῦ ἐστε καὶ τὸ πνεῦμα τοῦ θεοῦ οἰκεῖ ἐν ὑμῖν</u> (*Pan* 69.27.7)

    εἴπερ πνεῦμα θεοῦ οἰκεῖ ἐν ὑμῖν (*Pan* 74.5.12; from *Anc*)

    ναὸς τοῦ[267] θεοῦ ἐστε καὶ τὸ πνεῦμα τοῦ θεοῦ οἰκεῖ ἐν ὑμῖν (*Pan* 74.5.18; from *Anc*)

    καί·
    ὑμεῖς ναὸς θεοῦ ἐστε, καὶ τὸ πνεῦμα κυρίου οἰκεῖ ἐν ὑμῖν (*Pan* 74.13.6)

---

    a. οἰκεῖ ἐν ὑμῖν Epiph TR 𝔐 𝔓^{46} ℵ A C D F G L 049 81 104 699 1594 it^{d.e.f.g}
    b. ἐν ὑμῖν οἰκεῖ B P 33 1739

---

[264] Merk cites 6 incorrectly in support of the omission of τοῦτον.
[265] *add* κυρίου it^f vg.
[266] L^{epiph} J; ἐστε *Pan*. Holl.
[267] τοῦ with 104 Clem.

1 Corinthians 3:20
    οἶδε γὰρ ὁ θεὸς <u>τοὺς λογισμοὺς τῶν σοφῶν</u>[268] ὅτι εἰσὶ μάταιοι (*Pan* 76.20.14)

1 Corinthians 4:5
    ἕως ἂν ἔλθῃ ὁ[269] κύριος, ὃς[270] καὶ ἀποκαλύψει τὰ κρυπτὰ τῆς καρδίας· καὶ τότε ὁ ἔπαινος ἑκάστου φανερὸς γενήσεται (*Pan* 59.5.7)

1 Corinthians 4:12
    ἐργάζεσθαι δὲ ταῖς ἰδίαις χερσίν (*Pan* 80.4.2)

1 Corinthians 4:15
    ὅμοιον ὡς εἶπε Παῦλος·
    ἐν γὰρ Χριστῷ Ἰησοῦ ἐγὼ ὑμᾶς ἐγέννησα (*Anc* 72.8)

    ὡς καὶ ὁ Παῦλός φησι·
    εἰ γὰρ καὶ πολλοὺς διδασκάλους ἔχετε, <u>ἀλλ' οὐ πολλοὺς πατέρας. ἐν γὰρ Χριστῷ Ἰησοῦ</u>[271] <u>διὰ τοῦ εὐαγγελίου ἐγὼ ὑμᾶς ἐγέννησα</u> (*Pan* 66.63.7)

    ὅμοιον ὡς εἶπε Παῦλος·
    ἐν γὰρ Χριστῷ Ἰησοῦ ἐγὼ ἐγέννησα ὑμᾶς (*Pan* 74.9.8; from *Anc*)

1 Corinthians 5:5
    τῷ σατανᾷ εἰς ὄλεθρον τῆς σαρκός, ἵνα τὸ πνεῦμα σωθῇ ἐν τῇ ἡμέρᾳ τοῦ κυρίου (*Pan* 59.4.11)

    ἀλλά·
    παραδοῦναι τὸν τοιοῦτον[272] (*Pan* 66.86.9)

1 Corinthians 5:7
    <u>τὸ πάσχα ἡμῶν ἐτύθη Χριστός</u> κατὰ τὸ γεγραμμένον (*Pan* 42.12.3 *refut.* 18)

    τὸ γὰρ πάσχα ἡμῶν[273] ἐτύθη Χριστός (*Pan* 75.3.4)

---

[268] σοφῶν] ἀνθρώπων 33.

[269] *om* ὁ D*.

[270] ὃς καί U Foll; *om* ὅς M. In this loose allusion, one cannot be certain that Epiphanius reads ὃς καί with TR 𝔐 𝔓⁴⁶ ℵ A B L P 049 33 81 104 699 1594 1739 rather than καί with D* F G it^{d.e.f.g}.

[271] *om* Ἰησοῦ B Clem.

[272] τὸν τοιοῦτον] αὐτόν F G it^g.

1 Corinthians 5:7 cont.

ὥς φησι·
τὸ πάσχα ἡμῶν ἐτύθη Χριστός (*Pan* 75.6.1)

---

a. τὸ πάσχα ἡμῶν   Epiph ℵ* A B C* D F G 33 81 1739 Euseb Or
b. τὸ πάσχα ἡμῶν ὑπὲρ ἡμῶν   TR 𝔐 ℵ^c C^c L P 049 699 1594 Meth
c. τὸ πάσχα ἡμῶν ὑπὲρ ὑμῶν   104

---

1 Corinthians 6:11

δικαιωθέντες δὲ <u>ἐν τῷ ὀνόματι τοῦ κυρίου ἡμῶν Ἰησοῦ Χριστοῦ^{274} καὶ ἐν^{275} πνεύματι τοῦ θεοῦ ἡμῶν</u> (*Anc* 69.1)

δικαιωθέντες δὲ <u>ἐν τῷ ὀνόματι τοῦ κυρίου ἡμῶν Ἰησοῦ Χριστοῦ καὶ ἐν τῷ πνεύματι τοῦ θεοῦ ἡμῶν</u> (*Pan* 74.6.1; from *Anc*)

---

a. ἡμῶν Ἰησοῦ Χριστοῦ   Epiph B C^{vid} P 33 81 104 1739 it^t
b. Ἰησοῦ Χριστοῦ   𝔓^{46} ℵ D* it$^{d.e}$
c. Ἰησοῦ   TR 𝔐 A D^c L 699 1594

---

1 Corinthians 6:13

ὁ δὲ ἅγιος ἀπόστολος ... ἔφη·
τὰ βρώματα τῇ κοιλίᾳ καὶ ἡ κοιλία τοῖς βρώμασιν· ὁ δὲ θεὸς καὶ ταύτην καὶ ταῦτα καταργήσει (*Pan* 47.2.7)

τὰ βρώματα τῇ κοιλίᾳ καὶ ἡ κοιλία τοῖς βρώμασιν, ὁ δὲ θεὸς καὶ ταύτην καὶ ταῦτα καταργήσει (*Pan* 66.69.4)

1 Corinthians 6:16–17

16) ὡς <u>ὁ κολλώμενος τῇ πόρνῃ ἓν σῶμά ἐστι</u> 17) καὶ <u>ὁ κολλώμενος τῷ κυρίῳ ἓν πνεῦμά ἐστιν</u> (*Pan* 66.86.4)

---

^{273} ἡμῶν Holl; ὑμῶν J.
^{274} τοῦ κυρίου ἡμῶν Ἰησοῦ Χριστοῦ_L^{epiph} Holl; Ἰησοῦ Χριστοῦ τοῦ κυρίου ἡμῶν J.
^{275} τῷ *Pan* Holl; *om* τῷ L^{epiph} J.

1 Corinthians 6:20
φάσκων ὅτι·
τιμῆς ἠγοράσθητε (*Pan* 66.79.3)

1 Corinthians 7:2
διὰ γὰρ τὰς πορνείας[276] ἕκαστος τὴν ἑαυτοῦ γυναῖκα ἐχέτω (*Pan* 67.2.5)

1 Corinthians 7:5
ὁ ἅγιος ἀπόστολος λέγων, ἵνα·
πρὸς καιρὸν σχολάσωσι[277] τῇ προσευχῇ (*Pan* 59.4.7)

---

a. τῇ προσευχῇ Epiph $\mathfrak{P}^{46}$ ℵ* A B C D F G P 33 81 104 1739 it$^{d.e.f.g}$ Meth Or
b. τῇ νηστείᾳ καὶ τῇ προσευχῇ TR $\mathfrak{M}$ ℵ^c K L 699 1594

---

1 Corinthians 7:7–9
7) θέλω πάντας εἶναι ὡς[278] ἐμαυτόν 9) ἔλεγεν <u>εἰ οὐκ ἐγκρατεύονται, γαμείτωσαν</u>[279] (*Pan* 61.5.9)

7) θέλω, φησί, πάντας εἶναι ὡς ἐμαυτόν (*Pan* 67.2.5)

8) καὶ Παῦλος λέγων·
λέγω δὲ τοῖς ἀγάμοις ὅτι καλὸν αὐτοῖς, ἐὰν μείνωσιν οὕτως[280] καθὼς κἀγώ· 9) εἰ δὲ οὐκ ἐγκρατεύονται,[281] γαμησάτωσαν (*Pan* 58.4.8)

---

[276] τὰς πορνείας] τὴν πορνείαν F G it$^{f.g}$ vg Tert.

[277] Epiphanius cites accurately, transposing ἵνα to be the introduction and consciously altering the second person σχολάσητε to the third person σχολάσωσι to fit his argument. In arguing against the Purists who do not accept second marriages, Epiphanius states that they bind what is applicable to priests upon the laity. So, he says, "If the holy apostle directs even the laity to 'give themselves to prayer for a time'," priests should be even more unencumbered in order to perform "the godly exercise" of "spiritual employments," such as prayer.

[278] ὡς 221] ὡς καί *rell.*

[279] γαμείτωσαν M Holl] γαμησάτωσαν U. Epiphanius cites brief portions of vv. 7 and 9 loosely in *Pan* 61.5.9, whereas in *Pan* 58.4.8 he argues against Valesian castrations and misunderstandings of Matt 19:12 by citing 1 Cor 7:8–9 as evidence that Paul was not a eunuch. He deletes the widows from v. 8 as unnecessary to his argument and cites accurately that portion of v. 9 essential to his case.

[280] μείνωσιν οὕτως with 81 104] οὕτως μείνωσιν C Meth; μείνωσιν *rell.*

1 Corinthians 7:7–9 cont.
8) ἔλεγε·
λέγω δὲ τοῖς ἀγάμοις καὶ ταῖς χήραις, καλὸν²⁸² αὐτοῖς ἐὰν μείνωσιν ὡς κἀγώ (*Pan* 61.6.1)

(8)_____

a. αὐτοῖς Epiph 𝔓⁴⁶ ℵ A B C D* F G P 33 81 Meth CyrJer
b. αὐτοῖς ἐστιν TR 𝔐 Dᶜ L 104 699 1594
c. ἐστιν K
d. *om* 1739

(9)_____

a. γαμησάτωσαν Epiph TR 𝔐 𝔓⁴⁶ ℵ A B C D K L P 33 81* 699 1594 1739 Or CyrJer
b. γαμείτωσαν F G 81ᶜ 104 Chr

1 Corinthians 7:10
ὡς ἂν εἴποι·
λέγω δὲ οὐκ ἐγώ, ἀλλ᾽ ὁ κύριος, γυναῖκα ἀπὸ ἀνδρὸς μὴ χωρισθῆναι (*Anc* 68.5)

λέγω δὲ οὐκ ἐγώ, ἀλλ᾽ ὁ κύριος, γυναῖκα ἀπὸ ἀνθρώπου μὴ χωρισθῆναι (*Pan* 74.5.5; from *Anc*)

a. χωρισθῆναι Epiph TR 𝔐 ℵ B C K L P 81 104 699 1594 1739
b. χωρίζεσθαι A D F G Or
c. χωριζέσθω 𝔓⁴⁶

1 Corinthians 7:18
παρὰ τῷ ἁγίῳ ἀποστόλῳ, ὦ φιλοκαλώτατε, δι᾽ ὧν αὐτοῖς ῥήμασιν ὧδέ πως λέγει·
<u>περιτετμημένος τις ἐκλήθη, μὴ ἐπισπάσθω. ἐν ἀκροβυστίᾳ τις</u> ὑπάρχει; <u>μὴ περιτεμνέσθω</u>²⁸³ (*Mensur. pond.* P.G. 43 [1864]: 264 C.6)

---

²⁸¹ οὐ κρατεύονται F G.
²⁸² ὅτι καλόν A.
²⁸³ Arguing against second circumcisions, Epiphanius cites v. 18 accurately, with the conscious alteration of κέκληται to ὑπάρχει, which changes the original

1 Corinthians 7:18, cont.

a. τις ἐκλήθη^{pr} Epiph TR 𝔐 𝔓^{46} ℵ A B C K L P 33 81 104 699 1594 1739
b. ἐκλήθη τις D F G

1 Corinthians 7:25
ποῦ δὲ παρὰ σοὶ πεπλήρωται τό·
<u>περὶ τῶν παρθένων ἐπιταγὴν κυρίου οὐκ ἔχω, γνώμην δὲ δίδωμι ὡς ἠλεημένος</u>, τὸ καλὸν οὕτως εἶναι (*Pan* 25.6.7)

1 Corinthians 7:27
δέδεσαι γυναικί, μὴ ζήτει λύσιν· λέλυσαι ἀπὸ γυναικός, μὴ ζήτει γυναῖκα (*Pan* 61.5.9)

πῶς οὖν πάλιν ἔλεγε·
δέδεσαι γυναικί, μη ζήτει λύσιν (*Pan* 61.6.2)

1 Corinthians 7:29
ὡς ἔτι·
<u>ὁ καιρὸς συνεσταλμένος ἐστίν</u> ὥς φησιν ὁ ἱερὸς ἀπόστολος (*Anc* 107.1)[284]

1 Corinthians 7:34
καὶ πάλιν·
<u>ἡ παρθένος μεριμνᾷ τὰ τοῦ κυρίου, πῶς ἀρέσει τῷ κυρίῳ,</u>[285] <u>ἵνα ᾖ ἁγία ἐν σώματι καὶ ἐν πνεύματι</u>[286] (*Pan* 25.6.7)

---

meaning of Paul's "when you were called" to the "present state" of Epiphanius' readers, thus turning the verse into a polemic against second circumcisions. The unaffected portion reflects Epiphanius' biblical exemplar. This means that Epiphanius cannot be cited for the unit of variation involving κέκληταί τις, τις κέκληται, or τις ἐκλήθη.

[284] Epiphanius appears to support ὁ καιρός with ℵ B 𝔐 against ὅτι ὁ καιρός in D F G. However, as this omission occurs at the beginning of the citation, Epiphanius should be cited for neither reading. The same is true for ἐστίν, the last word in his citation. It is impossible to ascertain whether he read ἔστιν λοιπόν with 𝔓^{15}, ἔστιν τὸ λοιπόν with ℵ A, or ἔστιν λοιπὸν ἔστιν with F G. All that can be deduced is that apparently he did not read τὸ λοιπὸν ἔστιν with D^c E K L, and due to the brevity of the citation, one cannot be certain ever of that.

[285] Epiph 547; *om* πῶς ἀρέσει τῷ κυρίῳ *rell*. Rather than Epiphanius or a later corrector of Epiphanius having used a text similar to 547, it is likely that

1 Corinthians 7:34 cont.
ὡς τοῦ ἀποστόλου λέγοντος πῆ μέν·
ὁ ἄγαμος καὶ ἡ παρθένος μεριμνᾷ τὰ τοῦ κυρίου, πῶς ἀρέσει τῷ κυρίῳ (*Pan* 26.16.1)

ὑπὸ τοῦ ἁγίου ἀποστόλου ἐπαινουμένη, ὅτι·
ἡ παρθένος καὶ ἡ ἄγαμος μεριμνᾷ τὰ τοῦ κυρίου, πῶς ἀρέσει τῷ κυρίῳ, ἵνα ᾖ ἁγία τῷ σώματι καὶ τῇ ψυχῇ (*Pan* 63.4.2)

λέγει ὅτι·
ἡ ἄγαμος μεριμνᾷ τὰ τοῦ κυρίου πῶς ἀρέσει τῷ κυρίῳ καὶ ἡ παρθένος· ἡ δὲ γαμήσασα μεριμνᾷ ἡ δὲ γαμήσασα μεριμνᾷ, καὶ μεμέρισται[287] (*Pan* 67.2.3)

1 Corinthians 7:36
πόθεν δὲ τῷ ἀποστόλῳ τὸ εἰρημένον τό·
ἐάν νομίζῃ ἀσχημονεῖν ἐπὶ τὴν ἰδίαν παρθένον[288] καὶ οὕτως ὀφείλει ποιῆσαι, γαμείτω· οὐχ ἁμαρτάνει (*Pan* 61.4.9)

καὶ τοῦτο ὀφείλει ποιῆσαι, γαμείτω, φησίν, <u>οὐχ ἁμαρτάνει. γαμείτω</u>,[289] ᾧ δ' ἂν εὐποροίεν, οὐχ ἁμαρτάνει (*Pan* 61.5.8)

1 Corinthians 7:37
φησὶ οὖν·
ἔστηκεν ἑδραῖος[290] ἐν τῷ ἰδίῳ νῷ (*Pan* 61.5.8)

Epiphanius conflated vv. 32 and 34, making the same sort of error found in 547. Accordingly, it is uncertain from these loose conflations whether the exemplar of Epiphanius read ἡ ἄγαμος *post* ἡ παρθένος with D F G K L Ψ or *post* ἡ γυνή with B P, or perhaps the entire phrase ἡ γυνὴ ἡ ἄγαμος καὶ ἡ παρθένος ἡ ἄγαμος with 𝔓⁴⁶ ℵ A.

[286] In this allusion, involving a conflation with v. 32, one cannot be certain that Epiphanius' exemplar read καὶ σώματι καὶ πνεύματι with TR 𝔐 F G K L 104 699 1594 1739 rather than τῷ σώματι καὶ τῷ πνεύματι with 𝔓⁴⁶ ℵ A P 33, or καὶ τῷ σώματι καὶ τῷ πνεύματι ℵ B 81, or σώματι καὶ πνεύματι D.

[287] Due to imprecision in this allusion, one cannot be certain that Epiphanius' exemplar read καὶ μεμέρισται with 𝔓⁴⁶ ℵ A B D* P 33 81 104 1739 rather than μεμέρισται with 𝔐 Dᶜ F G K L 699 1594.

[288] νομίζει *ante* ἐπί D it^(d.e.f.g); νομίζει *post* αὐτοῦ *rell*.

[289] While Epiphanius may appear to agree with D* F G syrᵖ arm Aug in reading γαμείτω against γαμείτωσαν of 𝔓⁴⁶ ℵ A B K L P Ψ 𝔐, it is probable that the third person singular present imperative is simply an adaptation to ὀφείλει in the patristic sentence structure.

1 Corinthians 7:39

φησὶ γάρ·
γυνὴ δέδεται νόμῳ ἐφ᾽ ὅσον χρόνον ζῇ ὁ²⁹¹ ἀνὴρ αὐτῆς. ἐὰν δὲ ἀποθάνῃ²⁹² ὁ ἀνήρ, ἐλευθέρα ἐστὶν ᾧ θέλει γαμηθῆναι²⁹³ (Pan 59.6.4)

---

a. δέδεται νόμῳ Epiph TR 𝔐 ℵᶜ Dᶜ F* G L P 104 699 1594 itᶠ·ᵍ Chr
b. δέδεται γάμῳ K
c. δέδεται 𝔓⁴⁶ ℵ* A B D* Fᶜ 33 81 1739 Or

---

a. ἐὰν δέ Epiph TR 𝔓⁴⁶ ℵ A B D* K P 33 81 104 1594 1739 Or Chr
b. ἐὰν δὲ καί 𝔐 Dᶜ F G L 699

---

a. ὁ ἀνήρˢᵉᶜ Epiph 𝔐 𝔓⁴⁶ ℵ A B K P 81 699 1594 Or
b. ὁ ἀνὴρ αὐτῆς TR D F G L 33 104 1739

---

1 Corinthians 7:40

καί φησι·
μακαριωτέρα²⁹⁴ δέ ἐστιν, ἐὰν μείνῃ οὕτως (Pan 59.6.6)

1 Corinthians 8:5–6

ὁ γὰρ ἀπόστολος φήσας·
5) εἴπερ εἰσὶ λεγόμενοι θεοί (Pan 25.6.2)

φησιν·
5) εἴπερ εἰσὶ λεγόμενοι θεοὶ πολλοὶ καὶ κύριοι πολλοί 6) <u>ἡμῖν δὲ εἷς θεός, ἐξ οὗ τὰ πάντα, καὶ εἷς κύριος, Ἰησοῦς Χριστός, δι᾽ οὗ τὰ πάντα.</u> εἰ δέ <u>δι᾽ οὗ τὰ πάντα</u> καὶ <u>ἡμεῖς εἰς αὐτόν</u> (Pan 54.6.3)

καὶ αὐτὸς ὁ ἀπόστολός φησιν·
εἷς θεός, ἐξ οὗ τὰ πάντα, καὶ εἷς κύριος Ἰησοῦς Χριστός, δι᾽ οὗ τὰ πάντα (Pan 55.9.7)

---

²⁹⁰ μακαριωτέρα M; ἑδραίως U. While Epiphanius may appear to agree with ἑδραῖος *post* ἕστηκεν in ℵᶜ K L Ψ 𝔐 against ἑδραῖος *post* αὐτου in ℵ* A B D P, this reference to 7:37 preceding the general reference to 7:36 gives only the gist.

²⁹¹ ὁ] om F*.
²⁹² ἀποθάνῃ A Clem] κοιμήθη rell.
²⁹³ γαμηθῆναι MU with 𝔐] γαμηθῇ F G itᵈ·ᵉ·ᶠ·ᵍ.
²⁹⁴ μακαριωτέρα] μακαρία 𝔓⁴⁶.

1 Corinthians 8:6 cont.

τοῦ ἁγίου ἀποστόλου φάσκοντος ὅτι·
ἡμῖν²⁹⁵ εἷς θεὸς ὁ πατήρ, ἐξ οὗ τὰ πάντα καὶ ἡμεῖς εἰς αὐτόν, καὶ εἷς κύριος Ἰησοῦς Χριστός,²⁹⁶ δι' οὗ τὰ πάντα καὶ ἡμεῖς δι' αὐτοῦ²⁹⁷ (*Pan* 56.3.1)

εἷς θεός, ἐξ οὗ τὰ πάντα καὶ ἡμεῖς εἰς αὐτόν, καὶ εἷς κύριος Ἰησοῦς Χριστός, δι' ὃν τὰ πάντα καὶ ἡμεῖς δι' αὐτοῦ²⁹⁸ (*Pan* 57.5.1)

εἷς θεὸς ὁ πατήρ, ἐξ οὗ τὰ πάντα, καὶ εἷς κύριος Ἰησοῦς Χριστός, δι' οὗ τὰ πάντα (*Pan* 57.5.9)

εἷς πατὴρ ἐξ οὗ τὰ πάντα καὶ εἷς κύριος Ἰησοῦς Χριστός, δι' οὗ τὰ πάντα (*Pan* 66.69.12)

ὡς καὶ ὁ ἀπόστολος φάσκει·
εἷς θεός, ἐξ οὗ τὰ πάντα, καὶ ἡμεῖς δι' αὐτοῦ· καὶ εἷς κύριος Ἰησοῦς Χριστός, δι' οὗ τὰ πάντα, καὶ ἡμεῖς δι' αὐτοῦ (*Pan* 76.8.11)

εἷς θεὸς ἐξ οὗ τὰ πάντα, καὶ εἷς κύριος δι' οὗ τὰ πάντα (*Pan* 76.9.5)

---

a. λεγόμενοι θεοί   Epiph TR 𝔐 𝔓⁴⁶ ℵ A B P 33 81 104 699 1594 1739 (Or)
b. οἱ λεγόμενοι θεοί   F G K it^{f.g}
c. λεγόμενοι θεοὶ καὶ κύριοι   D it^{d.e}
d. θεοί   L

---

1 Corinthians 9:7

ἀλλ'·
οὐκ ἐν πᾶσιν ἡ γνῶσις κατὰ τὸν ἀποστολικὸν λόγον (*Anc* 26.6)

---

²⁹⁵ Note ἡμῖν δέ in *Pan.* 25 and in the adaptation in *Pan.* 54, but ἡμῖν with 𝔓⁴⁶ B in the verbally precise citation in *Pan* 56.

²⁹⁶ Ἰησοῦς ὁ Χριστός P.

²⁹⁷ As αὐτοῦ concludes the citation, there is no way to ascertain whether Epiphanius' text ended here with ℵ A B D F and TR or added καὶ ἐν πνεῦμα ἅγιον ἐν ᾧ τὰ πάντα καὶ ἡμεῖς ἐν αὐτῷ with 0142. He does not read εἰς αὐτόν with 104.

²⁹⁸ M; Ἰησοῦς Χριστὸς καὶ ἡμεῖς δι' αὐτοῦ δι' ὃν τὰ πάντα καὶ ἡμεῖς δι' αὐτοῦ U. The scribe of U accidentally omitted δι' ὃν τὰ πάντα after Χριστοῦ and wrote in δι' ὃν τὰ πάντα, thus producing a reversal of the phrases. He added καὶ ἡμεῖς δι' αὐτοῦ in its proper position, but failed to erase the first καὶ ἡμεῖς δι' αὐτοῦ.

1 Corinthians 9:7,cont.
τίς²⁹⁹ ποιμαίνει ποίμνην καὶ ἐκ τοῦ γάλακτος αὐτῆς οὐκ ἐσθίει; ἢ τίς φυτεύει ἀμπελῶνα, καὶ ἐκ τοῦ καρποῦ αὐτοῦ οὐ μεταλαμβάνει   (*Pan* 80.5.5)

---

a. ἐκ τοῦ καρποῦ Epiph TR 𝔐 𝔓⁴⁶ ℵᶜ Dᶜ K L 81 104 699 1594 it^{d.e} Chr
b. τὸν καρπόν ℵ* A B C* D* F G P 33 1739 it^{f.g} Or
c. τῶν καρπῶν Cᶜ

---

a. γάλακτος αὐτῆς Epiph D* F G Chr
b. γάλακτος τῆς ποίμνης P 𝔐 ℵ A B C K L P 33 81 104 699 1594 1739
c. γάλακτος 𝔓⁴⁶

---

1 Corinthians 9:8–9
8) μετηλλαγμένος ἀντὶ γὰρ τοῦ <u>καὶ ὁ νόμος ταῦτα οὐ λέγει</u>, φησὶν ἐκεῖνος, εἰ³⁰⁰ <u>καὶ ὁ νόμος Μωϋσέως ταῦτα οὐ λέγει</u> (*Pan* 42.11.8 *schol* 1 Cor)

8) καὶ ὁ νόμος ταῦτα οὐ λέγει· 9) ἐν γὰρ τῷ νόμῳ γέγραπται·³⁰¹ οὐ φιμώσεις βοῦν ἀλοῶντα (*Pan* 42.12.3 *refut* 15)

9) μετηλλαγμένως· ἀντὶ γὰρ τοῦ <u>ἐν τῷ νόμῳ</u> λέγει ἐν τῷ Μωϋσέως νόμῳ. λέγει δὲ πρὸ τούτου, ἢ καὶ ὁ νόμος ταῦτα οὐ λέγει (*Pan* 42.12.3 *schol* 15)

---

²⁹⁹ As this loose citation begins with τίς, one cannot know whether Epiphanius read τίς with B D F G or ἢ τίς with 𝔓⁴⁶ ℵ A C K L P. Although the remainder is verbally precise until the concluding verb, the last two clauses are switched. However, within the clauses, Epiphanius' reading is accurate.

³⁰⁰ V and M indicate that the interpolation of "Moses" belongs in v. 8, but in Pan 42.12.3 *schol* 15, Epiphanius alters the *scholion*, putting the interpolation in v. 9. Holl omits the text given by Epiphanius at Pan 42.11.8 *schol. 1 Cor* and prints instead the text of *Pan* 42.12.3 *schol* 15. He notes, "Die hier gebotene Form is wohl der Versuch eines Abschreibers, das dem Epiphanius zugestossene Versehen zu verbessern." Adolf von Harnack, *Marcion* (2nd ed.; Leipzig: J. C. Hinrich's, 1924): 3.86, states, "er wirst dem M. vor, er habe Μωσέως v. 8 eingeschoben; hier wird es bei M. wirklich gestanden und in v. 9 gefehlt haben." It seems best to accept the text of Epiphanius as it exists in the MSS at both points rather than Holl's conjecture.

³⁰⁵ ἐν γὰρ τῷ νόμῳ γέγραπται 𝔓⁴⁶] γέγραπται γάρ D* F G it^{d.e.f.g} Cr; ἐν γὰρ τῷ Μωϋσέως νόμῳ γέγραπται *rell*.

1 Corinthians 9:8–9, cont.
9) γὰρ ὁ ἀπόστολος . . . εἰρηκέναι·
μὴ τῶν βοῶν μέλει τῷ θεῷ 10) ἢ πάντως δι' ἡμᾶς[302] εἴρηκεν (*Pan* 42.12.3 *refut* 15)

(8)_____

    a. καὶ ὁ νόμος ταῦτα οὐ λέγει Epiph $\mathfrak{P}^{46}$ ℵ A B C D 81 1739 it[d.e]
    b. καὶ ὁ νόμος ταῦτα λέγει F G it[f.g]
    c. οὐχὶ καὶ ὁ νόμος ταῦτα λέγει TR $\mathfrak{M}$ K L P 104 699 1594

(9)_____

    a. φιμώσεις Epiph TR $\mathfrak{M}$ $\mathfrak{P}^{46}$ ℵ A B[c] C D[c] K L P 33 81 104 699 1594
    b. κημώσεις B* D* F G 1739

    a. τῶν βοῶν Epiph TR $\mathfrak{M}$ $\mathfrak{P}^{46}$ ℵ A B C K L P 81 699 1594 1739 Or
    b. περὶ τῶν βοῶν D F G 104

1 Corinthians 9:26
    deshalb sagt der apostel:
    οὕτω πυκτεύω ὡς οὐκ ἀέρα δέρων (*Mensur. pond. lag.* 60.19)

1 Corinthians 10:6–7
    λέγων·
    6) ταῦτα δὲ τύποι ἡμῶν ἐγενήθησαν, πρός τὸ μὴ εἶναι ἡμᾶς ἐπιθυμητὰς κακῶν, καθὼς καὶ ἐκεῖνοι ἐπεθύμησαν, 7) μηδὲ εἰδωλολάτραι γίνεσθε, καθώς τινες αὐτῶν[303] (*Pan* 42.12.3 *refut* 17)

    7) ἐπιφέρει ὡς γέγραπται φήσας ἐκάθισεν ὁ λαὸς φαγεῖν καὶ πιεῖν καὶ ἀνέστησαν[304] παίζειν (*Pan* 42.12.3 *refut* 17)
(7)_____

    a. ὡς Epiph TR C D* P 81
    b. ὥσπερ $\mathfrak{M}$ $\mathfrak{P}^{46}$ ℵ A B D[c] K L 104 699 1594 1739 Chr
    c. καθώς F 33
    d. *om* G

---

    [302] ἡμᾶς] ὑμᾶς 33 Euseb.
    [303] τινες αὐτῶν] τινες ἐξ αὐτῶν A it[d.e]; *om* F G it[f.g].
    [304] ἀνέστησαν] ἀνέστη F G.

1 Corinthians 10:9
εἶτα πάλιν <u>μηδὲ πειράζωμεν</u>[305] <u>τὸν κύριον</u>. ὁ δὲ Μαρκίων ἀντὶ τοῦ κύριον Χριστὸν ἐποίησε (*Pan* 42.12.3 *refut* 17)

a. κύριον Epiph ℵ B C P 33 104 Hymenaeusbriefe
b. Χριστόν TR 𝔐 $\mathfrak{P}^{46}$ D F G K L 699 1594 1739 it$^{d.f.3}$ Marcion Clem Iren Or^{1739mg} Euseb Ephr
c. θεόν A 81

1 Corinthians 10:10
φησὶ γὰρ ἡ θεία γραφή·
μηδὲ γογγύζετε καθάπερ τινὲς ἐγόγγυσαν καὶ ἀπώλοντο ὑπὸ τοῦ ὀλοθρευτοῦ (*Ep. ad Johannes*, 8)

a. γογγύζετε Epiph TR 𝔐 A B C K L P 81^{vid} 104 699 1594 1739 it^f
b. γογγύζωμεν ℵ D F G 33 it$^{d.e}$ Or Chr

a. καθάπερ Epiph $\mathfrak{P}^{46}$ ℵ B P Or
b. καθώς TR 𝔐 A C D F G K L 33 81 104 699 1594 1739

1 Corinthians 10:11
<u>ἐκείνοις τυπικῶς συνέβαινεν, ἐγράφη δὲ ἡμῖν εἰς νουθεσίαν, εἰς οὓς τὰ τέλη τῶν αἰώνων κατήντησεν</u>, ὥς φησιν ὁ ἁγιώτατος ἀπόστολος, περί τε περιτομῆς λέγων· καὶ σαββάτου καὶ τῶν ἄλλων (*Pan* 33.11.12)

πάλιν ὁ ἅγιος ἀπόστολος ... φησιν·
ταῦτα δὲ τυπικῶς συνέβαινεν ἐκείνοις, ἐγράφη δὲ ἡμῖν εἰς νουθεσίαν (*Pan* 42.12.3 *refut* 17)

τύποι μὲν γὰρ συνέβαινον ἐκείνοις, ἐγράφη δὲ πρὸς νουθεσίαν ἡμῶν, εἰς οὓς τὰ τέλη τῶν αἰώνων κατήντησεν wie die apostolischen worte leren (*Mensur. pond. La𝔷.* 35.24)[306]

---

[305] πειράζωμεν 33 Chr] ἐκπιράσωμεν F G; ἐκπειρςζωμεν rell.
[306] As *Mensur. pond. La𝔷.* 35.24 is from Migne's *Patrologia Graece*, the texts from Holl's edition of *Pan* are accepted as Epiphanius' text. Writing against Ptolemaeans who stress τυπικῶς in v. 11 and argue that the Law was written by an intermediate god and that much of it must be understood allegorically,

1 Corinthians 10:11, cont.

---

a. ταῦτα δέ Epiph A B 33 1739 (CyrJer γάρ)
b. ταῦτα δὲ πάντα TR 𝔐 C K L P 104 699 1594 it^d
c. πάντα δὲ ταῦτα ℵ D F G 81 it$^{f.g}$

---

a. συνέβαινεν Epiph 𝔓$^{46\text{vid}}$ ℵ B C K P 33 81 104 1739 Or
b. συνέβαινον TR 𝔐 A D F G L 699 1594

---

a. κατήντησεν Epiph TR 𝔐 A C D^c K L 33 104 699 1594 Or Chr
b. κατήντηκεν 𝔓^{46} ℵ B D* F G 81 1739
c. κατήντησαν P

---

1 Corinthians 10:19-20
19) τί οὖν φημι; εἰδωλόθυτον τί ἐστιν; [307] 20) ἀλλ' ὅτι ἅ[308] θύουσι, δαιμονίοις θύουσι καὶ οὐ θεῷ (*Pan* 42.12.3 *refut* 18)

(19)_____

a. ὅτι εἰδωλόθυτόν τί ἐστιν Epiph 𝔓^{46} (ℵ* *om* τί) A C* vg
b. ὅτι εἴδωλόν τί ἐστιν 33
c. ὅτι εἰδωλόθυτόν τί ἐστιν ἢ ὅτι εἴδωλόν τί ἐστιν B C^c P 81 104 1739 it$^{d.e.f.(g)}$
d. ὅτι εἴδωλόν τί ἐστιν ἢ ὅτι εἰδωλόθυτόν τί ἐστιν TR 𝔐 K L 699 1594
e. ὅτι εἰδωλόθυτόν ἐστιν τί οὐχ ὅτι εἴδωλόν ἐστιν τί D* (D^c τί ἐστιν^{pr})
f. ὅτι εἰδωλόθυτόν ἐστιν τί οὐχ ὅτι εἰδωλόθυτόν ἐστιν τί F G

Epiphanius states in *Pan* 33 that while v. 11 does refer to circumcision and the Sabbath, etc., this does not support their attribution of the Law to the demiurge. So, he transposes ἐκείνοις to the beginning of the citation and alters πρὸς νουθεσίαν ἡμῶν to ἡμῖν εἰς νουθεσίαν to place emphasis on the fact that these were written "for our instruction." He retains the last clause accurately. Writing in *Pan* 42 against Marcion, Epiphanius retains the wording in the first clause, and similarly adjusts the wording of the second to emphasize the contemporary application of the text (*Elenchus* 17).

[307] Epiphanius reports Marcion's text to read ὅτι ἱερόθυτον τί ἐστιν ἢ εἰδωλόθυτον τί ἐστιν;

[308] ἃ δέ D E; ἀλλὰ ἃ F G.

1 Corinthians 10:19–20, cont.
  (20)

  a. θύουσι^pr Epiph B D F G
  b. θύουσι τὰ ἔθνη $\mathfrak{P}^{46}$ ℵ A C P 33 81 104 1739
  c. θύει τὰ ἔθνη TR $\mathfrak{M}$ K L 699 1594

  a. θύουσι καὶ οὐ θεῷ Epiph D F G 104
  b. καὶ οὐ θεῷ θύουσι ℵ A B C P 33 81 1739
  c. θύει καὶ οὐ θεῷ TR $\mathfrak{M}$ K L 699 1594 Chr

1 Corinthians 10:22
  ὅμοιον τῷ εἰπεῖν·
  μὴ παραζηλοῦμεν τὸν κύριον; μὴ ἰσχυρότεροι αὐτοῦ ἐσμεν (*Anc* 69.3)

  ὅμοιον τῷ εἰπεῖν·
  ἢ παραζηλοῦμεν τὸν κύριον; μὴ ἰσχυρότεροι αὐτοῦ ἐσμεν; (*Pan* 74.6.3; from *Anc*)

1 Corinthians 10:31
  <u>πάντα</u>, γάρ φησιν, <u>εἰς δόξαν θεοῦ</u>[309] <u>γινέσθω</u> (*Pan* 67.7.8)

1 Corinthians 11:1
  ὅθεν καὶ ὁ ἅγιος Παῦλος ἔλεγεν·
  μιμηταί μου γένεσθε καθὼς κἀγὼ Χριστοῦ (*Pan* 30.33.8)

  καὶ τοῦ Παύλου λέγοντος·
  μιμηταί μου γίνεσθε, καθὼς κἀγὼ Χριστοῦ (*Pan* 48.12.5)

1 Corinthians 11:2
  ὥς φησιν ὁ ἅγιος ἀπόστολος·
  ὡς παρέδωκα[310] ὑμῖν[311] (*Pan* 61.6.5)

1 Corinthians 11:3
  <u>κεφαλὴ παντὸς ἀνθρώπου Χριστός, κεφαλὴ δὲ γυναικὸς</u>[312] <u>ὁ ἀνήρ, κεφαλὴ δὲ Χριστοῦ ὁ θεός</u>,[313] κατὰ τὸν ἀπόστολον (*Pan* 37.8.4)

---

[309] From this loose reference, it is unclear whether Epiphanius' text read θεοῦ with $\mathfrak{P}^{46}$ F G or θεοῦ ποιεῖτε with ℵ A B C D TR.

[310] παρέδωκα] παραδέδωκα ℵ.

[311] ὑμῖν] *om* F G it^g.

1 Corinthians 11:3, cont.

---

a. Χριστοῦ   Epiph TR 𝔐 $\mathfrak{P}^{46}$ C F G K L P 104 699 1594 1739 Or
b. τοῦ Χριστοῦ   ℵ A B D 33 81

---

1 Corinthians 11:7
καὶ πάλιν ἐν ἄλλῳ τόπῳ ὁ αὐτὸς ἀπόστολος·
<u>ἀνὴρ οὐκ ὀφείλει</u> κομᾶν, <u>δόξα καὶ εἰκὼν θεοῦ ὑπάρχων</u> (*Pan* 66.54.4)

<u>ἀνὴρ οὐκ ὀφείλει</u> κομᾶν, <u>εἰκὼν καὶ δόξα θεοῦ ὑπάρχων</u> (*Pan* 70.3.7)

<u>ἀνήρ</u>, γάρ φησιν, <u>οὐκ ὀφείλει</u> κομᾶν, <u>εἰκὼν καὶ δόξα θεοῦ ὑπάρχων</u> (*Pan* 80.6.6)

1 Corinthians 11:8
οὐ γάρ ἐστιν ἀνὴρ ἐκ γυναικός, ἀλλὰ[314] γυνὴ ἐξ ἀνδρός[315] (*Pan* 49.3.3)

1 Corinthians 11:14
φησιν ὁ ἀπόστολος·
αὕτη ἡ φύσις οὐ διδάσκει ὑμᾶς ὅτι ἀνὴρ μὲν ἐὰν[316] κομᾷ, ἀτιμία αὐτῷ ἐστι; (*Pan* 80.7.3)

---

a. αὕτη ἡ φύσις   Epiph TR 𝔐 D^c K L 104 699 1594 it$^{d.e.f.g}$ Chr
b. ἡ φύσις αὐτή $\mathfrak{P}^{46}$ ℵ A B C D* P 33 81 1739
c. ἡ φύσις   F G

---

1 Corinthians 11:16
λέγει δέ·
εἴ τις δοκεῖ φιλόνεικος εἶναι, ἡμεῖς τοιαύτην συνήθειαν οὐκ ἔχομεν οὔτε αἱ ἐκκλησίαι τοῦ θεοῦ (*Pan* 80.7.4)

---

[312] *om* δέ with P.
[313] ὁ θεός] ὁ Χριστός C. As the first part of this citation is loosely rendered, it is uncertain whether Epiphanius omitted ἡ before κεφαλή with 33 or whether he omitted the article before Χριστός with B D F G. The remainder of the citation is accurate.
[314] ἀλλά U] ἀλλὰ ἡ M.
[315] *om* v. 8 K.
[316] ἀνὴρ μὲν ἐάν] ἀνὴρ μὲν ἄν D*; ἀνὴρ μὲν γὰρ ἐὰν ℵ*; ἀνήρ.

1 Corinthians 11:19
ἵνα φησίν οἱ δόκιμοι φανεροὶ γένωνται³¹⁷ (Pan 75.1.2)

1 Corinthians 11:25
ἐπειδὴ δὲ λέγει·
τοῦτο ποιεῖτε³¹⁸ εἰς τὴν ἐμὴν ἀνάμνησιν (Pan 69.77.5)

1 Corinthians 12:3
οὐδεὶς γὰρ δύναται εἰπεῖν κύριος Ἰησοῦς, εἰ μὴ ἐν πνεύματι ἁγίῳ (Anc 3.1)

οὐδεὶς δύναται εἰπεῖν κύριον Ἰησοῦν, εἰ μὴ ἐν πνεύματι ἁγίῳ (Anc 69.2)

οὐδεὶς δύναται εἰπεῖν κύριον Ἰησοῦν, εἰ μὴ ἐν πνεύματι ἁγίῳ (Pan 74.6.2; from Anc)

---

a. κύριος Ἰησοῦς Epiph 𝔓⁴⁶ ℵ A B C 33 81 104 1739 it^f Or
b. κύριον Ἰησοῦν Epiph TR 𝔐 D F G K L P 699 1594 it^{d.e.g}

---

1 Corinthians 12:4–6
4) διαιρέσεις γὰρ χαρισμάτων εἰσὶ τὸ δὲ αὐτὸ πνεῦμα, 5) καὶ διαιρέσεις διακονιῶν εἰσιν, ὁ δὲ αὐτὸς κύριος, 6) καὶ διαιρέσεις ἐνεργημάτων εἰσίν, ὁ δὲ αὐτὸς θεός, ὁ ἐνεργῶν τὰ πάντα ἐν πᾶσι (Anc 7.4)

4) διαιρέσεις δὲ χαρισμάτων εἰσί, τὸ δὲ αὐτὸ πνεῦμα, 5) καὶ διαιρέσεις διακονιῶν εἰσιν, ὁ δὲ αὐτὸς κύριος, 6) καὶ διαιρέσεις ἐνεργημάτων εἰσίν, ὁ δὲ αὐτὸς θεός, ὁ ἐνεργῶν τὰ πάντα ἐν πᾶσι (Anc 69.2)

4) διαιρέσεις δὲ χαρισμάτων εἰσί, τὸ δὲ αὐτὸ πνεῦμα, 5) καὶ διαιρέσεις διακονιῶν εἰσίν, ὁ δὲ αὐτὸς κύριος, 6) καὶ διαιρέσεις ἐνεργημάτων εἰσίν, ὁ δὲ αὐτὸς θεός, ὁ ἐνεργῶν τὰ πάντα ἐν πᾶσι (Pan 74.6.2; from Anc)

---

[317] As Epiphanius adds ὁρᾶσιν, one cannot know whether his exemplar read ἵνα οἱ δόκιμοι with 𝔐 or ἵνα καὶ οἱ δόκιμοι with 𝔓⁴⁶ B D* 33 1739. Similarly, as this citation concludes with γένωνται, it cannot be ascertained whether Epiphanius actually omits ἐν ὑμῖν after γένωνται with 𝔓⁴⁶ C or includes it with 𝔐.

[318] ποιεῖτε P 81] ποιεῖτε, ὁσάκις ἐὰν πίνητε 𝔓⁴⁶ ℵ B C 33 1739; ποιεῖτε, ὁσάκις ἂν πίνητε rell.

1 Corinthians 12:4–6, cont.
4) διαιρέσεις γὰρ χαρισμάτων εἰσί, τὸ δὲ αὐτὸ πνεῦμα, 5) καὶ διαιρέσεις διακονιῶν εἰσιν, ὁ δὲ αὐτὸς[319] κύριος, 6) καὶ διαιρέσεις[320] ἐνεργημάτων εἰσίν, ὁ δὲ αὐτὸς θεὸς ὁ ἐνεργῶν τὰ πάντα ἐν πᾶσι (*Pan* 74.12.4; from *Anc*)
(6)_____

a. ὁ δὲ αὐτὸς θεός   Epiph ℵ* A P 33
b. ὁ αὐτὸς δὲ θεος   D F G
c. καί ὁ αὐτὸς θεός $\mathfrak{P}^{46}$ B C 81 1739 Or
d. ὁ δὲ αὐτὸς ἐστιν θεός   TR 𝔐 ℵ^c K L 104 699 1594 Cyr

1 Corinthians 12:8,10–11
8) <u>ᾧ μὲν γάρ φησί δίδοται λόγος σοφίας, ᾧ δὲ λόγος διδασκαλίας</u> (*Anc* 16.7)

κατὰ τὸ εἰρημένον ὅτι·
8) ᾧ μὲν δίδοται σοφία διὰ τοῦ πνεύματος, 10) τῷ δὲ γένη γλωσσῶν ἐν τῷ αὐτῷ πνεύματι, τῷ δὲ ἑρμηνεία γλωσσῶν,[321] 11) τῷ δὲ δύναμις, τῷ δὲ διδασκαλία, ἕν δέ ἐστι τὸ πνεῦμα τὸ διαιροῦν ἑκάστῳ ὡς βούλεται (*Pan* 69.58.4)

11) τὸ δὲ αὐτὸ πνεῦμα τὸ διαιροῦν ἑκάστῳ ὡς βούλεται (*Anc* 16.7)

11) ἕν δὲ καὶ τὸ αὐτὸ πνεῦμα, διαιροῦν ἑκάστῳ ὡς βούλεται (*Anc* 72.8)

11) ἕν γάρ ἐστι τὸ ἅγιον πνεῦμα, τὸ διαιροῦν ἑκάστῳ ὡς βούλεται (*Pan* 48.12.12)

11) καὶ πάλιν ὁ ἀπόστολος λέγει·
ἕν δέ ἐστιν τὸ πνεῦμα τὸ διαιροῦν ἑκάστῳ ὡς βούλεται πρὸς τὸ συμφέρον (*Pan* 55.9.9)

11) ἕν δὲ καὶ τὸ αὐτὸ πνεῦμα, διαιροῦν ἑκάστῳ ὡς βούλεται (*Pan* 74.9.7 from *Anc*)

---

[319] ὁ δὲ αὐτὸς 33] καί ὁ αὐτός *rell* (A *om* ὁ).
[320] διαιρέσεις] διακρίσις C.
[321] γένη γλωσσῶν ... ἑρμηνεία γλωσσῶν] γένη γλωσσῶν ... διερμηνεία γλωσσῶν A; γένη γλωσσῶν ... διερμηνεία γένη γλωσσῶν D*; *om* ἄλλῳ δὲ ἑρμηνεία γλωσσῶν B K.

1 Corinthians 12:8, 10–11, cont.
11) _____

    a. διαιροῦν Epiph 𝔓⁴⁶ F G it^{d.e.f.g} Or
    b. διαιροῦν ἰδίᾳ TR 𝔐 ℵ A B C K L P 33 81 104 1594 1739 CyrJer
    c. διαιρούμενα D

1 Corinthians 12:18
    ὁ αὐτὸς ἀπόστολός φησιν·
    ὁ θεὸς ἔθετο ἐν σώματι πάντα τὰ μέλη, ἕκαστον καθὼς ἠθέλησε (*Pan* 66.86.6)

1 Corinthians 12:27
    ὡς καὶ ἡμεῖς σῶμα Χριστοῦ ἐσμεν καὶ μέλη ἐκ μέλους (*Pan* 66.86.7)

1 Corinthians 13:9–10
    9) ἐκ μέρους γὰρ γινώσκομεν καὶ ἐκ μέρους προφητεύομεν (*Anc* 94.2)

    ὡς τοῦ ἁγίου ἀποστόλοι φήσαντος·
    9) ἀπὸ μέρους γινώσκομεν καὶ ἀπὸ μέρους προφητεύομεν, 10) ὅταν ἔλθῃ τὸ τέλειον, τὸ ἀπὸ[322] μέρους καταργηθήσεται (*Pan* 66.61.2)
9) _____

    a. μέρους γάρ Epiph TR 𝔓⁴⁶ ℵ A B D F G P 33 81 104 1739
    b. μέρους δέ 𝔐 K L 049 699 1594

(10) _____

    a. καταργηθήσεται *post* μέρους Epiph TR 𝔐 𝔓⁴⁶ ℵ A B K L P 049 33 81 104 699 1594 1739 Euseb Or
    b. καταργηθήσεται *ante* τὸ ἐκ μέρους D F G it Meth

1 Corinthians 13:12
    τότε πρόσωπον πρὸς πρόσωπον (*Pan* 66.61.8)

1 Corinthians 13:13
    πίστις καὶ ἐλπὶς καὶ ἀγάπη κατὰ τὸ γεγραμμένον (*Pan* 76.38.13)

---

[322] ἀπό] τό ἐκ ℵ A B D F G P 33 81 104 1739; τότε τό ἐκ TR *rell*.

1 Corinthians 14:14
ἐὰν ψαλῶ πάλιν τῷ πνεύματι, <u>ὁ δὲ νοῦς μου ἄκαρπός ἐστι</u>   (*Pan 77.27.8*)

1 Corinthians 14:15
ὅτι·
ψαλῶ τῷ νοΐ, ψαλῶ τῷ πνεύματι (*Anc 56.3*)

φησὶν ὅτι·
ψαλῶ τῷ πνεύματι, ψαλῶ δὲ καὶ[323] τῷ νοΐ (*Anc 76.5*)

πάλιν τίνι τῷ λόγῳ λέγει·
ψαλῶ τῷ πνεύματι, ψαλῶ καὶ τῷ νοΐ (*Anc 77.7*)

τοῦ ἀποστόλου σαφῶς λέγοντος·
ψαλῶ τῷ νοΐ, ψαλῶ καὶ τῷ πνεύματι (*Pan 77.23.6*)

διὰ τὸ εἰπεῖν·
ψαλῶ τῷ νοΐ, ψαλῶ καὶ τῷ πνεύματι (*Pan 77.24.1*)

ψαλῶ τῷ νοΐ, ψαλῶ τῷ πνεύματι (*Pan 77.27.8*)

---

a. ψαλῶ τῷ πνεύματι Epiph TR 𝔐 ℵ A B D K L 049 33 81 104 1594 1739 Or
b. ψαλῶ πνεύματι F G P
c. *om* 699

---

a. ψαλῶ δὲ καί Epiph TR 𝔐 ℵ A D K L P 049 33 81 104 1594 1739
b. ψαλῶ καί Epiph B F G it[f.g]
c. *om* 699

---

1 Corinthians 14:32
καί·
πνεύματα δὲ προφητῶν προφήταις ὑποτάσσεται (*Anc 72.4*)

---

[323] καί L[epiph*]; *om* καί J. In accord with criteria for recovering patristic data, brief, accurate citations with introductions are preferred.

1 Corinthians 14:32, cont.
καί·
πνεύματα δὲ προφητῶν προφήταις ὑποτάσσεται³²⁴ (*Pan* 74.9.4; from *Anc*)

---

a. πνεύματα   Epiph TR 𝔐 $\mathfrak{P}^{46}$ ℵ A B K L 049 33 81 104 699 1594 1739 it^f Or Chr
b. πνεῦμα   D F G it^{d.e.g}

---

1 Corinthians 15:2
τίνι λόγῳ εὐηγγελισάμην ὑμῖν (*Pan* 42.12.3 *refut* 24)

εἰ κατέχετε, ἐκτὸς εἰ μὴ εἰκῇ ἐπιστεύσατε (*Pan* 61.6.5)

---

a. εἰ κατέχετε   Epiph TR 𝔐 $\mathfrak{P}^{46}$ ℵ A B K L P 049 33 81 104 699 1594 1739
b. ὀφείλετε κατέχειν   D F G it^{d.e.g}

---

1 Corinthians 15:3-4
3) ὅτι Χριστὸς ἀπέθανεν ὑπὲρ τῶν ἁμαρτιῶν ἡμῶν κατὰ τὰς γραφάς (*Pan* 42.12.3 *refut* 24)

3) ὅτι Χριστὸς ἀπέθανεν 4) καὶ ἐτάφη καὶ ἐγήγερται τῇ τρίτῃ ἡμέρᾳ³²⁵ (*Pan* 42.12.3 *refut* 24)

1 Corinthians 15:8
καὶ·
ὡσπερεί τῷ³²⁶ ἐκτρώματι ὤφθη κἀμοί (*Pan* 30.33.8)

1 Corinthians 15:9
λέγει γὰρ ὅτι·
ἐγώ εἰμι ὁ ἐλάχιστος τῶν ἀποστόλων (*Pan* 30.33.8)

---

³²⁴ ὑποτάσσεται] ὑποτάσσεσθαι 88; ὑποτάσσονται L.
³²⁵ Because Epiphanius only gives the gist of these two verses in this allusion, it is not possible to determine whether his exemplar read τῇ τρίτῃ ἡμέρᾳ with TR 𝔐 F G K L P 049 699 1594 or τῇ ἡμέρᾳ τῇ τρίτῃ with $\mathfrak{P}^{46}$ ℵ A B D 33 81 104 1739.
³²⁶ *om* τῷ F G.

1 Corinthians 15:11
λέγων·
οὕτως κηρύσσομεν καὶ οὕτως ἐπιστεύσατε³²⁷ (*Pan* 42.12.3 *refut* 24)

1 Corinthians 15:12–15
ὁ ἅγιος ἀπόστολος τὴν ἡμῶν ἐλπίδα, φήσας ὅτι·
12) πῶς λέγουσί τινες ἐν ὑμῖν ὅτι ἀνάστασις νεκρῶν οὐκ ἔστιν; 13) εἰ δὲ ἀνάστασις νεκρῶν ουκ ἔστι, οὐδὲ Χριστὸς ἐγήγερται 14) εἰ δὲ Χριστὸς οὐκ ἐγήγερται, κενὸν ἄρα καὶ τὸ κήρυγμα ἡμῶν, ματαία καὶ ἡ πίστις ἡμῶν. 15) εὑρισκόμεθα δὲ καὶ ψευδομάρτυρες τοῦ θεοῦ, ὅτι εἴπαμεν ὅτι ἤγειρε τὸν Χριστὸν ὃν οὐκ ἤγειρε (*Pan* 64.68.2)

14) εἰ Χριστὸς οὐκ ἐγήγερται,³²⁸ μάταιον τὸ κήρυγμα ἡμῶν, ματαία καὶ ἡ πίστις ἡμῶν 15) εὑρισκόμεθα δε καὶ³²⁹ ψευδομάρτυρες τοῦ θεοῦ,³³⁰ ὅτι ἤγειρεν τὸν Χριστόν,³³¹ εἴπερ οὐκ ἤγειρεν (*Pan* 28.6.3)

14) καὶ εἰ Χριστὸς οὐκ ἐγήγερται, μάταιον τὸ κήρυγμα ἡμῶν (*Pan* 42.12.3 *refut* 24)

(12)_____

    a. τινές ἐν ὑμῖν   Epiph TR 𝔐 D F G K L 049 104 699 1594
    b. ἐν ὑμῖν τινές   𝔓⁴⁶ ℵ A B P 33 81 1739 Or

(13)_____

    a. εἰ δὲ ἀνάστασις νεκρῶν ουκ ἔστι, οὐδὲ Χριστὸς ἐγήγερται
        Epiph TR 𝔐 𝔓⁴⁶ ℵᶜ A B D F G K L P 049 104 699 1594 1739
    b. *om* v. 13 ℵ* 33 81

(14)_____

    a. ἄρα καί Epiph ℵ* A D F G K P 049 33 81 699 itᵍ
    b. ἄρα TR 𝔐 𝔓⁴⁶ ℵᶜ B L 104 1594 1739 itᵈ·ᵉ·ᶠ Chr CyrJer

---

³²⁷ ἐπιστεύσατε] πιστεύσατε ℵ*.
³²⁸ εἰ Χριστὸς οὐκ ἐγήγερται U Holl] *om* M.
³²⁹ δὲ καί V] *om* δέ M; *om* καί D 81; ἄρα.
³³⁰ τοῦ θεοῦ V M] *add* ὅτι ἐμαρτυρήσαμεν κατὰ τοῦ θεοῦ Holl *al fere omn; om* ψευδομάρτυρες τοῦ θεοῦ **and** *add* καὶ ψευδομαρτυροῦμεν *post* θεοῦˢᵉᶜ 81.
³³¹ τὸν Χριστόν] τὸν Χριστὸν αὐτοῦ ℵ*.

1 Corinthians 15:14, cont.

---

   a. πίστις ἡμῶν Epiph B D* 049 33 81 699 1739 Cy-Jer
   b. πίστις ὑμῶν TR 𝔐 ℵ A D^c F G K L P 104 1594

---

1 Corinthians 15:16
καὶ ὁ ἀπόστολος . . . ἔλεγεν·
εἰ νεκροὶ οὐκ ἐγείρονται,[322] οὐδὲ Χριστὸς ἐγήγερται (*Pan* 28.6.2)

εἰ νεκροὶ οὐκ ἐγείρονται, οὐδὲ Χριστὸς ἐγήγερται (*Pan* 42.12.3 *refut* 24)

1 Corinthians 15:20
πῶς οὖν λέγει·
ἀνέστη Χριστὸς ἀπαρχὴ τῶν κεκοιμημένων; (*Anc* 92.2)

καὶ πάλιν ὅτι·
Χριστὸς ἐγήγερται ἀπαρχὴ τῶν κεκοιμημένων[333] (*Pan* 28.6.8)

ἀνέστη γὰρ Χριστὸς ἐκ[334] νεκρῶν, ἀπαρχὴ τῶν κεκοιμημένων (*Pan* 64.64.10)

1 Corinthians 15:23
ὅμοιον τῷ εἰπεῖν·
ἀπαρχὴ Χριστός (*Anc* 68.13)

ἕκαστον γὰρ κατὰ τὸ ἴδιον τάγμα (*Pan* 67.6.3)

ὅμοιον τῷ εἰπεῖν·
ἀπαρχὴ Χριστός (*Pan* 74.5.13; from *Anc*)

1 Corinthians 15:24–28
   24) εἶτα τὸ τέλος, ὅταν παραδιδῷ τὴν βασιλείαν τῷ θεῷ καὶ πατρί, ὅταν καταργήσῃ πᾶσαν ἀρχὴν καὶ πᾶσαν ἐξουσίαν καὶ δύναμιν 25) δεῖ γὰρ αὐτὸν βασιλεύειν ἄχρις οὗ θῇ πάντας τοὺς ἐχθροὺς αὐτοῦ ὑπὸ τοὺς πόδας αὐτοῦ[335] 26) ἔσχατος ἐχθρὸς καταργεῖται ὁ θάνατος 27) ὅταν δὲ εἴπῃ ὅτι πάντα

---

[332] εἰ γὰρ νεκροὶ οὐκ ἐγείρονται] *om* P it^r.
[333] ἐγένετο is omitted at the end of the citation, as in K L TR.
[334] ἐκ U *rell*.] ἐκ τῶν M with F G.
[335] τοὺς πόδας αὐτοῦ] *om* F G it^g.

1 Corinthians 15:24–28, cont.

> αὐτῷ[336] ὑποτέτακται, δῆλον ὅτι ἐκτὸς τοῦ ὑποτάξαντος αὐτῷ τὰ πάντα 28) ὅταν δὲ ὑποταγῇ αὐτῷ τὰ πάντα,[337] τότε καὶ αὐτὸς ὁ υἱὸς ὑποταγήσεται τῷ ὑποτάξαντι[338] αὐτῷ τὰ πάντα, ἵνα ᾖ[339] ὁ θεὸς τὰ πάντα ἐν πᾶσιν (*Pan* 69.74.2–3)

> καὶ τό·
> 24) ἄχρις οὗ παραδιδῷ τὴν βασιλείαν τῷ θεῷ καὶ πατρί (*Pan* 69.75.1)

> ὅτι·
> 24) ὅταν παραδιδῷ τὴν βασιλείαν τῷ θεῷ καὶ πατρί, ὅταν καταργήσῃ πᾶσαν ἀρχὴν καὶ ἐξουσίαν καὶ δύναμιν (*Pan* 69.75.10)

> 25) καὶ τό·
> δεῖ αὐτὸν βασιλεύειν ἄχρις οὗ θῇ πάντας τοὺς ἐχθροὺς ὑπὸ τοὺς πόδας αὐτοῦ (*Pan* 69.75.10)

> 26) ἔσχατος ἐχθρὸς καταργεῖται ὁ θάνατος[340] (*Pan* 69.76.1)

> φησιν·
> 26) ἔσχατος ἐχθρὸς καταργεῖται ὁ θάνατος 27) ὅταν δὲ εἴπῃ, ὅτι πάντα αὐτῷ ὑποτέτακται (*Pan* 69.76.1)

> 27) καὶ φησι·
> πάντα ὑπέταξεν ὑπὸ τοὺς πόδας αὐτοῦ (*Pan* 69.76.1)

> 27) ὅταν εἴπῃ πάντα αὐτῷ ὑποτέτακται, δηλονότι ἐκτὸς τοῦ ὑποτάξαντος αὐτῷ τὰ πάντα (*Pan* 69.77.2)

> 28) ἵνα ᾖ ὁ θεὸς τὰ πάντα ἐν πᾶσι (*Pan* 69.77.5)

---

[336] αὐτῷ ὑποτέτακται] αὐτῷ *post* ὑποτέτακται F G; *om* αὐτῷ *rell*.

[337] ὅταν δὲ ὑποταγῇ αὐτῷ τὰ πάντα] ὅταν δὲ αὐτῷ ὑποταγῇ τὰ πάντα D; *om* ℵ* 699.

[338] τῷ ὑποτάξαντι] *om* 1836.

[339] ᾖ *post* ὁ θεός D* it[d.e].

[340] The lengthy and precise citation available for this verse places it properly after v. 25. It is unlikely that this brief reference reflects Epiphanius' use of a text such as ℵ[c] D* it[d.e] that places v. 26 in v. 27.

TEXT AND APPARATUS 115

1 Corinthians 15:24–28, cont.
(24)_____

    a. παραδιδῷ Epiph 𝔓⁴⁶ ℵ A D P 104 1739 Or
    b. παραδιδοῖ B F G
    c. παραδῷ TR 𝔐 K L 049 81 699 1594

(25)_____

    a. ἄχρις οὗ Epiph 𝔓⁴⁶ ℵ* A B D* F G P 33 81 104 1739 Euseb
    b. ἄχρις οὗ ἄν TR 𝔐 ℵᶜ Dᶜ K L 049 699 1594 CyrJer

---

    a. ἐχθροὺς αὐτοῦ Epiph A F G 33 104 it^{f.g}
    b. ἐχθρούς TR 𝔐 𝔓⁴⁶ ℵ B D K L P 049 81 699 1594 1739 it^{d.e}

(27)_____

    a. ὅτι πάντα Epiph TR 𝔐 A D F G K L P 049 81 104 699 1594 1739 it^{f.g} Or Cyr̄er
    b. πάντα 𝔓⁴⁶ B 33 it^{d.e} Chr
    c. ὅτι τὰ πάντα ℵ

(28)_____

    a. τότε καὶ αὐτός Epiph TR 𝔐 ℵ A Dᶜ K L P 049 81 104 699 1594 it^{f} CyrJer
    b. τότε αὐτός B D* F G 33 1739 it^{d.e.g} Or

---

    a. τὰ πάντα ἐν πᾶσιν Epiph TR 𝔐 ℵ Dᶜ F G K L P 049 104 699 1594
    b. πάντα ἐν πᾶσιν A B D* 33 81 1739

---

1 Corinthians 15:29

    φησι τὸν αὐτὸν ἅγιον ἀπόστολον εἰρηκέναι·
    εἰ ὅλως νεκροὶ οὐκ ἐγείρονται, τί καὶ βαπτίζονται ὑπὲρ αὐτῶν; (*Pan* 28.6.5)

---

    a. ὑπὲρ αὐτῶν Epiph 𝔓⁴⁶ ℵ A B D* F G K P 33 81 104 1739 it^{d.e.f.g} Or
    b. ὑπὲρ τῶν νεκρῶν^{sec} TR 𝔐 Dᶜ L 049 699 1594

---

1 Corinthians 15:32
καὶ τὸ· φάγωμεν καὶ πίωμεν· αὔριον γὰρ ἀποθνήσκομεν[341] (*Pan* 28.6.2)

1 Corinthians 15:33
καὶ τὸ· μὴ πλανᾶσθε· φθείρουσιν ἤθη χρηστὰ ὁμιλίαι κακαί (*Pan* 28.6.2)

1 Corinthians 15:35
λέγοντα·
πῶς ἡ ἀνάστασις γίνεται; ποίῳ δὲ σώματι ἔρχονται;[342] (*Pan* 42.5.5)

ἀλλὰ ἐρεῖς μοι, πῶς ἐγείρονται οἱ νεκροί; ποίῳ δὲ σώματι ἔρχονται (*Pan* 64.68.9)

1 Corinthians 15:36–38
φησὶν ἡ ἁγία γραφή·
36) ἄφρων, σὺ ὃ σπείρεις οὐ ζωογονεῖται, ἐὰν μὴ ἀποθάνῃ,[343] 37) καὶ οὐκ αὐτὸ τὸ γενησόμενον σῶμα σπείρει. ἀλλ' εἰ τύχοι κόκκον σίτου ἢ τῶν ἄλλων σπερμάτων, 38) καὶ ὁ θεὸς δίδωσιν αὐτῷ σῶμα ὡς ἠθέλησε (*Anc* 90.2)

εἶτά φησιν·
36) ἄφρων, σὺ ὃ σπείρεις οὐ ζωογονεῖται, ἐὰν μὴ ἀποθάνῃ, 37) καὶ ὃ σπείρεις, οὐ τὸ γενησόμενον σῶμα σπείρεις ἀλλὰ γυμνὸν κόκκον εἰ τύχοι σίτου ἢ τῶν ἄλλων σπερμάτων, καὶ οὐ ζωογονεῖται, ἐὰν μὴ ἀποθάνῃ.[344] 38) ὁ δὲ θεὸς δίδωσιν αὐτῷ σῶμα ὡς ἠθέλησε, καὶ ἑκάστῳ τῶν σπερμάτων ἴδιον σῶμα (*Pan* 64.68.10)

36) ἐὰν γὰρ μὴ ἀποθάνῃ, οὐ ζωογονεῖται (*Anc* 83.4)

36) φησιν·
ἄφρων, σὺ ὃ σπείρεις οὐ ζωογονεῖται,[345] ἐὰν μὴ ἀποθάνῃ (*Pan* 42.5.5)

---

[341] Text V] the itacistic variant φάγομεν καὶ πίομεν in M is of no real textual significance, but occurs elsewhere in 915 917 1836. It is also assumed that ἀποθνήσκομεν / -ωμεν (L) is itacistic.

[342] ἔρχονται] ἐγείρονται 81.

[343] ἀποθάνῃ] πρῶτον ἀποθάνῃ F G it^{d.f.g}; ἀποθάνῃ πρῶτον D E.

[344] Although most of the citation is precise, Epiphanius alters τὸ σῶμα τὸ γενησόμενον to τὸ γενησόμενον σῶμα, precluding certainty whether his exemplar read γενησόμενον with TR 𝔐 ℵ A B D K L P 049 33 81 104 699 1594 1739, or γεννησόμενον with 𝔓^{46} F G it^{d.e.g}, since the variation occurs in the affected portion of text.

[345] This early alteration is preserved also in A Chr; 𝔐 reads ζωοποιεῖται.

1 Corinthians 15:36–38, cont.
(36)_____

    a. ἄφρων Epiph 𝔓⁴⁶ ℵ A B D F G P 33 81 104
    b. ἄφρον TR 𝔐 K L 049 699 1594 1739 Or

(38)_____

    a. δίδωσιν αὐτῷ Epiph 𝔓⁴⁶ ℵ A B P 33 81 104 it^f Or
    b. αὐτῷ δίδωσιν TR 𝔐 D F G K L 049 699 1594 1739 it$^{d.e.g}$

    a. ἴδιον Epiph ℵ* A B D F G P 33 81 104 1739 Or
    b. τὸ ἴδιον TR 𝔐 ℵ^c K L 049 699 1594 Chr

1 Corinthians 15:40
λέγει γάρ·
σώματα ἐπουράνια καὶ σώματα³⁴⁶ ἐπίγεια· ἀλλ᾽ ἑτέρα μὲν ἡ τῶν ἐπουρανίων δόξα, ἑτέρα δὲ ἡ τῶν ἐπιγείων (*Pan* 66.45.9)

1 Corinthians 15:42
ἐπειδή·
σπείρονται ἐν φθορᾷ, ἐγείρονται ἐν ἀφθαρσίᾳ (*Par.* 42.12.3 *refut* 11)

σπείρεται ἐν φθορᾷ, ἐγείρεται ἐν ἀφθαρσίᾳ (*Pan* 77.29.3)

1 Corinthians 15:43
σπείρεται ἐν ἀτιμίᾳ, ἐγείρεται ἐν δόξῃ· σπείρεται ἐν ἀσθενείᾳ, ἐγείρεται ἐν δυνάμει (*Pan* 64.69.8)

1 Corinthians 15:44
σπείρεται σῶμα ψυχικόν, ἐγείρεται σῶμα πνευματικόν (*Pan* 77.29.3)

τὰ νῦν σπειρόμενα ψυχικῶς ἐγείρεσθαι πνευματικα (*Pan, De fide* 17.9)

1 Corinthians 15:47
ὅτι καὶ ὁ ἀπόστολος εἴρηκεν·
ὁ πρῶτος ἄνθρωπος³⁴⁷ ἐκ γῆς χοϊκός, καὶ ὁ δεύτερος³⁴⁸ ἀπ᾽ οὐρανοῦ³⁴⁹
(*Pan* 71.3.2)

---

    ³⁴⁶ σώματα] *om* F G it^g.
    ³⁴⁷ ἄνθρωπος] ἄνθρωπος ᾽Αδάμ C*.

1 Corinthians 15:49
καθὼς ἐφορέσαμεν τὴν εἰκόνα τοῦ χοϊκοῦ φορέσωμεν[350] καί[351] τὴν εἰκόνα τοῦ ἐπουρανίου[352] (*Pan* 70.3.3)

1 Corinthians 15:50
καὶ μή τις λάβηται τοῦ ἁγίου ἀποστόλου εἰπόντος·
σὰρξ καὶ αἷμα βασιλείαν θεοῦ οὐ κληρονομήσουσιν[353] (*Pan* 42.12.3 *refut* 6)

γέγραπται·
σὰρξ καὶ αἷμα βασιλείαν θεοῦ οὐ κληρονομήσουσι (*Pan* 66.87.1)

1 Corinthians 15:52
σαλπίσει γάρ, καὶ οἱ νεκροὶ ἐγερθήσονται ἄφθαρτοι (*Anc* 95.4)

σαλπίσει γάρ, φησί, καὶ οἱ νεκροὶ ἀναστήσονται (*Pan* 51.32.9)

σαλπίσει, καὶ οἱ νεκροὶ ἀναστήσονται (*Pan* 64.70.2)

---

a. ἀναστήσονται Epiph A D F G P
b. ἐγερθήσονται Epiph TR 𝔐 $\mathfrak{P}^{46}$ ℵ B C K L 049 33 81 104 699 1594 1739 Cyr

---

1 Corinthians 15:53
ὁ ἀπόστολος διεβεβαιοῦτο λέγων·
δεῖ γὰρ τὸ φθαρτὸν τοῦτο ἐνδύσασθαι ἀφθαρσίαν[354] (*Anc* 90.1)

---

[348] Epiphanius implies but does not read ἄνθρωπος, so there is no way to tell if his exemplar read ἄνθρωπος with ℵ* B C D* F G 33 1739* it$^{d.e.f.g}$ Or, or ἄνθρωπος ὁ κύριος TR 𝔐 ℵ^c A D^c K L P 049 81 104 699 1594 1739^{mg} Chr, or ἄνθρωπος πνευματικός with $\mathfrak{P}^{46}$.
[349] ἀπ' οὐρανοῦ] ἐξ οὐρανοῦ ὁ οὐράνιος F G it$^{f.g}$; ἐξ οὐρανοῦ TR *rell.*
[350] φορέσωμεν] φορέσομεν B.
[351] καί] *om* 1739.
[352] ἐπουρανίου] ἐπουρανοῦ G.
[353] οὐ κληρονομήσουσι with F G] κληρονομῆσαι οὐ δύναται ℵ B P; κληρονομῆσαι οὐ δύνανται TR 𝔐 *rell.*
[354] Text L^{epiph} J] *add* καὶ τὸ θνητὸν ἐνδύσασθαι ἀθανασίαν Holl.

1 Corinthians 15:53, cont.

φάσκων·
δεῖ τὸ[355] φθαρτὸν τοῦτο ἐνδύσασθαι ἀφθαρσίαν καὶ τὸ θνητὸν τοῦτο[356] ἐνδύσασθαι ἀθανασίαν (*Pan* 28.6.8)

δεῖ γὰρ τὸ θνητὸν τοῦτο ἐνδύσασθαι ἀθανασίαν, καὶ τὸ φθαρτὸν τοῦτο ἐνδύσασθαι ἀφθαρσίαν (*Pan* 42.12.3 *refut* 24)

ἄκουε τοῦ ἀποστόλου λέγοντός ὅτι·
δεῖ τὸ φθαρτόν[357] τοῦτο ἐνδύσασθαι ἀφθαρσίαν καὶ τὸ θνητὸν τοῦτο ἐνδύσασθαι ἀθανασίαν (*Pan* 44.6.4)

ὅτι·
δεῖ τὸ φθαρτὸν τοῦτο ἐνδύσασθαι ἀφθαρσίαν καὶ τὸ θνητὸν τοῦτο ἐνδύσασθαι ἀθανασίαν (*Pan* 56.2.10)

λέγων·
δεῖ τὸ φθαρτὸν τοῦτο ἐνδύσασθαι ἀφθαρσίαν καὶ τὸ θνητὸν τοῦτο ἐνδύσασθαι ἀθανασίαν (*Pan* 64.68.3)

ὅταν τὸ φθαρτὸν εἰς ἀφθαρσίαν μεταβληθῇ καὶ τὸ θνητὸν εἰς ἀθανασίαν (*Pan* 66.61.8)

δεῖ γὰρ τὸ φθαρτὸν τοῦτο ἐνδύσασθαι ἀφθαρσίαν καὶ τὸ θνητὸν τοῦτο ἐνδύσασθαι ἀθανασίαν (*Pan* 66.87.6)

λέγει·
δεῖ τὸ φθαρτὸν τοῦτο ἐνδύσασθαι ἀφθαρσίαν καὶ τὸ θνητὸν τοῦτο ἐνδύσασθαι ἀθανασίαν (*Pan* 77.27.6)

1 Corinthians 15:54
τότε γενήσεται ὁ λόγος ὁ γεγραμμένος, κατεπόθη ὁ θάνατος εἰς νῖκος[358] (*Pan* 42.12.3 *refut* 24)

---

[355] τό] ὁ F G.
[356] τοῦτο] om F G it^g.
[357] Text V M] ἐν τούτῳ post φθαρτόν erased V^c.
[358] Frederick Danker, *A Greek-English Lexicon* (3rd ed.; Chicago: Univ. of Chicago Press, 2000): 667, states that νεῖκος "in 1 Cor 15:54f is not the word for 'strife' w. the same spelling (Hom. et al.), but an itacistic form of νῖκος." Consequently, the reading νεῖκος in 𝔓^{46} B should not be cited as a variant reading of νῖκος Epiph TR 𝔐 ℵ A et al.

1 Corinthians 15:55
   ποῦ σου θάνατος τὸ κέντρον; ποῦ σου "Αιδη τὸ νῖκος (*Pan 66.78.4*)

---

   a. κέντρον; ποῦ σου, ᾅδη τὸ νῖκος; Epiph TR 𝔐 ℵ^c A^c K L P 049 104 699 1594 Or Chr
   b. νῖκος; ποῦ σου, θάνατε, τὸ κέντρον; 𝔓⁴⁶ ℵ* B C 1739*vid
   c. νῖκος; ποῦ σου, ᾅδη τὸ κέντρον; 33 81 1739^c CyrJer
   d. κέντρον; ποῦ σου, θάνατε, τὸ νῖκος; D* (D^c *om* θάνατε) F G it^{d.f.g}

---

2 Corinthians 1:7
ὁ ἅγιος ἀπόστολος λέγων ὅτι·
καθάπερ κοινωνοί ἐστε τῶν παθημάτων τοῦ Χριστοῦ, οὕτως[359] καὶ τῆς δόξης[360] (Pan 42.12.3 refut 7)

2 Corinthians 2:7
ἵνα μὴ τῇ περισσοτέρᾳ λύπῃ καταποθῇ ὁ τοιοῦτος (Pan 59.4.11)

2 Corinthians 2:8
κυρώσατε εἰς αὐτὸν ἀγάπην (Pan 59.4.11)

2 Corinthians 2:10–11
ἔλεγε γὰρ πάλιν·
10) ᾧ τι χαρίζεσθε, κἀγώ· διότι εἴ τι κεχάρισμαι, δι' ὑμᾶς κεχάρισμαι ἐν προσώπῳ κυρίου, 11) ἵνα μὴ πλεονεκτηθῶμεν ὑπὸ τοῦ σατανᾶ. οὐ γὰρ αὐτοῦ τὰ νοήματα ἀγνοοῦμεν (Pan 59.4.12)

2 Corinthians 3:6
τὸ γράμμα, γάρ φησιν ἀποκτένει,[361] τὸ δὲ πνεῦμα ζωοποιεῖ (Anc 22.5)

2 Corinthians 3:7
διὰ τὸ εἰρηκέναι τὸν ἀπόστολον·
εἰ δὲ διαθήκη τοῦ θανάτου ἐν γράμμασιν ἐντετυπωμένη λίθοις ἐγενήθη ἐν δόξῃ[362] (Pan 66.73.1)

ἐγένετο δὲ ἐν δόξῃ (Pan 66.73.4)

εἶτά φησιν ὅτι ὁ νόμος·
διακονία ἦν τοῦ θανάτου (Pan 66.80.1)

---

[359] om οὕτως F G it^(d.e.g).

[360] In this allusion, one cannot be certain that Epiphanius read ἐστε τῶν παθημάτων with TR 𝔐 𝔓⁴⁶ ℵ A B C K L P 049 33 81 104 699 1594 1739 rather than τῶν παθημάτων ἐστε D F G.

[361] Epiphanius reads ἀποκτένει rather than ἀποκτέννει or ἀποκτείνει, all orthographical variations of the third person singular present active indicative. He does not read ἀποκτενεῖ, which is a future indicative. The apparatus of NA²⁷ is confusing, as with no accents it is impossible to distinguish the future from the indicative, which would be the only genuine variation. It is unclear why NA²⁷ lists the orthographical variations within the indicative as "variants."

[362] As Epiphanius prefaces this citation by saying, "Mani declares that the covenant [διαθήκην] of the Law is the testament of death, since the apostle has said . . . ." The alteration of διακονία to διαθήκη is a conscious adjustment to the patristic argument. The remainder is accurate.

2 Corinthians 3:7 cont.

a. ἐν γράμμασιν Epiph TR 𝔐 𝔓⁴⁶ ℵ A C Dᶜ K L P 049 81 104 699 1594 1739 it^{d.e.f} Or Chr
b. ἐν γράμματι B D* F G
c. ἐγγεγραμμένη 33

a. λίθοις Epiph 𝔓⁴⁶ ℵ* A B C D* F G P 33 81 it^g
b. ἐν λίθοις TR 𝔐 ℵᶜ Dᶜ K L 049 104 699 1594 1739 it^{d.e.f}

2 Corinthians 3:17
ὁ δὲ ἀπόστολος σαφῶς περὶ αὐτοῦ λέγει·
ὁ δὲ κύριός ἐστι τὸ πνεῦμα, οὗ δὲ³⁶³ τὸ πνεῦμα κυρίου, ἐκεῖ ἐλευθερία (*Pan* 74.13.6)

a. ἐκεῖ ἐλευθερία Epiph TR 𝔐 ℵᶜ Dᶜ F G K L P 049 104 699 1594 it^{d.e.f.g} Chr
b. ἐλευθερία 𝔓⁴⁶ ℵ* A B C D* 33 81 1739

2 Corinthians 3:18
καί·
ἀπὸ δόξης εἰς δόξαν, καθάπερ ἀπὸ κυρίου πνεύματος (*Anc* 69.2)

ἵνα·
ἀπὸ δόξης εἰς δόξαν, καθάπερ ἀπὸ κυρίου πνεύματος (*Pan* 66.73.6)

καί·
ἀπὸ δόξης εἰς δόξαν, καθὼς ἀπὸ κυρίου πνεύματος (*Pan* 74.6.2; from *Anc*)

2 Corinthians 4:4
καὶ πάλιν παρὰ τῷ ἀποστόλῳ ὅτι·
ὁ θεὸς τοῦ αἰῶνος τούτου ἐτύφλωσε τὰ νοήματα τῶν ἀπίστων, πρὸς τὸ μὴ καταυγάσαι³⁶⁴ τὸν φωτισμὸν τοῦ εὐαγγελίου τῆς δόξης (*Pan* 66.66.1)

---

³⁶³ οὗ δέ *bis* J; ποῦ δέ F G.
³⁶⁴ καταυγάσαι with C D.

2 Corinthians 4:4, cont.
ὅτι·
ὁ θεὸς, φησι, τοῦ αἰῶνος τούτου ἐτύφλωσε τὰ νοήματα τῶν ἀπίστων, τοῦ μὴ καταυγάσαι εἰς τὸν φωτισμὸν τοῦ εὐαγγελίου (*Pan* 66.68.1)

---

a. om αὐτοῖς *post* αὐγάσαι Epiph 𝔓⁴⁶ ℵ A B C D* F G 33 81 1739 it^{d.e.f.g} CyrJer
b. αὐτοῖς TR 𝔐 Dᶜ K L P 049 104 699 1594 Chr

---

2 Corinthians 4:7
κατὰ τὸ εἰρημένον·
ἔχοντες τὸν θησαυρὸν τοῦτον ἐν ὀστρακίνοις σκεύεσι (*Anc* 89.2)

2 Corinthians 4:13
ἔχοντες δὲ τὸ αὐτὸ πνεῦμα τῆς πίστεως καὶ ἡμεῖς πιστεύομεν, διὸ καὶ λαλοῦμεν. ἐξέκοψεν δὲ τὸ κατὰ τὸ γεγραμμένον³⁵⁵ (*Pan* 42.12.3 *schol* 2 Cor.; from 42.11.8 *schol* 2 Cor.)

ἔχοντες δὲ τὸ αὐτὸ πνεῦμα τῆς πίστεως καὶ ἡμεῖς πιστεύομεν, διὸ καὶ λαλοῦμεν. ἐξέκοψεν δὲ τὸ κατὰ τὸ γεγραμμένον (*Pan* 42.12.3 *schol* 27)

2 Corinthians 5:10
ἑκάστῳ καθὰ ἔπραξεν, ἤτοι ἀγαθὸν ἤτοι φαῦλον (*Pan* 66.37.7)

δεῖ γὰρ πάντας στῆναι ἐνώπιον τοῦ βήματος αὐτοῦ (*Pan* 76.42.8)

ἵνα ἕκαστος ἀπολάβῃ πρὸς ἃ ἔπραξεν³⁶⁶ (*Pan, De fide* 18.1)

2 Corinthians 5:15
ἵνα οἱ ζῶντες μηκέτι ἑαυτοῖς ζῶσιν, ἀλλὰ τῷ ὑπὲρ ἡμῶν ἀποθανόντι καὶ ἐγερθέντι (*Anc* 65.5)

ἵνα οἱ ζῶντες μηκέτι ἑαυτοῖς ζῶσιν, ἀλλὰ τῷ ὑπὲρ ἡμῶν ἀποθανόντι καὶ ἀναστάντι (*Pan* 74.2.5; from *Anc*)

---

³⁶⁵ Epiphanius attributes the omission of κατὰ τὸ γεγραμμένον to Marcion.
³⁶⁶ Since the quotations of 5:10 are merely loose allusions, one cannot know whether Epiphanius read πρὸς ἃ ἔπραξεν with TR 𝔐 𝔓⁴⁶ ℵ B C K L P 049 33 81 104 1594 1739 or ἔπραξεν with D F G; nor can one know whether he read φαῦλον with ℵ C 33 81 1739 or κακόν with TR 𝔐 𝔓⁴⁶ B D F G K L P 049 104 699 1594.

2 Corinthians 5:19
θεὸς ἦν ἐν Χριστῷ κόσμον καταλλάσσων ἑαυτῷ μὴ λογιζόμενος αὐτοῖς τὰ παραπτώματα αὐτῶν (*Anc* 65.5)

ὅτι·
θεος ἦν ἐν Χριστῷ, κόσμον καταλλάσσων ἑαυτῷ. μὴ λογιζόμενος αὐτοῖς τὰ παραπτώματα (*Pan* 66.74.8)

ὁ θεὸς ἦν ἐν Χριστῷ, κόσμον καταλλάσσων ἑαυτῷ, μὴ λογιζόμενος αὐτοῖς τὰ παραπτώματα αὐτῶν (*Pan* 74.2.5 from *Anc*)

2 Corinthians 6:16
ὅμοιον τῷ εἰπεῖν·
ἐνοικήσω ἐν αὐτοῖς καὶ ἐμπεριπατήσω, καὶ ἔσομαι αὐτῶν θεὸς καὶ αὐτοὶ ἔσονταί μοι λαός (*Anc* 68.18)

ὅτι·
κατασκηνώσω ἐν αὐτοῖς καὶ ἐμπεριπατήσω (*Pan* 51.32.6)

ὅμοιον τῷ εἰπεῖν·
ἐνοικήσω ἐν αὐτοῖς καὶ ἐμπεριπατήσω, καὶ ἔσομαι αὐτῶν θεὸς καὶ αὐτοὶ ἔσονται μοι λαός[367] (*Pan* 74.5.18; from *Anc*)

---

a. ἔσομαι αὐτῶν Epiph TR 𝔐 $\mathfrak{P}^{46}$ ℵ B C D K L 049 33 81 104 699 1594 1739 it$^{d.e.f}$ CyrJer
b. ἔσομαι αὐτοῖς F G P it^g Or

---

a. ἔσονται μοι Epiph TR 𝔐 D F G K L 049 104 699 1594 it CyrJer
b. ἔσονται μου $\mathfrak{P}^{46}$ ℵ B C P 33 81 1739 Or

---

2 Corinthians 10:3
ὡς λέγει·
ἐν σαρκὶ γὰρ περιπατοῦντες οὐ κατὰ σάρκα στρατευόμεθα (*Pan* 66.87.4)

---

[367] It is unclear whether *Pan* 51.32.6 cites 2 Cor 6:16 or Lev 26:11, but the *Pan* 74.5.18 citation is clearly from 2 Cor, as in this context Epiphanius states that 1 Cor 2:12 is similar to 2 Cor 13:5 and that 1 Cor 2:16 is similar to 2 Cor 6:16.

2 Corinthians 10:3, cont.

a. περιπατοῦντες Epiph TR 𝔐 ℵ B Cᶜ D K L P 049 33 104 699 1594 1739 Or
b. περιπατοῦντας 𝔓⁴⁶ F G

2 Corinthians 10:5
πᾶν ὕψωμα ἐπαιρόμενον κατὰ τῆς γνώσεως³⁶⁸ τοῦ θεοῦ (*Pan* 55.2.4)

2 Corinthians 10:13
τὸ παρὰ τῷ ἀποστόλῳ εἰρημένον·
τὸ μέτρον τοῦ κανόνος οὗ δέδωκεν ἡμῖν ὁ θεὸς μέτρου (*Anc* 1.2)

a. ἡμῖν Epiph TR 𝔐 𝔓⁴⁶ ℵ B D K P 049 33 81 104 1594 1739
b. *om* F G L itᵍ

2 Corinthians 11:3
γὰρ ὁ ἅγιος ἀπόστολος . . . λέγων·
<u>φοβοῦμαι δὲ μή πως ὡς ὁ ὄφις ἠπάτησεν Εὔαν ἐν τῇ πανουργίᾳ αὐτοῦ,</u>
<u>φθαρῇ τὰ νοήματα ὑμῶν ἀπὸ τῆς ἁπλότητος</u> καὶ ἁγνείας Χριστοῦ καὶ δικαιοσύνης (*Pan* 37.8.10)

ὅτι·
φοβοῦμαι μή πως ὡς ὁ ὄφις ἐξηπάτησεν Εὔαν ἐν τῇ πανουργίᾳ, οὕτω φθαρῇ τὰ νοήματα ὑμῶν ἀπὸ τῆς ἁγνότητος καὶ τῆς ἁπλότητος³⁶⁹ τῆς εἰς τὸν Χριστόν (*Pan* 66.54.3)

a. μή πως Epiph TR 𝔐 ℵ B K L P 049 33 104 1594 Or Euseb
b. μήποτε F G 1739 Chr
c. μή D

a. ἐξηπάτησεν Εὔαν Epiph ℵ B F G P 33 81 104 1739 itᵍ
b. Εὔαν ἐξηπάτησεν TR 𝔐 D K L 049 1594 itᵈ·ᵉ·ᶠ

---

³⁶⁸ γνώσεως] δόξης 33.
³⁶⁹ ἀπὸ τῆς ἁγνότητος «καὶ τῆς ἁπλότητος» with D* E itᵈ·ᵉ] ἀπὸ τῆς ἁπλότητος καὶ τῆς ἁγνότητος 𝔓⁴⁶ ℵ* B F G 33 81 104; ἀπὸ τῆς ἁπλότητος TR 𝔐 ℵᶜ K L P 049.

2 Corinthians 11:3, cont.

---

a. οὕτω Epiph TR 𝔐 D^c K L 049 104 1594 1739 it^f Or Chr
b. *om* Epiph 𝔓^46 ℵ B D* F G P 33 81 it^{d.e.g} Euseb

---

a. εἰς τὸν Χριστόν Epiph TR 𝔐 𝔓^46 B D K L P 049 33 81 104 1594 Or Chr
b. εἰς Χριστόν ℵ F G 1739

---

2 Corinthians 11:6
ἰδιωτῶν τῷ λόγῳ, ἀλλ' οὐ τῇ γνώσει (*Pan* 77.31.2)

2 Corinthians 11:13
καὶ οὗτοί εἰσιν οἱ παρὰ τῷ ἀποστόλῳ Παύλῳ εἰρημένοι·
ψευδαπόστολοι, ἐργάται δόλιοι, μετασχηματιζόμενοι εἰς[370] ἀποστόλους Χριστοῦ (*Pan* 28.4.6)

2 Corinthians 11:22
καὶ ἐν ἄλλῳ τόπῳ λέγει·
Ἰσραηλῖταί εἰσι, κἀγώ· σπέρμα Ἀβραάμ εἰσι, κἀγώ (*Pan* 30.25.3)

2 Corinthians 12:2
τοῦ ἁγίου ἀποστόλου εἰρημένου ὅτι·
οἶδα ἄνθρωπον πρὸ ἐτῶν δεκατεσσάρων, εἴτε ἐν[371] σώματι οὐκ οἶδα, εἴτε ἐκτὸς τοῦ[372] σώματος οὐκ οἶδα, ὁ θεός οἶδεν, ἁρπαγέντα τὸν τοιοῦτον ἕως τρίτου οὐρανοῦ (*Anc* 54.3)

2 Corinthians 12:3–4
καί φησιν·
3) οἶδα τὸν τοιοῦτον ἄνθρωπον 4) ἁρπαγέντα εἰς τὸν παράδεισον καὶ ἀκούσαντα ῥήματα ἃ οὐκ ἐξὸν ἀνθρώπῳ εἰπεῖν (*Anc* 54.4)

4) ἄρρητα ῥήματα, ἃ οὐκ ἐξὸν ἀνθρώπῳ λαλῆσαι (*Anc* 11.5)

4) καὶ ἀκηκοέναι ἄρρητα ῥήματα, ἃ οὐκ ἐξὸν ἀνθρώπῳ λαλῆσαι (*Pan* 38.2.5)

---

[370] *om* εἰς F G.
[371] ἐν τῷ D* E*.
[372] *om* τοῦ B.

2 Corinthians 12:21
    φησί·
    καὶ πενθήσω πολλοὺς τοὺς ἐν ὑμῖν παραπεσόντας καὶ μὴ μετανοήσαντας (*Pan* 59.5.2)

2 Corinthians 13:3
    ὅμοιον ὡς εἶπε Παῦλος·
    εἰ δοκιμὴν ζητεῖτε τοῦ ἐν ἐμοὶ λαλοῦντος Χριστοῦ; (*Anc* 68.7)

    ὅμοιον ᾧ εἶπε Παῦλος·
    εἰ δοκιμὴν ζητεῖτε τοῦ ἐν[373] ἐμοὶ λαλοῦντος Χριστοῦ (*Pan* 74.5.7; from *Anc*)

2 Corinthians 13:4
    λέγει αὐτὸς ὁ ἀπόστολος ὅτι·
    εἰ καὶ ἀπέθανεν ἐξ ἀσθενείας, ζῇ δὲ ἐκ δυνάμεως (*Pan* 69.59.7)

2 Corinthians 13:5
    ὅμοιον τῷ εἰπεῖν·
    ἑαυτοὺς δοκιμάζετε εἰ ὁ Χριστὸς ἐν ὑμῖν (*Anc* 68.17)

    ὅμοιον τῷ εἰπεῖν·
    ἑαυτοὺς δοκιμάζετε[374] εἰ ὁ Χριστὸς ἐν ὑμῖν[375] (*Pan* 74.5.17; from *Anc*)

---

[373] ἐν ἐμοί *post* λαλοῦντος F G it^g.

[374] ἑαυτοὺς δοκ.μάζετε] *om* A.

[375] As ὑμῖν occurs at the end, it is unclear whether Epiphanius read ὑμῖν with $\mathfrak{P}^{46}$ B D* or ὑμῖν ἐστιν with ℵ A F G K L P.

Galatians 1:8
ὁ αὐτὸς ἀπόστολος ἔλεγεν·
κἄν τε ἡμεῖς ἢ ἄγγελος εὐαγγελίσηται ὑμῖν[376] παρ' ὃ παρελάβετε, ἀνάθεμα ἔστω (*Pan* 42.12.3 refut. 24)

Galatians 1:14
περισσοτέρως ζηλωτὴς ὑπάρχων τῶν πατρικῶν μου παραδόσεων (*Pan* 30.25.2)

Galatians 1:15–16
ὅμοιον τῷ εἰπεῖν·
15) ὅτε εὐδόκησεν ὁ ἀφορίσας με ἐκ κοιλίας μητρός μου διὰ τῆς χάριτος αὐτοῦ, 16) ἀποκαλύψαι τὸν υἱὸν αὐτοῦ ἐν ἐμοί (*Anc* 68.16)

ὅμοιον τῷ εἰπεῖν·
15) ὅτε εὐδόκησεν ὁ ἀφορίσας με ἐκ κοιλίας μητρός μου διὰ τῆς χάριτος αὐτοῦ 16) ἀποκαλύψαι τὸν υἱὸν αὐτοῦ ἐν ἐμοί (*Pan* 74.5.16; from *Anc*)

---

a. εὐδόκησεν   Epiph 𝔓⁴⁶ B F G it^{f.g}
b. εὐδόκησεν ὁ θεός   TR 𝔐 ℵ A D K L P 049 33 81 104 699 1594 1739 it^{d.e} Or

---

Galatians 2:3–5
διὸ καὶ Παῦλος λέγει·
3) ἀλλ' οὐδὲ Τίτος ὁ[377] σὺν ἐμοί,[378] Ἕλλην ὤν, ἠναγκάσθη περιτμηθῆναι, 4) διὰ δὲ τοὺς παρεισάκτους ψευδαδέλφους, οἵτινες παρεισῆλθον κατασκοπῆσαι τὴν ἐλευθερίαν ἡμῶν ἣν ἔχομεν ἐν Χριστῷ, 5) οἷς οὐδὲ[379] πρὸς ὥραν εἴξαμεν τῇ ὑποταγῇ[380] (*Pan* 28.4.2)

5) παρὰ τῷ ἁγίῳ ἀποστόλῳ Παύλῳ· φάσκει γὰρ οὕτως·
οἷς οὐδὲ πρὸς ὥραν εἴξαμεν τῇ ὑποταγῇ (*Pan* 28.4.3)

5) οὐδὲ πρὸς ὥραν εἶξαι (*Pan* 70.3.5)

---

[376] εὐαγγελίσηται ὑμῖν ℵ^c A 81] εὐαγγελίζηται ὑμῖν TR (D* ὑμᾶς) D^c L 33 1594; ὑμῖν εὐαγγελίζηται B 1739; εὐαγγελίζεται ὑμῖν 𝔐 K P 049 104; εὐαγγελίσηται ℵ*; εὐαγγελίζηται F (G).
[377] *om* ὁ B.
[378] *om* ὁ σὺν ἐμοί 𝔓⁴⁶.
[379] *om* οἷς οὐδὲ D* it^{d.e}.
[380] *om* τῇ ὑποταγῇ 𝔓⁴⁶.

Galatians 2:9
πάλιν δὲ ὁ ἅγιος Παῦλος μαρτυρεῖ καὶ αὐτὸς τοῖς περὶ Πέτρον λέγων·
Ἰάκωβος καὶ Ἰωάννης καὶ Κηφᾶς, οἱ δοκοῦντες στῦλοι εἶναι, δεξιὰς
ἔδωκαν ἐμοί[381] τε καὶ Βαρνάβᾳ κοινωνίας[382] (*Pan* 30.25.5)

---

a. Ἰάκωβος καὶ Κηφᾶς καὶ Ἰωάννης (Epiph 1.3.2) TR 𝔐 ℵ B C K L
   P 049 33 81 104 699 1594 1739 Chr
b. Πέτρος καὶ Ἰάκωβος καὶ Ἰωάννης ($\mathfrak{P}^{46}$ 2.1.3) D F G it$^{d.f.g}$ Or
c. Ἰάκωβος καὶ Ἰωάννης A

Galatians 3:2
γέγραπται·
<u>ἐξ ἀκοῆς πίστεως</u>[383] τὸ πνεῦμα τοῦ Χριστοῦ (*Pan* 74.4.3)

Galatians 3:10
πεπλάνηνται δὲ καὶ οὗτοι περιτομὴν αὐχοῦντες, καὶ ἔτι οἱ τοιοῦτοι <u>ὑπὸ
κατάραν εἰσί</u>, μὴ δυνάμενοι τὸν νόμον πληρῶσαι (*Pan* 29.8.1)

λέγων·
ἐπικατάρατος ὃς οὐκ ἐμμένει πᾶσι τοῖς γεγραμμένοις[384] λόγοις ἐν τῷ
βιβλίῳ τούτῳ τοῦ ποιῆσαι αὐτούς (*Pan* 29.8.3)

Galatians 3:11
μάθετε ὅτι ὁ δίκαιος ἐκ πίστεως ζήσεται (*Pan* 42.12.3 refut. 1)

Galatians 3:13
τὸ τοῦ ἀποστόλου ῥητόν, ὅτι·
Χριστὸς ἡμᾶς ἐξηγόρασεν ἐκ τῆς κατάρας τοῦ νόμου, γενόμενος ὑπὲρ
ἡμῶν κατάρα (*Pan* 42.8.1)

φάσκων ὅτι ὁ Χριστὸς ἐξηγόρασεν ἡμᾶς ἀπὸ τῆς κατάρας τοῦ νόμου,
γενόμενος ὑπὲρ ἡμῶν κατάρα (*Pan* 66.79.1)

καὶ οὕτως αἰσχρῶς περὶ τοῦ <u>ἐξαγοράσαντος ὑμᾶς</u>, εἴ γε ἐξηγόρασε,
διανοεῖσθε (*Pan* 69.31.4)

---

[381] μοι F G.
[382] Κηφᾶς is inadvertently transposed after Ἰωάννης due to the discussion in 30.22–25; the remainder is accurate. Although in the discussion Πέτρος is used of Peter, Κηφᾶς is retained here and likely represents the biblical exemplar.
[383] J Holl; πιστῇ *Anc.* according to Holl.
[384] ἐνγεγραμμένοις B.

Galatians 3:24
 ὡς καὶ ὁ ἅγιος ἀπόστολός φησι·
 παιδαγωγὸς ἡμῖν γέγονεν[385] ὁ νόμος εἰς Χριστόν[386] (*Pan* 42.11.17 *refut.* 62)

 καὶ ὁ ἀπόστολος λέγει ὅτι·
 παιδαγωγὸς ἡμῶν γέγονεν ὁ νόμος εἰς τὴν τοῦ κυρίου παρουσίαν (*Pan* 66.75.6)

 παιδαγωγὸς εἰς Χριστὸν ἡμῖν γέγονεν (*Pan* 77.38.2)

Galatians 3:28
 καὶ ἅγιος τοῦ θεοῦ ἀπόστολος Παῦλος ... λέγων ὅτι·
 ἐν Χριστῷ Ἰησοῦ οὐ βάρβαρος οὐ Σκύθης, οὐχ <u>Ἕλλην, οὐκ Ἰουδαῖος</u>[387] (*Pan* 8.3.3)

 φησίν·
 ἐν γὰρ Χριστῷ Ἰησοῦ οὔτε ἄρσεν[388] οὔτε θῆλυ (*Pan* 49.2.5)

Galatians 4:3
 ἵνα μηκέτι·
 ὑπὸ τὰ στοιχεῖα τοῦ κόσμου ὦμεν δεδουλωμένοι (*Anc* 2.4)

Galatians 4:4
 κατὰ τὸ εἰρημένον <u>γενόμενος ἐκ γυναικός</u> (*Anc* 30.4)

 καὶ διὰ τοῦτό φησιν ὁ ἀπόστολος·
 γενόμενος ἐκ γυναικός, γενόμενος ὑπὸ νόμον (*Anc* 80.3)

 καὶ πάλιν·
 γενόμενος ἐκ γυναικός, γενόμενος ὑπὸ νόμον (*Pan* 54.6.2)

 ὡς μαρτυρεῖ Παῦλος ὁ ἅγιος λέγων·
 γενόμενος ἐκ γυναικός, γενόμενος ὑπὸ νόμον (*Pan* 56.2.9)

 γενόμενος ἐκ γυναικός, γενόμενος ὑπὸ νόμον (*Pan, De fide* 15.4)

---

[385] γέγονεν] ἐγένετο 𝔓⁴⁶ B.

[386] Because the add/omit occurs at the end of the citation, one cannot know whether Epiphanius read εἰς Χριστόν with TR 𝔐 𝔓⁴⁶ ℵ A B C K L P 049 33 81 104 699 1594 1739 or εἰς Χριστὸν Ἰησοῦν with D* F G it^(d.e.f.g).

[387] Conflation of material from Gal 3:28, 6:15, and Col 3:11.

[388] ἄρσεν] ἄρσης F G; ἄρρεν ℵ.

Galatians 4:4, cont.

a. γενόμενον Epiph^vid TR 𝔐 𝔓^46 ℵ A B C D F G L P 049 33 81 1739 it^d.e.f.g Meth CyrJer Chr
b. γεννώμενον (K -ομενον) 104 699 1594

Galatians 4:24–25
φησὶ γὰρ ὁ ἀπόστολος·
24) ἡ πρώτη διαθήκη ἐκ τοῦ ὄρους Σινᾶ ἐδόθη, <u>εἰς δουλείαν γεννῶσα</u>,
25) τὸ γὰρ ὄρος[389] Σινᾶ ἐστιν ἐν τῇ Ἀραβίᾳ (*Pan* 66.74.6)

Galatians 5:2
ἔλεγεν·
μὴ περιτέμνεσθε[390] <u>ὅτι ἐὰν περιτέμνησθε, Χριστὸς ὑμᾶς οὐδὲν ὠφελήσει</u> (*Pan* 28.4.2)

καὶ ὅτι·
ἐὰν περιτέμνησθε, Χριστὸς ὑμᾶς οὐδὲν ὠφελήσει (*Pan* 28.5.3)

λέγοντος Παύλου τοῦ ἁγίου ἀποστόλου ὅτι·
ἐὰν περιτέμνησθε, Χριστὸς ὑμᾶς οὐδὲν ὠφελήσει (*Pan* 29.8.7)

ποῦ οὖν τὸ παρὰ τῷ ἀποστόλῳ εἰρημένον ὅτι·
ἐὰν περιτέμνησθε, Χριστὸς ὑμᾶς οὐδὲν ὠφελήσει (*Pan* 77.37.5)

Galatians 5:4
διὰ τὸ εἰρηκέναι·
ὅσοι ἐν νόμῳ δικαιοῦσθε, τῆς χάριτος ἐξεπέσατε (*Pan* 28.5.3)

οἵτινες ἐν νόμῳ καυχᾶσθε, τῆς χάριτος ἐξεπέσατε (*Pan* 29.8.7)

καὶ·
οἵτινες ἐν νόμῳ δικαιοῦσθε, τῆς χάριτος ἐξεπέσατε (*Pan* 77.37.5)

---

[389] ὄρος ἐστιν] ὄρος 1739. In giving the gist of portions of vv. 24, 25, Epiphanius does not provide sufficient verbal accuracy to enable one to know whether his exemplar read γὰρ Σινᾶ with ℵ C F G 1739 it^f.g; δὲ Ἀγὰρ Σινᾶ with A B D; γὰρ Ἀγὰρ Σινᾶ with TR 𝔐 K L P 049 33 104 699 1594; or δὲ Σινᾶ with 𝔓^46.

[390] V; *om* μή M; περιτεμνῆσθαι F G; περιτέμνησθε *rell*.

Galatians 5:9
ἀντὶ τοῦ <u>μικρὰ ζύμη ὅλον τὸ</u>[391] <u>φύραμα ζυμοῖ</u> ἐποίησε δολοῖ (*Pan* 42.11.8 *schol. Gal.*)

Galatians 5:19
φανερὰ δὲ τὰ ἔργα τῆς σαρκός (*Anc* 79.1)

καὶ οὐκ οἶδεν ὁ ἄπειρος κατὰ πάντα ὅτι <u>τὰ ἔργα τῆς σαρκὸς πορνεία μοιχεία</u>[392] <u>ἀσέλγεια</u> καὶ τὰ τούτοις ὅμοια (*Pan* 66.86.3)

<u>τῆς γὰρ σαρκός</u> φησιν οἱ καρποὶ <u>πορνεία μοιχεία ἀσέλγεια</u> καὶ τὰ τούτων ὅμοια (*Anc* 76.5)

Galatians 5:25
διὰ τοῦ εἰρημένου·
εἰ ζῶμεν πνεύματι, πνεύματι καὶ στοιχῶμεν (*Pan* 64.63.16)

---

a. ζῶμεν πνεύματι Epiph TR 𝔐 𝔓^{46} ℵ A B C K P 049 33 81 104 699 1594 1739
b. πνεύματι ζῶμεν D F G it$^{d.e.g}$ Or
c. ζῶμεν ἐν πνεύματι L

---

a. πνεύματι καί Epiph TR 𝔐 ℵ A B C D K L P 049 33 81 104 699 1594 1739
b. πνεύματι 𝔓^{46} F G it$^{d.e.g}$

---

a. στοιχῶμεν Epiph TR 𝔐 𝔓^{46} ℵ A B C D* F G P 049 33 81 104 699 1594
b. στοιχοῦμεν D^c K L 1739

---

[391] τό] *om* 𝔓^{46}.
[392] Epiphanius knows the reading μοιχεία, but neither of these allusions reflects an intention to cite an exemplar. At an earlier period, he might have gotten the gist from a text reading μοιχεία, as reflected in Irenaeus, *Adv. haer.* 5.11.1, and later adopted by Byzantine scribes. This memorized allusion was used in arguing "flesh" versus "spirit," as in Irenaeus. See also *Pan* 66.87.7. Nothing in the arguments of Irenaeus or Epiphanius is predicated upon μοιχεία. One cannot know whether Epiphanius' text read μοιχεία with TR 𝔐 ℵ^c D F G K L 049 104 699 1594 or *om* with ℵ* A B C P 33 81 1739*.

Galatians 6:1
προληφθῇ ἔν τινι παραπτώματι, ὡς λέγει ὁ ἀπόστολος, ὑμεῖς οἱ πνευματικοὶ καταρτίζετε τὸν τοιοῦτον ἐν πνεύματι πραότητος, σκοπῶν ἑαυτόν,³⁹³ μὴ καὶ σὺ πειρασθῇς (*Pan* 59.5.5)

---

a. σὺ πειρασθῇς Epiph TR 𝔐 𝔓⁴⁶ ℵ A B C K (L -θεις) P (33 -θεις) 81 (104 -θεις) 699 1594 1739
b. αὐτὸς πειρασθῇς D* (F G -θῇ)
c. *om* phrase 049

Galatians 6:7
καὶ ὅτι δικαιοκρισία ἐστὶ καὶ θεὸς οὐ μυκτηρίζεται (*Anc* 110.1)

οὐ γὰρ μυκτηρίζεται ὁ θεός, ὡς προεῖπον (*Anc* 114.3)

Galatians 6:10
ὡς καὶ γέγραπται·
ποιεῖν τὸ ἀγαθὸν πρῶτον εἰς τοὺς οἰκείους τῆς πίστεως (*Pan* 42.16.3)

Galatians 6:17
τοῦ λοιποῦ³⁹⁴ τοίνυν μηδεὶς ἡμῖν κόπους παρεχέτω (*Anc* 63.1)

---

³⁹³ ἑαυτόν M] σεαυτόν U 𝔐; *add* ἕκαστος F G: *om* phrase 049.
³⁹⁴ τὸ λοιπόν D*.

Ephesians 1:10

παρεγένετο τοίνυν·
εἰς οἰκονομίαν τοῦ πληρώματος τῶν καιρῶν (Anc 65.7)

παρεγένετο τοίνυν·
εἰς οἰκονομίαν³⁹⁵ τοῦ πληρώματος τῶν καιρῶν (Pan 74.2.7; from Anc)

Ephesians 1:21

ἐπάνω πάσης ἀρχῆς καὶ ἐξουσίας, δυνάμεως καὶ παντὸς ὀνόματος ὀνομαζομένου (Anc 81.1)

ὑπεράνω πάσης ἀρχῆς καὶ ἐξουσίας³⁹⁶ καὶ κυριότητος καὶ παντὸς ὀνόματος ὀνομαζομένου (Pan 62.7.8)

Ephesians 2:2

<u>ἐνεργεῖται ἐν τοῖς υἱοῖς τῆς ἀπειθείας</u> κατὰ τὸ γεγραμμένον (Pan 66.79.5)

Ephesians 2:6

κατὰ τὸν ἀποστολικὸν λόγον ὅτι·
ὁ θεὸς ἤγειρε καὶ συνεκάθισεν ἐν τοῖς ἐπουρανίοις³⁹⁷ (Pan 44.5.12)

Ephesians 2:14–15

14) δι' αὐτοῦ ποιήσας τὰ ἀμφότερα ἕν. ἦλθε γὰρ ἡ εἰρήνη ἡμῶν, καὶ τὸ μεσότοιχον τοῦ φραγμοῦ λύσας, τὴν ἔχθραν ἐν τῇ σαρκὶ αὐτοῦ, 15) τὸν νόμον τῶν ἐντολῶν ἐν δόγμασι καταργήσας, ἵνα τοὺς δύο κτίσῃ εἰς ἕνα καινὸν ἄνθρωπον (Anc 65.8)

14) δι' αὐτοῦ ποιήσας τὰ ἀμφότερα ἕν. ἦλθε γὰρ ἡ εἰρήνη ἡμῶν, καὶ τὸ μεσότοιχον τοῦ φραγμοῦ λύσας τὴν ἔχθραν ἐν τῇ σαρκὶ αὐτοῦ, 15) τὸν νόμον τῶν ἐντολῶν ἐν δόγμασι καταργήσας,³⁹⁸ ἵνα τοὺς δύο κτίσῃ ἐν ἑαυτῷ εἰς ἕνα καινὸν ἄνθρωπον (Pan 74.2.8; from Anc)

(15)_____

a. ἐν ἑαυτῷ Epiph TR 𝔐 ℵᶜ D G K L 049 81 699 1594 Euseb
b. ἐν αὐτῷ 𝔓⁴⁶ ℵ* A B F P 33 104 1739

---

³⁹⁵ εἰς] κατὰ τὴν οἰκονομίαν A.
³⁹⁶ ἀρχῆς καὶ ἐξουσίας] ἐξουσίας καὶ ἀρχῆς B.
³⁹⁷ Epiphanius omits ἐν Χριστῷ Ἰησοῦ after ἐπουρανίοις with F G itᵍ, but the omission occurs at the end of his citation and cannot be used.
³⁹⁸ καταργήσας] καταρτίσας D* E*.

Ephesians 2:14–15 cont.
(15)_____

    a. καινόν Epiph TR 𝔐 ℵ A B D L P 049 33 81^vid 104 699 1594 1739
    b. κοινόν 𝔓^46 F G
    c. καὶ μόνον K

_____

Ephesians 2:16
ἀποκατήλλαξε δὲ ἐν τῷ σώματι τῆς σαρκὸς αὐτοῦ (*Anc* 65.8)

ἀποκατήλλαξε δὲ ἐν τῷ σώματι τῆς σαρκὸς αὐτοῦ (*Pan* 74.2.8; from *Anc*)

Ephesians 3:6
εἶναι τε τὰ ἔθνη σύσσωμα καὶ συμμέτοχα καὶ συγκληρονόμα τῆς ἐπαγγελίας (*Anc* 65.8)

εἶναι δὲ τὰ ἔθνη σύσσωμα καὶ συμμέτοχα καὶ συγκληρονόμα τῆς ἐπαγγελίας[399] (*Pan* 74.2.8 from *Anc*)

Ephesians 3:15
ἢ ὥς ἄν εἴποι τις·
ἐξ οὗ πᾶσα πατριὰ ἐν οὐρανῷ[400] καὶ ἐπὶ γῆς (*Anc* 71.3)

πατρὸς ὄντος τοῦ κυρίου ἡμῶν Ἰησοῦ Χριστοῦ, <u>ἐξ οὗ πᾶσα πατριὰ ἐν οὐρανῷ καὶ ἐπὶ γῆς ὀνομάζεται</u> (*Pan* 66.70.2)

ἢ ὥς ἄν εἴποι τις·
ἐξ οὗ τὰ πατριὰ ἐν οὐρανοῖς[401] καὶ ἐπὶ τῆς γῆς (*Pan* 74.8.3; from *Anc*)

καὶ ἐπὶ τῷ·
ἀφ᾽ οὗ πᾶσα πατριὰ ἐν οὐρανῷ καὶ ἐπὶ γῆς ὀνομάζεται (*Pan* 76.25.8)

_____

[399] In both citations of this verse, Epiphanius omits αὐτοῦ after ἐπαγγελίας with ℵ B C D* P 33 it Or. However, the omission occurs at the end of the quotation and cannot be used as datum.

[400] οὐρανῷ L^epiph J; οὐρανοῖς Holl.

[401] As the singular is read in all the other citations, the plural here appears to be due to lack of care when copying that section of *Anc* into the *Pan*. Further lack of attention is exhibited by the addition of the article before γῆς. This quotation does not reflect Epiphanius' exemplar.

Ephesians 3:15, cont.

---

a. ἐν οὐρανῷ Epiph P 81 104 Meth
b. ἐν οὐρανοῖς TR 𝔐 $\mathfrak{P}^{46}$ ℵ A B C D F G K L 049 33 699 1594 1739 CyrJer

---

Ephesians 4:10
τὸ εἰρημένον·
ὁ καταβὰς αὐτός ἐστιν καὶ ὁ ἀναβὰς ὑπεράνω[402] (*Pan* 62.7.8)

ὁ καταβὰς αὐτὸς καὶ ὁ ἀναβὰς ἐπάνω πάντων[403] τῶν οὐρανῶν (*Pan* 66.73.7)

Ephesians 4:25
καὶ καθὼς ὁ ἅγιος ἀπόστολός φησιν·
ἀλήθειαν λαλείτω ἕκαστος μετὰ τοῦ[404] πλησίον αὐτοῦ (*Pan* 73.27.2)

Ephesians 4:28
ἐργαζόμενοι ταῖς ἰδίαις χερσίν, ἵνα δυνηθῆτε καὶ τοῖς μὴ ἔχουσι μεταδοῦναι[405] (*Pan* 26.11.2)

Ephesians 4:30
καὶ·
μὴ λυπεῖτε τὸ πνεῦμα τὸ ἅγιον, ἐν ᾧ ἐσφραγίσθητε εἰς ἡμέραν ἀπολυτρώσεως (*Anc* 69.3)

καὶ·
μὴ λυπεῖτε τὸ πνεῦμα τὸ ἅγιον, ἐν ᾧ ἐσφραγίσθητε εἰς ἡμέραν ἀπολυτρώσεως (*Pan* 74.6.3; from *Anc*)

---

a. τὸ πνεῦμα τὸ ἅγιον Epiph TR 𝔐 $\mathfrak{P}^{46}$ ℵ A B K L P 049 33 81 104 699 1594 1739 CyrJer
b. τὸ ἅγιον πνεῦμα D F G it[d.e.g]

---

[402] ὑπεράνω is common to 4:10 and 1:21, and is also included as the first word in the quotation of 1:21.
[403] πάντων] *om* P.
[404] μετὰ τοῦ] πρὸς τὸν ℵ*.
[405] This citation is too loose to indicate Epiphanius' agreement with μεταδοῦναι in D F G against μεταδιδόναι in TR 𝔐 $\mathfrak{P}^{46}$ ℵ et al.

Ephesians 5:12
αἰσχρόν ἐστι καὶ λέγειν (*Pan* 24.5.3)

ὡς καὶ που ὁ ἁγιώτατος ἀπόστολός φησι·
τὰ γὰρ κρυφῇ γινόμενα ὑπ᾽ αὐτῶν αἰσχρόν ἐστι καὶ λέγειν (*Pan* 25.2.5)

αἰσχρόν ἐστι καὶ λέγειν (*Pan* 26.4.4)

Ephesians 5:14
τὸ εἰρημένον·
ἔγειρε ὁ καθεύδων καὶ ἀνάστα ἐκ τῶν νεκρῶν καὶ ἐπιφαύσει σοι ὁ Χριστός (*Pan* 46.5 9)

τὸ γεγραμμένον·
ἔγειρε ὁ καθεύδων καὶ ἀνάστα ἐκ τῶν νεκρῶν καὶ ἐπιφαύσει σοι ὁ Χριστός (*Pan* 64.71.19)

Ephesians 5:16
ὅμοιον δὲ τούτῳ ὁ αὐτὸς ἅγιος ἀπόστολός φησιν·
ἐξαγοραζόμενοι τὸν καιρόν, ὅτι αἱ ἡμέραι πονηραί εἰσι (*Pan* 42.8.6)

Ephesians 5:31
ὡς καὶ ὁ ἀπόστολος λέγει ὅτι ὁ ἀπ᾽ ἀρχῆς συζεύξας τὰ ἀμφότερα εἶπεν, <u>ἀντὶ τούτου καταλείψει ἄνθρωπος τὸν πατέρα αὐτοῦ καὶ τὴν μητέρα αὐτοῦ,</u>[406] <u>καὶ κολληθήσεται τῇ γυναικὶ αὐτοῦ, καὶ ἔσονται οἱ δύο εἰς σάρκα μίαν</u> (*Pan* 66.86.4)

---

a. τὸν πατέρα αὐτοῦ Epiph TR 𝔐 ℵ^c A D^c K L P 049 104 699 1594
b. τὸν πατέρα 𝔓^{46} ℵ* 33 81 1739 Or
c. πατέρα B D* F G

---

a. κολληθήσεται Epiph ℵ^c D F G
b. προσκολληθήσεται TR 𝔐 𝔓^{46} ℵ* A B K L P 049 33 81 104 699 1594 1739 Meth

---

a. τῇ γυναικί αὐτοῦ Epiph 𝔓^{46} (ℵ* *om* αὐτοῦ) A D* F G 33 81 (1739 *om* αὐτοῦ) Meth

b. πρὸς τὴν γυναῖκα αὐτοῦ TR 𝔐 ℵ^c B D^c K L (P) 049 104 699 1594 Or

---

[406] τὴν μητέρα αὐτοῦ with F 104; μητέρα B D* F G; τὴν μητέρα *rell*.

Ephesians 5:32
καὶ ὁ ἅγιος ἀπόστολος . . . λέγει·
τὸ μυστήριον τοῦτο μέγα ἐστίν. ἐγὼ δὲ[407] λέγω εἰς Χριστὸν καὶ τὴν ἐκκλησίαν[408] (*Pan* 66.56.5)

Ephesians 6:2
πάλιν λέγει·
ὁ τιμῶν πατέρα καὶ μητέρα· αὕτη γάρ ἐστιν ἐν ἐπαγγελίαις πρώτη ἐντολὴ ὑπάρχουσα (*Pan* 61.6.3)

---

[407] δέ] om 81.
[408] Epiphanius reads τὴν ἐκκλησίαν with B K Clem Iren Tert against εἰς τὴν ἐκκλησίαν *rell*.

Philippians 1:1
πάλιν δὲ ἐν ἄλλῳ τόπῳ·
ἐπισκόποις⁴⁰⁹ καὶ διακόνοις (*Pan* 75.4.4.)

Philippians 1:10
ὅμοιον τῷ εἰπεῖν·
ὁ δὲ κύριος ἁγιάσαι ὑμᾶς, ἵνα ἦτε εἰλικρινεῖς καὶ ἀπρόσκοποι εἰς ἡμέραν Χριστοῦ⁴¹⁰ (*Anc* 68.15)

ὅμοιον τῷ εἰπεῖν·
ὁ δὲ κύριος ἁγιάσαι ὑμᾶς, ἵνα ἦτε εἰλικρινεῖς καὶ ἀπρόσκοποι εἰς ἡμέραν κυρίου⁴¹¹ (*Pan* 74.5.15; from *Anc*)

Philippians 2:6–7
6) ὃς <u>οὐχ ἁρπαγμὸν ἡγήσατο τὸ εἶναι ἴσα θεῷ</u>, 7) ἀλλ' ἑαυτὸν ἐκένωσε, μορφὴν δούλου λαβών (*Anc* 44.5)

φησὶ γὰρ περὶ αὐτοῦ Παῦλος·
6) ὃς ἐν μορφῇ θεοῦ ὑπάρχων οὐχ ἁρπαγμὸν ἡγήσατο τὸ εἶναι ἴσα θεῷ,
7) ἀλλ' ἑαυτὸν ἐκένωσε⁴¹² μορφὴν δούλου λαβών (*Pan* 65.7.8)

6) ἐν μορφῇ θεοῦ ὑπάρχοντος (*Pan* 76.34.8)

7) ἐκένωσεν ἑαυτὸν μορφὴν δούλου λαβών (*Anc* 40.2)

7) καὶ πάλιν·
ἐν σχήματι εὑρεθεὶς ὡς ἄνθρωπος (*Anc* 80.3)

7) μορφὴν δούλου λαβών (*Pan* 74.3.6; from *Anc*)

(6)_____

   a. τὸ εἶναι Epiph TR 𝔐 ℵ A B C D K L P 049 33 81 104 699 1594
      1739 Or
   b. εἶναι 𝔓⁴⁶ F G Euseb

---

⁴⁰⁹ ἐπισκόποις] συνεπισκόποις Bᶜ Dᶜ K.
⁴¹⁰ Χριστοῦ] Χριστοῦ Ἰησοῦ F G itᶠ·ᵍ.
⁴¹¹ J; Χριστοῦ Holl. The first part of this citation is free, but ἵνα … κυρίου is exact, as in *Anc.* 68.15, where Χριστοῦ is read.
⁴¹² ἐκένωσε] ἐκαίνωσε F G is probably an orthographical variant but it does result in the plausible reading, καινόω.

Philippians 2:8
ὁ δὲ ἅγιος Παῦλός φησι·
γευσάμενος θανάτου, θανάτου δὲ σταυρου (*Pan* 24.9.5)

θανάτου, θανάτου δὲ σταυροῦ (*Pan* 69.62.6)

Philippians 2:9
ὡς καὶ τὸ εἰρημένον·
ἔδωκεν αὐτῷ ὄνομα τὸ[413] ὑπὲρ πᾶν ὄνομα (*Pan* 69.38.1)

---

a. ὄνομα Epiph TR 𝔐 D F G K L P 049 81 104 699 1594
b. τὸ ὄνομα 𝔓⁴⁶ ℵ A B C 33 1739

Philippians 2:10–11
10) καὶ πᾶν γόνυ κάμψει ἐπουρανίων καὶ ἐπιγείων καὶ καταχθονίων, 11) καὶ πᾶσα γλῶσσα ἐξομολογήσεται, ὅτι κύριος Ἰησοῦς Χριστὸς[414] εἰς δόξαν θεοῦ πατρός (*Pan* 69.18.3)

10) ᾧ κάμπτει[415] πᾶν γόνυ ἐπουρανίων καὶ ἐπιγείων καὶ καταχθονίων (*Anc* 37.4)

γὰρ·
10) κάμψει πᾶν γόνυ ἐπουρανίων καὶ ἐπιγείων καὶ καταχθονίων (*Pan* 42.11.17 *refut.* 65)

10) καὶ πάλιν·
αὐτῷ κάμψει πᾶν γόνυ ἐπουρανίων καὶ ἐπιγείων καὶ καταχθονίων (*Pan* 69.75.6)

11) καὶ·
πᾶσα γλῶσσα ἐξομολογήσεται ὅτι κύριος Ἰησοῦς Χριστός (*Pan* 76.42.8)

11) πάσης γλώσσης ἐξομολογουμένης ὅτι Ἰησοῦς Χριστὸς εἰς δόξαν θεοῦ πατρός (*Pan* 76.53.15)

---

[413] τό] εἰς τὸ F G.

[414] κύριος Ἰησοῦς Χριστός] κύριος Ἰησοῦς F G; Χριστὸς κύριος K; εἰς κύριος Ἰησοῦς Χριστός 1739.

[415] As κάμψει is read at all other places by Epiphanius, κάμπτει has no substantial claim to represent a text known to him. In minuscule script, ψ often appears to read very much like τ.

Philippians 2:11, cont.
(11)_____

    a. ἐξομολογήσεται Epiph A C D F G K L P 049 33 81 104 Or
    b. ἐξομολογήσηται TR 𝔐 $\mathfrak{P}^{46}$ ℵ B 699 1594 1739 Euseb

---

Philippians 3:1
    ἐμοὶ μὲν οὐκ ὀκνηρόν, τοῖς δὲ ἐντυγχάνουσιν ἀσφαλὲς ἔσται[416] (*Pan* 69.45.1)

Philippians 3:5
    πῶς οὖν αὐτὸς λέγει περὶ ἑαυτοῦ ὅτι·
    Ἑβραῖος ἐξ Ἑβραίων, ἐκ σπέρματος Ἀβραάμ, φυλῆς Βενιαμίν, κατὰ νόμον[417] Φαρισαῖος (*Pan* 30.25.2)

    περιτομῇ ὀκταήμερος καὶ ἀνατεθραμμένος παρὰ τοὺς πόδας Γαμαλιὴλ καὶ Ἑβραῖος ἐξ Ἑβραίων (*Pan* 30.25.3)

Philippians 3:19
    ὡς καὶ ἐν ἄλλῳ τόπῳ λέγει·
    ὧν ὁ θεὸς ἡ κοιλία καὶ ἡ δόξα ἐν τῇ αἰσχύνῃ αὐτῶν (*Pan* 66.69.2)

Philippians 3:21
    μετασχηματίσει τὸ σῶμα τῆς ταπεινώσεως ἡμῶν εἰς τὸ γενέσθαι σύμμορφον[418] τῆς δόξης αὐτοῦ κατὰ τὴν ἐνέργειαν τοῦ δύνασθαι καὶ ὑποτάξαι αὐτῷ τὰ πάντα (*Anc* 65.11)

    μετασχηματίσει τὸ σῶμα τῆς ταπεινώσεως ἡμῶν εἰς τὸ γενέσθαι σύμμορφον τῆς δόξης αὐτοῦ κατὰ τὴν ἐνέργειαν τοῦ δύνασθαι καὶ ὑποτάξαι αὐτῷ τὰ πάντα (*Pan* 74.2.11; from *Anc*)

---

[416] In this allusion, one cannot know whether Epiphanius' exemplar read ἀσφαλές with TR $\mathfrak{P}^{46}$ ℵ A^{vid} B C D F G K L P 33 81 1594 1739 or τὸ ἀσφαλές with 𝔐 104 699.

[417] Epiphanius cannot be cited as evidence against τὸν νόμον of F G because of the fragmentary nature of the citation.

[418] In his citation of three verses, Epiphanius includes, as usual, only that which is essential to his point. For instance, in v. 9 he omits αὐτό following γενέσθαι and τῷ σώματι, but clearly evidencing awareness of the longer text form. The presence or absence of αὐτό was not considered by John Chrysostom to be essential to the verse either, as he cites the longer text five times with and twice without αὐτό.

Philippians 3:21, cont.

---

a. εἰς τὸ γενέσθαι αὐτὸ σύμμορφον (Epiph) TR 𝔐 D^c K L P 049 33 104 699 1594 Chr
b. σύμορφον ℵ A B D* F G 81 1739 it^{d.e.f.g} Euseb

---

a. αὐτῷ Epiph ℵ* A B D* F G K P 049 33 81 1739 it^{d.e.g} Euseb
b. ἑαυτῷ TR 𝔐 ℵ^c D^c L 104 699 1594 it^f

Colossians 1:13
λέγει δὲ αὐτὸν ὁ ἀπόστολος . . .·
<u>ὃς ἐρρύσατο ἡμᾶς</u>⁴¹⁹ φησίν <u>ἐκ τῆς ἐξουσίας τοῦ σκότους καὶ μετέστησεν εἰς τὴν βασιλείαν τοῦ υἱοῦ τῆς ἀγάπης αὐτοῦ</u> (*Anc* 50.1)

Colossians 1:18
καὶ γὰρ·
<u>πρωτότοκός ἐστιν ἐκ</u>⁴²⁰ <u>τῶν νεκρῶν</u>, ὡς εἶπεν ἡ θεία γραφή (*Pan* 69.66.8)

Colossians 1:19–20
19) ὅτι ἐν αὐτῷ εὐδόκησε πᾶν τὸ πλήρωμα κατοικῆσαι, 20) καὶ δι' αὐτοῦ ἀποκαταλλάξαι τὰ πάντα εἰς αὐτόν, εἰρηνοποιήσας διὰ τοῦ αἵματος τοῦ σταυροῦ (*Anc* 65.6)

19) ὅτι ἐν αὐτῷ εὐδόκησε πᾶν τὸ πλήρωμα κατοικῆσαι, 20) καὶ δι' αὐτοῦ ἀποκαταλλάξαι τα πάντα εἰς αὐτόν, εἰρηνοποιήσας διὰ τοῦ αἵματος τοῦ σταυροῦ (*Pan* 74.2.6; from *Anc*)

Colossians 1:26
μυστήριον τὸ ἀπόκρυφον πρὸ τῶν αἰώνων καὶ γενεῶν (*Anc* 65.10)

μυστήριον τὸ ἀπόκρυφον πρὸ τῶν αἰώνων καὶ γενεῶν (*Pan* 74.2 10; from *Anc*)

Colossians 2:3
ἐν ᾧ πάντες οἱ θησαυροὶ τῆς σοφίας ἀπόκρυφοι (*Anc* 70.6)

ἐν ᾧ πάντες οἱ θησαυροὶ τῆς σοφίας ἀπόκρυφοι (*Pan* 74.7.6; from *Anc*)

Colossians 2:6
ὅμοιον τῷ εἰπεῖν·
καθὼς ἐλάβετε Χριστόν, ἐν αὐτῷ περιπατεῖτε (*Anc* 68.12)

ὅμοιον τῷ εἰπεῖν·
καθὼς ἐλάβετε Χριστόν, ἐν αὐτῷ περιπατεῖτε (*Pan* 74.5.12; from *Anc*)

Colossians 2:9
ὅτι ἐν αὐτῷ κατοικεῖ πᾶν τὸ πλήρωμα τῆς θεότητος σωματικῶς (*Anc* 65.11)

---

[419] ἡμᾶς] ὑμᾶς P 104.
[420] *om* ἐκ 𝔓⁴⁶ ℵ*.

Colossians 2:9, cont.
ἐν ᾧ εὐδόκησε πᾶν τὸ πλήρωμα τῆς θεότητος κατοικῆσαι σωματικῶς (*Anc* 80.2)

ἐν τῷ γὰρ κυρίῳ ηὐδόκησε πᾶν τὸ πλήρωμα τῆς θεότητος κατοικῆσαι σωματικῶς[421] (*Pan* 48.11.7)

ὅτι ἐν αὐτῷ κατοικεῖ πᾶν τὸ πλήρωμα τῆς θεότητος σωματικῶς (*Pan* 74.2.11; from *Anc*)

Colossians 2:11
ὅμοιον τῷ εἰπεῖν·
καὶ περιετμήθητε περιτομῇ ἀχειροποιήτῳ ἐν τῇ ἀπεκδύσει τοῦ σώματος τῶν ἁμαρτιῶν, ἐν περιτομῇ τοῦ Χριστοῦ (*Anc* 68.11)

περιτομὴν Χριστοῦ ἐν τῇ ἀπεκδύσει τοῦ σώματος τῶν ἁμαρτιῶν (*Anc* 73.8)

ὅμοιον τῷ εἰπεῖν·
καὶ[422] περιετμήθητε περιτομῇ ἀχειροποιήτῳ ἐν τῇ ἀπεκδύσει τοῦ σώματος τῶν ἁμαρτιῶν[423] ἐν τῇ περιτομῇ τοῦ Χριστοῦ (*Pan* 74.5.11; from *Anc*)

περιτομὴν Χριστοῦ ἐν τῇ ἀπεκδύσει τοῦ σώματος τῶν ἁμαρτιῶν (*Pan* 74.10.8; from *Anc*)

Colossians 2:14–15
14) ἐξαλείψας τὸ καθ᾽ ἡμῶν χειρόγραφον, τοῖς δόγμασιν ὃ ἦν ὑπεναντίον ἡμῶν, ἦρκεν ἐκ μέσου[424] καὶ προσηλώσας τῷ σταυρῷ, 15) ἀπεκδυσάμενος τὰς ἀρχὰς καὶ τὰς ἐξουσίας, ἐδειγμάτισεν[425] ἐν παρρησίᾳ, θριαμβεύσας αὐτὰς ἐν αὐτῷ (*Anc* 65.2)

14) ἐξαλείψας τὸ καθ᾽ ἡμῶν χειρόγραφον τοῖς δόγμασιν, ὃ ἦν ὑπεναντίον ἡμῶν,[426] ἦρκεν ἐκ μέσου προσηλώσας αὐτὸ τῷ σταυρῷ,

---

[421] σωματικῶς *ante* θεότητος 81.
[422] καί] *om* F G it⁸ arm.
[423] τοῦ σώματος τῶν ἁμαρτιῶν] τοῦ σώματος τῆς σαρκός 𝔓⁴⁶ ℵ* A B C D* F G P 33 81 1739; τοῦ σώματος τῶν ἁμαρτιῶν τῆς σαρκός TR 𝔐 ℵᶜ Dᶜ K L 049 104 699 1594.
[424] ἐκ μέσου with A 1739] ἐκ τοῦ μέσου *rell*.
[425] Holl (*Pan* 74.2.2); παρεδειγμάτισεν Lᵉᵖⁱᵖʰ J.
[426] ἡμῶν with ℵ*] ὑμῖν P 104; ἡμῖν *rell*.

Colossians 2:14–15, cont.
15) ἀπεκδυσάμενος τὰς ἀρχὰς καὶ⁴²⁷ τὰς εξουσίας,⁴²⁸ ἐδειγμάτισεν ἐν παρρησίᾳ, θριαμβεύσας αὐτοὺς ἐν αὐτῷ (*Pan* 74.2.2; from *Anc*)

14) σχίσας τὸ καθ' ἡμῶν χειρόγραφον καὶ προσηλώσας αὐτὸ τῷ σταυρῷ (*Pan* 77.32.8)

15) ἐν γὰρ τῷ σταυρῷ <u>ἐθριάμβευσεν ἀρχὰς καὶ ἐξουσίας</u> (*Pan* 66.73.6)

15) καί·
θριαμβεύσῃ πᾶσαν ἀρχήν καὶ ἐξουσίαν (*Pan* 69.62.6)

(14)_____

a. ἦρκεν Epiph TR 𝔐 𝔓⁴⁵ ℵ A B C K L 049 33 81 104 699 1739 Chr
b. ἦρεν D* F G 1594 Or   c. ἦρκται P

Colossians 2:19
<u>μὴ κρατῶν τὴν κεφαλήν,</u>⁴²⁹ <u>ἐξ ἧσπερ πᾶν τὸ σῶμα συναρμολογούμενον αὔξει</u> κατὰ τὸ γεγραμμένον (*Pan* 48.11.10)

<u>τὴν κεφαλὴν τῆς πίστεως, ἐξ οὗ πᾶν τὸ σῶμα διὰ τῶν ἁφῶν καὶ τῶν συνδέσμων ἐπιχορηγούμενον καὶ συμβιβαζόμενον αὔξει τὴν αὔξησιν τοῦ θεοῦ,</u> ὡς ὁ ἀπόστολος λέγει (*Pan* 77.15.1)

Colossians 3:5
λέγει·
<u>νεκρώσατε τὰ μέλη τὰ ἐπὶ τῆς γῆς,</u> ἅτινά ἐστι πορνεία μοιχεία ἀσέλγεια καὶ τὰ ἐξῆς. (*Pan* 66.87.7)

_____

a. τὰ μέλη Epiph 𝔓⁴⁶ ℵ* B C* 33 81 1739 Or Euseb
b. τὰ μέλη ὑμῶν TR 𝔐 ℵᶜ A Cᶜ D F G K L P 049 104 699 1594

_____

Colossians 3:11
φησὶ γάρ·
ἐν Χριστῷ Ἰησοῦ οὐ βάρβαρος, οὐ Σκύθης, οὐχ Ἕλλην, οὐκ Ἰουδαῖος⁴³⁰ (*Pan* 1.9)

_____

⁴²⁷ τὰς ἀρχὰς καί] τὴν σάρκα F G itᵍ.
⁴²⁸ *add* καὶ 𝔓⁴⁶ B.
⁴²⁹ *add* Χριστόν D itᵈ.
⁴³⁰ This is a conflation of Col 3:11, Gal 3:28, 6:15.

1 Thessalonians 4:17
  ἡμεῖς ἁρπαγησόμεθα⁴³¹ εἰς συνάντησιν⁴³² αὐτῷ εἰς ἀέρα (*Pan* 64.70.2)

  ὁ ἅγιος ἀπόστολος ... ·
  ἡμεῖς ἁρπαγησόμεθα ἐν νεφέλαις εἰς συνάντησιν αὐτοῦ (*Pan* 64.70.3)

1 Thessalonians 5:2
  ὡς κλέπτης ἐν νυκτὶ ἔρχεται ἡ ἡμέρα ἐκείνη (*Anc* 21.2)

1 Thessalonians 5:4
  καὶ φησιν·
  οὐκ ἔστε ἐν νυκτί, ἵνα ἡ ἡμέρα ἐν σκότει ἡμᾶς⁴³³ καταλάβῃ (*Anc* 21.2)

  καὶ ὁ ἅγιος ἀπόστολός φησιν·
  οὐκ ἐστὲ σκότους τέκνα, ἀλλὰ ἡμέρας, <u>ἵνα ἡ ἡμέρα ὑμᾶς μὴ ὡς κλέπτης</u>⁴³⁴ <u>καταλάβῃ</u> (*Pan* 69.44.1)

---

  a. ἡ ἡμέρα ὑμᾶς Epiph TR 𝔐 ℵ B K L P (33 *om* ἡ) 81 104 699 1594 Chr
  b. ὑμᾶς ἡ ἡμέρα A D 1739 Euseb
  c. ὑμᾶς ἡ ἡμέρα ἐκείνη F G it^(d.e.f.g)

---

1 Thessalonians 5:5
  καὶ ὁ ἅγιος ἀπόστολος λέγων·
  ὑμεῖς δὲ ἡμέρας ἐστὲ τέκνα καὶ τέκνα φωτός (*Pan, De fide* 6.3)

1 Thessalonians 5:23
  ὡς λέγει ὁ ἀπόστολος·
  ἵνα ὁλόκληρον ὑμῶν τὸ πνεῦμα καὶ ἡ ψυχὴ καὶ τὸ σῶμα ἐν τῇ ἡμέρᾳ τοῦ κυρίου ἡμῶν Ἰησοῦ Χριστοῦ τηρηθείη⁴³⁵ (*Anc* 77.4)

---

[431] ἁρπαγησόμεθα] ἁρπαγησώμεθα L 81.
[432] συνάντησιν] ὑπάντησιν D* E* F G; ἀπάντησιν *rell*.
[433] ἡμᾶς L^epiph J; ὑμᾶς Holl.
[434] κλέπτης] κλέπτας A B.
[435] τηρηθείη] *om* F it^g (space left vacant).

2 Thessalonians 2:2–3
ὅτι·
μηδὲν ὑμᾶς πτυρέτω ἐν λόγῳ ἐν ἐπιστολῇ, ὡς ὅτι ἡ ἡμέρα ἐνέστηκε τοῦ κυρίου.[436] 3) ἐὰν γὰρ μὴ ἀποκαλυφθῇ ὁ υἱὸς τῆν ἀνομίας, ὁ ἄνθρωπος τῆς ἀδικίας (*Pan* 66.61.3)

2 Thessalonians 3:10
ὁ μὴ ἐργαζόμενος μηδὲ ἐσθιέτω (*Pan* 66.53.3)

ὁ μὴ ἐργαζόμενος μηδὲ ἐσθιέτω (*Pan* 80.4.3)

2 Thessalonians 3:11
μηδὲν ἐργαζόμενοι, ἀλλὰ περιεργαζόμενοι (*Pan* 66.53.2)

περιεργαζομένων καὶ μηδὲν ἀγαθὸν ἐργαζομένων (*Pan* 69.25.5)

---

[436] In this loose allusion, one cannot know whether Epiphanius' exemplar read τοῦ κυρίου with ℵ A B D* L 81 104 1739, τοῦ κυρίου Ἰησοῦ with 33, κυρίου F G P, or τοῦ Χριστοῦ TR 𝔐 D^c K 699 1594. As the reminiscence continues into v. 3, one cannot know whether Epiphanius reads τῆς ἀνομίας with ℵ B 81 104 1739 or τῆς ἁμαρτίας with TR 𝔐 A D F G K L P 699 1594.

1 Timothy 1:7
μὴ νοοῦντες μήτε ἃ λέγουσι μήτε περὶ τίνων διαβεβαιοῦνται (*Pan* 40.8.4)

οὐ γὰρ ἃ λέγουσιν οἴδασιν οὔτε περὶ τίνων διαβεβαιοῦνται (*Pan* 50.1.2)

μήτε ἃ λέγουσι νοοῦντες μήτε περὶ τίνων διαβεβαιοῦνται (*Pan* 51.4.1)

τὸ εἰρημένον ὑπὸ τοῦ ἁγίου ἀποστόλου·
μήτε ἃ λέγουσι νοοῦντες μήτε περὶ τίνων διαβεβαιοῦνται (*Pan* 57.6.4)

1 Timothy 1:9-10
ἀλλ' ὅτι·
9) ὁ νόμος δικαίῳ οὐ κεῖται, ἀλλὰ πατραλοίαις καὶ μητρολοίαις 10) καὶ ἐπιόρκοις, καὶ εἴ τι ἀντίκειται τῇ ὑγιαινούσῃ διδασκαλίᾳ (*Pan* 66.73.2)

9) δικαίῳ γὰρ νόμος οὐ κεῖται, ἀλλὰ πατρολῴοις καὶ μητρολῴοις καὶ λοιποῖς (*Pan* 75.3.6)

1 Timothy 1:12
ὅμοιον τῷ εἰπεῖν·
χάριν ἔχω τῷ ἐνδυναμώσαντί με Χριστῷ Ἰησοῦ τῷ κυρίῳ ἡμῶν, ὅτι πιστόν με ἡγήσατο θέμενος εἰς διακονίαν (*Anc* 69.10)

ὅμοιον τῷ εἰπεῖν·
χάριν ἔχω τῷ ἐνδυναμώσαντί με Χριστῷ Ἰησοῦ τῷ κυρίῳ ἡμῶν, ὅτι πιστόν με ἡγήσατο εἰς διακονίαν θέμενος (*Pan* 74.6.10; from *Anc*)

1 Timothy 1:17
πῶς οὖν·
θεῷ μόνῳ σοφῷ ἀοράτῳ[437] (*Anc* 43.2)

1 Timothy 2:5
τούτῳ τῷ λόγῳ Παῦλος ὁ ἅγιος ἀπόστολος φάσκων·
εἷς θεός, εἷς καὶ μεσίτης θεοῦ καὶ ἀνθρώπων, ἄνθρωπος Ἰησοῦς Χριστός (*Anc* 44.5)

ἄνθρωπος δὲ Χριστὸς Ἰησοῦς, μεσίτης δὲ θεοῦ καὶ ἀνθρώπων (*Pan* 30.31.8)

---

[437] From this allusion, one cannot be certain that Epiphanius read μόνῳ σοφῷ with TR 𝔐 ℵc Dc K L P 81 104 699 rather than μόνῳ with ℵ* A D* F G 33 1739.

1 Timothy 2:5, cont.

ἀλλ' ἵνα δείξῃ ὅτι·
μεσίτης θεοῦ καὶ ἀνθρώπων, ἄνθρωπος Χριστὸς Ἰησοῦς (*Pan* 42.11.17 refut. 5)

1 Timothy 2:12

ὁ ἀποστολικὸς λόγος ὅτι·
γυναικὶ οὐκ ἐπιτρέπω λαλεῖν οὔτε αὐθεντεῖν ἀνδρός (*Pan* 49.3.3)

1 Timothy 2:14–15

καὶ μετὰ ταῦτά φησιν·
14) Ἀδὰμ οὐκ ἐξηπατήθη, ἀλλ' ἡ γυνὴ ἐν παραβάσει γενομένη ἡμάρτηκε·[438] 15) σωθήσεται δὲ διὰ τῆς τεκνογονίας ἐὰν ἐμμείνωσιν ἐν τῇ πίστει (*Pan* 66 54.5)

14) ὁ Ἀδὰμ οὐκ ἠπάτηται, ἀλλ' ἡ Εὔα πρώτη ἀπατηθεῖσα ἐν παραβάσει γέγονεν (*Pan* 49.3.3)

15) φάσκει . . . ὁ αὐτὸς ἀπόστολος ὅτι·
σωθήσεται διὰ τῆς τεκνογονίας, ἐὰν μείνωσιν ἐν πίστει καὶ δικαιοσύνῃ (*Pan* 46.3.10)

1 Timothy 3:2,8

ἀκηκοότες γὰρ ὅτι·
2) δεῖ[439] τὸν ἐπίσκοπον ἀνεπίληπτον εἶναι, μιᾶς γυναικὸς ἄνδρα, ἐγκρατῆ 8) ὡσαύτως καὶ τὸν διάκονον (*Pan* 59.4.1)

1 Timothy 3:15

ὁ ἁγιώτατος Παῦλος γράφων τῷ Τιμοθέῳ διὰ τούτων τῶν λόγων·
ὅπως γινώσκοις πῶς δεῖ[440] ἐν οἴκῳ κυρίου[441] περιπατεῖν, ἥτις[442] ἐστὶν ἐκκλησία θεοῦ ζῶντος, στῦλος καὶ ἑδραίωμα τῆς ἀληθείας (*Pan* 40.8.4)

καὶ·
πίστις καὶ ἑδραίωμα τῆς ἀληθείας (*Pan* 80.11.6)

---

[438] One cannot tell from these allusions whether Epiphanius read ἀπατηθεῖσα with TR 𝔐 ℵ^c D^c K L 699 1594 or ἐξαπατηθεῖσα ℵ* A D* F G P 33 81 104 1739.
[439] δεῖ] δεῖ δὲ F G it$^{f.g}$; δεῖ οὖν rell.
[440] δεῖ] δεῖ σε D* it$^{d.f.}$
[441] κυρίου with P; θεοῦ rell.
[442] ἥτις] εἴ τις C P.

1 Timothy 3:16

ἤ· ἐφανερώθη⁴⁴³ ἐν σαρκί, ἐδικαιώθη ἐν πνεύματι (*Anc* 69.8)

ἤ· ὅς⁴⁴⁴ ἐφανερώθη ἐν σαρκί, ἐδικαιώθη ἐν πνεύματι (*Pan* 74.6.8; from *Anc*)

a. ὅς   Epiph ℵ* A*vid C* F G 33 Or
b. ὅ   D* it^{d.f}
c. θεός   TR 𝔐 ℵᶜ Aᶜ Cᶜ Dᶜ K L P 81 104 699 1594 1739 Chr

1 Timothy 4:1

τὸ δὲ πνεῦμα ῥητῶς λέγει (*Anc* 69.4)

φησιν ὁ ἁγιώτατος Παῦλος ὁ ἀπόστολος·
ἐν ὑστέροις⁴⁴⁵ καιροῖς ἀποστήσονταί τινες τῆς διδασκαλίας,⁴⁴⁶ προσέχοντες μύθοις καὶ διδασκαλίαις δαιμόνων (*Pan* 31.34.5)

προσέχοντες πνεύμασι πλάνης⁴⁴⁷ καὶ διδασκαλίαις δαιμονίων (*Pan* 48.1.4)

Παῦλος δὲ ὁ ἁγιώτατος ἀπόστολος προφητεύων ἔλεγε·
τὸ⁴⁴⁸ δὲ πνεῦμα ῥητῶς λέγει (*Pan* 48.8.6)

καὶ πάλιν ἄλλοτε ὅτι·
ἀποστήσονταί τινες τῆς ὑγιαινούσης διδασκαλίας, προσέχοντες πλάνοις καὶ⁴⁴⁹ διδασκαλίαις⁴⁵⁰ δαιμόνων (*Pan* 48.8.7)

τὸ δὲ πνεῦμα ῥητῶς λέγει (*Pan* 74.6.4; from *Anc*)

---

⁴⁴³ L^{epiph} J; *add* ὅς *ante* ἐφανερώθη Holl. It is unclear why Holl inserted ὅς here and substituted θεός for ὅς in *Pan* with no MS support for either alteration.

⁴⁴⁴ J; θεός Holl; *om Anc* 8. Holl incorrectly substitutes θεός (with TR) for ὅς of J which clearly agrees with ℵ* A*vid C* G Or.

⁴⁴⁵ ὑστέροις] ἐσχάτοις 33.
⁴⁴⁶ *add* καὶ; K.
⁴⁴⁷ πλάνης with P 104.
⁴⁴⁸ τὸ] ὁ F G.
⁴⁴⁹ καὶ] *om* D*.
⁴⁵⁰ διδασκαλίαις] διδασκαλίας ℵ* P.

1 Timothy 4:2–3
2) κεκαυτηριασμένων τὴν συνείδησιν,[451] 3) καὶ κωλυόντων γαμεῖν, ἀπέχεσθαι βρωμάτων, ἃ ὁ θεὸς εἰς μετάληψιν ἐποίησεν (*Pan* 67.8.2)

καὶ πάλιν·
2) κωλυόντων γαμεῖν, κεκαυτηριασμένων τὴν συνείδησιν (*Pan* 26.16.3)

3) κωλυόντων γαμεῖν, ἀπέχεσθαι βρωμάτων, ἃ ὁ θεὸς ἔκτισεν εἰς μετάληψιν ἡμῖν[452] τοῖς μετὰ εὐχαριστίας[453] (*Pan* 48.8.7)

3) κατὰ τὸ εἰρημένον·
κωλυόντων γαμεῖν (*Pan* 48.9.7)

1 Timothy 4:4
ὅτι πάντα καλὰ καὶ ἡδέα, καὶ οὐδὲν ἀπόβλητον παρὰ θεῷ (*Pan* 67.8.2)

1 Timothy 4:5
ἁγιάζεται γὰρ διὰ λόγου θεοῦ ζῶντος καὶ ἐντεύξεως[454] (*Pan* 67.8.2)

1 Timothy 4:14
καὶ τῷ ἐπισκόπῳ φησί·
μὴ ἀμέλει τοῦ ἐν σοὶ χαρίσματος,[455] οὗ ἔλαβες διὰ χειρῶν τοῦ πρεσβυτερίου[456] (*Pan* 75.4.4)

1 Timothy 5:1
ὡς λέγει Τιμοθέῳ ἐπισκόπῳ ὄντι·
πρεσβυτέρῳ[457] μὴ ἐπιπλήξῃς, ἀλλὰ παρακάλει ὡς πατέρα[458] (*Pan* 75.5.8)

1 Timothy 5:11–12
11) χήρας φησίν νεωτέρας παραιτοῦ· μετὰ γὰρ τὸ καταστρηνιᾶσαι[459] τοῦ Χριστοῦ γαμεῖν θέλουσιν, 12) ἔχουσαι κρίμα, ὅτι τὴν πρώτην πίστιν ἠθέτησαν (*Pan* 26.14.2)

---

[451] τὴν συνείδησιν] τὴν συνείδησιν ἑαυτῶν D; τὴν οἰκίαν συνείδησιν 81; τὴν ἰδίαν συνείδησιν rell.
[452] ἡμῖν U Holl; om ἡμῖν M.
[453] Text M U; add λαμβάνουσιν Holl.
[454] ἐντεύξεως] ἐντεύξεσιν D*.
[455] χαρίσματος] χρίσματος P.
[456] πρεσβυτερίου] πρεσβυτέρου ℵ*.
[457] πρεσβυτέρῳ Holl from lines 29, 32] πρεσβυτρ' J.
[458] πατέρα] om ℵ*.
[459] καταστρηνιᾶσαι] καταστρηνιάσουσι A F G P 104; καταστρηνιάσωσι rell.

1 Timothy 5:11-12, cont.
   11) ὡς καὶ ὁ ἅγιος ἀπόστολος . . . ὅτι·
   νεωτέρας χήρας παραιτοῦ· μετὰ γὰρ τὸ καταστρηνιάσαι τοῦ Χριστοῦ γαμεῖν θέλουσιν, 12) ἔχουσαι τὸ[460] κρίμα, ὅτι τὴν πρώτην πίστιν ἠθέτησαν (*Pan* 48.9.9–10)

   ὡς λέγει·
   11) νεωτέρας χήρας παραιτοῦ. μετὰ γὰρ τὸ καταστρηνιᾶσαι τοῦ Χριστοῦ γαμεῖν ἐθέλουσιν, 12) ἔχουσαι κρίμα, ὅτι τὴν πρώτην πίστιν ἠθέτησαν (*Pan* 67.6.7)

   ὁ αὐτὸς ἀπόστολος λέγων·
   11) νεωτέρας χήρας παραιτοῦ. μετὰ γὰρ τὸ καταστρηνιάσαι τοῦ Χριστοῦ γαμεῖν θέλουσιν, 12) ἔχουσαι κρίμα, ὅτι τὴν πρώτην πίστιν ἠθέτησαν (*Pan* 61.6.8)

   11) λέγων διὰ Τιμοθέου·
   νεωτέρας χήρας παραιτοῦ· μετὰ γὰρ τὸ καταστρηνιάσαι τοῦ Χριστοῦ γανεῖν θέλουσι (*Pan* 23.5.7)

1 Timothy 5:14
   καὶ μεθ' ἕτερα·
   γαμείτωσαν τεκνογονείτωσαν οἰκοδεσποτείτωσαν (*Pan* 23.5.7)

   ἀλλὰ γαμείτωσαν τεκνοποιείτωσαν οἰκοδεσποτείτωσαν (*Pan* 26.14.2)

   ἔλεγεν ὁ ἀπόστολος ταῖς χήραις·
   γαμείτωσαν τεκνογονείτωσαν οἰκοδεσποτείτωσαν (*Pan* 59.4.11)

   γαμείτωσαν, τοίνυν, τεκνοποιείτωσαν,[461] οἰκοδεσποτείτωσαν (*Pan* 61.7.1)

   τί οὖν φησιν;·
   ἀλλὰ γαμείτωσαν τεκνογονείτωσαν οἰκοδεσποτείτωσαν (*Pan* 67.6.8)

1 Timothy 5:19
   ὡς καὶ πάλιν λέγει·
   κατὰ πρεσβυτέρου[462] μὴ ταχέως κατηγορίαν δέχου,[463] εἰ μή τι ἐπὶ[464] δύο καὶ[465] τριῶν μαρτύρων (*Pan* 75.5.9)

---
[460] τό M Holl; *om* U.
[461] τεκνοποιείτωσαν M Holl; τεκνογονείτωσαν U.
[462] πρεσβυτέρου] πρεσβυτέρους L.

1 Timothy 6:1
καὶ·
ὑπὸ ζυγὸν δουλείας⁴⁶⁶ (*Pan* 75.3.6)

1 Timothy 6:10
καὶ ὁ ἀπόστολος λέγει·
ῥίζα πάντων τῶν⁴⁶⁷ κακῶν ἐστιν ἡ φιλαργυρία (*Pan* 66.69.4)

1 Timothy 6:16
οἰκῶν φῶς⁴⁶⁸ τὸ ἀπρόσιτον (*Anc* 70.5)

φῶς⁴⁶⁹ οἰκῶν τὸ ἀπρόσιτον (*Pan* 74.7.5; from *Anc*)

---

⁴⁶³ δέχου with 104] παραδέχου *rell.*
⁴⁶⁴ ἐπί] *om* F G it^{d.g.}.
⁴⁶⁵ καί with 1739] ἤ *rell.*
⁴⁶⁶ δουλείας] δούλου F G; δοῦλοι *rell.*
⁴⁶⁷ *om* τῶν D*.
⁴⁶⁸ οἰκῶν φῶς L^{epiph} J; φῶς εἰκῶν Holl.
⁴⁶⁹ *add* καὶ *ante* φῶς D* E* it, but Epiphanius should not be cited for the ommission as it occurs at the beginning of the citation.

2 Timothy 1:15
ὧν ἐστι Φύγελος καὶ Ἑρμογένης (Pan 40.8.5)

2 Timothy 2:5
ἐὰν γὰρ ἀθλῇ τις, οὐ στεφανοῦται, ἐὰν μὴ νομίμως ἀθλήσῃ (Pan 67.2.7)

2 Timothy 2:6
τὸν κοπιῶντα γεωργὸν δεῖ πρῶτον[470] τῶν καρπῶν μεταλαμβάνειν (Pan 80.5.5)

2 Timothy 2:7
νόει ὃ λέγω. δώσει γάρ σοι ὁ[471] κύριος σύνεσιν ἐν πᾶσιν (Pan 20.2.3)

---

a. ὃ λέγω   Epiph ℵ* A C F G P 33 1739 it^g Chr
b. ἃ λέγω   TR 𝔐 ℵ^c D K L 81 104 699 1594 it$^{d.e.f}$

---

a. δώσει   Epiph ℵ A C* D F G 33 1739 it$^{d.e.f.g}$
b. δῴη   TR 𝔐 C^c K L P 81 104 699 1594

---

2 Timothy 2:19
ἔγνω κύριος τοὺς ὄντας αὐτοῦ (Anc 20.9)

οὕτω καὶ ἐν τῇ θείᾳ γραφῇ·
ἔγνω κύριος τοὺς ὄντας[472] αὐτοῦ (Pan 69.46.7)

2 Timothy 3:1–2, 4
ἐν τῇ πρὸς Τιμόθεον ἐπιστολῇ ... λέγει ὅτι·
1) ἐν ἐσχάταις ἡμέραις ἐνστήσονται καιροὶ χαλεποί· 2) ἔσονται γὰρ[473] οἱ ἄνθρωποι, 4) φιλήδονοι (Pan 26.16.3)

1) ἐν[474] ἐσχάταις ἡμέραις ἐνστήσονται καιροὶ χαλεποί (Pan 48.8.6)

---

[470] πρῶτον] πρωότερον ℵ*.
[471] om ὁ 81.
[472] τοὺς ὄντας] πάντας τοὺς ὄντας ℵ*.
[473] om γάρ 104.
[474] add ταῖς P.

2 Timothy 3:5
μόρφωσιν μόνον κεκτημένοι, τὴν δὲ δύναμιν αὐτῆς τῆς εὐσεβείας ἠρνημένοι (*Pan* 47.3.1)

2 Timothy 3:6
τὸ σωρευόμενον ἁμαρτήμασι καὶ ἀγόμενον ἐπιθυμίαις[475] ποικίλαις (*Pan* 26.11.9)

2 Timothy 3:15
διὸ ... Τιμοθέῳ γράφων ἔλεγεν·
ὅτι ἀπὸ νεότητος ἱερὰ γράμματα ἔμαθες[476] (*Pan* 42.12.3 refut. 21)

2 Timothy 4:4
ἣν οἱ πολλοὶ ἀφέντες εἰς μύθους καὶ εἰς μωρολογίας ἐξετράπησαν (*Pan* 40.8.4)

2 Timothy 4:10
λέγει ἐν ταῖς αὐτοῦ ἐπιστολαῖς ὁ αὐτὸς Παῦλος·
Κρήσκης, φησίν, ἐν τῇ Γαλλίᾳ· οὐ γὰρ ἐν τῇ Γαλατίᾳ, ὥς τινες πλανηθέντες νομίζουσιν, ἀλλὰ ἐν τῇ Γαλλίᾳ (*Pan* 51.11.7)

---

a. Γαλλίαν   Epiph ℵ C 81 104 Euseb
b. Γαλατίαν TR 𝔐 A D F G K L P 33 699 1594 1739 it[d.e.f.g]

---

[475] ἐπιθυμίαις καὶ ἡδόναις A syr[h].
[476] ἔμαθες] οἶδες D E; οἶδας *rell*. Due to the looseness of this allusion, one cannot know whether Epiphanius' exemplar read ἱερά with ℵ C[c] D* F G 33 or τὰ ἱερά with TR 𝔐 A C* D[c] K L P 81 104 699 1594 1739.

Titus 1:12
καὶ·

Κρῆτες ἀεὶ ψεῦσται (*Anc* 77.2)

καὶ πάλιν φήσαντος·
εἶπέν[477] τις[478] ἴδιος αὐτῶν[479] προφήτης· Κρῆτες ἀεὶ ψεῦσται, κακὰ θηρία, γαστέρες[480] ἀργαί (*Pan* 42.12.3 *refut.* 21)

Titus 2:10–13
ἤ·
10) ἵνα τὴν διδασκαλίαν τοῦ σωτῆρος[481] ἡμῶν θεοῦ κοσμήσωσιν,[482] 11) ἤ· ἐπεφάνη ἡ χάρις τοῦ θεου καὶ σωτῆρος πᾶσιν ἀνθρώποις, 12) παιδεύουσα ἡμᾶς, 13) ἤ· προσδεχόμενοι τὴν μακαρίαν ἐλπίδα καὶ ἐπιφάνειαν τῆς δόξης τοῦ κυρίου καὶ σωτῆρος ἡμῶν Ἰησοῦ Χριστοῦ (*Anc* 69.9)

ἤ·
10) ἵνα τὴν διδασκαλίαν τοῦ σωτῆρος ἡμῶν κοσμήσωσιν, 11) ἤ· ἐπεφάνη ἡ χάρις τοῦ θεοῦ καὶ σωτῆρος[483] πᾶσιν ἀνθρώποις, 12) διδάσκουσα ἡμᾶς, 13) ἤ· δεχόμενοι τὴν μακαρίαν ἐλπίδα καὶ ἐπιφάνειαν τῆς δόξης τοῦ μεγάλου θεοῦ καὶ σωτῆρος ἡμῶν Ἰησοῦ Χριστοῦ (*Pan* 74.6.9; from *Anc*)

10)_____

   a. τὴν διδασκαλίαν Epiph TR 𝔐 K L P 104 699 1594 1739
   b. τὴν διδασκαλίαν τήν ℵ A C D F G 33 81 Chr

---

[477] As the initial portion of this citation is less than verbally exact, one cannot be certain that Epiphanius' exemplar read εἶπεν with TR 𝔐 ℵ^c A C D K L P 33 104 699 1594 1739 rather than εἶπεν δέ with ℵ* F G 81 it^f.g. This is easily seen below in Epiphanius' citations of Tit 2:11, where γάρ occurs at the beginning of the citation in *Anc* 65.1, but is omitted when Epiphanius copies that portion of *Anc* into *Pan* 74.2.1.

[478] τις with 1739] τις ἐξ *rell.*

[479] αὐτῶν] *om* F G.

[480] γαστέρες] γαστέραις 1594.

[481] Text Holl] πατρός L^epiph J.

[482] Text Holl] κοσμήσωμεν L^epiph J; κοσμῶσιν ἐν πάσιν *rell.*

[483] σωτῆρος with ℵ* (*add* ἡμῶν F G)] σωτηρίος *rell.*

Titus 2:11–14

11) ἐπεφάνη γὰρ ἡ χάρις τοῦ κυρίου ἡμῶν καὶ σωτῆρος, 12) διδάσκουσα ἡμᾶς, ἵνα ἀρνησάμενοι τὴν ἀσέβειαν καὶ τὰς κοσμικὰς ἐπιθυμίας σωφρόνως καὶ εὐσεβῶς καὶ δικαίως ζήσωμεν ἐν τῷ νῦν αἰῶνι, 13) προσδεχόμενοι τὴν μακαρίαν ἐλπίδα καὶ ἐπιφάνειαν τῆς δόξης τοῦ μεγάλου θεοῦ καὶ σωτῆρος ἡμῶν Ἰησοῦ Χριστοῦ· 14) ὃς ἔδωκεν ἑαυτὸν ὑπὲρ ἡμῶν, ἵνα λυτρώσηται ἡμᾶς ἀπὸ πάσης ἀνομίας, καὶ καθαρίσῃ ἑαυτῷ λαὸν περιούσιον, ζηλωτὴν καλῶν ἔργων (*Anc* 65.1)

11) ἐπεφάνη[484] ἡ χάρις τοῦ κυρίου ἡμῶν Ἰησοῦ Χριστοῦ 12) διδάσκουσα ἡμᾶς, ἵνα ἀρνησάμενοι τὴν ἀσέβειαν καὶ τὰς[485] κοσμικὰς ἐπιθυμίας σωφρόνως καὶ εὐσεβῶς καὶ δικαίως ζήσωμεν ἐν τῷ νῦν αἰῶνι, 13) προσδεχόμενοι τὴν μακαρίαν ἐλπίδα καὶ[486] ἐπιφάνειαν τῆς δόξης τοῦ μεγάλου θεοῦ καὶ σωτῆρος ἡμῶν Ἰησοῦ Χριστοῦ· 14) ὃς ἔδωκεν ἑαυτὸν ὑπὲρ ἡμῶν,[487] ἵνα λυτρώσηται[488] ἡμᾶς ἀπὸ πάσης ἀνομίας, καὶ καθαρίσῃ ἑαυτῷ λαὸν περιούσιον, ζηλωτὴν καλῶν ἔργων (*Pan* 74.2.1; from *Anc*)

13)_____

    a. Ἰησοῦ Χριστοῦ Epiph TR 𝔐 ℵ^c A C D K L P 33 81 104 699 1594 it$^{d.e.f}$ CyrJer
    b. Χριστοῦ Ἰησοῦ ℵ* F G it^g
    c. Ἰησοῦ 1739

---

[484] Text J with 104] incl. γὰρ *rell*.
[485] τάς] *om* D* 1739.
[486] *add* τήν 33.
[487] ἑαυτὸν ὑπὲρ ἡμῶν] αὐτὸν ὑπὲρ ἡμῶν ℵ*; ὑπὲρ ἡμῶν ἑαυτόν D it$^{d.e}$.
[488] λυτρώσηται] λυτρώσεται P.

Philemon 1
    ὡς ἂν εἴποι·
    Παῦλος δέσμιος Ἰησοῦ Χριστοῦ (*Anc* 68.8)

    ὡς ἂν εἴποι·
    Παῦλος δέσμιος[489] Ἰησοῦ Χριστοῦ (*Pan* 74.5.8; from *Anc*)

---

  a. Ἰησοῦ Χριστοῦ Epiph D* L 699 1739
  b. Χριστοῦ Ἰησοῦ TR 𝔐 ℵ A D^c F G K P 33 81 104 1594

---

[489] δέσμιος] ἀπόστολος D* it^{d.e}.

Hebrews 1:3
ἀπαύγασμα τῆς δόξης, ὁ χαρακτὴρ τῆς ὑποστάσεως[490] (*Anc* 19.1)

ἀπαύγασμα τῆς δόξης καὶ χαρακτὴρ τῆς ὑποστάσεως αὐτοῦ (*Pan* 69.72.2)

Hebrews 1:6
ὡς ἡ γραφὴ λέγει περὶ αὐτοῦ ὅτι·
ὅταν εἰσαγάγῃ τὸν πρωτότοκον εἰς τὴν οἰκουμένην, λέγουσα, καὶ προσκυνησάτωσαν αὐτῷ πάντες ἄγγελοι θεοῦ (*Pan* 69.75.6)

Hebrews 1:14
ἀλλὰ· λειτουργικὰ πνεύματα εἰς διακονίαν[491] ἀποστελλόμενα[492] διὰ τοὺς μέλλοντας κληρονομεῖν σωτηρίαν (*Pan* 40.4.2)

Hebrews 2:9
καὶ ... τοῦ ἀποστόλου ἐνταῦθα πάλιν εἴρηκε·
τὸν δὲ βραχύ τι παρ' ἀγγέλους ἠλαττωμένον βλέπομεν Ἰησοῦν διὰ τὸ πάθημα τοῦ θανάτου δόξῃ καὶ τιμῇ ἐστεφανωμένον (*Pan* 69.38.3)

Hebrews 2:11
ἵνα ὑπὲρ ἡμῶν ὁ ἰφ' ἡμῶν γενόμενος προσφορὰ τῷ ἰδίῳ πατρὶ θεῷ τοὺς μαθητὰς <u>ἀδελφοὺς καλέσῃ</u> (*Anc* 41.6)

Hebrews 2:14
καταργήσῃ δὲ τὸν τὸ κράτος ἔχοντα τοῦ θανάτου τουτέστι τὸν διάβολον (*Pan* 69.62.6)

Hebrews 3:1–2
πῶς οὖν γέγραπται·
1) δέξασθε τὸν <u>ἀρχιερέα τῆς ὁμολογίας ἡμῶν</u>, 2) πιστὸν ὄντα τῷ ποιήσαντι αὐτόν (*Anc* 41.1)

1) δέξασθε, γάρ, τὸν ἀρχιερέα, 2) πιστὸν ὄντα τῷ ποιήσαντι αὐτόν (*Anc* 41.6)

---

[490] Epiphanius' omission of αὐτοῦ after ὑποστάσεως is not in agreement with 0121, as in this loose citation the "omission" occurs at the end. The verbally precise citation in *Pan* 69.72.2 includes αὐτοῦ.

[491] διακονίαν] διακονίας B.

[492] ἀποστελλόμενα] ἀποστελλόμενοι 104.

Hebrews 3:1–2, cont.
τὸ ἐν τῷ ἀποστόλῳ γεγραμμένον τό·
1) δέδασθαι τὸν ἀρχιερέα τῆς ὁμολογίας ἡμῶν, 2) πιστὸν ὄντα τῷ ποιήσαντι αὐτόν (*Pan* 69.14.2)

φασὶ τοῦτο τὸ ῥητὸν παρερμηνεύοντες τό·
1) δέξασθε τὸν ἀρχιερέα ὑμῶν, 2) πιστὸν ὄντα τῷ ποιήσαντι αὐτόν (*Pan* 69.37.1)

2) δῆθεν ἀπὸ τοῦ εἰρημένου ὅτι·
πιστὸν ὄντα τῷ ποιήσαντι αὐτόν (*Pan* 69.37.2)

Hebrews 4:12–13
λέγοντος τοῦ ἀποστόλου ὅτι·
12) ζῶν ὁ λόγος τοῦ θεοῦ καὶ ἐνεργὴς καὶ τομώτερος ὑπὲρ πᾶσαν μάχαιραν δίστομον καὶ διϊκνούμενος ἄχρι μερισμῶν ψυχῆς (*Anc* 56.1)

12) <u>τῇ ὑπὲρ πᾶσαν μάχαιραν δίστομον καὶ διϊκνουμένῃ ἄχρι μερισμῶν ψυχῆς καὶ πνεύματος, ἁρμῶν τε καὶ μυελῶν</u> κατὰ τὸ γεγραμμένον (*Pan* 42.15.3)

12) ζῶν γὰρ ὁ λόγος (*Pan* 54.5.4)

12) ζῶν γὰρ ἐστιν ὁ λόγος καὶ ἐνεργὴς καὶ τομώτερος ὑπὲρ πᾶσαν μάχαιραν δίστομον (*Pan* 69.59.9)

φησὶ γὰρ ὁ ἀπόστολος·
12) ζῶν γὰρ ὁ λόγος τοῦ θεοῦ καὶ ἐνεργὴς καὶ τομώτερος ὑπὲρ πᾶσαν μάχαιραν δίστομον, καὶ διϊκνούμενος μέχρι μερισμοῦ ψυχῆς καὶ μυελῶν, καὶ κριτικὸς ἐνθυμήσεων[493] καὶ ἐννοιῶν. 13) καὶ οὐκ ἔστι κτίσις ἀφανὴς ἐνώπιον αὐτοῦ (*Pan* 70.4.4)

12)_____

    a. ψυχῆς Epiph 𝔓⁴⁶ ℵ A B C L P 33 81 104 1739 Or Euseb
    b. ψυχῆς τε TR 𝔐 D K 699 1594

Hebrews 4:15
ὡς γέγραπται·
πεπειραμένος κατὰ πάντα ὡς ἄνθρωπος, χωρὶς ἁμαρτίας (*Pan* 69.25.8)

---

[493] ἐνθυμήσεων] ἐνθυμήσεως C* D* it^{d.e}.

Hebrews 4:15, cont.
τὸ εἰρημένον·
πεπειραμένος[494] κατὰ πάντα ὡς ἄνθρωπος, χωρὶς ἁμαρτίας (*Pan* 77.17.2)

πεπειραμένος κατὰ πάντα ὡς ἄνθρωπος, χωρὶς ἁμαρτίας (*Pan* 77.27.2)

Hebrews 5:1–2
1) <u>πᾶς γὰρ ἱερεὺς ἀπὸ ἀνθρώπων λαμβανόμενος ὑπὲρ ἀνθρώπων καθίσταται</u> κατὰ τὸ γεγραμμένον (*Anc* 93.2)

1) φάσκει . . . ὅτι·
πᾶς ἀρχιερεὺς ἐξ ἀνθρώπων λαμβανόμενος ὑπὲρ ἀνθρώπων καθίσταται, εἰς τὸ προσφέρειν δῶρά ⁻ε[495] καὶ θυσίας, 2) δυνάμενος μετριοπαθεῖν (*Pan* 69.37.6)

1) ὁ ἀπόστολός φησι·
πᾶς γὰρ ἀρχιερεὺς ἐξ ἀνθρώπων λαμβανόμενος τὰ ὑπὲρ[496] ἀνθρώπων καθίσταται, εἰς τὸ προσφέρειν δῶρα καὶ θυσίας (*Anc* 41.5)

Hebrews 5:6
<u>ἱερεύς</u> τοίνυν, ὡς ἔφην, ὁ κύριος ἡμῶν Ἰησοῦς Χριστός <u>εἰς τὸν αἰῶνα κατὰ τὴν τάξιν Μελχισεδέκ</u>[497] (*Pan* 29.4.5)

Hebrews 5:7
καὶ πάλιν·
ὅς[498] ἐν ταῖς ἡμέραις τῆς σαρκὸς αὐτοῦ δεήσεις καὶ ἱκεσίας ἐποιεῖτο, φησί, πρὸς τὸν δυνάμενον αὐτὸν σῶσαι[499] (*Pan* 55.9.15)

Hebrews 6:2
<u>ἐπιθέσεως</u>[500] <u>χειρῶν</u>, κατὰ τὸ γεγραμμένον (*Pan* 77.38.4)

---

[494] In this loose allusion, it is unclear whether Epiphanius' exemplar actually read πεπειραμένον with TR 𝔐 C K L P 33 104 699 1594 or πεπειρασμένον with 𝔓⁴⁶ ℵ A B D 1739.

[495] It is uncertain whether Epiphanius read τε after δῶρα with 𝔐 or omitted it with 𝔓⁴⁶ B.

[496] ὑπέρ] περί 𝔓⁴⁵.

[497] This citation from Psa. 109:4 occurs later in Heb 7:17.

[498] add ὦν D*.

[499] σῶσαι] σώζειν αὐτόν *rell*.

[500] *om* τε with 6| *add* τε *rell*.

Hebrews 6:4–8

τὸ ῥητὸν τοῦ ἀποστόλου τὸ εἰρημένον·
4) ἀδύνατον γὰρ τοὺς ἅπαξ φωτισθέντας, 5) καὶ καλὸν γευσα-μένους[501] θεοῦ ῥῆμα[502] δυνάμεις[503] τε τοῦ μέλλοντος αἰῶνος 6) καὶ

παραπεσόντας[504] πάλιν ἀνακαινίζειν εἰς μετάνοιαν, ἀνασταυροῦντας ἑαυτοῖς τὸν υἱὸν τοῦ θεοῦ καὶ παραδειγματίζοντας,[505] 7) γῆ γὰρ ἡ πιοῦσα πολλάκις[506] τὸν ἐπ᾽ αὐτῆς ἐρχόμενον ὑετὸν καὶ τίκτουσα βοτάνην εὔθετον ἐκείνοις, δι᾽ οὓς καὶ[507] γεωργεῖται, μεταλαμβάνει εὐλογίας· 8) ἐκφέρουσα δὲ ἀκάνθας καὶ τριβόλους ἀδόκιμος καὶ[508] κατάρας ἐγγύς, ἧς τὸ τέλος εἰς καῦσιν (Pan 59.2.1–2)

Hebrews 6:9–10

ὁ ἅγιος ἀπόστολος ... φησι·
9) πεπείσμεθα δὲ[509] περὶ ὑμῶν, ἀγαπητοί,[510] τὰ κρείττονα καὶ ἐχόμενα σωτηρίας, εἰ καὶ οὕτως λαλοῦμεν. 10) οὐ γὰρ ἄδικος ὁ θεὸς ἐπιλαθέσθαι τοῦ ἀγαθοῦ ἔργου ὑμῶν (Pan 59.2.4)

Hebrews 7:3

φασιν ὅτι ἀμήτωρ, ἀπάτωρ,[511] ἀγενεαλόγητος ἐκ τῆς πρὸς Ἑβραίους τοῦ ἁγίου Παύλου ἐπιστολῆς (Pan 55.1.4)

εὑρίσκεται δὲ εὐθὺς λέγων·
ἀφομοιούμενος τῷ υἱῷ τοῦ θεοῦ μένει ἱερεὺς εἰς τὸ διηνεκές (Pan 55.1.7)

ἀφομοιούμενος, φησί, τῷ υἱῷ τοῦ θεοῦ μένει ἱερεὺς εἰς τὸ διηνεκές (Pan 55.5.2)

ὡς ἔχει ἡ θεία γραφὴ ὅτι·
ἀφομοιούμενος τῷ υἱῷ τοῦ θεοῦ μένει ἱερεὺς εἰς τὸ διηνεκές (Pan 55.7.4)

---

[501] Haplography has resulted in an abbreviated text.
[502] θεοῦ ῥῆμα] ῥῆμα θεοῦ P.
[503] δυνάμεις] δύναμις 𝔓⁴⁶.
[504] παραπεσόντας] παραπεσόντος D*.
[505] παραδειγματίζοντας] παραδειγματίζοντες D.
[506] M Holl; πολλάκις post ἐπ᾽ αὐτῆς U.
[507] καί] om D* it^{d.e.f.}.
[508] U Holl; om ἀδόκιμος καί M.
[509] U Holl; om δέ M.
[510] ἀγαπητοί] ἀδελφοί ℵ*.
[511] ἀμήτωρ, ἀπάτωρ U Holl with 𝔐; ἀπάτωρ, ἀμήτωρ M.

Hebrews 7:3, cont.
μένει ἱερεὺς εἰς τὸ διηνεκές (*Pan* 67.3.2)

φησὶν ὁ ἀπόστολος·
ἀπάτωρ ἀμήτωρ ἀγενεαλόγητος (*Pan* 67.3.3)

ἀφωμοιωμένος δὲ τῷ υἱῷ τοῦ θεοῦ μένει ἱερεὺς εἰς τὸ διηνεκές (*Pan* 67.3.3)

τὸ εἰρημένον·
ἀφωμοιωμένος τῷ υἱῷ τοῦ θεοῦ μένει ἱερεὺς εἰς τὸ διηνεκές (*Pan* 67.3.5)

καὶ τῷ εἰπεῖν·
ἀφωμοιωμένος τῷ υἱῷ τοῦ θεοῦ μένει ἱερεὺς εἰς τὸ διηνεκές (*Pan* 67.7.2)

<u>ἀρχὴν ἡμερῶν</u> κατὰ τὸ γεγραμμένον (*Pan* 69.72.6)

Hebrews 7:6
φάσκει γὰρ οὕτως·
ὁ δὲ μὴ γενεαλογούμενος ἐξ αὐτῶν δεδεκάτωκε τὸν πατριάρχην (*Pan* 55.3.2)

τῷ ὄντι δὲ·
ὁ μὴ γενεαλογούμενος ἐξ αὐτῶν τὸν Ἀβραὰμ δεδεκάτωκεν (*Pan* 55.7.5)

ὁ ἅγιος ἀπόστολος . . . ἔφη·
<u>ὁ δὲ μὴ γενεαλογούμενος ἐξ αὐτῶν</u> (δῆλον δέ· ἀλλὰ εξ ἐτέρων) <u>δεδεκάτωκε τὸν Ἀβραά</u>_ (*Pan* 55.9.15)

ὁ ἀπόστολος . . . λέγων·
ὁ δὲ μὴ γενεαλογούμενος ἐξ αὐτῶν δεδεκάτωκε τὸν Ἀβραὰμ τὸν πατριάρχην (*Pan* 67.7.6)

---

a. τὸν Ἀβραάμ   Epiph ⁻R 𝔐 ℵᶜ A Dᶜ K L P 81 104 699 1594 1739
b. Ἀβραάμ   𝔓⁴⁶ ℵ* B C D* 33

Hebrews 7:12
μετατιθεμένης γάρ, φησι, τῆς ἱερωσύνης ἐξ ἀνάγκης καὶ νόμου[512] μετάθεσις γίνεται (*Pan* 77.38.5)

Hebrews 7:14
καὶ πάλιν ὁ ἀπόστολος·
δῆλον ὅτι ἐξ Ἰούδα ἀνατέταλκεν ὁ κύριος (*Pan* 66.63.13)

Hebrews 7:19
εἰ γάρ·
ὁ νόμος οὐδένα ἐτελείωσε (*Pan* 77.38.2)

Hebrews 8:13
καὶ τό·
πεπαλαιωμένον καὶ ἐγγὺς ἀφανισμοῦ γεγονός (*Anc* 94.5)

τοῦ ἀποστόλου λέγοντος ὅτι·
πᾶν τὸ παλαιούμενον καὶ γηράσκον ἐγγὺς ἀφανισμοῦ γίνεται (*Pan* 77.38.4)

Hebrews 9:17–19
καί φησι·
17) διαθήκη δὲ ἐπὶ νεκροῖς βεβαία ἐστί, 18) διὸ καὶ ἡ πρώτη ἄνευ αἵματος οὐκ ἐγένετο, 19) ἔλαβε γὰρ Μωυσῆς τὸ αἷμα τῶν τράγων καὶ ἐρράντισεν αὐτὸ τὸ βιβλίον καὶ τὸν λαόν (*Pan* 66.74.7)

Hebrews 10:12
ἀλλ᾽·
ἐκάθισεν ἐν δεξιᾷ τοῦ πατρός (*Anc* 81.8)

ἐκάθισεν ἐν δεξιᾷ[513] τοῦ πατρός (*Pan* 69.39.4)

καὶ πάλιν·
ἐκάθισεν ἐν δεξιᾷ τοῦ πατρός (*Pan* 69.75.6)

ἐκάθισεν ἐν δόξῃ ἐν δεξιᾷ τοῦ πατρός κατὰ τὸ γεγραμμένον (*Pan* 70.8.7)

---

[512] καὶ νόμου] *om* B.
[513] ἐν δεξιᾷ] ἐκ δεξιῶν A 104.

Hebrews 11:4–5
4) πρῶτον τὸ τοῦ "Αβελ αἷμα κηρύττει· μετὰ γὰρ τὸ ἀποθανεῖν ἔτι λαλεῖ,[514] ὥς φησιν ἡ γραφή, 5) 'Ενὼχ μετετέθη καὶ οὐχ ηὑρίσκετο καὶ οὐκ εἶδε θάνατον· εὐηρέστησε γὰρ τῷ θεῷ (*Anc* 94.4)

Hebrews 11:6
τῷ ἀποστόλῳ εἰρημένον, ὅτι·
δεῖ τὸν προσερχόμενον θεῷ πιστεύειν ὅτι ἔστι καὶ τοῖς ἀγαπῶσιν αὐτὸν μισθαποδότης γίνεται (*Pan* 70.6.4)

ὅτι·
πιστεύειν δεῖ τὸν προσερχόμενον θεῷ[515] ὅτι ἔστι καὶ τοῖς ἐκζητοῦσιν[516] αὐτὸν μισθαποδότης γίνεται (*Pan* 76.37.14)

ὅτι·
ἔστι καὶ τοῖς ἀγαπῶσιν αὐτὸν μισθαποδότης γίνεται (*Pan* 76.54.22)

Hebrews 11:25
ὡς Μωυσῆς;
μᾶλλον εἵλετο συγκακουχεῖσθαι τῷ λαῷ τοῦ θεοῦ ἤπερ ἀπολαύειν (*Pan* 80.5.2)

Hebrews 11:32
ὅρα τὸν ἀπόστολον λέγοντα περὶ ἀρχαίων προφητῶν·
ἐπιλείψει μοι ὁ χρόνος διηγουμένῳ περὶ[517] Γεδεών, Βαράκ, Σαμψών, 'Ιεφθάε, Δαυὶδ καὶ λοιπῶν προφητῶν[518] (*Pan* 66.81.7)

Hebrews 11:37–38
37) οἵτινες περιῆλθον ἐν μηλωταῖς, ἐν αἰγείοις δέρμασι, κακουχούμενοι στενοχωρούμενοι θλιβόμενοι, 38) ὧν οὐκ ἦν ἄξιος ὁ κόσμος (*Pan* 66.81.7)

---

[514] This citation is too loose to permit the conclusion that Epiphanius' exemplar read λαλεῖ with 𝔓⁴⁶ ℵ A P 33 81 104 1739 rather than λαλεῖται with TR 𝔐 D K L 699 1594.

[515] θεῷ with ℵ* Dᶜ 33] τῷ θεῷ rell.

[516] ἐκζητοῦσιν] ζητοῦσιν P.

[517] add δέ D*.

[518] As Epiphanius gives the gist of vv. 32, 37, 38, his lack of verbal precision makes it questionable whether his exemplar read Βαράκ with 𝔓⁴⁶ ℵ A 33 1739 itᶠ, Βαράκ τε with TR 𝔐 Dᶜ K L P 104 699 1594, or καὶ Βαράκ with D* itᵈ·ᵉ. It is similarly uncertain whether he read Σαμψών with 𝔓⁴⁶ ℵ A 33 1739 itᵈ·ᵉ·ᶠ or καὶ Σαμψών with TR 𝔐 D K L P 81 104 699 1594, and likewise 'Ιεφθάε with 𝔓⁴⁶ ℵ A 33 81 104 1739 or καὶ 'Ιεφθάε TR 𝔐 D K L P 699 1594.

Hebrews 12:13
κατὰ τὸ γεγραμμένον·
μὴ ἐκτραπῆναι τὸ χωλόν, ἰαθῆναι δὲ μᾶλλον (*Pan* 68.3.1)

Hebrews 12:14
ὅταν εἴπῃ ὅτι·
καὶ τὸν ἁγιασμὸν ὑμῶν, οὗ χωρὶς τὸν θεόν[519] οὐδεὶς ὄψεται (*Pan* 67.2.1)

Hebrews 12:21
ὡς ὁ Μωυσῆς φησιν·
ἔμφοβός εἰμι καὶ ἔντρομος (*Pan* 48.7.8)

Hebrews 13:4
εἶτα ὁ ἅγιος ἀπόστολος·
τίμιος ὁ γάμος[520] καὶ ἡ κοίτη ἀνίαντος (*Pan* 23.5.7)

λέγοντος·
τίμιος ὁ γάμος καὶ ἡ κοίτη ἀμίαντος, πόρνους δὲ καὶ μοιχοὺς κρινεῖ ὁ θεός (*Pan* 26.16.1)

καὶ τοῦ ἀποστόλου φάσκοντος·
τίμιος ὁ γάμος καὶ ἡ κοίτη ἀμίαντος (*Pan* 47.2.2)

τίμιος ὁ γάμος καὶ ἡ κοίτη ἀμίαντος (*Pan* 61.3.5)

πῶς ὁ ἀπόστολος ἔφη·
τίμιος ὁ γάμος καὶ ἡ κοίτη ἀμίαντος, πόρνους δὲ καὶ μοιχοὺς κρινεῖ ὁ θεός (*Pan* 67.2.2)

πῶς γὰρ οὐκ ἔσται <u>τίμιος ὁ γάμος</u> (*Pan* 67.6.4)

---

a. πόρνους δέ Epiph TR 𝔐 C D^c K L 33 104 699 1594 it^f Euseb
b. πόρνους γάρ 𝔓⁴⁶ ℵ A D* P 81 1739^{vid} it^d

Hebrews 13:5
ὧδε λέγων·
οὐ μή σε ἀνῶ, οὐδ' οὐ μή σε ἐγκαταλίπω[521] (*Pan* 69.66.1)

---

[519] θεόν with it^d] κύριον *rell.*
[520] V Holl; *add* ἐν πᾶσι M.
[521] ἐγκαταλίπω] ἐγκαταλείπω *rell.* See Deut 31:6.

Revelation 1:1
ὡς καὶ ὁ ἅγιος Ἰωάννης ἐν τῇ Ἀποκαλύψει ἔλεγε·
τάδε ἀπεκάλυψε κύριος τοῖς αὐτοῦ δούλοις διὰ τοῦ δούλου αὐτοῦ
Ἰωάννου, καί τάδε λέγει κύριος (*Pan* 48.10.1)

Revelation 1:8
ἐπείπερ ἔφη ὁ σω⁻ήρ·
ἐγώ εἰμι τὸ ᾱ καὶ[522] ἐγώ εἰμι τὸ ω̄ (*Pan* 51.20.3)

καὶ πάλιν φησὶν ἐν τῇ Ἀποκαλύψει·
ὁ ὢν ἀπ' ἀρχῆς καὶ ἐρχόμενος παντοκράτωρ (*Pan* 57.9.3)

φησίν· ἐγώ εἰμι τὸ ἄλφα καὶ τὸ ω̄ (*Pan* 62.7.8)

Revelation 2:6
φησιν·
ἔχεις δέ τι καλόν, ὅτι μισεῖς τὰ ἔργα τῶν Νικολαϊτῶν, ἃ[523] κἀγὼ μισῶ
(*Pan* 25.3.1)

Revelation 2:18–21
18) οὕτω γὰρ εὐθὺς διελέγχει ὁ κύριος ἐν τῇ Ἀποκαλύψει λέγων·
γράψον τῷ ἀγγέλῳ τῆς[524] ἐν Θυατείροις[525] ἐκκλησίας·[526] τάδε λέγει ὁ
ἔχων τοὺς ὀφθαλμοὺς αὐτοῦ[527] ὡς φλόγα[528] πυρὸς καὶ οἱ πόδες αὐτοῦ
ὅμοιοι χαλκολιβάνῳ· 19) οἶδά σου τὰ ἔργα καὶ τὴν πίστιν καὶ ἀγάπην
καὶ τὴν διακονίαν,[529] καὶ ὅτι τὰ ἔσχατά σου πλείονα τῶν πρώτον. 20)
ἔχω δὲ κατὰ σοῦ,[530] ὅτι ἀφεῖς[531] τὴν γυναῖκα[532] Ἰεζάβελ ἀπατᾶν τοὺς
δούλους μου, λέγουσαν[533] ἑαυτὴν[534] προφῆτιν,[535] διδάσκουσαν φαγεῖν
εἰδωλόθυτα[536] καὶ πορνεύειν.

---

[522] καί with ℵ*.
[523] ἅ] om A.
[524] τῆς with TR 𝔐 ℵ P] τῷ A syr^h; om C.
[525] Θυατείροις TR 𝔐 ℵ A C P] Θυατείρη B.
[526] ἐκκλησίας] om A.
[527] αὐτοῦ TR 𝔐 ℵ C P] om A.
[528] φλόγα TR 𝔐 A C P] φλόξ ℵ.
[529] καὶ τὴν διακονίαν] om ℵ*.
[530] add πολυ ℵ.
[531] ἀφεῖς] ἀφήκες ℵ^c; ἐᾶς TR.
[532] Text with TR ℵ C P] γυναῖκα σου 𝔐 046; add τήν A.
[533] τὴν λέγουσαν TR ℵ^c P; ἡ λέγουσα ℵ* A C; ἢ λέγει 𝔐 B.
[534] ἑαυτήν TR 𝔐 A C P] αὐτήν ℵ 046.
[535] προφῆτιν TR 𝔐 ℵ A C] προφήτην P.
[536] εἰδωλόθυτα φαγεῖν TR.

Revelation 2:18–21, cont.
21) καὶ ἔδωκα αὐτῇ χρόνον μετανοῆσαι καὶ οὐ θέλει[537] μετανοῆσαι ἐκ τῆς πορνείας αὐτῆς. (*Pan* 51.33.6–7)

Revelation 4:8
ἀλλὰ τρεῖς φωνὰς ἑνικάς, τὸ <u>ἅγιος ἅγιος ἅγιος</u>· . . . εἷς γάρ ἐστι θεός, πατὴρ ἐν υἱῷ, υἱὸς ἐν πατρὶ σὺν ἁγίῳ πνεύματι (*Anc* 10.3)

Revelation 9:14, 16–17
συνᾴδουσι γὰρ καὶ αὗται τῷ εὐαγγελίῳ καὶ τῇ Ἀποκαλύψει, καί φασιν ὅτι·
14) εἶδον, καὶ εἶπε τῷ ἀγγέλῳ· λῦσον τοὺς τέσσαρας ἀγγέλους τοὺς ἐπὶ τοῦ Εὐφράτου, 16) καὶ ἤκουσα τὸν ἀριθμὸν τοῦ στρατοῦ, μύριαι μυριάδες καὶ χίλιαι χιλιάδες 17) καὶ ἦσαν ἐνδεδυμένοι θώρακας πυρίνους καὶ θειώδεις καὶ ὑακινθίνους (*Pan* 51.34.1–2)

14) <u>λῦσον τοὺς τέσσαρας ἀγγέλους τοὺς ἐπὶ τοῦ Εὐφράτου</u>, ἐφισταμένους δηλονότι (*Pan* 51.34.6)

Revelation 22:2
διὸ καὶ ἐν ἀποκρύφοις ἀναγινώσκοντες ὅτι·
εἶδον δένδρον φέρον δώδεκα καρποὺς τοῦ ἐνιαυτοῦ καὶ εἶπέν μοι τοῦτό ἐστι τὸ ξύλον τῆς ζωῆς (*Pan* 26.5.1)

---

[537] καὶ οὐ θέλει 𝔐 A C P] οὐκ ἠθέλησεν A.

CHAPTER 3

METHODOLOGY OF TEXTUAL ANALYSIS

1. EARLIER APPROACHES TO TEXTUAL ANALYSIS

Indispensable to textual research is a sound method. Conclusions are determined by the data selected for use, as well as the principles that govern the study of those data. Proper procedures must be followed in order to ensure valid and trustworthy results. Several methodologies have been used in various textual researches in attempts to locate textual witnesses within the New Testament manuscript tradition.[1]

A. VARIANTS FROM THE *TEXTUS RECEPTUS*.

Studies of the texts of the Greek Fathers demonstrate textual relationships with evidence from the Greek manuscripts and the early versions. Many of these studies employed a secondary methodology based upon locating variants from the TR and analyzing them in terms of agreements with a large number of manuscripts whose readings are found in various *apparatus critici* of the Greek Testament. This method is described and advocated by Greenlee.[2] Since the text of the TR is Koine in character, those variants from it in a textual witness are expected to be mainly non-Koine readings. If the differences between the witness and the TR are relatively few, it is understood that the witness may safely be considered primarily Koine in character. On the other hand, if the witness varies frequently from the TR, its variants should then be examined to assess its affinities with non-Koine forms of the text.

---

[1] See Bart D. Ehrman, "Methodological Developments in the Analysis and Classification of New Testament Documentary Evidence," *NovT* 29 (1987): 22–45, for a survey of the history of textual analysis of the NT. See also Eldon J. Epp, *The New Testament and Its Modern Interpreters* (ed. E. Epp and G. MacRae; Atlanta: Scholars Press, 1989), 75–126.

[2] J. Harold Greenlee, *Introduction to New Testament Textual Criticism* (Grand Rapids: Eerdmans, 1964), 135–41, advocates the study of variants from the TR as a proper method of discovering the textual affinities of a witness, yet he recognizes that due consideration must be given to the variants with which the witness does not agree. See especially p. 141, and the revised edition (Peabody, Mass.: Hendrickson, 1995), 138–39.

Colwell noted that "the nineteenth century's battle with the TR fastened attention upon that text, and study of variation from it was a natural development."[3] The principal weakness of the method is that it omits a significant amount of evidence, especially readings that a witness has in common with the TR. An analysis in terms of differences from the TR is useless when adequate control is not used.[4] Fee notes correctly, "although this method might work accidentally—when a Father's text is particularly close to a given manuscript of text type—, it is especially inadequate in texts with an appreciable amount of 'mixture.'"[5] Metzger's criticism signaled the doom of this method.[6] He proposed an alternative:

> The proper method of determining the relation of a hitherto unknown manuscript to the Neutral, Western, Caesarean, and Byzantine families is not merely to count how many of its variants from the Textus Receptus (or from any given norm) agree with B ℵ D Θ W, etc. Such a procedure is indeed necessary and not uninstructive, but the only really satisfactory method is to reconstruct the text of each of the major families and to determine precisely what proportion of variants from the Textus Receptus in such a reconstructed text is also present in the manuscript to be analyzed.[7]

Fee's critique of the inadequacy of the method of analyzing variants from the TR, as illustrated from the text of John in Origen and Cyril of Alexandria, is equally instructive.[8] Should Epiphanius be in agreement

---

[3] E. C. Colwell, "The Significance of Grouping of New Testament Manuscripts," *NTS* 4 (1958): 90; repr. "Method in Grouping New Testament Manuscripts," in *Studies in Methodology in Textual Criticism of the New Testament* (NTTS 9; ed. B. Metzger; Leiden: Brill, 1969), 24.

[4] Bruce M. Metzger, *The Text of the New Testament: Its Transmission, Corruption, and Restoration* (3rd ed.; Oxford: Oxford University Press, 1992), 179.

[5] Gordon D. Fee, "The Text of John in Origen and Cyril of Alexandria: A Contribution to Methodology in the Recovery and Analysis of Patristic Citations," *Bib* 52 (1971): 364.

[6] Bruce Metzger, "The Caesarean Text of the Gospels," *JBL* 64 (1945): 488.

[7] Bruce Metzger, *Chapters in the History of N.T. Textual Criticism* (Grand Rapids: Eerdman's, 1963), 71–72.

[8] With reference to Cyril, Fee, *Biblica*, (1971), 365, states, "In this chapter his text varies from the TR 35 times, three of which are singular and one sub-singular (4, 37, word order with 579). In the remaining 31 his text has the following agreements: B 22, L 22, ℵ 21, D 19, Origen 18. However, by simply adding one other factor, one may see how totally misleading such 'agreements' are. Cyril's text has the following number of agreements *with the TR against these MSS.*: B 19, L 11, ℵ 46, D 35, Origen 18. This means that ultimately his text should

with the TR where the TR itself agrees with the papyri and/or non-Koine witnesses, but is in disagreement with the mass of Koine witnesses, one would erroneously assume his text to be in agreement with the Koine textual tradition. In this event, one would be led to overlook the truly significant textual data with which Epiphanius was in actual agreement.

B. HUTTON'S TRIPLE READINGS METHOD

Hutton proposed a "triple readings method"[9] based upon selecting variants that present at least three alternative readings, each of which has support from one of the three principal types of text (*i.e.*, "Western," Alexandrian, and Syrian [Byzantine]).[10] The affinities of a witness are known by the proportion of readings of each textual group supported by the witness in these passages. Hutton listed over 200 such passages and presented the readings of each of the three text types in them.[11]

Metzger observes, "with the multiplication of the number of identifiable textual groups, it is desirable to seek a higher degree of precision than Hutton's method permits."[12] The "triple reading" method limits the scope of usable evidence in the case of incomplete texts as are often found in patristic quotations. This criticism is significant in that Epiphanius' quotations from the Apostolos yield only a small number of passages with triple readings. This slight data is not substantial enough to peermit a valid assessment of the textual affinities of Epiphanius' quotations. The only apparent contribution of Hutton's method to textual criticism is that it later became the basis for the "multiple readings method" devised by Merrill Parvis and E. C. Colwell.[13]

---

be more like codex L than the others. But even these figures will not tell the whole story until the various agreements among these mss *vs.* Cyril and the TR are noted. The final absurdity of all this is that in the first set of figures, Origen has extant text only at 25 points of variation, so that apart from the giving of percentages even the number of agreements *vs.* TR is misleading." Fee states further that it is precisely this methodological failure which renders almost valueless a large proportion of the unpublished dissertations on the Father's texts, especially Zervopoulos' study of Athanasius, Linss' analysis of the text of Didymus, and the examination of the text of Cyril by Witherspoon. These three studies were done at Boston University, the first two in 1955 and the last in 1962.

[9] E. A. Hutton, *An Atlas of Textual Criticism* (Cambridge: Cambridge University Press, 1911).

[10] Hutton, *An Atlas of Textual Criticism*, 4.

[11] Hutton, *An Atlas of Textual Criticism*, 67–125.

[12] Metzger, *The Text of the New Testament*, 180.

[13] E. C. Colwell, "Method in Locating a Newly-Discovered Manuscript Within the Manuscript Tradition of the Greek New Testament," in Kurt Aland,

C. COLWELL'S MULTIPLE READINGS METHOD

A higher degree of precision than Hutton's method permits is desirable. Parvis and Colwell observed that classification of MSS in terms of how much they diverge from the TR is limited in scope, as this method does not consider instances in which MSS in readings in which they do not diverge from the TR. Parvis and Colwell advocate the collation of a number of MSS and establishing their relationships to one another in terms of percentages of agreement in all units of variation in which at least two MSS agree against the others. A textual group can be identified on the basis of agreement in genetically significant readings among several witnesses, regardless of relation to an external norm. Three steps are involved.

First, Parvis and Colwell proposed that "multiple readings" be employed, by which they mean a reading,

> in which the minimum support for each of at least three variant forms of the text is either one of the major strands of the tradition, or the support of a previously established group (such as Family 1, Family P, the Ferrar Group, K^1, K^i, K^r), or the support of some one of the ancient versions (such as af, it, sy^s, sy^c, bo, or sa), or the support of some single manuscript of an admittedly distinctive character (such as D).[14]

Second, they proposed evaluating the document's support for distinctive group readings, arguing, "a group is not a group unless it has unique elements."[15] Third, they argue that quantitative analysis is required, for "Members of a group must agree with one another in a large majority of the total number of existing variant readings."[16]

In collaboration with Ernest Tune,[17] Colwell refined his method of establishing quantitative relationships. Working with John 11, they

---

ed., *Studia Evangelica*, (TU 74; Berlin: Akademie-Verlag, 1959): 757–777 (see especially p. 759); repr. "Method in Locating a Newly-Discovered Manuscript," in Colwell, *Studies in Methodology in Textual Criticism of the New Testament*, 26–44.

[14] Colwell, *Studia Evangelica* (1959): 759.
[15] *Ibid.* 30.
[16] *Ibid.* 31.
[17] E. C. Colwell and Ernest W. Tune, "The Quantitative Relationships Between MS Text-Types," in *Biblical and Patristic Studies in Memory of Robert Pierce Casey* (ed. J. N. Birdsall and R. W. Thomson; Freiburg: Herder, 1963), 25–32; repr. "Method in Establishing Quantitative Relationships Between Text-Types of New Testament Manuscripts," in *Studies in Methodology in Textual Criticism of the New Testament*, 56–62.

worked to demonstrate the inter-relationships of the MSS by percentages of agreement in genetically significant readings. Colwell and Tune held that group members normally agree in 70% or more of all readings, while maintaining a separation from non-group members by at least 10%. Of Colwell's three steps, only his emphasis upon the quantitative relationships of MSS has influenced current textual theory.

Colwell's method was used by Fee[18] in his investigation of $\mathfrak{P}^{66}$, who insisted that variations be weighed after counting rather than before. Of genetically-significant units of variation. Fee says,

> Genetic relationships must ultimately be built upon firmer ground than on agreements, for example, in the addition / omission of articles, possessives, conjunctions, or the tense change of verbs (usually), or certain kinds of word order, or in many instances of harmonization.[19]

Hurtado[20] used Fee's procedure in his study of Codex Washingtonianus, and concluded that there is no Pre-Caesarean text in the gospel of Mark. Richards'[21] followed this suggestion in his study of the Johannine Epistles, and it was used also in Osburn's[22] study of the Pauline Epistles in Hippolytus and Ehrman's[23] study of the Gospels in Didymus.

Textual research has relied upon "leading" representatives of the various textual groups whose claim to inclusion are based upon analyses

---

[18] Gordon D. Fee, *Papyrus Bodmer II ($\mathfrak{P}^{66}$): Its Textual Relationships and Scribal Characteristics* (SD 34; Salt Lake City: University of Utah Press, 1968). Fee advocated the procedure in his "Codex Sinaiticus in the Gospel of John: A Contribution to Methodology in Establishing Textual Relationships," *NTS* 15 (1968): 23–44, and *idem*, "The Text of John in Origen and Cyril of Alexandria: A Contribution to Methodology in the Recovery and Analysis of Patristic Citations," *Bib* 52 (1971): 357–94.

[19] Gordon D. Fee, "On the Types, Classification, and Presentation in Textual Variation," in *Studies in the Theory and Method of New Testament Textual Criticism* (SD 45; ed. E. Epp and G. Fee: Grand Rapids: Eerdmans, 1993), 67–68. This point was made earlier by Bruce M. Metzger, "The Caesarean Text of the Gospels," *JBL* 64 (1945): 489; repr. *Chapters in the History of New Testament Textual Criticism* (Leiden: Brill, 1963), 42–72.

[20] Larry Hurtado, *Text-Critical Methodology and the Pre-Caesarean Text* (Grand Rapids: Eerdmans, 1981).

[21] W. Larry Richards, *The Classification of the Greek Manuscripts of the Johannine Epistles* (SBLDS 35; Missoula, Mont.: Scholars Press, 1977)

[22] Carroll D. Osburn, 'The Text of the Pauline Epistles in Hippolytus of Rome," *SecC* 2 (1982): 97–124.

[23] Bart D. Ehrman, *Didymus the Blind and the Text of the Gospels* (SBLNTGF 1; Atlanta: Scholars Press, 1986).

other than the quantitative method.[24] Ehrman observed correctly, "The point is that the 'representative' witnesses themselves must be subjected to quantitative analyses before they can be *used* as representative witnesses."[25]

Further, Richards[26] concluded that it is not possible to posit a given percentage of agreement prior to an analysis. This means that Colwell and Tune's theory that MSS of the same group will agree in 70% or more of the genetically significant variation and will be separated from MSS of other groups by at least 10 % cannot be relied upon. Instead, textual groups will be found to have their own percentages of agreement that might not fit a preconceived norm.

2. RECENT APPROACHES TO ANALYSIS AND GROUPING OF MSS

It is clear that the quantitative method of analysis is, in itself, inadequate for analyzing textual relationships. The need exists to classify NT MSS by determining their proportional relationship to individual witnesses of established textual groups (the quantitative analysis portion of the task), but also to consider their attestation of characteristic group readings. A step in this direction was Fee's[27] work on Origen and Cyril, in which he attempted to classify all variant readings according to different combinations of group witnesses. Osburn used this procedure in his study of Hippolytus,[28] although Ehrman[29] misunderstood him to be using Hutton's "triple readings" method. Fee's profile method was useful, but not directly applicable to other research.

A. THE CLAREMONT PROFILE METHOD

Paul McReynolds and Frederick Wisse, in Ph.D. dissertations written under the supervision of Colwell at Claremont, developed

---

[24] These groupings of witnesses are those of Metzger, *Text of the New Testament*, 213–16; M.-J. Lagrange, *Introduction a l'etude du nouveau testament*, 2. *critique textuelle*: 466–87; and Greenlee, *Introduction to New Testament Textual Criticism*, 118.

[25] Ehrman, "Methodological Developments," *NovT* (1987): 40.

[26] Richards, *Classification of the Greek Manuscripts of the Johannine Epistles*, 43–129, concluded that Byzantine MSS tend to agree in about 90% of variation, while Alexandrian MSS agreed in about 70% of variation.

[27] Fee, "Text of John in Origen and Cyril," *Bib* 52 (1971): 357–94.

[28] Osburn, "Pauline Epistles in Hippolytus," *SecC* (1982): 97–124.

[29] Ehrman, "Methodological Developments," *NovT* (1987): 42, n. 68.

another method of grouping NT MSS.³⁰ The Claremont Profile Method assesses manuscripts in terms of selected test readings in sample portions of a given NT book. McReynolds and Wisse were searching for representative MSS in von Soden's *Kappa* groups to be used in the extensive critical apparatus for the Gospel of Luke being prepared by the International Greek New Testament Project.³¹ In the Claremont Profile Method, patterns of readings are not based upon the determination of distinctive readings for each group, but on the identification of characteristic readings for each group. In this way, each group reveals a particular pattern of variations formed by readings that are characteristic of, but not necessarily distinctive to, the group.

Although the method proved useful for the rapid classification of manuscripts as Byzantine, it has certain inadequacies. One significant problem is in the inability of the method to detect block mixture within a MS. That is to say, when McReynolds and Wisse analyze profiles drawn from chapters 1, 10, and 20 of Luke, they could recognize a change in textual affinity between chapters 1 and 10 and between chapters 11 and 20. However, if textual affinity changes within a block of text within chapters 2–9 or 11–19 or 21–24, that change would go undetected. A second criticism of the Claremont Profile Method is that it leads to incorrect pairings, e.g. Codex Bezae and Codex Vaticanus.³²

B. THE ALAND'S FIVE CATEGORIES

Kurt and Barbara Aland assign MSS to one of five categories they have developed on the basis of 1,000 test passages in which the Byzantine text differs from that of non-Byzantine MSS.³³ In *Text und*

---

[30] See E. J. Epp, "The Claremont Profile-Method for Grouping New Testament Minuscule Manuscripts," in *Studies in the History and Text of the New Testament* (ed. B. Daniels and M. J. Suggs; SD 29; Salt Lake City: University of Utah Press, 1967), 27–38; and Frederick Wisse, *The Profile Method for Classification and Evaluation of Manuscript Evidence* (SD 44; Grand Rapids: Eerdmans, 1982). See also O. M. Kvalheim *et al.*, "A Data-Analytical Examination of the Claremont Profile Method for Classifying and Evaluating Manuscript Evidence," *Symbolae Osloenses*, 63 (1988): 133–44.

[31] See now *The New Testament in Greek: The Gospel According to St. Luke. Part One: Chapters 1–12; Part Two: Chapters 13–24* (Oxford: Clarendon Press, 1984, 1987).

[32] Frederik Wisse, *The Profile Method for Classification and Evaluation of Manuscript Evidence* (SD 44; Grand Rapids: Eerdmans, 1982), 119.

[33] Kurt Aland and Barbara Aland, *The Text of the New Testament* (2nd ed.; trans. E. Rhodes; Grand Rapids: Eerdmans, 1989), 317–37.

Textwert der griechischen Handschriften,[34] the Aland's include data from 1000 test passages. On this basis, the five categories are:[35]

I — MSS with a very high proportion of the early text, presumably the original text, which has not been preserved in its purity in any one manuscript. To this category are assigned all MSS to the beginning of the fourth century, regardless of further distinctions.

II — MSS with a considerable proportion of the early text, but which are marked by alien influences, e.g., smoother readings.

III — MSS with a small but not a negligible proportion of early readings, with a considerable encroachment of polished readings.

IV — MSS of the "Western" text.

V — MSS with a predominantly Byzantine text.

This classification has been criticized, however, for enabling text critics to arrive at conclusions that are, in fact, their presuppositions.[36]

3. PROBLEMS AND SOLUTIONS IN TEXTUAL ANALYSIS

A. THE IMPORTANCE OF FULL COLLATIONS

W. J. Elliott has cautioned correctly that, instead of falling into the trap of collecting selected evidence to fit a preconceived notion, textual scholars should quote individual manuscripts in full rather than

---

[34] Kurt Aland, *Text und Textwert der griechischen Handschriften des Neuen Testaments. I: Die Katholischen Briefe* (ANTF 9–11; Berlin: de Gruyter, 1987), vols. 1–3, includes 98 test passages in 540 MSS.

[35] See Kurt Aland and Barbara Aland, *The Text of the New Testament*, 317–37, esp. 335–36.

[36] Metzger, *The Text of the NT*, 290, states, "The Aland's system, furthermore, involves a procedural circularity, for the classifying of manuscripts in terms of how helpful they have been in determining the original text tells us nothing about their textual relations or characteristics." See also Bart Ehrman, "A Problem of Textual Circularity: The Alands on the Classification of New Testament Manuscripts," *Bib* 70 (1989): 377–88; and Eldon J. Epp, "New Testament Textual Criticism, Past, Present, and Future," *HTR* 82 (1989): 213–29.

cursorily or selectively. "It is," he says, "the detailed, word for word, evidence of the MSS themselves that our editors need."[37]

B. CRITIQUE AND LIMITATIONS OF STATISTICAL ANALYSIS

Jean Duplacy worked on methodological questions presented by the critical apparatus of Aland's *editio maior critica*.[38] Duplacy was interested in the selection of units of variation and their boundaries. The selection of units of variation must include truly significant variation units. If this is done rigorously, agreements between the different text forms can be detected with relative certainty. However, Duplacy observes that agreement between two forms of a text can vary greatly, even from one chapter to the next, and statistical data can be easily misleading. This means that provisional classification of a manuscript cannot be done without first taking into account the section of text used, the selection of units of variation and the choice of the forms of text used for comparison. Thus taxonomical grouping does not yield the desired conclusion unless rigorous controls have been brought to bear

For Duplacy, taxonomy has considerable value, but the careful selection of text forms is mandatory. Only certain MSS should be used for classifying forms of the text, and it is not always the most known MSS that should be used for this purpose. Rather than start with dubious family tree constructions of a half-century ago, data must be interpreted to see what textual groupings are needed.

C. UNITS OF VARIATION

In the *Festschrift* for G. D. Kilpatrick,[39] Eldon Epp sought to clarify the term "textual variant." The simplistic assumption that any reading that disagrees with another reading in the same unit of text is a "textual

---

[37] W. J. Elliott, "The Need for an Accurate and Comprehensive Collation of all Known Greek NT Manuscripts," *Studies in New Testament Language and Text* (NovTSupp 44; ed. J. K. Elliott; Leiden: Brill, 1976), 143.

[38] See Jean Duplacy, "Histoire des manuscrits et histoire du texte du Nouveau Testament," *NTS* 12 (1965): 124–39; idem, "Classification des états d'un texte, mathématiques et informatique: repères historiques et recherches méthodologiques," *RHT* 5 (1975): 249–309. Both articles are included in Jean Duplacy, *Études du critique textuelle du Nouveau Testament* (BETL, 78; Leuven: Leuven University Press, 1987), esp. 39–54, 193–257.

[39] Eldon J. Epp, "Toward the Clarification of the Term 'Textual Variant,'" in *Studies in New Testament Text and Language: Essays in Honour of George D. Kilpatrick* (ed. J. K. Elliott: Leiden: Brill, 1976), 152–173, reprinted in *Studies in the Theory and Method of New Testament Textual Criticism*, 47–61.

variant" will not suffice, he argues. Rather, Epp stresses, the term "textual variant" must mean *"significant* textual variant." Following the lead of Colwell and Tune,[40] Epp says, "a 'variation-unit' is not the same as a 'variant', for 'a variant . . . is one of the possible alternative readings which are found in a variation-unit.'" He concludes, "In New Testament textual criticism, *a variation unit is that segment of text where our Greek manuscripts present at least two variant forms and where, after insignificant readings have been excluded, each variant form has the support of at least two manuscripts*" (157). Insignificant readings include nonsense readings, demonstrable scribal errors, orthographic differences and singular readings. Significant readings, then, are those variation-units of genuine usefulness in the text critical enterprise.

D. EVALUATION OF READINGS

In a paper read in 1974, but not published until 1993, Gordon Fee[41] addressed the concept of textual variation as it relates to the quantitative analysis of textual variants. Accepting Colwell and Tune's understanding of "variation unit" and their caveat that "one scholar may subdivide what another scholar regards as a single unit,"[42] Fee notes,

> within one variation-unit where the elements of expression go together there is sometimes a second or a third set of variants which also belong together. That is, a single variation-unit may contain more than one set of variants, which are (or may be) genetically unrelated (63).

Fee observes that all variation is one of three kinds: add-omit, substitution, or word order. In some instances, any two or even three of these may occur in combination in any set of variants. He concludes,

> My experience is that a count of agreements in variation-units in itself will reveal clear patterns of relationships, while a count including sets of variants refines the details of agreements within major groups (66).

---

[40] E. C. Colwell and E. W. Tune, "Variant Readings: Classification and Use," *JBL* 83 (1964): 253–62; repr. "Method in Classifying and Evaluating Variant Readings," in Colwell, *Studies in Methodology in Textual Criticism of the New Testament*, 96–105.

[41] Gordon D. Fee, "On the Types, Classification, and Presentation of Textual Variation," *Studies in the Theory and Method of New Testament Textual Criticism*, 62–79.

[42] Colwell and Tune, "Variant Readings," *JBL* (1964): 255.

Whereas Colwell and Tune list nonsense readings, dislocated readings and singular readings as types of insignificant variant readings that need to be eliminated from textual analysis,[43] Fee adds orthographical and singular readings, as well as sub-singular readings, which he defines as, "non-genetic, accidental agreement in variation between two MSS which are not otherwise closely related" (66-67). Genetic relationships must be built, Fee argues, on firmer agreement than the addition/omission of articles, possessives, conjunctions, or the tense change of verbs (usually), or certain kinds of word order or harmonization.[44] On the other hand, he suggests that large addition/omission variants, certain kinds of substitutions, as well as several kinds of word order variants must be recognized as the genetically significant data from which to construct stemmata of textual relationships.

In terms of statistical analysis, Ehrman[45] notes Colwell's accepted norm that a group witness should agree in approximately 70% of all variation with other group members, and exhibit a ±10% disparity between groups. In his study of Didymus, however, available data did not fall within those figures. Consequently, Ehrman proposes that, in view of the special character of patristic citations that occur frequently but sporadically, the figures for patristic writers should be adjusted to ±65% with a 6–8% disparity between groups.

Additionally, Ehrman[46] proposes "to evaluate a MS's support of group readings only after its proportional relationship to individual representatives of the known textual groups has been established." This so-called "Comprehensive Profile Method" goes beyond the Claremont Profile Method in classifying MSS not only according to readings found extensively among members of the various textual groups, but also those occurring uniquely within each of the groups. Ehrman notes,

> all categories of group readings apply only to units of genetically significant variation in which two or more of the representative witnesses agree against the rest (478).

In his work on Didymus the Blind,[47] Ehrman found from a quantitative analysis that Didymus' text demonstrates Alexandrian tendencies, possibly even Early Alexandrian. However, Ehrman concludes that it is

---

[43] *Ibid.* 257.

[44] See also Metzger, "Caesarean Text of the Gospels," *JBL* (1945): 489

[45] Ehrman, *Didymus the Blind*, 202.

[46] Bart Ehrman, "The Use of Group Profiles for the Classification of New Testament Documentary Evidence," *JBL* 106 (1987): 465–86.

[47] Ehrman, *Didymus the Blind and the Text of the Gospels*, 223–53.

important to refrain from classifying Didymus as Early Alexandrian until an analysis of his characteristic group readings is completed. Ehrman uses three approaches to evaluate these group readings.

First, an "Inter-Group Profile" reckons a document's attestation of readings found among representative witnesses of only one of the known textual groups. In this connection, two sets of readings are noted: 1) those readings attested *mainly* in witnesses of only one group, which he calls "primary" readings, and 2) those attested *only* in witnesses of one group. This latter group of readings is divided into two sub-categories: 1) those attested by most group members, yet by no others, which he calls "distinctive" readings, and 2) those attested by at least two group members, but no others, which he calls "exclusive" readings.[48]

Second, an "Intra-Group Profile" reckons a document's support of readings among members of a given textual group, no matter how well they are supported by witnesses of other groups. Two sets of readings are noted: 1) those attested by *all* the representative witnesses of a group ("uniform" witnesses), and 2) those attested by at least *two-thirds* of these representative witnesses, ("predominant" readings). In order for a reading to be included in this "Intra-Group Profile" it must vary from at least one other reading that is also supported by at least two representatives from any group. This would tend to exclude instances of accidental agreement among otherwise unrelated MSS (481).

Third, a "Combination Profile" reckons a document's attestation of readings found uniformly or predominantly among representatives of a group (from the Intra-Group Profile), but in few or no other witnesses (as determined by the Inter-Group Profile).

4. THE METHOD OF ANALYSIS USED IN THIS STUDY

In order to secure trustworthy results, a sound method of analysis must be devised which can account adequately for all data that emerge.[49] A critical investigation of the text of the Apostolos in Epiphanius aimed at discovering the textual affinities of his biblical citations should involve statistical data, profiles, and analysis of specific readings.[50]

---

[48] Ehrman, "The Use of Group Profiles," *JBL* (1987): 478.

[49] Fee, "Text of John in Origen and Cyril," *Bib* (1971): 364.

[50] See on the limitations of statistical analysis in textual criticism, Günther Zuntz, *Text of the Epistles: A Disquisition Upon the Corpus Paulinum* (London: Oxford University Press, 1953), 58–60, and Duplacy, "Classification des états d'un texte, mathématiques et informatique," *RHT* (1975): 249–309.

A. STATISTICAL ANALYSIS OF EPIPHANIUS' CITATIONS

Statistical information alone is insufficient to establish adequately the textual affinities of a patristic writer such as Epiphanius. Such data can indicate general trends and provide a *point d' appui* for the detailed examination and analysis of specific readings that have significant claim to be more than loose citations or adaptations. A preliminary quantitative analysis of the data presented in Chapter Three should provide a general indication of textual affinity.

B. PROFILE ANALYSIS OF EPIPHANIUS' CITATIONS

Initially, Romans was analyzed following Ehrman's constructive lead in profile analysis. In the inter-group readings, Epiphanius agreement with the Egyptian text was 50%, Byzantine 63.6% and "Western" only 21.7%. However, in the intra-group readings, the Egyptian was 92.3%, while Byzantine was only 65.0%, and the "Western" only 29.6%. The significant rise in support for the Egyptian text raised the question of why the Egyptian was so low in the inter-group readings, yet the Byzantine remained the same in both profiles. The combination profile showed the same difficulties as the inter-group profile.

The 40% variance in the Egyptian analysis required explanation. Splitting the Egyptian witnesses into two groups and isolating the so-called "Western" cursives, enabled a clearer picture to emerge. In a second attempt at an intra-group profile, Old Egyptian uniform (83.3%) and predominant readings (23.1%) had a total 42.1% agreement, while the Late Egyptian uniform (100%) and predominant (91.7%) totaled 93.8%. Although the percentage for the Late Egyptian group does not vary from the entire Egyptian group in the first attempt, it became clear that the Old Egyptian witnesses were guilty of skewing the inter-group percentages, except when uniform. So distinguishing between Old and Late Egyptian support went some distance toward solving a problem inherent within the profile method itself.

Subsequent assessment of two works following Ehrman's profile procedure clarified the problem further. Mullen[51] found the procedure to be useful in his analysis of Cyril, but careful reading of his analysis indicates that he faced similar problems with the method. Mullen's inter-group profile of the Pauline corpus is illustrative:[52]

---

[51] Roderic L. Mullen, *The New Testament Text of Cyril of Jerusalem* (SBLNTGF 7; Atlanta: Scholars Press, 1997). See also Darrell D. Hannah, *The Text of 1 Corinthians in the Writings of Origen* (SBLNTGF 4; Atlanta: Scholars Press, 1997).

[52] Mullen, *NT Text of Cyril*, 378.

Text-type	Distinctive	Exclusive	Primary	Totals
Alexandrian	9/23 (39.1%)	6/25 (24.0%)	23/42 (54.8%)	38/90 (42.2%)
Byzantine	5/21 (23.8%)	2/7 (33.3%)	31/47 (65.9%)	38/75 (50.7%)
"Western"	1/22 (4.5%)	0/0 (——)	1/8 (12.5%)	2/30 (6.7%)

Because primary Byzantine support is significantly higher than the Alexandrian support, he concludes, "primary readings are generally less indicative of text-type than are distinctive readings because primary readings are shared with one or more witnesses of other textual groups." In his intra-group profile, the data clearly show an affinity with the Alexandrian group (uniform 77.8%; predominant 65.3%) rather than with the Byzantine (uniform 66.9%; predominant 51.3%). Data are obviously skewed in some way. So Mullen disregards exclusive, primary and totals data in the inter-group profile and concentrates solely on the distinctive readings column, as well as on the intra-group profile, where Alexandrian support agrees with the statistical conclusions reached on the preceding page.[53] This same problem was encountered in my initial attempt to analyze Romans in Epiphanius with this method.

Ehrman's procedure has made a significant contribution to the analysis of patristic citations, and revisions continue to be made to it. Two difficulties exist in Ehrman's procedure that skew data. First, the question arises as to why exclusive inter-group readings are included to profile a Father's total agreements with a particular group, when by definition an exclusive reading is a secondary or minority reading for that group. Although it is important to be aware of such readings, especially when a Father agrees with one, including them in the total agreement for the inter-group profile does not represent accurately a Father's agreement with a group. Ehrman's combination of the inter-group and intra-group profiles eliminates these minority readings, but the independent value of the inter-group profile is lessened greatly. This explains partially why Mullin focused upon distinctive readings rather than the exclusive or primary readings of the inter-group profile in his analysis. In this study, this difficulty is recognized but not resolved.

Second, a problem exists regarding how primary readings are reckoned. Ehrman's profile for uniform primary readings allows mixed readings to be counted as primary for a group in that he allows another group to support the reading predominantly.[54] In such a case, if one group uniformly supports a reading, a second group is allowed to have

---

[53] The same problem can be seen clearly in the analysis of the text of John in Mullen, *NT Text of Cyril*. 336–37.

[54] Ehrman, "The Use of Group Profiles," *JBL* (1987): 478 n. 30.

every witness for that group except one support the same reading, yet the group having uniform support for the reading still counts as primary. Such a reading, which is supported by significant majority of two groups, appears to be a mixed reading rather than a primary reading for either group. The accounts for the reason Mullen did not rely on the primary readings in the inter-group profile. This problem is more significant than the previous one in that the combined profile does not filter out these readings as it did the exclusive ones. Clearly, a revision to the method is necessary to provide accurate data.

In this investigation, the procedure has been revised as follows. Distinctive readings are treated precisely as Ehrman suggests—most (greater than 50%) of group members and no others. Exclusive readings are the same as in Ehrman—at least two group members (less than 50%) and no others. Primary readings, though, are treated differently. Concerning primary readings, Ehrman has at least two group members and greater group than non-group support, either uniform (100%; no other uniform group and only one 2/3 group), predominant (2/3; no uniform group and no other 2/3 group), or less than 2/3 (more group than non-group). This study understands primary as most (greater than 50%) and twice as much group support (in %) as non-group (in %).

> *Uniform* (100%). No other uniform (100%) or Predominant (2/3) group. If there is another predominant group, it is a mixed reading and not primary for either group.
>
> *Predominant* (2/3; less than 100%) group. No uniform (100%) group; no other predominant (2/3) group; no more than 1/3 of any other single group.
>
> *Majority* (more than 1/2 and less than 2/3) group. No uniform or predominant groups; no more than 1/4 any single group, and total of all non-group witnesses must not exceed 1/3 of the total MSS for that reading.

In determining primary readings, if the "Western" text is uniform, but has only one witness for the reading, it is not allowed to cancel the group that has a primary reading on that variant.

C. INSTANCES OF VARIATION KNOWN TO EPIPHANIUS

Several instances occur in which Epiphanius mentions the existence of variant readings in contemporary copies of the NT. Such references enable one to assess the critical acumen of Epiphanius in choosing among the readings, as well as providing indisputable evidence for the existence of alternative readings in the Eastern Mediterranean during the fourth century C.E.[55] Occasionally, Epiphanius accuses another patristic writer of falsifying scripture. Just how far those charges reflect fact and how far they reflect accumulating errors in the NT manuscript tradition remains unclear. There is no doubt that Marcion introduced numerous changes into his text. Occasionally, however, such a charge against a heretic is unjustified, as the alteration was actually made by an orthodox writer.[56] This study will include an analysis of 1 Cor 10:9 and 2 Tim 4:10 in this regard.

---

[55] See Bruce M. Metzger, "The Practice of Textual Criticism Among the Church Fathers," *Studia Patristica XII* (TU 115; Berlin: Akademie Verlag, 1975): 340–49.

[56] Bart D. Ehrman, *The Orthodox Corruption of Scripture: The Effect of Early Christological Controversies on the Text of the New Testament* (Oxford: Oxford University Press, 1993).

CHAPTER 4

EPIPHANIUS' TEXT OF ACTS

The observation of Klijn[1] over three decades ago, that "there has never been so little agreement about the nature of the original text [of Acts] as at the moment," remains true even today. The textual history of Acts is not at all certain. From at least the time of Bengel in 1725, efforts to classify NT MSS into groups eventually achieved classical formulation in the work of Westcott and Hort.[2] Basically, three types of text emerged, one best represented by the uncials ℵ and B, another by D, and a third by the mass of Byzantine cursives. The types of text in B and D differ so markedly that Blass[3] proposed that these reflect two editions of Acts, both by Luke. While Blass' theory of two Lukan editions of Acts did not become widely accepted,[4] the significant differences between these two types of text led Ropes[5] to opt for the B type of text as the original form of Acts, and Clark[6] to argue vigorously for the text of D as more nearly the original.

Most twentieth-century scholarship viewed B as the product of a fourth century revision.[7] The discovery of $\mathfrak{P}^{75}$ required a drastic revision of that understanding for the portion of text for which it is extant,

---

[1] A. F. J. Klijn, "In Search of the Original Text of Acts,"in *Studies in Luke-Acts: Essays Presented in Honor of Paul Schubert* (ed. L. E. Keck and J. L. Martyn; Nashville: Abingdon. 1966), 108.

[2] B. F. Westcott and F. J. A. Hort, *The New Testament in the Original Greek* (Cambridge: Macmillan, 1881, 1882).

[3] F. Blass, *Acta Apostolorum sive Lucae ad Theophilum liber alter* (Leipzig: Teubner, 1896).

[4] See now E. Delebecque, "Les deux prologues des Actes des Apôtres," *RevThom* 80 (1980): 628–34; and W. A. Strange, *The Problem of the Text of Acts* (SNTSMS 71; Cambridge: Cambridge University Press, 1992).

[5] James Hardy Ropes, *The Beginnings of Christianity*. III. *The Text of Acts* (ed. F. Foakes Jackson and K. Lake; London: Macmillan, 1926).

[6] A. C. Clark, *The Acts of the Apostles* (Oxford: Clarendon, 1933).

[7] See Kenneth Clark, "The Effect of Recent Textual Criticism upon New Testament Studies," in *The Background of the New Testament and its Eschatology* (ed. W. D. Davies and D. Daube. Cambridge: Cambridge University Press, 1956), 37.

pushing the date of the B type of text back from c. 350 to 200, but failing to answer the question whether the B text was the result of a late second-century revision or not. Fee[8] argues strongly that there was no such revision. On the other hand, the actual existence of a "Western" text has been debated vigorously. No uncial exists with a *purely* "Western" text, The so-called "Western" cursives are actually primarily Byzantine with only a few "Western" readings.[9] Boismard[10] attempts to demonstrate the "Western" text in Acts have achieved only dubious results.[11] The riddle of the "Western" text remains.

Geer's research on Family 1739 in Acts has added another valuable dimension to the textual history of Acts. Geer countered the suggestion of Lake,[12] that 1739 might "represent the Origenian-Caesarean text of the epistles. . . . It is natural to presume that the same may be true of Acts, but here the evidence fails." Even Haenchen[13] thought that 1739 might represent a "Caesarean" text in Acts. Geer,[14] however, contends that 1739 is a weak Alexandrian witness that reflects a small amount of Byzantine and Western influence in Acts. It is improbable that a distinctive and independent text of Acts ever existed in Roman Palestine. Epiphanius' relationship to 1739 in Acts is of significant interest.

Ropes[15] concluded that Origen's text of Acts was Egyptian in character, as was that of Eusebius. Even so, he mentioned von Soden's opinion that Cyril of Jerusalem and Epiphanius used texts of the "Western" type.[16]

---

[8] Gordon D. Fee, "$\mathfrak{P}^{75}$, $\mathfrak{P}^{66}$, and Origen: The Myth of Early Textual Recension in Alexandria," in *New Dimensions in New Testament Studies* (ed. R. Longenecker and M. Tenney; Grand Rapids: Zondervan, 1974), 31–44.

[9] Thomas C. Geer, Jr. "An Investigation of a Select Group of So-called Western Cursives in Acts" (Ph.D. dissertation, Boston University, 1985).

[10] M.-E. Boismard and A. Lamouille, *Le texte occidentale des Actes des Apôtres: Reconstruction et réhabilitation* (Paris: Éditions recherche sur les civilisations, 1984).

[11] See Thomas C. Geer, "The Presence and Significance of Lucanisms in the 'Western' Text of Acts," *JSNT* 39 (1990): 59–76, for problems with the approach of Boismard and Lamouille.

[12] Kirsopp Lake, J. de Zwaan, and Morton S. Enslin, "Codex 1739," *Six Collations of New Testament Manuscripts* (HTS, 17; ed. K. Lake and S. New; Cambridge: Harvard University Press, 1932), 145.

[13] Ernst Haenchen, "Zum Text der Apostelgeschichte," *ZTK* 54 (1957): 54–55.

[14] See Thomas C. Geer, Jr., "Codex 1739 in Acts and Its Relationship to Manuscripts 945 and 1891," *Bib* 69 (1988): 31, 41–42.

[15] Ropes, *The Beginnings of Christianity*, 3. clxxxix–cxci, cxcviii.

[16] *Ibid.*, cxc–cxci.

1. QUANTITATIVE ANALYSIS OF ACTS IN EPIPHANIUS

The twenty witnesses selected as representative of the various textual traditions in Acts are:

Egyptian
    Old Egyptian – $\mathfrak{P}^{74}$ ℵ B
    Later Egyptian – A C 81 1175
        Family 1739 – 630 945 1704 1739 1891
"Western" uncials – D E + old Latin or Vulgate
Byzantine – 𝔐 H L P 049 1073 1352

The general classification of MSS according to textual grouping is that of Metzger,[17] Lagrange,[18] and Greenlee.[19] Research conducted at Abilene Christian University for the text of Acts in *Novum Testamentum Graecum Editio Critica Maior* indicates that the so-called "Western" cursives are not, in fact, "Western" at all, but Byzantine MSS with certain readings characteristic of the "Western" text. Accordingly, they are not included in this study.

---

[17] Bruce M. Metzger, *The Text of the New Testament* (3rd ed.; Oxford: Oxford University Press, 1992), 213–16.

[18] M.-J. Lagrange, *Introduction à l'étude du Nouveau Testament. 2 Critique textuelle* (Paris: Lecoffre, 1935), 466–87.

[19] J. Harold Greenlee, *Introduction to New Testament Textual Criticism* (rev. ed.; Peabody, Mass.: Hendrickson, 1995), 117–18.

Table 1

The Complete Corpus of Acts 1-28

	Epiph	TR	𝔐	𝔓74	ℵ	A	B	C	D	E	H	L	P	049	81	630	945	1073	1175	1352	1704	1739	1891
Epiph	-																						
TR	41.2	-																					
𝔐	38.2	91.2	-																				
𝔓74	66.7	26.7	26.7	-																			
ℵ	58.8	20.6	17.6	83.3	-																		
A	58.8	20.6	20.6	90.0	88.2	-																	
B	67.6	14.7	11.8	80.0	91.2	85.3	-																
C	50.0	25.0	32.1	70.8	64.3	78.6	71.4	-															
D	38.7	29.0	29.0	51.9	45.2	51.6	41.9	61.5	-														
E	50.0	64.7	64.7	53.3	38.2	50.0	38.2	46.4	35.5	-													
H	35.3	94.1	91.2	23.3	14.7	17.6	8.8	21.4	29.0	61.8	-												
L	33.3	91.7	91.7	20.8	16.7	16.7	8.3	27.8	33.3	50.0	95.8	-											
P	41.9	87.1	96.8	23.3	16.1	19.4	16.1	40.0	28.6	58.1	87.1	87.5	-										
049	47.1	85.3	88.2	36.7	26.5	29.4	20.6	32.1	32.3	64.7	85.3	87.5	83.9	-									
81	70.0	16.7	16.7	69.2	76.7	73.3	86.7	58.3	42.9	40.0	16.7	9.5	18.5	26.7	-								
630	55.9	50.0	44.1	63.3	44.1	50.0	41.2	53.6	41.9	55.9	52.9	45.8	35.5	50.0	40.0	-							
945	61.8	47.1	41.2	56.7	41.2	47.1	44.1	57.1	41.9	50.0	50.0	45.8	41.9	44.1	43.3	88.2	-						
1073	29.4	88.2	91.2	16.7	14.7	11.8	8.8	28.6	32.3	55.9	88.2	91.7	87.1	79.4	13.3	41.2	38.2	-					
1175	61.8	29.4	26.5	73.3	79.4	79.4	82.4	78.6	51.6	50.0	23.5	25.0	25.8	35.3	73.3	55.9	52.9	17.6	-				
1352	44.1	85.3	88.2	26.7	17.6	20.6	17.6	39.3	32.3	64.7	85.3	79.2	90.3	76.5	23.3	50.0	52.9	85.3	26.5	-			
1704	64.7	44.1	44.1	63.3	47.1	52.9	50.0	64.3	38.7	52.9	47.1	45.8	45.2	47.1	50.0	88.2	94.1	35.3	58.8	50.0	-		
1739	69.7	36.4	30.3	66.7	51.5	57.6	54.5	63.0	46.7	51.5	39.4	33.3	32.3	36.4	51.7	87.9	87.9	27.3	60.6	42.4	87.9	-	
1891	71.0	35.5	35.5	69.0	51.6	58.1	54.8	64.0	42.9	58.1	38.7	33.3	36.7	38.7	51.9	87.1	83.9	25.8	61.3	41.9	90.3	96.8	-

Table 2

The Text of Acts 1-12

	Epiph	TR	𝔐	𝔓74	ℵ	A	B	C	D	E	H	L	P	049	81	630	945	1073	1175	1352	1704	1739	1891
Epiph																							
TR	46.7																						
𝔐	53.3	93.3	-																				
𝔓74	63.6	27.3	36.4																				
ℵ	60.0	13.3	20.0	90.9	-																		
A	66.7	20.0	26.7	100.0	93.3	-																	
B	66.7	13.3	20.0	81.8	93.3	86.7	-																
C	63.6	18.2	27.3	85.7	81.8	90.9	81.8	-															
D	42.9	14.3	7.1	50.0	57.1	64.3	50.0	60.0	-														
E	53.3	73.3	80.0	45.5	26.7	33.3	26.7	27.3	14.3	-													
H	40.0	93.3	86.7	18.2	6.7	13.3	6.7	9.1	14.3	66.7	-												
L	40.0	80.0	80.0	0.0	0.0	0.0	0.0	0.0	0.0	20.0	00.0	80.0											
P	58.3	91.7	100.0	36.4	25.0	33.3	25.0	37.5	9.1	75.0	83.3	60.0	-										
049	66.7	80.0	86.7	54.5	33.3	40.0	33.3	36.4	14.3	80.0	73.3	0.0	27.3	-									
81	78.6	21.4	28.6	70.0	78.6	71.4	55.7	60.0	46.2	35.7	71.4	40.0	33.3	42.9	-								
630	40.0	53.3	46.7	54.5	40.0	46.7	33.3	45.5	28.6	40.0	60.0	60.0	33.3	53.3	35.7	-							
945	46.7	53.3	46.7	45.5	40.0	46.7	33.3	45.5	35.7	33.3	60.0	40.0	41.7	46.7	35.7	80.0	-						
1073	33.3	86.7	80.0	9.1	13.3	6.7	13.3	18.2	14.3	60.0	80.0	60.0	75.0	66.7	21.4	40.0	40.0	-					
1175	80.0	26.7	33.3	81.8	80.0	86.7	86.7	90.9	50.0	40.0	20.0	20.0	41.7	46.7	71.4	46.7	46.7	13.3	-				
1352	46.7	100.0	93.3	27.3	13.3	20.0	13.3	18.2	14.3	73.3	93.3	80.0	91.7	80.0	21.4	53.3	53.3	86.7	26.7	-			
1/04	53.3	46.7	53.3	63.6	53.3	60.0	46.7	63.6	28.6	40.0	53.3	60.0	50.0	53.3	50.0	80.0	86.7	33.3	60.0	46.7	-		
1739	57.1	35.7	28.6	63.6	57.1	64.3	50.0	60.0	46.2	28.6	42.9	20.0	25.0	35.7	53.8	85.7	78.6	21.4	61.3	35.7	78.6	-	
1891	58.3	33.3	41.7	70.0	58.3	66.7	50.0	62.5	36.4	41.7	41.7	20.0	36.4	41.7	54.5	83.3	66.7	16.7	66.7	33.3	83.3	91.7	-

Table 3

The Text of Acts 13-28

	Epiph	TR	𝔐	𝔓74	ℵ	A	B	C	D	E	H	L	P	049	81	630	945	1073	1175	1352	1704	1739	1891
Epiph	-																						
TR	36.8	-																					
𝔐	26.3	89.5	-																				
𝔓74	68.4	26.3	21.1	-																			
ℵ	57.9	26.3	15.8	78.9	-																		
A	52.6	21.1	15.8	84.2	84.2	-																	
B	68.4	15.8	5.3	78.9	89.5	-	-																
C	41.2	29.4	35.3	64.7	52.9	70.6	64.7	-															
D	35.3	41.2	47.1	52.9	35.3	41.2	35.3	62.5	-														
E	47.4	57.9	52.6	57.9	47.4	63.2	47.4	58.8	52.9	-													
H	31.6	94.7	94.7	26.3	21.1	21.1	10.5	29.4	41.2	57.9	-												
L	31.6	94.7	94.7	26.3	21.1	21.1	10.5	29.4	41.2	57.9	100.0	-											
P	31.6	84.2	94.7	15.8	10.5	10.5	10.5	41.2	41.2	47.4	89.5	89.5	-										
049	31.6	89.5	89.5	26.3	21.1	21.1	10.5	29.4	47.1	52.6	94.7	94.7	84.2	-									
81	62.5	12.5	6.2	68.8	75.0	75.0	87.5	57.1	40.0	43.8	12.5	12.5	12.5	12.5	-								
630	68.4	47.4	42.1	68.4	47.4	52.6	47.4	58.8	52.9	68.4	47.4	47.4	36.8	47.4	43.8	-							
945	73.7	42.1	36.8	63.2	42.1	47.4	52.6	64.7	47.1	63.2	42.1	42.1	42.1	42.1	50.0	94.7	-						
1073	26.3	89.5	100.0	21.1	15.8	15.8	5.3	35.3	47.1	52.6	94.7	94.7	94.7	89.5	6.2	42.1	36.8	-					
1175	47.4	31.6	21.1	68.4	78.9	73.7	78.9	70.6	52.9	57.9	26.3	26.3	15.8	26.3	75.0	63.2	57.9	21.1	-				
1352	42.1	73.7	84.2	26.3	21.1	21.1	21.1	52.9	47.1	57.9	78.9	78.9	89.5	73.7	25.0	47.4	52.6	84.2	26.3	-			
1704	73.7	42.1	36.8	63.2	42.1	47.4	52.6	64.7	47.1	63.2	42.1	42.1	42.1	42.1	50.0	94.7	100.0	36.8	57.9	52.6	-		
1739	78.9	36.8	31.6	68.4	47.4	52.6	57.9	64.7	47.1	68.4	36.8	36.8	36.8	36.8	50.0	89.5	94.7	31.6	57.9	47.4	94.7	-	
1891	78.9	36.8	31.6	68.4	47.4	52.6	57.9	64.7	47.1	68.4	36.8	36.8	36.8	36.8	50.0	89.5	94.7	31.6	57.9	47.4	94.7	100.0	-

Table 4

Epiphanius' Percentages of Agreement with Control Witnesses in Significant Variation in Acts

(Witness; % Agreement with Epiphanius; No. Occurrences)

Chapters 1–28			Chapters 1–12			Chapters 13–28		
1891	71.0	31	1175	80.0	15	1739	78.9	19
81	70.0	30	81	78.6	14	1891	78.9	19
1739	69.7	33	A	66.7	15	945	73.7	19
B	67.6	34	B	66.7	15	1704	73.7	19
$\mathfrak{P}^{74}$	66.7	30	049	66.7	15	$\mathfrak{P}^{74}$	68.4	19
1704	64.7	34	$\mathfrak{P}^{74}$	63.6	11	B	68.4	19
945	61.8	34	C	63.6	11	630	68.4	19
1175	61.8	34	ℵ	60.0	15	81	62.5	16
ℵ	58.8	34	P	58.3	12	ℵ	57.9	19
A	58.8	34	1891	58.3	12	A	52.6	19
630	55.9	34	1739	57.1	14	E	47.4	19
C	50.0	28	𝔐	53.3	15	1175	47.4	19
E	50.0	34	E	53.3	15	1352	42.1	19
049	47.1	34	1704	53.3	15	C	41.2	17
1352	44.1	34	TR	46.7	15	TR	36.8	19
P	41.9	31	945	46.7	15	D	35.3	17
TR	41.2	34	1352	46.7	15	H	31.6	19
D	38.7	31	D	42.9	14	L	31.6	19
𝔐	38.2	34	H	40.0	15	P	31.6	19
H	35.3	34	L	40.0	5	049	31.6	19
L	33.3	24	630	40.0	15	𝔐	26.3	19
1073	29.4	34	1073	33.3	15	1073	26.3	19

Table 5
% of Agreement of Witnesses with Epiphanius in Acts 1–28

A. Egyptian

Witness	Agreements	Comparisons
$\mathfrak{P}^{74}$	20	30
ℵ	20	34
B	23	34
A	20	34
C	14	28
81	21	30
630	19	34
945	21	34
1175	21	34
1704	22	34
1739	23	33
1891	<u>22</u>	<u>31</u>
Total	246	390

% Agreement: 63.1

B. Old Egyptian

Witness	Agreements	Comparisons
$\mathfrak{P}^{74}$	20	30
ℵ	20	34
B	<u>23</u>	<u>34</u>
Total:	63	98

% Agreement: 64.3

C. Later Egyptian

Witness	Agreements	Comparisons
A	20	34
C	14	28
81	21	30
1175	<u>21</u>	<u>34</u>
Total	76	126

% Agreement: 60.3

D. Family 1739

Witness	Agreements	Comparisons
630	19	34
945	21	34
1704	22	34
1739	23	33
1891	<u>22</u>	<u>31</u>
Total	107	166

% Agreement: 64.5

E. "Western"

Witness	Agreements	Comparisons
D	12	31
E	<u>17</u>	<u>34</u>
Total	29	65

% Agreement: 44.6

F. Byzantine witnesses

Witness	Agreements	Comparisons
𝔐	13	34
H	12	34
L	8	24
P	13	31
049	16	34
1073	10	34
1352	<u>15</u>	<u>34</u>
Total	87	225

% Agreement: 38.7

If Family 1739 had not been included and only a composite of chapters 1–28 taken into account, one could conclude only that Epiphanius has more agreement with the Old Egyptian text than with the other textual traditions, but the 64.3% agreement with the Old Egyptian text is somewhat low. When Family 1739 is included in this composite, it is clear that Epiphanius has substantially more agreement with this family than with the other textual traditions. Epiphanius has the highest overall percentage of agreement with 1891, followed closely by 1739, both of which are primary members of Family 1739. Two other members of Family 1739, 945 and 1704, also rank quite high. From these data, Epiphanius does not have the 70% agreement with Family 1739 required for membership in this group.[20] However, Ehrman[21] suggests that the special character of patristic citations and allusions that occur frequently but sporadically means that the 70% figure should be "lowered perhaps to a ±65% agreement of a witness with group members with a 6–8% disparity between groups." If this suggestion is followed regarding chapters 1-28, then the 64.5% agreement with Family 1739, followed by the Old Egyptian text at 64.3%, places Epiphanius close to Family 1739. The data in Table 4, however, show a different affinity in the two halves of Acts.

---

[20] Ernest C. Colwell and Ernest W. Tune, "The Quantitative Relationships between MS Text-types," *Biblical and Patristic Studies in Memory of Robert Pierce Casey* (ed. J. N. Birdsall and R. W. Thompson; Freiburg: Herder, 1963), 29.

[21] Bart D. Ehrman, *Didymus the Blind and the Text of the Gospels* (SBLNTGF 1; Atlanta: Scholars Press, 1986), 202.

Table 6

% of Agreement of Witnesses with Epiphanius in Acts 1–12

A. Egyptian

Witness	Agreements	Comparisons
$\mathfrak{P}^{74}$	7	11
ℵ	9	15
B	10	15
A	10	15
C	7	11
81	11	14
630	6	15
945	7	15
1175	12	15
1704	8	15
1739	8	14
1891	7	12
Total	102	167

% of Agreement   61.2

B. Old Egyptian

Witness	Agreements	Comparisons
$\mathfrak{P}^{74}$	7	11
ℵ	9	15
B	10	15
Total	26	41

% Agreement: 63.4

Table 6, cont.

C. Later Egyptian

Witness	Agreements	Comparisons
A	10	15
C	7	11
81	11	14
1175	<u>12</u>	<u>15</u>
Total	40	55

% Agreement: 72.7

C. Family 1739

Witness	Agreements	Comparisons
630	6	15
945	7	15
1704	8	15
1739	8	14
1891	<u>7</u>	<u>12</u>
Total	36	71

% Agreement: 50.7

E. "Western" uncials

Witness	Agreements	Comparisons
D	6	14
E	<u>8</u>	<u>15</u>
Total	14	29

% Agreement: 48.3

Table 6, cont.

F. Byzantine witnesses

Witness	Agreements	Comparisons
𝔐	8	15
H	6	15
L	2	5
P	7	12
049	10	15
1073	5	15
1352	7	15
Total	45	92

% Agreement: 48.9

Table 7

% of Agreement of Witnesses with Epiphanius in Acts 13–28

A. Egyptian

Witness	Agreements	Comparisons
$\mathfrak{P}^{74}$	13	19
ℵ	11	19
B	13	19
A	10	19
C	7	17
81	10	16
630	13	19
945	14	19
1175	9	19
1704	14	19
1739	15	19
1891	15	19
Total	144	223

% Agreement: 64.6%

Table 7, cont.

B. Old Egyptian

Witness	Agreements	Comparisons
$\mathfrak{P}^{74}$	13	19
ℵ	11	19
B	<u>13</u>	<u>19</u>
Total	37	57

% Agreement: 64.9

C. Later Egyptian

Witness	Agreements	Comparisons
A	10	19
C	7	17
81	10	16
1175	<u>9</u>	<u>19</u>
Total	36	71

% Agreement: 50.7

D. Family 1739

Witness	Agreements	Comparisons
630	13	19
945	14	19
1704	14	19
1739	15	19
1891	<u>15</u>	<u>19</u>
Total	71	95

% Agreement: 74.7

Table 7, cont.

E. "Western" uncials

Witness	Agreements	Comparisons
D	6	17
E	9	19
Total	15	36

% Agreement: 41.7

F. Byzantine witnesses

Witness	Agreements	Comparisons
𝔐	5	19
H	6	19
L	6	19
P	6	19
049	6	19
1073	5	19
1352	8	19
Total	42	133

% Agreement: 31.6

Table 8

Summary of Statistical Data in Tables 5–7

Groups	Acts 1–28	Acts 1–12	Acts 13–28
Egyptian	63.1	61.2	64.6
Old Egyptian	64.3	63.4	64.9
Later Egyptian	60.3	72.7	50.7
Family 1739	64.5	50.7	74.7
"Western" uncials	44.6	48.3	41.7
Byzantine	38.7	48.9	31.6

From Table 8, it is clear that Epiphanius has highest agreement with Family 1739, followed closely by the Old Egyptian witnesses. Epiphanius does not have significant agreement in Acts with either the "Western" uncials or the Byzantine tradition.

This analysis, however, presupposes a uniformity of text type throughout Acts. As Geer[22] observed, MS 33 is usually understood to be a good witness for the Egyptian textual group in Acts. A closer examination, though, discloses that 33 is actually Byzantine in chapters 1–11 and Egyptian in chapters 12–28. Its textual affinities in Acts change between 11:25 and 11:26. Reasons for a change at this particular point appear to be incidental. In view of Geer's observation, it is important to note that chapters 1–12 deal with Peter and 13–28 with Paul. It is assumed that if this phenomenon exists with a single MS, it might also exist in the wider manuscript tradition. Indeed, this proves to be the case, as Tables 6–8 demonstrate.

When Acts is analyzed in two sections, certain very important observations emerge. In Table 6 (1–12) Epiphanius' agreement with Family 1739 is not high (50.7%), his agreement being with the Later Egyptians (72.7%). The Old Egyptian agreement is only 64.3%, and agreement with the "Western" uncials and Byzantines is negligible. In Table 7 (13–28), however, Epiphanius has strong agreement with Family 1739 (74.7%). Agreement with the Later Egyptians drops significantly (50.7%), and Old Egyptian agreement remains about the same as in 1–12 (64.9%). Agreement with the "Western" uncials and Byzantine witnesses remains negligible.

When chapters 1–12 and 13–28 are analyzed separately, Epiphanius' agreement in 1–12 is decidedly Later Egyptian. The 72.7% agreement with the Later Egyptians and a 23.8% disparity between the top two groups permits a firm conclusion that Epiphanius' text of Acts 1–12 is Egyptian in character, and specifically Later Egyptian.

In Acts 13–28, Epiphanius' 64.6% agreement with the Old Egyptian text, followed by the Later Egyptian at 50.7% and the "Western" uncials at 41.7%, would be sufficient to establish his text of Acts as definitely Egyptian. Agreement with $\mathfrak{P}^{74}$ and B (68.4%), followed by ℵ A C 1175 is important. However, Epiphanius' higher (74.7%) agreement with Family 1739 modifies that conclusion significantly. So while Epiphanius' text of Acts 13–28 may be said to have some affinity with the Egyptian text, that agreement is precisely with Family 1739. Epiphanius has no real affinity with the "Western" or Byzantine texts in the last half of Acts.

---

[22] Thomas C. Geer, Jr., "The Two Faces of Codex 33 in Acts," *NovT* 31 (1989): 39–47.

2. PROFILE ANALYSIS OF ACTS IN EPIPHANIUS

For Acts, Epiphanius' Inter-group relationships are analyzed in terms of three types "distinctive" (readings shared by more than half of the extant and usable members of a group with no support from outside the group), "exclusive" (readings shared by at least two members of a group with no support from outside the group), and "primary" (readings shared by at least two members of a group, with greater support from within the group than from outside it, and no other group being uniform). "Greater support" means 1) in the case of "uniform" primary readings, readings supported neither uniformly by another group, nor predominantly by more than one other group, nor by two other groups when one of them supports it predominantly, and 2) in the case of "predominant" primary readings, readings supported neither uniformly nor predominantly by another group, and 3) in all other instances, readings supported by more group than non-group witnesses.[23]

In order to ascertain the strength of a MSS group's support for a particular reading, those readings must be analyzed that occur only among the witnesses of that group. Thus, Intra-group readings may or may not be attested by members of another group. Epiphanius' Intra-group relationships are analyzed in terms of two types: "uniform" (readings that are shared by all extant and usable group members), and "predominant" (readings that are shared by at least two-thirds of the members extant and usable at a given point).

Table 9

Epiphanius' Inter-group Relationships in Acts

	Distinctive	Exclusive	Primary	Total
Egyptian	2/5 (40.0%)	5/8 (62.5%)	8/10 (80.0%)	15/23 (65.2%)
"Western"	—	0/3 (0.0%)	1/1 (100.0%)	1/4 (25.0%)
Byzantine	1/5 (20.0%)	—	7/17 (41.2%)	8/22 (36.4%)

---

[23] Adapted from Bart D. Ehrman, "The Use of Group Profiles for the Classification of New Testament Documentary Evidence," *JBL* 106 (1987): 478.

Table 10

Epiphanius' Intra-group Relationships in Acts

	Uniform	Predominant	Total
Egyptian	6/7 (85.7%)	10/14 (71.4%)	16/21 (76.2%)
Old Egyptian	19/26 (73.1%)	2/7 (28.6%)	21/33 (63.6%)
Late Egyptian	7/8 (87.5%)	10/16 (62.5%)	17/24 (70.8%)
A C 81 1175	13/19 (68.4%)	5/10 (50.0%)	18/29 (62.1%)
Family 1739	18/26 (69.2%)	2/3 (66.7%)	20/29 (69.0%)
"Western"	7/14 (50.0%)	0/3 (0.0%)	7/17 (41.2%)[24]
Byzantine	8/21 (38.1%)	3/10 (30.0%)	11/31 (35.5%)

Table 11

Epiphanius' Agreements with Uniform or Predominant Readings that are also Distinctive, Exclusive or Primary in Acts

	Uniform	Predominant	Total
Egyptian	4/5 (80.0%)	5/8 (62.5%)	9/13 (69.2%)
"Western"	1/1 (100.0%)	–	1/1 (100.0%)
Byzantine	8/16 (50.0%)	0/5 (0.0%)	8/21 (38.1%)

The Inter-group relationships in Table 9 confirm that Epiphanius' text of Acts 1–28 is Egyptian, rather than Byzantine or "Western." Intra-group relationships in Table 10 indicate negligible support by the Byzantine (35.5%) and "Western" traditions (41.2%). Principal support, however, is found in the Egyptian tradition (76.2%). Among the Egyptians, Epiphanius has 70.8% agreement with the Later Egyptians, as opposed to only 63.6% with the Old Egyptians. Further, among the Late Egyptians, Epiphanius has 69.0% agreement with Family 1739, but only 62.1% with A C 81 1175. His agreement with "uniform" or "predominant" readings that are also "distinctive," "exclusive," or "primary" confirms Epiphanius' agreement with the Later Egyptian text-form. However, the relationship with Family 1739 remains unclear.

---

[24] There are few "Western" Intra-group readings because only D and E, which often do not agree, are used, and also because the Old Latin is used to assist with group readings and often it^d and it^e do not agree.

Table 12

Epiphanius' Inter-group Relationships in Acts 1–12

	Distinctive	Exclusive	Primary	Total
Egyptian	0/2 (0.0%)	1/2 (50.0%)	5/6 (83.3%)	6/10 (60.0%)
"Western"	–	0/2 (50.0%)	1/1 (100%)	1/3 (33.3%)
Byzantine	1/1 (100%)	–	3/9 (33.3%)	4/10 (40.0%)

Table 13

Epiphanius' Intra-group Relationships in Acts 1–12

	Uniform	Predominant	Total
Egyptian	2/2 (100%)	6/9 (66.7%)	8/11 (72.7%)
Old Egyptian	9/13 (69.2%)	0/2 (0.0%)	9/15 (60.0%)
Late Egyptian	2/2 (100%)	6/9 (66.7%)	8/11 (72.7%)
A C 81 1175	8/9 (88.9%)	4/6 (66.7%)	12/15 (80.0%)
Family 1739	18/26 (69.2%)	2/3 (66.7%)	20/29 (69.0%)
"Western"	2/3 (66.7%)	0/2 (0.0%)	2/5 (40.0%)
Byzantine	4/8 (50.0%)	3/6 (50.0%)	7/14 (50.0%)

Table 14

Epiphanius' Agreements with Uniform or Predominant Readings that are also Distinctive, Exclusive or Primary in Acts 1–12

	Uniform	Predominant	Total
Egyptian	2/2 (100%)	3/6 (50.0%)	5/8 (62.5%)
"Western"	1/1 (100%)	–	1/1 (100%)
Byzantine	4/8 (50.0%)	0/2 (0.0%)	4/10 (40.0%)

Although only fifteen variants exist for these profiles, Epiphanius' text of Acts 1–12 is Egyptian in character, especially Late Egyptian (80.0%), but affinity with Family 1739 is much lower (69.0%). The Old Egyptians have only 60.0% agreement, while "Western" and Byzantine agreements are negligible.

Table 15

Epiphanius' Inter-group Relationships in Acts 13–28

	Distinctive	Exclusive	Primary	Total
Egyptian	2/3 (66.7%)	4/6 (66.7%)	3/4 (75.0%)	9/13 (69.2%)
"Western"	–	0/1 (0.0%)	–	0/1 (0.0%)
Byzantine	0/4 (0.0%)	–	5/9 (55.6%)	5/13 (38.5%)

Table 16

Epiphanius' Intra-group Relationships in Acts 13–28

	Uniform	Predominant	Total
Egyptian	4/5 (80.0%)	4/5 (80.0%)	8/10 (80.0%)
Old Egyptian	10/14 (71.4%)	2/5 (40.0%)	12/19 (63.2%)
Late Egyptian	5/6 (83.3%)	5/8 (62.5%)	10/14 (71.4%)
A C 81 1175	5/10 (50.0%)	2/5 (40.0%)	7/15 (46.7%)
Family 1739	13/17 (76.5%)	1/1 (100%)	14/18 (77.8%)
"Western"	5/11 (45.5%)	0/1 (0.0%)	5/12 (41.7%)
Byzantine	5/14 (35.7%)	0/4 (0.0%)	5/18 (27.8%)

Table 17

Epiphanius' Agreements with Uniform or Predominant Readings that are also Distinctive, Exclusive or Primary in Acts 13–28

	Uniform	Predominant	Total
Egyptian	2/3 (66.7%)	2/2 (100%)	4/5 (80.0%)
"Western"	–	–	–
Byzantine	5/9 (55.6%)	0/3 (0.0%)	5/12 (41.7%)

In the nineteen units of variation available, these profiles indicate that in Acts 13–28, Epiphanius' text is primarily Late Egyptian (71.4%) rather than Old Egyptian (63.2%), but within the Later Egyptian group there is very high agreement with Family 1739 (77.8%). It is more than interesting that in both quantitative and qualitative analyses, Epiphanius' text of Acts 1–12 is strongly Late Egyptian with no significant affinity with Family 1739, but in Acts 13-28 his text is primarily that of Family 1739.

3. *Summary and Conclusion*

In terms of quantitative analysis, important differences emerge between Acts 1–12 and 13–28. In 1–12, Epiphanius' agreement with the Later Egyptians is significant (72.7%), but agreement with Family 1739 is relatively weak at only 50.7%. Agreement with the Old Egyptians is not so high in 1–12 (63.4%), and agreement with the "Western" uncials (48.3%) and Byzantines (48.9%) is negligible. In Acts 13–28, however, Epiphanius exhibits strong agreement with Family 1739, at 74.7%, but surprisingly agreement with the Later Egyptians drops significantly to 50.7%. Agreement with the Old Egyptian text in 13-28 remains similar to that in 1–12 (64.9%). Epiphanius seems to have no appreciable affinity with the Later Egyptian text in 13–28, nor with the "Western" (41.7%) or Byzantine (31.6%) texts.

The qualitative analysis of Epiphanius' text of Acts 1–28 confirms principal agreement with the Later Egyptian tradition. However, when Acts 1–12 and 13–28 are analyzed separately, the profiles indicate a strong relationship with the Late Egyptian text in 1–12 (80.0%), and somewhat weaker affinity with Family 1739 and the Old Egyptians (60.0%). In 13–28, however, the Late Egyptian relationship remains strong (71.4%), but affinity with Family 1739 increases dramatically (77.8%). Affinity with the Old Egyptians remains approximately the same throughout Acts. "Western" (41.2%) and Byzantine (35.5%) influence is negligible.

From these analyses, one can conclude that Epiphanius' text of Acts is certainly not "Western," as von Soden proposed, nor Old Egyptian, as Ropes held. Instead, Epiphanius has primary relationship with the Later Egyptian MSS in chapters 1–12 and especially with Family 1739 in 13–28. There is no Byzantine affinity. As efforts to link 1739 with Caesarea have not been conclusive, Epiphanius' text cannot be said to be Caesarean.[25] His fourth-century text does reflect alterations common to the Later Egyptian tradition, but only occasionally readings peculiar to the "Western" and developing Byzantine traditions. One can conclude that

---

[25] Kirsopp Lake, J. de Zwaan, and Morton S. Enslin, "Codex 1739," *Six Collations of New Testament Manuscripts*, 145, note that 1739 was copied from early MSS connected with Origen (esp. in Romans). Ernst Haenchen. "Zum Text der Apostelgeschichte," *ZTK* 54 (1957): 54–55, considered the possibility that 1739 might represent a "Caesarean" text type in Acts. However, in *idem*, *The Acts of the Apostles* (Philadelphia: Westminster, 1971), 50, he did not pursue this matter. Thomas Geer, *Family 1739 in Acts* (SBLMS 48; Atlanta: Scholars Press, 1994), 63–64, 113–14, found 1739 to be Later Egyptian in textual affinity.

either Epiphanius used separate MSS of Acts 1–12 and 13–28, or the copyist of his exemplar relied upon different MSS in the two halves of Acts.

CHAPTER 5

EPIPHANIUS' TEXT OF THE CATHOLIC EPISTLES

1. QUANTITATIVE ANALYSIS OF THE CATHOLIC EPISTLES IN EPIPHANIUS

The MSS representative of the Egyptian textual tradition in the Catholic Epistles are those found in Greenlee,[1] although the studies of Blakely,[2] Richards,[3] and others, have been instructive. Von Soden thought the textual relationships in Acts and the Catholic Epistles were the same from MS to MS.[4] While Gallagher[5] concluded that P "offers weak attestation to the H-text," but still has some significant relation to that text, Kubo[6] concluded that P is not Egyptian in 1 and 2 Peter and Jude. Similarly, Richards[7] noted that 1175 is Alexandrian in James and 1 and 2 Peter, but Byzantine in Jude and the Johannine Epistles. MSS P and 1175 are omitted from this study. MS 1739 has been classified as Alexandrian in James by Gallagher,[8] in 1 and 2 Peter and Jude by Kubo[9] and in the Johannine Epistles by Richards.[10]

---

[1] J. Harold Greenlee, *Introduction to New Testament Textual Criticism* (2nd ed.; Peabody, Mass.: Hendrickson, 1995), 118.

[2] Wayne A. Blakely, "Manuscript Relationships as Indicated by the Epistles of Jude and II Peter" (Ph.D. dissertation, Emory University, 1964).

[3] W. Larry Richards, *The Classification of the Greek Manuscripts of the Johannine Epistles* (SBLDS 35; Missoula, Mont.: Scholars Press, 1977).

[4] Hermann von Soden, *Die Schriften des Neuen Testaments in ihrer ältesten erreichbaren Textgestalt* (Göttingen: Vandenhoeck und Ruprecht, 1911), 1.3.1840–41.

[5] J. Tim Gallagher, "A Study of von Soden's H-Text in the Catholic Epistles," *AUSS* 8 (1970): 97–119, esp. 107.

[6] Sakae Kubo, "A Comparative Study of $\mathfrak{P}^{72}$ and Codex Vaticanus" (Ph.D. dissertation, University of Chicago, 1964), 259.

[7] W. Larry Richards, "Gregory 1175: Alexandrian or Byzantine in the Catholic Epistles?" *AUSS* 21 (1983): 155–68, esp. 161.

[8] Gallagher, "von Soden's H-Text in the Catholic Epistles," *AUSS* (1970): 79-119.

[9] Kubo, "A Comparative Study of $\mathfrak{P}^{72}$ and Codex Vaticanus," 259.

[10] Richards, *Classification of the Greek MSS of the Johannine Epistles*, 200.

The selection of Byzantine MSS is based upon the analysis of Wachtel[11] and upon unpublished research of Osburn and Geer.

The "Western" text is not discernible in the Catholic Epistles.[12] Duplacy[13] did mention briefly the possibility of a "Western" text in the Catholic Epistles. Also, Amphoux[14] posited the existence of four textual groupings in the Catholic Epistles, two of which make up one taxonomic group.[15]

In 1970, Carder[16] posited the existence of a Caesarean text in the Catholic Epistles, but Kurt Aland[17] argued convincingly that there is no evidence to support this thesis.[18]

The following witnesses are used as representative:

Egyptian $\mathfrak{P}^{72}$ ℵ A B C Ψ 33 81 323 1739

Byzantine   𝔐 L 049 105 201 325 1022 1352

Selected MSS from Family 1739 in Acts are included in the quantitative analysis because of the close relationship of Epiphanius' text of Acts to that group. However, as will be seen, Epiphanius' text of the Catholic Epistles has no significant relationship to 1739 or to Family 1739, and the group is not included in the Inter-group and Intragroup profiles. From the following investigation, it appears that each of these manuscripts may exhibit different textual affinities from epistle to epistle, and certainly there is no basis for assuming that

---

[11] Klaus Wachtel, *Der Byzantinische Text der Katholischen Briefe* (ANTT 24; Berlin: de Gruyter, 1995).

[12] Metzger, *Text of the NT*, 213–14, *contra* Greenlee, *Introduction to NT Textual Criticism*, 118.

[13] Jean Duplacy, "Le Texte 'occidental' des épîtres catholiques," *NTS* 16 (1969): 397–99.

[14] C.-B. Amphoux, "Le Texte des épîtres catholiques. Essais de classement des états de texte, préparatoires à une histoire du texte de ces épîtres" (Ph.D. dissertation, Paris-Sorbonne, 1981).

[15] Leon Vaganay, *An Introduction to New Testament Textual Criticism* (2nd ed., rev. C.-B. Amphoux; trans. J. Heimerdinger; Cambridge: Cambridge University Press, 1982), 71–73.

[16] Muriel M. Carder, "A Caesarean Text in the Catholic Epistles," *NTS* 16 (1970): 252-70, which summarizes the work in her Th.D. dissertation at Victoria University.

[17] Kurt Aland, "Bemerkungen zu den gegenwärtigen möglichkeiten textkritiscsher Arbeit aus Anlass einer Untersuchung zum Cäsarea-Text der Katholischen Briefe," *NTS* 17 (1970): 1-9.

[18] See also the critique in Richards, *Classification of the Greek MSS of the Johannine Epistles*, 202-06.

there is a necessary affinity of textual grouping between Acts and the Catholic Epistles in a MS. Since in this study there are insufficient data to conduct an analysis epistle by epistle, the data from the Catholic Epistles are analyzed collectively to see what, if any, conclusions can be drawn.

Table 19

Proportional Relationship of all Witnesses in the Corpus of the Catholic Epistles

	Epiph	TR	𝔐	𝔓72	ℵ	A	B	C	L	ψ	049	33	105	201	323	325	1022	1739
Epiph	-																	
TR	90.0	-																
𝔐	80.0	90.0	-															
𝔓72	33.3	33.3	33.3	-														
ℵ	30.0	20.0	30.0	33.3	-													
A	60.0	60.0	50.0	33.3	50.0	-												
B	40.0	30.0	20.0	100.0	60.0	60.0	-											
C	55.6	44.4	33.3	66.7	22.2	44.4	66.7	-										
L	80.0	80.0	90.0	33.3	30.0	60.0	20.0	33.3	-									
ψ	70.0	60.0	50.0	66.7	30.0	50.0	70.0	88.9	50.0	-								
049	70.0	80.0	90.0	33.3	30.0	40.0	20.0	33.3	80.0	50.0	-							
33	66.7	77.8	66.7	33.3	44.4	88.9	55.6	50.0	55.6	55.6	55.6	-						
105	80.0	90.0	100.0	33.3	30.0	50.0	20.0	33.3	90.0	50.0	90.0	66.7	-					
201	80.0	90.0	100.0	33.3	30.0	50.0	20.0	33.3	90.0	50.0	90.0	66.7	100.0	-				
323	40.0	50.0	60.0	33.3	40.0	30.0	20.0	44.4	50.0	30.0	60.0	44.4	60.0	60.0	-			
325	90.0	100.0	90.0	33.3	20.0	60.0	30.0	44.4	80.0	60.0	80.0	77.8	90.0	90.0	50.0	-		
1022	80.0	90.0	100.0	33.3	30.0	50.0	20.0	33.3	90.0	50.0	90.0	66.7	100.0	100.0	60.0	90.0	-	
1739	40.0	30.0	20.0	33.3	60.0	60.0	50.0	66.7	20.0	50.0	20.0	55.6	20.0	20.0	60.0	30.0	20.0	-

Table 20

Epiphanius' Percentages of Agreement with Control Witnesses in Genetically Significant Variation in the Catholic Epistles
(Witness; % Agreement with Epiphanius; No. Occurrences)

[TR	90.0	10]		33	66.7	9
325	90.0	10		A	60.0	10
𝔐	80.0	10		C	55.6	9
L	80.0	10		B	40.0	10
105	80.0	10		323	40.0	10
201	80.0	10		1739	40.0	10
1022	80.0	10		𝔓72	33.3	3
ψ	70.0	10		ℵ	30.0	10
049	70.0	10				

Table 21

Percentage of Agreement of Witnesses with Epiphanius in the Catholic Epistles

A. Egyptian Agreements with Epiphanius

Witnesses	Agreements	Comparisons
$\mathfrak{P}^{72}$	1	3
ℵ	3	10
B	4	10
A	6	10
C	5	9
Ψ	7	10
33	6	9
323	4	10
1739	4	10
Total	40	81

% Agreement: 49.4

B. Byzantine Agreements with Epiphanius

Witnesses	Agreements	Comparisons
L	8	10
049	7	10
105	8	10
201	8	10
325	9	10
1022	8	10
Total	48	60

% Agreement: 80.0 ($\mathfrak{M}$ 80.0)

In the Catholic Epistles, 1739 demonstrates 4 agreements with Epiphanius and 6 disagreements, resulting in only 40.0% agreement. From these meager data, the relationship of Epiphanius' text to 1739 in Acts does not carry over to the Catholic Epistles.

Table 22

Summary of Statistical Data in Tables 18–20

Groups	Catholic Epistles
Egyptian	49.4
Byzantine	80.0
Family 1739	58.8

The results of Table 21 suggest that Epiphanius' citations of the Catholic Epistles have primary affinity with the Byzantine text. The separation of 30.6 % between the Byzantine and the Egyptian text leaves little to the imagination.

2. PROFILE ANALYSIS OF THE CATHOLIC EPISTLES IN EPIPHANIUS

Table 23

Epiphanius' Inter-group Relationships in the Catholic Epistles

	Distinctive	Exclusive	Primary	Total
Egyptian	1/5 (20.0%)	0/5 (0.0%)	1/2 (50.0%)	2/12 (16.7%)
Byzantine	1/1 (100.0%)	—	6/8 (75.0%)	—

Epiphanius reads only one of five distinctive Egyptian readings and none of the five exclusive Egyptian readings. His support of Egyptian readings in the Inter-group profile is in only one of two primary texts. Agreeing with the one exclusive Byantine reading, Epiphanius also reads six of eight primary Byzantine texts.

Table 24

Epiphanius Intra-Group Relationships in the Catholic Epistles

	Uniform	Predominant	Total
Egyptian	—	4/7	4/7
Byzantine	9/9	2/4	11/13

More instructive are Epiphanius' Intra-group Relationships, where he only reads four of seven predominant Egyptian readings (57.1%), but all eight of the Byzantine uniform readings and two of four Byzantine predominant readings (83.3%). This tends to confirm the earlier quantitative analysis favoring Epiphanius' agreement with the Byzantine text-form in the Catholic Epistles.

Epiphanius' support of uniform or predominant readings that are also distinctive, exclusive or primary in the Catholic Epistles, shows agreement with all five Byantine uniform readings and one of three predominant readings (75%), while showing only one agreement in four Egyptian predominant readings (25%).

Coupled with the 80% agreement with the Byzantine text in the quantitative data, as opposed to only 49.2% with the Egyptian text, the slight evidence of the ten readings in these citations lead to the likelihood that Epiphanius' text of the Catholic Epistles is Byzantine in character. However, one must use restraint in this conclusion, as the database is too small to provide a definitive characterization.

CHAPTER 6

EPIPHANIUS' TEXT OF THE PAULINE EPISTLES

1. THE QUANTITATIVE ANALYSIS

The following witnesses are used as representative of the major textual groupings in the Pauline epistles:

Old Egyptian — $\mathfrak{P}^{46}$ ℵ B 1739
Late Egyptian — A C P 33 81 104
"Western" uncials — D F G
Byzantine— 𝔐 K L 049 699 1594

The MSS selected as representative of the Egyptian textual tradition in the Pauline Epistles are those found in Metzger[1] and Greenlee,[2] with certain exceptions. MS 1739 is included as an Old Egyptian witness on the basis of the study of Zuntz.[3] Based on Morrill's analysis,[4] which concluded that Ψ and 6 have mixed texts in 1 Corinthians much closer to the Byzantine tradition and that 1908 is definitely Byzantine in character in 1 Corinthians, those MSS are not included in this study, lest they skew the data. The so-called "Western cursives" were included in the earlier stages of the investigation, but were omitted from the study when the results were decidedly negative. Bover[5] discusses the possibility of a Caesarean text in the Pauline Epistles, but efforts to identify it have been unsuccessful.

---

[1] Bruce M. Metzger, *The Text of the New Testament* (3rd ed.; Oxford: Oxford University Press, 1992), 216, and *idem, A Textual Commentary on the Greek New Testament* (2nd ed.; New York: UBS, 1994), 15*-16*.

[2] J. Harold Greenlee, *Introduction to New Testament Textual Criticism* (2nd ed.; Peabody, Mass.: Hendrickson, 1995), 118.

[3] Günther Zuntz, *The Text of the Epistles: A Disquisition Upon the Corpus Paulinum* (London: Oxford University Press, 1953), 68–84, esp. 78.

[4] Bruce Morrill, "The Classification of the Greek Manuscripts of First Corinthians" (M.A. thesis, Harding Graduate School of Religion, 1981), 266 pp., analyzed full collations of MSS.

[5] J. M. Bover, *Novi Testamenti Biblia Graeca et Latina* (5th ed.; Madrid: Gráficas Cóndor, 1968), xlvi–xlvii.

Table 25

Complete Corpus of the Pauline Epistles

	Epiph	TR	𝔐	𝔓46	ℵ	A	B	C	D	F	G	K	L	P	049	33	81	104	699	1594	1739
Epiph	-																				
TR	59.7	-																			
𝔐	58.1	96.0	-																		
𝔓46	54.6	39.4	39.4	-																	
ℵ	61.2	41.6	41.6	76.6	-																
A	62.2	45.7	45.7	65.5	80.2	-															
B	56.2	40.2	40.2	73.1	74.4	65.7	-														
C	66.3	44.4	43.2	68.3	77.8	75.6	73.0	-													
D	45.7	38.4	34.4	45.7	48.0	52.6	50.4	43.2	-												
F	40.3	27.5	25.8	39.3	35.8	39.6	37.2	31.6	67.5	-											
G	41.1	28.3	26.7	38.2	35.0	38.7	36.3	31.6	68.3	98.3	-										
K	54.6	85.6	87.5	37.7	41.3	45.3	42.7	47.5	35.6	24.8	25.7	-									
L	55.0	89.6	92.0	35.1	38.4	44.8	37.6	45.7	36.0	26.7	27.5	85.6	-								
P	68.3	64.8	63.9	51.1	59.8	61.1	56.1	57.5	39.3	35.9	35.0	62.7	60.7	-							
049	63.2	85.7	88.1	34.4	44.0	45.3	41.7	50.0	46.4	27.7	28.9	90.6	85.7	66.7	-						
33	60.8	47.9	46.3	62.2	72.7	68.8	70.8	74.4	47.9	37.1	35.3	49.0	46.3	66.9	55.4	-					
81	66.1	51.2	49.6	66.7	78.0	73.3	70.4	74.1	52.0	32.2	33.1	51.0	48.0	65.0	52.4	70.6	-				
104	69.8	74.4	72.0	45.7	52.0	54.3	47.9	53.1	36.0	33.3	32.5	69.2	70.4	70.5	66.7	56.2	61.0	-			
699	57.4	89.9	94.1	36.7	38.7	42.6	37.8	42.5	34.5	24.6	25.4	85.7	89.9	60.3	87.3	44.3	48.3	67.2	-		
1594	57.4	93.6	96.0	37.2	40.8	44.8	37.6	42.0	33.6	23.3	24.2	87.5	88.0	63.1	84.5	44.6	48.8	72.8	91.6	-	
1739	54.3	51.2	49.6	64.9	67.2	64.7	71.8	61.7	45.6	32.5	31.7	49.0	48.0	56.6	51.2	65.3	65.0	52.0	47.1	47.2	-

Table 26

Romans

	Epiph	TR	𝔐	𝔓46	ℵ	A	B	C	D	F	G	K	L	P	049	33	81	104	699	1594	1739
Epiph	-																				
TR	61.5	-																			
𝔐	61.5	92.3	-																		
𝔓46	0.0	25.0	25.0	-																	
ℵ	53.8	23.1	23.1	50.0	-																
A	53.8	23.1	23.1	50.0	100.0	-															
B	38.5	38.5	38.5	75.0	53.8	53.8	-														
C	60.0	20.0	20.0	50.0	60.0	60.0	50.0	-													
D	23.1	38.5	30.8	100.0	46.2	46.2	69.2	50.0	-												
F	23.1	38.5	30.8	75.0	15.4	15.4	53.8	20.0	61.5	-											
G	23.1	38.5	30.8	75.0	15.4	15.4	53.8	20.0	61.5	100.0	-										
K	44.4	88.9	88.9	33.3	22.2	22.2	55.6	42.9	44.4	33.3	33.3	-									
L	53.8	84.6	92.3	25.0	30.8	30.8	46.2	30.0	38.5	23.1	23.1	100.0	-								
P	63.6	90.9	100.0	0.0	18.2	18.2	27.3	22.2	18.2	27.3	27.3	87.5	90.9	-							
049	46.2	76.9	84.6	25.0	23.1	23.1	53.8	40.0	46.2	30.8	30.8	100.0	92.3	81.8	-						
33	46.2	76.9	84.6	25.0	23.1	23.1	38.5	30.0	30.8	30.8	30.8	100.0	92.3	90.9	84.6	-					
81	69.2	38.5	38.5	25.0	76.9	76.9	53.8	70.0	46.2	23.1	23.1	33.3	46.2	36.4	38.5	38.5	-				
104	76.9	76.9	69.2	25.0	38.5	38.5	30.8	40.0	38.5	30.8	30.8	55.6	61.5	63.6	53.8	53.8	53.8	-			
699	53.8	84.6	92.3	25.0	30.8	30.8	46.2	30.0	38.5	23.1	23.1	100.0	100.0	90.9	92.3	92.3	46.2	61.5	-		
1594	69.2	84.6	92.3	25.0	30.8	30.8	30.0	23.1	23.1	23.1	23.1	77.8	84.6	90.9	76.9	76.9	46.2	76.9	84.6	-	
1739	46.2	53.8	53.8	0.0	46.2	46.2	46.2	20.0	30.8	30.8	30.8	44.4	46.2	54.5	53.8	38.5	38.5	38.5	46.2	46.2	-

EPIPHANIUS' TEXT OF THE PAULINE EPISTLES 215

Table 27

1 Corinthians

	Epiph	TR	𝔐	𝔓46	ℵ	A	B	C	D	F	G	K	L	P	049	33	81	104	699	1594	1739
Epiph	-																				
TR	57.7	-																			
𝔐	54.9	94.1	-																		
𝔓46	60.0	39.7	39.7	-																	
ℵ	62.0	41.2	41.2	77.6	-																
A	64.3	46.3	46.3	66.7	77.6	-															
B	54.9	32.4	32.4	72.4	72.1	67.2	-														
C	60.9	47.7	45.5	65.0	75.0	76.7	70.5	-													
D	47.9	33.8	27.9	43.1	48.5	50.7	45.6	36.4	-												
F	43.5	28.8	27.3	32.1	34.8	38.5	33.3	28.6	74.2	-											
G	43.5	28.8	27.3	32.1	34.8	38.5	33.3	23.6	74.2	98.5	-										
K	51.9	82.4	86.3	42.9	45.1	46.0	37.3	51.9	27.5	25.5	25.5	-									
L	50.7	92.6	95.6	37.9	39.7	44.8	30.9	47.7	30.9	30.3	30.3	84.5	-								
P	70.0	56.7	53.7	56.1	67.2	65.2	56.7	66.2	41.8	36.9	36.9	54.0	52.2	-							
049	62.5	84.2	86.8	32.3	42.1	40.5	26.3	44.4	39.5	27.0	27.0	90.9	84.2	56.8	-						
33	58.2	37.5	32.8	59.3	75.0	73.0	70.3	73.2	48.4	35.5	33.9	36.2	34.4	63.5	40.5	-					
81	63.4	48.5	45.6	69.0	79.4	74.6	72.1	75.0	51.5	33.3	33.3	49.0	44.1	65.7	50.0	75.0	-				
104	69.0	67.6	64.7	51.7	55.9	58.2	47.1	56.8	36.8	40.9	40.9	60.8	66.2	67.2	57.9	56.2	58.8	-			
699	55.7	88.1	94.0	38.6	37.3	42.4	29.9	44.2	28.4	27.7	27.7	82.0	89.6	51.5	86.8	31.7	44.8	58.2	-		
1594	54.9	94.1	97.1	39.7	41.2	46.3	32.4	45.5	27.9	24.2	24.2	88.2	92.6	55.2	86.8	34.4	45.6	64.7	91.0	-	
1739	54.9	50.0	47.1	69.0	66.2	64.2	77.9	53.2	50.0	33.3	33.3	49.0	45.6	58.2	47.4	70.3	70.6	55.9	43.3	47.1	-

Table 28

2 Corinthians

	Epiph	TR	𝔐	𝔓46	ℵ	A	B	C	D	F	G	K	L	P	049	33	81	104	699	1594	1739
Epiph	-																				
TR	69.2	-																			
𝔐	69.2	100.0	-																		
𝔓46	63.6	40.0	40.0	-																	
ℵ	69.2	41.7	41.7	80.0	-																
A	75.0	25.0	25.0	100.0	100.0	-															
B	69.2	41.7	41.7	80.0	83.3	75.0	-														
C	66.7	33.3	33.3	100.0	100.0	100.0	83.3	-													
D	61.5	50.0	50.0	70.0	58.3	75.0	75.0	66.7	-												
F	46.2	16.7	16.7	40.0	41.7	50.0	41.7	33.3	41.7	-											
G	46.2	16.7	16.7	40.0	41.7	50.0	41.7	33.3	41.7	100.0	-										
K	69.2	100.0	100.0	40.0	41.7	25.0	41.7	33.3	50.0	16.7	16.7	-									
L	61.5	91.7	91.7	30.0	33.3	25.0	33.3	33.3	41.7	25.0	25.0	91.7	-								
P	69.2	58.3	58.3	60.0	56.7	50.0	66.7	50.0	41.7	41.7	41.7	58.3	50.0	-							
049	69.2	100.0	100.0	40.0	41.7	25.0	41.7	33.3	50.0	16.7	16.7	100.0	91.7	58.3	-						
33	69.2	41.7	41.7	80.0	83.3	75.0	91.7	83.3	66.7	33.3	33.3	41.7	33.3	66.7	41.7	-					
81	72.7	40.0	40.0	100.0	90.0	100.0	90.0	100.0	70.0	40.0	40.0	40.0	30.0	70.0	40.0	90.0	-				
104	76.9	91.7	91.7	40.0	50.0	25.0	50.0	33.3	41.7	25.0	25.0	91.7	83.3	66.7	91.7	50.0	50.0	-			
699	71.4	100.0	100.0	28.6	42.9	25.0	23.6	33.3	42.9	28.6	28.6	100.0	100.0	57.1	100.0	28.6	33.3	100.0	-		
1594	69.2	100.0	100.0	40.0	41.7	25.0	41.7	33.3	50.0	16.7	16.7	100.0	91.7	58.3	100.0	41.7	40.0	91.7	100.0	-	
1739	53.8	50.0	50.0	60.0	75.0	75.0	58.3	83.3	41.7	33.3	33.3	50.0	41.7	41.7	50.0	58.3	70.0	58.3	57.1	50.0	-

Table 29

Galatians through Hebrews

	Epiph	TR	𝔐	𝔓46	ℵ	A	B	C	D	F	G	K	L	P	049	33	81	104	699	1594	1739
Epiph	-																				
TR	59.4	-																			
𝔐	59.4	100.0	-																		
𝔓46	45.5	40.9	40.9	-																	
ℵ	59.4	50.0	50.0	77.3	-																
A	59.4	56.2	56.2	59.1	75.0	-															
B	62.5	62.5	62.5	71.4	87.5	66.7	-														
C	81.0	52.4	52.4	66.7	85.7	76.2	92.9	-													
D	43.8	43.8	43.8	31.8	43.8	56.2	41.7	47.6	-												
F	37.9	24.1	24.1	52.6	44.8	51.7	36.4	44.4	65.5	-											
G	41.4	27.6	27.6	47.4	41.4	48.3	31.8	44.4	69.0	96.6	-										
K	56.2	84.4	84.4	27.3	40.6	53.1	50.0	47.6	40.6	24.1	27.6	-									
L	62.5	84.4	84.4	31.8	40.6	53.1	54.2	52.4	43.8	20.7	24.1	81.2	-								
P	65.6	75.0	75.0	40.9	56.2	68.8	62.5	52.4	40.6	34.5	31.0	71.9	71.9	-							
049	71.4	85.7	85.7	36.8	61.9	71.4	61.9	75.0	57.1	33.3	38.1	81.0	81.0	81.0	-						
33	68.8	59.4	59.4	68.2	84.4	78.1	79.2	95.2	46.9	44.8	41.4	56.2	56.2	65.6	71.4	-					
81	68.8	65.6	65.6	54.5	71.9	65.6	66.7	66.7	50.0	31.0	34.5	62.5	62.5	71.9	71.4	68.8	-				
104	65.6	81.2	81.2	36.4	50.0	56.2	58.3	57.1	31.2	20.7	17.2	78.1	78.1	81.2	76.2	59.4	71.9	-			
699	59.4	93.8	93.8	36.4	43.8	50.0	58.3	47.6	43.8	17.2	20.7	84.4	84.4	68.8	81.0	53.1	59.4	81.2	-		
1594	53.1	93.8	93.8	31.8	43.8	50.0	54.2	42.9	43.8	24.1	27.6	84.4	78.1	71.9	76.2	53.1	59.4	81.2	93.8	-	
1739	56.2	53.1	53.1	68.2	75.0	71.9	75.0	61.9	43.8	31.0	27.6	50.0	56.2	59.4	57.1	68.8	62.5	46.9	53.1	46.9	-

Table 30

Agreement of Manuscripts with Epiphanius in the Pauline Epistles

Witness	No. Agreements	Total Occurrences	% Agreement
104	90	129	69.8
P	86	126	68.3
C	55	83	66.3
81	84	127	66.1
049	55	87	63.2
A	74	119	62.2
ℵ	79	129	61.2
33	76	125	60.8
TR	77	129	59.7
𝔐	75	129	58.1
699	70	122	57.4
1594	74	129	57.4
B	68	121	56.2
L	71	129	55.0
𝔓46	53	97	54.6
K	59	108	54.6
1739	70	129	54.3
D	59	129	45.7
G	51	124	41.1
F	50	124	40.3

Table 31

Agreement with Epiphanius in Rom, 1 Cor, 2 Cor. and Gal-Heb
(Witness; % Agreement with Epiphanius; No. Occurrences)

Romans			1 Corinthians			2 Corinthians			Galatians-Hebrews		
104	76.9	13	P	70.0	70	104	76.9	13	C	81.0	21
81	69.2	13	104	69.0	71	A	75.0	4	049	71.4	21
1594	69.2	13	A	64.3	70	81	72.7	11	33	68.8	32
P	63.6	11	81	63.4	71	699	71.4	7	81	68.8	32
TR	61.5	13	049	62.5	40	TR	69.2	13	P	65.6	32
𝔐	61.5	13	ℵ	62.0	71	𝔐	69.2	13	104	65.6	32
C	60.0	10	C	60.9	46	ℵ	69.2	13	B	62.5	24
ℵ	53.8	13	𝔓⁴⁶	60.0	60	B	69.2	13	L	62.5	32
A	53.8	13	33	58.2	67	K	69.2	13	ℵ	59.4	32
L	53.8	13	TR	57.7	71	P	69.2	13	A	59.4	32
699	53.8	13	699	55.7	70	049	69.2	13	TR	59.4	32
049	46.2	13	B	54.9	71	33	69.2	13	𝔐	59.4	32
33	46.2	13	1739	54.9	71	1594	69.2	13	699	59.4	32
1739	46.2	13	𝔐	54.9	71	C	66.7	6	K	56.2	32
K	44.4	9	1594	54.9	71	𝔓⁴⁶	63.6	11	1739	56.2	32
B	38.5	13	K	51.9	54	D	61.5	13	1594	53.1	32
D	23.1	13	L	50.7	71	L	61.5	13	𝔓⁴⁶	45.5	22
F	23.1	13	D	47.9	71	1739	53.8	13	D	43.8	32
G	23.1	13	F	43.5	69	F	46.2	13	G	41.4	29
𝔓⁴⁶	0.0	4	G	43.5	69	G	46.2	13	F	37.9	29

Table 32

% of Agreement of Witnesses with Epiphanius in the Pauline Epistles

A. Old Egyptian = 56.7%

Witness	Agreements	Comparisons
𝔓⁴⁶	53	97
ℵ	79	129
B	68	121
1739	70	129
Total	270	476

B. Later Egyptian = 65.6%

Witness	Agreements	Comparisons
A	74	119
C	55	83
P	86	126
33	76	125
81	84	127
104	90	129
Total	465	709

C. "Western" Unicals = 42.4%

Witness	Agreements	Comparisons
D	59	129
F	50	124
G	51	124
Total	160	377

Table 32, cont.

D. Byzantine Witnesses = 57.4%

Witness	Agreements	Comparisons
𝔐	75	129
K	59	108
L	71	129
049	55	37
699	70	122
1594	74	129
Total	404	704

Table 33

% of Agreement of Witnesses with Epiphanius in Romans

A. Old Egyptian = 41.9%

Witness	Agreements	Comparisons
$\mathfrak{P}^{46}$	0	4
ℵ	7	13
B	5	13
1739	6	13
Total	18	43

B. Later Egyptian = 61.6%

Witness	Agreements	Comparisons
A	7	13
C	6	10
P	7	11
33	6	13
81	9	13
104	10	13
Total	45	73

Table 33, cont.

C. "Western" Uncials = 23.1%

Witness	Agreements	Comparisons
D	3	13
F	3	13
G	3	13
Total	9	39

D. Byzantine witnesses = 55.4%

Witness	Agreements	Comparisons
𝔐	8	13
K	4	9
L	7	13
049	6	13
699	7	13
1594	9	13
Total	41	74

Table 34

% of Agreement of Witnesses with Epiphanius in 1 Corinthians

A. Old Egyptian = 57.9%

Witness	Agreements	Comparisons
$\mathfrak{P}^{46}$	36	60
ℵ	44	71
B	39	71
1739	39	71
Total	158	273

Table 34, cont.

B. Later Egyptian = 64.6%

Witness	Agreements	Comparisons
A	45	70
C	28	46
P	49	70
33	39	67
81	45	71
104	49	71
Total	255	395

C. "Western" Uncials = 45.0%

Witness	Agreements	Comparisons
D	34	71
F	30	69
G	30	69
Total	94	209

D. Byzantine witnesses = 54.6%

Witness	Agreements	Comparisons
𝔐	39	71
K	28	54
L	36	71
049	25	40
699	39	70
1594	39	71
Total	206	377

Table 35

% of Agreement of Witnesses with Epiphanius in 2 Corinthians

A. Old Egyptian = 64.0%

Witness	Agreements	Comparisons
$\mathfrak{P}^{46}$	7	11
ℵ	9	13
B	9	13
1739	<u>7</u>	<u>13</u>
Total	32	50

B. Later Egyptian = 71.7%

Witness	Agreements	Comparisons
A	3	4
C	4	6
P	9	13
33	9	13
81	8	11
104	<u>10</u>	<u>13</u>
Total	43	60

C. "Western" Uncials = 51.3%

Witness	Agreements	Comparisons
D	8	13
F	6	13
G	<u>6</u>	<u>13</u>
Total	20	39

Table 35, cont.

D. Byzantine witnesses = 68.1%

Witness	Agreements	Comparisons
𝔐	9	13
K	9	13
L	8	13
049	9	13
699	5	7
1594	<u>9</u>	<u>13</u>
Total	49	72

Table 36

% of Agreement of Witnesses with Epiphanius in Galatians — Hebrews

A. Old Egyptian = 56.4%

Witness	Agreements	Comparisons
𝔓⁴⁶	10	22
ℵ	19	32
B	15	24
1739	<u>18</u>	<u>32</u>
Total	62	110

B. Later Egyptian = 67.4%

Witness	Agreements	Comparisons
A	19	32
C	17	21
P	21	32
33	22	32
81	22	32
104	<u>21</u>	<u>32</u>
Total	122	181

Table 36, cont.

C. "Western" Uncials = 41.1%

Witness	Agreements	Comparisons
D	14	32
F	11	29
G	12	29
Total	37	90

D. Byzantine witnesses = 59.7%

Witness	Agreements	Comparisons
𝔐	19	32
K	18	32
L	20	32
049	15	21
699	19	32
1594	17	32
Total	108	181

[TR 59.4%]

Table 37

Summary of Statistical Data in Tables 23–27

Groups	Corpus	Romans	1 Cor	2 Cor	Gal–Hebrews
Old Egyptian	56.7	41.9	57.9	64.0	56.4
Later Egyptian	65.6	61.6	64.6	71.7	67.4
"Western" uncials	42.4	23.1	45.0	51.3	41.1
Byzantine	57.4	55.4	54.6	68.1	59.7

In Table 30, Epiphanius has highest agreement with Later Egyptian witnesses. The Byzantine witnesses follow, and it is evident that Epiphanius does not have significant agreement with the "Western" witnesses.

This analysis, however, presupposes a uniformity of text type throughout these epistles. In order to clarify the initial indication of textual affinity in individual epistles, separate analyses are made for Romans, 1 Corinthians and 2 Corinthians. The quotations from Galatians through Hebrews are grouped together. Percentages of agreement are given in Tables 31 and 32. As expected, Tables 31 and 32 maintain the general impression from Table 30 that the Egyptian witnesses are Epiphanius' primary agreement, followed by significantly less Byzantine support, and the "Western" uncials presenting only negligible support.

When the first three epistles are analyzed separately, some very important observations emerge. In Romans, there is very strong support for Epiphanius' text in the Later Egyptian witnesses (61.6%), while Older Egyptians exhibit very little agreement with Epiphanius (41.9%). The Byzantine text in Romans is not as strong (55.4%) as the Later Egyptians. The "Western" uncials show only negligible support (23.1%)

In 1 Corinthians, the Later Egyptian text is still prominent (64.6%), while the Old Egyptians increase considerably (57.9%). The Byzantine witnesses follow (54.6%), and the "Western" support is low (45.0%).

The pattern of agreement with the Later Egyptian text (71.7%) continues in 2 Corinthians, with the Old Egyptian text increasing to a surprising 64.0%. The Byzantine text is significantly higher (68.1%), but the "Western" uncials are not strong (51.3%).

From Galatians through Hebrews, grouped together because of the small number of variants in each of these smaller epistles, the Later Egyptian witnesses cluster convincingly at the top (67.4%), followed by the Byzantines (59.7%), and at a distance by the Old Egyptians (56.4%) and "Western" uncials (41.1%) decidedly at the bottom.

Six of the top eight witnesses in agreement with the text of Epiphanius in Table 30 are Later Egyptians. In Table 31, C P 81 104 show good support for Epiphanius throughout. A is strong in 1 and 2 Corinthians, but less so in Romans. In the citations of Epiphanius from the Pauline Epistles, A C P 81 104 demonstrate textual phenomena not found in $\mathfrak{P}^{46}$ B 1739.[6]

From these data, it appears that Epiphanius' text of Romans is Late Egyptian in character, with a certain Byzantine influence. There is no significant agreement with either the Old Egyptian tradition or with the "Western" manuscripts. Epiphanius' text of 1 and 2 Corinthians appears to be Late Egyptian, with some Byzantine influence. Epiphanius' text of Galatians-Hebrews, however, appears to be Late Egyptian in character with no significant Byzantine influence.

---

[6] See Zuntz, *Text of the Epistles*, 84–159.

2. THE QUALITATIVE ANALYSIS

Table 38

Epiphanius' Attestation of Inter-Group Readings in the Pauline Epistles (125 variants)

	Distinctive	Exclusive	Primary	Total	%
Egyptian	5/14	7/20	10/14	22/48	45.8
"Western"	2/18	0/5	10/34	12/57	21.1
Byzantine	0/9	–	19/41	19/50	38.0

Table 39

Epiphanius' Attestation of Intra-Group Readings in the Pauline Epistles

	Uniform	Predominant	Total	%
Egyptian	19/20	52/73	71/93	76.3
Old Egyptian	40/60	28/49	68/109	62.4
Late Egyptian	36/43	41/52	77/95	81.1
"Western"	38/84	9/31	47/115	40.9
Byzantine	58/96	13/22	71/118	60.2

Table 40

Epiphanius' Agreements with Uniform or Predominant Readings that are also Distinctive, Exclusive or Primary in the Pauline Epistles

	Uniform	Predominant	Total	%
Egyptian	4/4	8/18	12/22	54.5
"Western"	8/40	4/11	12/51	23.5
Byzantine	18/44	1/6	19/50	38.0

Table 41

Epiphanius' Attestation of Inter-Group Readings in Romans

	Distinctive	Exclusive	Primary	Total	%
Egyptian	1/1	1/4	2/2	4/7	57.1
"Western"	0/2	0/1	0/5	0/8	0.0
Byzantine	–	–	3/6	3/6	50.0

Table 42

Epiphanius' Attestation of Intra-Group Readings in Romans

	Uniform	Predominant	Total	%
Egyptian	–	5/6	5/6	83.3
Old Egyptian	4/5	2/12	6/17	35.3
Late Egyptian	1/1	7/8	8/9	88.9
"Western"	1/8	0/3	1/11	9.1
Byzantine	6/10	1/3	7/13	53.8

Table 43

Epiphanius' Agreements with Uniform or Predominant Readings that are also Distinctive, Exclusive or Primary in Romans

	Uniform	Predominant	Total	%
Egyptian	–	1/1	1/1	100.0
"Western"	0/5	0/2	0/7	0.0
Byzantine	3/6	–	3/6	50.0

Table 44

Epiphanius' Attestation of Inter-Group Readings in 1 Corinthians

	Distinctive	Exclusive	Primary	Total	%
Egyptian	3/9	4/14	6/8	13/31	41.9
"Western"	1/11	0/3	7/18	8/33	25.0
Byzantine	0/9	–	10/20	10/29	34.5

Table 45

Epiphanius' Attestation of Intra-Group Readings in 1 Corinthians

	Uniform	Predominant	Total	%
Egyptian	13/13	26/38	39/51	76.5
Old Egyptian	24/34	15/27	39/61	63.9
Late Egyptian	20/24	22/28	42/52	80.8
"Western"	25/50	6/15	31/65	47.7
Byzantine	31/53	6/11	37/64	57.8

Table 46

Epiphanius' Agreements with Uniform or Predominant Readings that are also Distinctive, Exclusive or Primary in 1 Corinthians

	Uniform	Predominant	Total	%
Egyptian	2/2	6/12	8/14	57.1
"Western"	5/23	3/5	8/28	28.6
Byzantine	9/25	1/4	10/29	34.5

Table 47

Epiphanius' Attestation of Inter-Group Readings in 2 Corinthians

	Distinctive	Exclusive	Primary	Total	%
Egyptian	0/1	–	1/2	1/3	33.3
"Western"	–	–	0/2	0/2	0.0
Byzantine	–	–	1/4	1/4	25.0

Table 48

Epiphanius' Attestation of Intra-Group Readings in 2 Corinthians

	Uniform	Predominant	Total	%
Egyptian	2/2	8/10	10/12	83.3
Old Egyptian	4/6	5/5	9/11	81.8
Late Egyptian	5/5	5/7	10/12	83.3
"Western"	4/5	1/5	5/10	50.0
Byzantine	8/11	1/1	9/12	75.0

Table 49

Epiphanius' Agreements with Uniform or Predominant Readings that are also Distinctive, Exclusive or Primary in 2 Corinthians

	Uniform	Predominant	Total	%
Egyptian	1/1	0/2	1/3	33.3
"Western"	0/1	0/1	0/2	0.0
Byzantine	1/4	–	1/4	25.0

Table 50

Epiphanius' Attestation of Inter-Group Readings in Galatians-Hebrews

	Distinctive	Exclusive	Primary	Total	%
Egyptian	1/3	2/2	1/2	4/7	57.1
"Western"	1/5	0/1	3/9	4/15	26.7
Byzantine	–	–	5/11	5/11	45.5

Table 51

Epiphanius' Attestation of Intra-Group Readings in Galatians-Hebrews

	Uniform	Predominant	Total	%
Egyptian	4/5	13/19	17/24	70.8
Old Egyptian	10/17	7/9	17/26	65.4
Late Egyptian	10/13	7/9	17/22	77.3
"Western"	8/21	2/8	10/29	34.5
Byzantine	13/22	5/7	18/29	62.1

Table 52

Epiphanius' Agreements with Uniform or Predominant Readings that are also Distinctive, Exclusive or Primary in Galatians-Hebrews

	Uniform	Predominant	Total	%
Egyptian	1/1	1/3	2/4	50.0
"Western"	3/11	1/3	4/14	28.6
Byzantine	5/9	0/2	5/11	45.5

A. EPIPHANIUS' TEXT OF THE PAULINE EPISTLES: GROUP PROFILES

Table 38 indicates Epiphanius' support for the distinctive, exclusive and primary readings of each textual group. As it is rare for all members of a textual group to agree on a particular reading, one cannot expect large totals or high percentages of agreement in these categories. These data suggest that the text of the Pauline Epistles used by Epiphanius was a good Egyptian text. Some Byzantine agreement is detectable, but there is no substantial "Western" agreement. In Table 39, the Intra-Group Profile treats majority readings of a group, regardless of how many other witnesses also support them. Here the results clearly show an Egyptian affinity (76.3%), more precisely a Late Egyptian affinity (81.1%). There is some Byzantine agreement (60.2%), but "Western" support is not strong (40.9%). When, in Table 40, one tabulates Epiphanius' agreements with uniform and predominant readings that are also distinctive, exclusive or primary, Epiphanius is decidedly Egyptian, but with fewer readings. Byzantine support is not strong, and "Western" support is slight.

The general picture emerging from the analysis is that his text was Egyptian in textual character, and specifically Later Egyptian. There is actually little Byzantine influence and no indication at all of relationship with the "Western" text.

B. EPIPHANIUS' TEXT OF ROMANS: GROUP PROFILE

The Inter-Group Profile of Romans in Table 41 indicates Egyptian affinity (57.1%) with some Byzantine support (50%), but no "Western" support. The Intra-Group Profile in Table 42 corroborates this finding, with strong Egyptian support (83.3%), primarily Late Egyptian (88.9%). Byzantine support is not strong (53.8%), and "Western" support is negligible (9.1%). The combination of readings in Table 43 confirms the Late Egyptian affinity of Epiphanius' text of Romans.

C. EPIPHANIUS' TEXT OF 1 CORINTHIANS: GROUP PROFILE

The Inter-Group Profile in Table 44 indicates Egyptian affinity in Epiphanius' citations of 1 Corinthians. Byzantine support is not strong, nor is "Western" support. The Intra-Group Profile in Table 45, treating majority readings of a group regardless of how many others also support those readings, confirms that Epiphanius' text has a strong Egyptian (76.5%) affinity, primarily Later Egyptian (80.8%). Byzantine support is not strong (57.8%) and "Western" support follows (47.7%). The combination of readings in Table 46 clearly demonstrates Egyptian affinity in Epiphanius' citations of 1 Corinthians, primarily Later Egyptian. Byzantine affinity is not strong, nor is "Western."

D. EPIPHANIUS' TEXT OF 2 CORINTHIANS: GROUP PROFILE

In the Inter-Group Profile in Table 47, Epiphanius has good Egyptian support in 2 Corinthians, but Byzantine support is not strong, and there is no "Western" support at all. In the Intra-Group Profile in Table 48, Epiphanius has sizeable support from the Egyptian traditions (83.3%), more so Later Egyptian (83.3%) but with significant support from the Old Egyptians (81.8%). Byzantine agreement is stronger than elsewhere (75%), but "Western" support is not appreciable (50%). The combination of readings in Table 49 confirms that Epiphanius' affinity in 2 Corinthians is principally with the Later Egyptian textual group.

E. EPIPHANIUS' TEXT OF GALATIANS-HEBREWS: GROUP PROFILE

The Inter-Group Profile in Table 50 indicates strong support in Epiphanius' quotations of the epistles from Galatians–Hebrews by the Egyptian text. Byzantine support is not strong, and "Western" support is slight. The Intra-Group Profile in Table 51 indicates, likewise, a strong Egyptian support (70.8%), primarily Late Egyptian (77.3%) rather than Old Egyptian (65.4%). There is some Byzantine agreement (62.1%), but "Western" support is not strong (34.5%). The combination of readings in Table 52 confirms a strong Egyptian affinity, primarily Later Egyptian.

F. SUMMARY OF GROUP PROFILES

Epiphanius' quoations of the Pauline epistles demonstrate a solid Egyptian affinity, more Later Egyptian than Old Egyptian. Support from the Byzantine tradition is not as strong as statistical data might indicate. Support from the "Western" tradition is negligible.

4. SELECTED READINGS UPON WHICH EPIPHANIUS COMMENTS

Occasionally, Epiphanius indicates an awareness of more than one reading in manuscripts known to him. For instance, in *Pan* 51.13.1 he cites John 1:28, noting, "'These things were done in Bethabara'—'Bethany' in other copies—beyond Jordan."

Rarely does he comment upon his preference for one particular reading as opposed to another. For instance, in *Pan* 51.11.6, he says that the text of 2 Tim 4:10, does not read "in Galatia," as some manuscripts have it, but "in Gaul," as his biblical exemplar reads. Epiphanius says of Marcion that "some of the sayings had been falsely entered by himself, in an altered form and different from the authentic copy of the Gospel and the meaning of the apostolic canon, but others were exactly like both the Gospel and Apostle—unchanged by Marcion, and yet capable of disproving his entire case" (*Pan* 42.10.4–5). One important instance involves the reading "Christ" or "lord" in 1 Cor 10:9.

These two units of variation upon which Epiphanius comments in the Apostolos illustrate the way he dealt with instances of known variation and what this contributes to our knowledge of his biblical exemplar.

A. EPIPHANIUS AND THE TEXTUAL PROBLEM IN 2 TIM 4:10

In *Pan* 51.11.6, Epiphanius says regarding 2 Tim 4:10 that Luke,

> preached in Dalmatia, Gaul, Italy and Macedonia first, but originally in Gaul, as Paul says of certain of his followers in his epistles, 'Crescens is in Gaul'. It does not say, 'in Galatia", as some wrongly believe, but 'in Gaul'.

The basic textual data for 4:10 are as follows:

Γαλλίαν   Epiph ℵ C 81 104 326 436 919 cop^{sa}

Γαλατίαν   A D F G K L P Ψ 33 88 181 383 614 699 915 917 1594 1739 1881 1908 1912 2127 2344 2495 𝔐 it$^{d.e.f.g}$ syr$^{p.h}$ cop$^{bo[mss]}$ Iren Ephr

Γαλιλαίαν cop$^{bo[mss]}$

Support for Γαλατίαν is early and widespread,[7] while support for Γαλλία is not earlier than the fourth century [Epiph ℵ cop^sa] and occurs primarily in Later Egyptian MSS. External data are strongly in favor of the reading Γαλατίαν.

Complicating the picture emerging from the textual apparatus is the fact that both UBSGNT[4] and NA[27] list Eusebius as support for Γαλλίαν. However, it is certain that Eusebius has no intent to cite the text of 2 Tim 4:10 in *EH* 3.4.8. Although most English translations read, "Crescens is mentioned by him as sent to Gaul," the Greek text reads Κρήσκης μὲν ἐπὶ τὰς Γαλλίας στειλάμενος ὑπ' αὐτοῦ μαρτυρεῖται, and ἐπὶ τὰς Γαλλίας should be rendered, "to the Gauls" instead of "to Gaul."[8]

Ancient writers spoke of that portion of Europe that is West of the Rhine with three terms: (1) Κέλται (or Κελτοί, Κελτική), (2) Γαλατία (Γαλάται), and (3) Γαλλία. When Greek writers did not use the older and more usual Κέλται,[9] they usually used Γαλατία for Gaul, so much so that eventually it became necessary to refer to the land of Galatia in Asia and its inhabitants specifically as οἱ ἐν 'Ασίᾳ Γαλάται[10] and Γαλλογραικοί / Γαλλογραῖκα.[11] Γαλατία, occurs as early as the third-century B.C.E. in reference to this region,[12] and is the more frequent term in Polybius, Diodorus, Strabo, Josephus, Plutarch, Appian, Pausanius, and Dio Cassius. It appears also in Clement of Alexandria and Origen.[13]

On the other hand, the customary Roman term for these people was *Galli*. Long ago, Zahn[14] observed that over the centuries Γαλατία with reference to the European Celts became a somewhat strange term, leading scribes to alter ΓΑΛΑΤΙΑ into ΓΑΛΛΙΑ.[15] Γαλλία occurs in the

---

[7] In a precise citation of vv. 10–11, Irenaeus' Latin text of *Adv. Haer.* 3.14 reads, "Crescens in Galatiam." See W. W. Harvey, *Sancti Irenaei* (Cambridge: Cambridge University Press, 1857), 2.75.

[8] Eduard Schwartz, *Eusebius Werke* (Leipzig: Hinrichs, 1903), 2.1.194.

[9] For example, see Hecataeus in C. and T. Müller, eds., *Fragmenta Historicum Graecorum* (Paris: Didot, 1841), 2; and for Herodotus, see A. D. Godley, *Herodotus* (LCL; London: Heinemann, 1960), 1.314 and 2.250.

[10] See Frank C. Babbitt, *Plutarch* (LCL; London: Heinemann, 1949), 3.536.

[11] See C. Müller and F. Dübner, eds., *Strabonis Geographica* (Paris: Didot, 1853), 107, 485.

[12] C. and T. Müller, *Fragmenta Historicum*, 200.

[13] J. B. Lightfoot, *Saint Paul's Epistle to the Galatians* (London: Macmillan, 1902), 3, n. 2.

[14] Theodor Zahn, *Introduction to the New Testament* (trans. M. W. Jacobus; Edinburgh: T&T Clark, 1909), 2.25, n. 8.

[15] Bernhard Weiss, *Die Briefe Pauli an Timotheus und Titus* (KEK 11; Göttingen: Vanderhoeck und Ruprecht, 1902), 319, suggests the alteration was unintentional and orthographical in nature.

Acts of Paul, about 170.[16] Galen, speaking of a quotation dating from the time of Nero in which Γαλατία is used of Gaul, writes about the various usages of the three possible terms, apparently with no reference to the Galatians in Asia Minor.[17] By the fourth century, Γαλλία had largely displaced Γαλατία with reference to this region.

Therefore, Eusebius' statement, Κρήσκης μὲν ἐπὶ τὰς Γαλλίας στειλάμενος ὑπ᾿ αὐτοῦ μαρτυρεῖται, is not a citation at all, but a reminiscence using the customary term for the European Celts. Certainly, ἐπὶ τὰς Γαλλίας refers to the inhabitants of the region, and should be understood as a patristicism rather than as the text of Eusebius' exemplar. Eusebius does not support Γαλλία in 2 Tim 4:10.

This means that Γαλλία is not known to exist in 2 Tim 4:10 prior to the fourth century. When the oldest extant MSS of the NT were copied, Greeks were already in the habit of following Roman precedent in referring to this area as Γαλλία. Certainly, early Christian interpretation understood the term Γαλατίαν with reference to Gaul. The limited attestation for Γαλλία suggests its intrusion into the MS tradition at least as early as the fourth century, especially in Later Egyptian MSS and some Coptic MSS in Egypt.[18] The alteration was made by a scribe who understood Γαλατία to refer to Gaul.[19] Γαλατία is now accepted correctly as the original reading, and is widely understood with reference to Gaul.[20] This reading is characteristic of Epiphanius' modernized biblical exemplar of Later Egyptian textual character.

---

[16] See R. A. Lipsius, *Acta Apostolorum Apocrypha* (Leipzig: Mendelssohn, 1891), 104.

[17] See C. G. Kühn, *Claudii Galeni: Opera Omnia* (Leipzig: in Officina Libraria Car. Cnoblochii, 1827), 14.80.

[18] Walter Lock, *The Pastoral Epistles* (ICC; Edinburgh: T&T Clark, 1924), 117, mentions a similar problem in 1 Macc 8:2. Theodore of Mopsuestia interprets ἅς ποιοῦσιν ἐν τοῖς Γαλάταις in that text with reference to the Gauls, saying τὰς νῦν καλουμένας Γαλλίας· οὕτως γὰρ αὐτὰς πάντες ἐκάλουν οἱ παλαιοί, and he appeals to the descriptive statement in Josephus' *Jewish War* 2.371, which reads, "especially the Gauls (Γαλάτας) with their magnificent natural ramparts, on the east the Alps, on the north the river Rhine, on the south the chain of the Pyrenees, on the west the ocean."

[19] Metzger, *Textual Commentary on the Greek NT*, 581; and R. V. G. Tasker, *The Greek New Testament* (Oxford: Oxford University Press, 1964), Appx., 441; and B. F. Westcott and F. J. A. Hort, *The New Testament in the Original Greek* (Cambridge: Macmillan, 1882), Appx. 135.

[20] Among those understanding Γαλατία with reference to Gaul, see the lengthy discussion of Ceslas Spicq, *Les Épîtres pastorales* (Paris: Lecoffre, 1969), 2.811–12. See full discussions in William D. Mounce, *Pastoral Epistles* (WBC 46; Nashville: Nelson, 2000), 590; and Gustav Wohlenberg, *Die Pastoralbriefe* (KNT

B. EPIPHANIUS AND THE TEXTUAL PROBLEM IN 1 COR 10:9

In the 1981 *Festschrift* for Bruce Metzger,[21] I held that Epiphanius' statement in *Pan* 42.12.3 regarding the text of 1 Cor 10:9, ὁ δὲ Μαρκίων ἀντὶ τοῦ κύριον Χριστὸν ἐποίησε, cannot be taken at face value. The *erratum* is attributable instead to Epiphanius, who, using a text that read κύριον, merely *assumed* Marcion to have made the substitution. Recently, Ehrman[22] argued that κύριον is, in fact, the original reading at 1 Cor 10:9, and that Χριστόν is an orthodox corruption against Adoptionism. The text critical issue at stake involves not only the reading of 1 Cor 10:9, but how textual data are analyzed.

Elliott[23] observes that, "most text critics claim to try to balance internal criteria or transcriptional probability with an assessment of the age, geographical spread, and reputation of the external (i.e., MS) evidence." Epp[24] suggests, however, that in practice most tend to fall to

---

13; Leipzig: Deichert, 1923), 337, n. 2. See also Gordon D. Fee, *1 and 2 Timothy, Titus* (NIBC; Peabody, Mass. Hendrickson, 1995), 294; J. N. D. Kelly, *The Pastoral Epistles* (London: Black, 1963), 213; and Martin Dibelius, *Die Pastoralbriefe* (HNT 13; Tübingen: Mohr. 1966), 92.

On the other hand, those understanding Γαλατία with reference to Asia Minor are unable to marshal evidence for their view. For instance, A. T. Hanson, *The Pastoral Letters* (Cambridge: Cambridge University Press, 1966), 100, says, without comment, "on the whole Galatia in Asia Minor is more likely," and J. Keith Elliott, *The Greek Text of the Epistles to Timothy and Titus* (SD 36; Salt Lake City: University of Utah Press, 1968): 164, notes without comment, "Γαλατίαν refers to Galatia as at 1 Cor 16:1 " See also, Raymond Collins, *1 & 2 Timothy and Titus* (NTL; Louisville: Westminster/John Knox, 2002), 279; and Donald Guthrie, *The Pastoral Epistles* (Grand Rapids: Eerdmans, 1957), 172, who notes only that Asiatic Galatia "seems to be the most probable here."

[21] See Carroll D. Osburn, "The Text of 1 Corinthians 10:9," in *New Testament Textual Criticism: Essays in Honour of Bruce M. Metzger* (ed. E. Epp & G. Fee; Oxford: Clarendon, 1981), 201–212.

[22] Bart D. Ehrman, *The Orthodox Corruption of Scripture: The Effect of Early Christological Controversies on the Text of the New Testament* (Oxford: Oxford University Press, 1993), 89–90.

[23] J. Keith Elliott, "Thoroughgoing Eclecticism in New Testament Textual Criticism," *The Text of the New Testament in Contemporary Research: Essays on the Status Quaestionis—A Volume in Honor of Bruce M. Metzger* (ed. B. Ehrman and M. Holmes; Grand Rapids: Eerdmans, 1995), 321.

[24] Eldon J. Epp, "The Eclectic Method in New Testament Textual Criticism: Solution or Symptom?" in *Studies in the Theory and Method of New Testament Textual Criticism* (ed. E. Epp and G. Fee; Grand Rapids: Eerdmans, 1993), 166.

one side or the other. Metzger,[25] for instance, argues for a balanced and reasoned eclecticism, yet tends to favor external considerations over internal, and this practice is evident among the UBSGNT committee. Among others, Duplacy[26] insists upon paying major attention to the historical *realia* of the MSS. Ehrman's procedure, on the other hand, certainly utilizes transcriptional probability as the decisive factor in analysis of textual variation in which he detects orthodox corruption. Admittedly, at times neither external data nor authorial intent is as conclusive as could be wished, necessitating greater reliance upon transcriptional probability; however, it is important to be clear about the circumstances and conditions in which this would be the case.[27] While it is obvious that deliberate alterations were sometimes made to the NT text by orthodox scribes, Ehrman has not established his case that this tendency was as common as he posits, and certainly not widespread enough to be turned into a text critical maxim that "the less orthodox reading is to be preferred as original." In view of this challenge to long-standing textual procedure that gives precedence to the MSS tradition, Ehrman's reassessment of the external evidence, internal evidence and transcriptional probabilities related to 1 Cor 10:9 necessitates a re-evaluation of this particular unit of variation.

1. External Evidence.

Textual criticism begins appropriately with the documentary evidence, as set out by Hort,[28] who wrote, "The first step towards obtaining a sure foundation is a consistent application of the principle that KNOWLEDGE OF DOCUMENTS SHOULD PRECEDE FINAL JUDGMENT UPON READINGS." See also Colwell,[29] Aland,[30] and many others,[31] contra Vaganay and Amphoux.[32]

---

[25] Bruce M. Metzger, *A Textual Commentary on the Greek New Testament* (2nd ed.; New York: United Bible Societies, 1994), 1*–16*.

[26] Jean Duplacy, "Histoire des manuscrits et histoire du texte du Nouveau Testament: Quelches réflexions méthodologiques," *NTS* 12 (1965/66): 125.

[27] Bruce M. Metzger, *The Text of the New Testament: Its Transmission, Corruption, and Restoration* (3rd ed.; Oxford: Oxford University Press, 1992), 207–19, esp. 209–10.

[28] B. F. Westcott and F. J. A. Hort, *The New Testament in the Original Greek* (Cambridge: Macmillan, 1882), Introduction, 31.

[29] E. C. Colwell, "Hort Redivivus—A Plea and a Program," in *Transitions in Biblical Scholarship* (ed. J. C. Rysaarsdam; Essays in Divinity 6; Chicago: University of Chicago Press, 1968), 131–55, argued for balance, viewing a one-sided emphasis upon internal considerations as inimical to sound scholarship.

κύριον appears in all of the principal critical editions of the Greek NT since Lachmann in 1831. However, UBSGNT³ introduced Χριστόν and is followed now by NA²⁷. The support for κύριον is basically Egyptian, but the Egyptian versions, corroborated by the particularly noteworthy evidence of Clement,³³ 𝔓⁴⁶ and 1739 readily demonstrate that it was probably not the original Egyptian reading. Furthermore, it was not the dominant Palestinian reading, since Origen and other Fathers in that vicinity based Christological arguments on the reading Χριστόν. On the other hand, Χριστόν, the reading of Marcion, is well attested as early as the second century and throughout the Mediterranean, including Alexandria.³⁴ Zuntz³⁵ comments poignantly that to adopt the reading κύριον under these circumstances is *fides non quarens intellectum*.

Ehrman admits that Χριστόν occurs in the majority of witnesses, including the earliest Alexandrian witness 𝔓⁴⁶, and that "the argument for its originality is certainly attractive." However, he does not consider the antiquity and widespread attestation for Χριστόν to be as significant as the attestation of κύριον in the four "best" Alexandrian witnesses (ℵ B C 33). Although κύριον does not occur in any Greek or versional source prior to B-ℵ, Ehrman posits nevertheless that it is the original reading of the text.

---

[30] Kurt Aland and Barbara Aland, *The Text of the New Testament* (2nd ed.; trans. E. Rhodes; Grand Rapids: Eerdmans, 1989), 281, state, "3. Criticism of the text must always begin from the evidence of the manuscript tradition and only afterward turn to a consideration of internal criteria."

[31] For example, see Michael W. Holmes, "Reasoned Eclecticism in New Testament Textual Criticism," *The Text of the New Testament in Contemporary Research*, 336–60.

[32] Léon Vaganay and Christian-Bernard Amphoux, *An Introduction to New Testament Textual Criticism* (2ⁿᵈ ed.; Cambridge: Cambridge University Press, 1991), 75.

[33] Clement of Alexandria, *Eclogae propheticae* 49.2 (GCS, 3.150).

[34] Gordon D. Fee, *The First Epistle to the Corinthians* (NIC; Grand Rapids: Eerdmans, 1987), 457, notes that Χριστόν "has the best external support (the combination of 𝔓⁴⁶, 1739, Clement, the Egyptian versions in Egypt; all the Western evidence; the earliest evidence from Palestine [Origen]; and Marcion)." Prior to UBSGNT³, C. K. Barrett, *The First Epistle to the Corinthians* (New York: Harper & Row, 1968), 225, [following Günther Zuntz, *The Text of the Epistles* (London: Oxford University Press, 1953), 126, 232] observed Χριστόν to be the original reading upon the basis of the strength of the external evidence.

[35] Zuntz, *Text of the Epistles*, 127. Similarly, Eberhard Nestle, *Einführung in das griechische Neue Testament* (Göttingen: Vandenhoeck und Ruprecht, 1899), 123, observed, "an dieser Stelle war der textus receptus besser als der unserer kritischen Ausgaben."

The following apparatus presents the essential data:[36]

Χριστόν 𝔓[46] D F G K L Ψ 6 69 88 105 201 221 325 356 383 498 547 614 699 915 1075 1241 1247 1594 1739 1881 1908 1912 2298 2344 2412 𝔐 it[d.e.f.g] vulg syr[p.h{txt}] cop[sa.bo] Marc Iren Clem Or Euseb Ephr Chrys Aug Pelag

κύριον ℵ B C P 0150 33 43 104 181 255[vid] 256 263 326 365 436 441 459 460 467 606 621 623 917 1175 1319 1573 1735 1836 1837 1838 1874 1875 1877 1939[vid] 1942 1945 1996 2004 2127 2242 2464 syr[h{mg}] arm eth Hymenaeus[37] Epiph Hesych Thdrt

θεόν A 2 61* 81 254 891* 1003 1115 1127 1524 1595 1649 1947 2012 2523

om 927 1729* 1985 2659

Θεόν appears to be a scribal correction conforming to the LXX.[38] The omission of any object of ἐκπειράζωμεν is likely accidental, although an intentional effort to render the passage ambiguous is possible. Neither θεόν nor the omission has serious claim to be the original reading.

The long-standing preference for κύριον was based upon the assumption that Χριστόν is merely a scribal gloss to explain the meaning of κύριον.[39] The more recent assumption is that the original Χριστόν was altered to κύριον because of the difficulty involved in supposing the ancient Israelites actually to have tempted Christ.[40]

---

[36] For full textual data pertaining to 1 Cor 10:9 in 560 MSS, see Osburn, "The Text of 1 Corinthians 10:9," *New Testament Textual Criticism*, 201–202.

[37] The text of the *Hymenaeusbriefe* against Paul of Samosata printed by M. J. Routh, *Reliquiae Sacrae* (2nd ed.; Oxford: Oxford University Press, 1846), 3.299, and the manuscript followed by Friedrich Loofs, *Paulus von Samosata* (TU 24.5; Leipzig: Hinrichs, 1924), 274, 329, have κύριον, as does the text of Eduard Schwartz, *Eine fingierte Korrespondenz mit Paulus dem Samosatener* (München: Bayerische Akademie der Wissenschaften, 1927), 46. Loofs conjectured that the text must have read Χριστόν originally. This conjecture had been noted earlier by Theodor Zahn, "Eine neue Quelle für die Textgeschichte des Neuen Testaments," *Theologisches Literaturblatt* (1899): 180.

[38] George Howard's, "The Tetragram and the New Testament," *JBL* 96 (1977): 81, suggestion that Paul wrote יהוה and that θεόν and κύριον were the first substitutes, and Χριστόν being a later scribal interpretation, is rather speculative.

[39] See Johannes Weiss, *Der erste Korintherbrief* (MeyerK; 9th ed.; Göttingen: Vandenhoeck & Ruprecht, 1910), 253, n. 2.

[40] Metzger, *Textual Commentary on the Greek New Testament*, 494.

The well-known statement of Epiphanius that Marcion altered κύριον to Χριστόν[41] has been adduced as prime evidence for the secondary nature of Χριστόν. For instance, Blackman cautiously allowed,

> There is a possibility of this being a Marcionite alteration as Epiphanius says, because Κύριον in this context refers to the Creator, and if Marcion was going to make any use of the passage at all he had to alter Κύριον here, as he could have no object in exhorting his followers not to tempt the Demiurge.[42]

Although this would provide a possible rationale for Epiphanius' allegation, Blackman's assumption that "Κύριον in this context refers to the Creator" is questionable, since elsewhere (e.g., 1 Cor 2:8; 4:5; 6:14; 10:16; 15:45, 47) Marcion retained or used κύριος with reference to Christ and could have done so quite easily here. Additionally, argument that Marcion could not have allowed an original κύριον to stand in his text because it would have been inconsistent with his doctrinal presuppositions is nullified by numerous instances in which he retained passages inimical to his theology, such as Lk 7:27; 10:27; 16:17 and Rom 13:8–10, which are inconsistent with his "dualism." In view of Marcion's retention of ἡ δὲ πέτρα ἦν ὁ Χριστός in v. 4 and his omission of ὁ θεός in v. 5, making Χριστός the subject of εὐδόκησεν, it is more reasonable to assume that Marcion, rather than falsifying the text at this point, actually found Χριστόν in his exemplar.[43]

If one accepts Epiphanius' attribution of Χριστόν to Marcion, one concomitantly accepts the difficult task of explaining the reading Χριστόν in Clement and the "presbyter" whom Irenaeus mentions.[44] It is highly unlikely that writers as early as Clement, Irenaeus and his "presbyter" were positively influenced by the text of Marcion. Keeping in mind the fact that apart from Epiphanius' statement about this being a Marcionite alteration, κύριον is otherwise unattested prior to the fourth century.

Epiphanius, using a text that read κύριον, merely *assumed* Marcion to have made the substitution. In view of the zealous hatred for all heresies that permeates the work of Epiphanius and the lack of critical

---

[41] See Adolf von Harnack, *Marcion: Das Evangelium vom fremden Gott* (TU 45; Leipzig: Hinrichs, 1921), 87*.

[42] E. C. Blackman, *Marcion and His Influence* (London: S.P.C.K., 1948), 164–5; cf. however, 47, n. 1.

[43] F. H. A. Scrivener, *A Plain Introduction to the Criticism of the New Testament* (3rd ed.; Cambridge: Deighton Bell, 1883), 506, n. 2; (4th ed; 1894: 2.260, n. 3), says, "In 1 Cor x.9 Marcion seems to uphold the true reading against the judgement of Epiphanius."

[44] Irenaeus, *Adv. Haer.* 4.27.3 (SC 100/2. 746–7).

acumen often reflected in his writings,⁴⁵ one cannot rely too heavily upon his allegation having a reliable basis. As a heresiologist, Epiphanius was motivated to controvert Marcion by any available means, and his allegation of a Marcionite alteration in 10:9 fits this agenda. Since Epiphanius provides no source of information upon which to base such an assertion, it remains an open question whether Epiphanius even relied upon a source at this point. Long ago, Hort⁴⁶ cautioned that, in the statements themselves the contemporary existence of the several variants mentioned is often all that can be safely accepted, and that consideration must be given to the Father's tendencies in referring to texts.

Epiphanius' lack of critical care in citing scripture is well known,⁴⁷ and his "fiery zeal in defense of the purity of ecclesiastical doctrine"⁴⁸ certainly reduces any claim to Epiphanius' impartiality. Epiphanius was aware of these two readings, but his allegation of a Marcionite alteration of κύριον to Χριστόν cannot be taken at face value. In fact, Epiphanius' strongest agreement in citations from the Pauline epistles is with the Later Egyptians (A C P 33 81 104), all of which read κύριον (except A 81, which read θεόν). The Later Egyptian text is characterized by alterations of just this sort. Within this group with which Epiphanius has strongest agreement, MSS P and 104 are the highest at 69–70%, whereas there is much weaker agreement with A and 81 (63–64%). Statistically, it is even less likely that Epiphanius is reliant upon the Old Egyptians (B-ℵ) in 1 Corinthians. There is no early evidence for the existence of κύριον, and Epiphanius, using a fourth-century MS containing a Later Egyptian type of text, simply attributes to Marcion the introduction of the reading Χριστόν, and does so, as usual, without substantiation for his assertion.⁴⁹

---

⁴⁵ See Wilhelm von Christ, *Geschichte der griechischen Literatur* in *Handbuch der Altertumswissenschaft* (6ᵗʰ ed.; Munich: Beck, 1961), 7.1446–51.

⁴⁶ Hort, *The New Testament in the Original Greek: Introduction, Appendix*, 87. Bruce Metzger, "Patristic Evidence and the Textual Tradition of the New Testament," *NTS* 18 (1972): 398–9, mentions the value of explicit patristic references to variant readings in the NT MSS that were known in antiquity, and notes Hort's caution.

⁴⁷ See among others, Gordon D. Fee, "The Use of Greek Patristic Citations in New Testament Textual Criticism: The State of the Question," in *Studies in the Theory and Method of New Testament Textual Criticism* (ed. G. Fee & E. Epp; Grand Rapids: Eerdmans, 1993), 345, who says that Epiphanius' work is "notoriously slovenly," and that his work has "a notorious number of singular readings."

⁴⁸ Johannes Quasten, *Patrology* (Utrecht: Spectrum, 1966), 3. 384.

⁴⁹ Ehrman, *Orthodox Corruption of Scripture*, 116, states, "Osburn . . . has effectively discounted Epiphanius' claim that the text was corrupted by Marcion."

Origen's use of 1 Cor 10:9 is important to note. The marginal reading in 1739 at 1 Cor 10:9 preserves a fragment of book four of Origen's lost *Stromateis*,[50] written in Alexandria sometime prior to A.D. 232, that uses 10:9 with the reading Χριστόν in a series of Christological texts against those who deny that Christ participated in the ancient wilderness experience mentioned in vv. 4–6. Origen ponders whether they will produce some ingenious interpretation of 10:9 to avoid the obvious implications of Christ's presence with the Jews during their wilderness wanderings.[51] Aparently Origen did not know a text of 10:9 that read other than Χριστόν or his argument would have had little or no force.

In the *Hymenaeusbriefe* against Paul of Samosata, written in A.D. 268, the bishops seeking Origen's condemnation used 1 Cor 10:9 with the reading κύριον as evidence against Paul of Samosata's erroneous view of the pre-existence of Christ. Κύριον appears in the text of 10:9 as part of a series of similar texts intended to counter any denial of the pre-existence of Christ. This is the earliest occurrence of the reading κύριον prior to ‍א B and Epiphanius, and κύριον is unquestionably interpreted with reference to Christ rather than to God.

The external textual data for the text of 1 Cor 10:9 demonstrate that Χριστόν, preserved in $\mathfrak{P}^{46}$ and 1739 is by far the oldest reading, occurring early in the East, found in both major Coptic versions, supported by Clement of Alexandria and Origen, and surviving in the so-called "Western" portions of the textual tradition (D E F G), as well as in the majority of Byzantine manuscripts. In basing his argument for the originality of κύριον on ‍א B C 33, Ehrman strangely omits reference to the Sahidic and Bohairic, as well as the important evidence of Clement and Origen, making $\mathfrak{P}^{46}$ appear to be the only Alexandrian witness for Χριστόν.[52] This misdirects the reader's attention from the fact that there is a paucity of pre-fourth century evidence for κύριον, even in Alexandria.

Unlike Χριστόν, κύριον does not enjoy such early and widespread support, occurring in B-‍א and a few later Byzantine witnesses. Although κύριον was the standard reading in printed editions from Lachmann in 1831 through UBSGNT² and NA²⁵, there is no external evidence that the reading even existed prior to the fourth century, apart from the textually-uncertain reference in *Hymenaeusbriefe*. External data overwhelmingly favor Χριστον as the original reading of 1 Cor 10:9.

---

[50] Eusebius, *H.E.* 6.24.3 (GCS 2/2.572).

[51] Darrell Hannah's, *The Text of 1 Corinthians in the Writings of Origen* (SBLNTGF 4; Atlanta: Scholars Press, 1997), failure to include this data is a significant oversight.

[52] Ehrman, *Orthodox Corruption of Scripture*, 116, n. 211.

2. Internal Evidence.

"Internal evidence is of two kinds, which cannot be too sharply distinguished from one another," Hort wrote, ". . . Intrinsic Probability, having reference to the author, and what may be called Transcriptional Probability, having reference to copyists."[53] While admittedly these two matters of textual concern are closely related, they can be confused. One must pay close attention not only to what a later scribe would likely have altered but to what a writer would likely have written in that context in terms of his thought and style. In recent discussions of text critical procedure, considerable attention is paid to the former, i.e., several maxims such as "lectio brevior," "lectio difficilior," and the reading that best explains the origin of the others.[54] However, in these discussions of internal evidence, intrinsic probability has received scant attention. Aland[55] mentions only that,

> Internal criteria (the context of the passage, its style and vocabulary, the theological argument of the author, etc.) can never be the sole basis for a critical decision, especially in opposition to external evidence.

Metzger[56] and Fee[57] also mention context, style and vocabulary of the author as intrinsic data, and both briefly mention problems in using these data, but they assume that text critics will apply these criteria using definitions and procedures established elsewhere.

Elliott[58] and other "thoroughgoing eclectics" who emphasize internal evidence, rather than concern "about the weight, provenance, and the alleged authority of the MSS supporting the variant," stress the importance of ascertaining an author's style. Thus, Kilpatrick[59] stresses the role of Atticism. Placing greater emphasis upon internal criteria than

---

[53] See Westcott and Hort, *New Testament in the Original Greek*, Appx. 20, followed on pp. 21–30 by critique of the limited usefulness of these categories.

[54] Metzger, *Text of the New Testament*, 209–10; Aland, *Text of the New Testament*, 281; Fee, *Studies in the Theory and Method of NT Textual Criticism*, 14.

[55] Aland and Aland, *Text of the New Testament*, 280.

[56] Metzger, *Text of the New Testament*, 210.

[57] Fee, *Theory and Method of NT Textual Criticism*, 14–15.

[58] J. Keith Elliott, "Thoroughgoing Eclecticism in New Testament Textual Research," *Text of the NT in Contemporary Research*, 322. See idem, *Essays and Studies in New Testament Textual Criticism* (Estudios de Filología Neotestamentaria 3; Cordoba: el Almendro, 1992).

[59] See J. Keith Elliott, *The Principles and Practice of New Testament Textual Criticism: Collected Essays of G. D. Kilpatrick* (BETL 96; Louvain: Louvain University Press, 1990).

upon external data has met criticism, but such attempts to clarify internal criteria are welcomed. Even so, Elliott states that stylistic criteria require more elaboration.[60]

With only a brief mention and no specification of criteria, however, the other aspect of intrinsic evidence is left ambiguous—*viz.*, contextual considerations, or what the author would likely have written in that context, given his theological understandings, style and vocabulary. Metzger suggests that attention be paid to "the immediate context,"[61] but this ambiguous reference does not serve well as a useful criterion for ascertaining authorial intent. Written at a time when exegetical procedure began with "defining the limits of the passage,"[62] much exegesis concentrated upon relatively brief units of text, with only minimal reference to the entire documents in which they occurred. Contextual considerations involve much more than merely "the immediate context." A text should be evaluated also in terms of what it contributes to the larger document of which it is a developing part.

In the Metzger *Festschrift*,[63] I argued that in terms of the Christological opening in 1–4, Paul argues in 8:1–11:1 that the Corinthians should avoid situations involving idol food, using 10:1–11 as a midrashic warning with regard to his principal point in 9:27 and 10:12. Directly related to his statement in 8:6 that there is but one Lord, *Jesus Christ*, the exhortation in 10:9 was made in view of the fact that the Corinthians must reckon with Christ. I concluded, "in view of the immediate context of 10:1–11, the developing argument in chs. 8–10, and Paul's dominant concern throughout the epistle, Χριστόν assumes intrinsic probability as the original reading of 10:9" (p. 209).

Ehrman says, "we must take serious account of intrinsic probabilities, specifically with regard to the broader literary context,"[64] and that, "Carroll Osburn provides an extensive argument for the superiority of Χριστός on just such contextual grounds." Since Ehrman has only slight external evidence for his proposal, however, he begins with internal evidence. In fact, he actually dismisses the broader epistolary context and concentrates instead upon the immediate context

---

[60] Elliott, "Thoroughgoing Eclecticism," *The Text of the NT in Contemporary Research*, 324.

[61] Metzger, *Textual Commentary on the Greek NT*, 14*.

[62] See Otto Kaiser and W. G. Kümmel, *Exegetical Method: A Student's Handbook* (trans. E Goetchius; New York: Seabury, 1963), 49; and John Reumann, "Methods in Studying the Biblical Text Today," *Concordia Theological Monthly* 40 (1969): 655–81.

[63] Osburn, "1 Cor 10.9," *New Testament Textual Criticism*, 205–09.

[64] Ehrman, *Orthodox Corruption of Scripture*, 90.

of 10:1–11. He attempts to reduce the contextual argument to mean, "because Paul calls Christ the rock in verse 4, he probably has 'Christ' in mind still in verse 9." He proposes instead that in v. 5 it is not Christ but "God" who is "not well pleased." Since v. 5 is closer to v. 9 than v. 4, Ehrman views the subject of v. 9 as "God." In order to make this argument, Ehrman also has to postulate the omission of ὁ θεός by a few witnesses in v. 5 as an orthodox corruption. His argument relating vv. 5 and 9 is based totally upon transcriptional probability rather than Pauline intent. In fact, Ehrman's internal evidence treats only 10:5, 9, and totally avoids the "serious account . . . of the broader literary context" which he otherwise advocates.

Ehrman correctly observes the vital importance of the "broader literary context." Advances in literary analysis facilitate understanding shorter texts in terms of their contribution to the larger document.[65] Rhetorical criticism is now brought to bear on NT texts.[66] Discourse analysis moves beyond individual words and verses and addresses the function of smaller units in a connected discourse to form increasingly larger units of text, providing meaning and structure for the entire document.[67]

a. *Literary Structure in 1 Corinthians.* The opening midrashic section of 1 Corinthians functions within the total structure of the epistle to overcome various objections and to reestablish his apostolic authority as the founder of the church at Corinth, in order that he might effectively answer the questions that had been raised, not as the champion of one group, but in terms of his Christological focus in order that he might bring about unity in the "body of Christ."[68] Conzelmann and Lindemann[69] observe correctly,

---

[65] See Stanley Stowers, *Letter Writing in Greco-Roman Antiquity* (Philadelphia: Westminster, 1986), and David Aune, *The New Testament in Its Literary Environment* (Philadelphia: Westminster, 1987).

[66] See Stanley Porter, ed., *Handbook of Classical Rhetoric in the Hellenistic Period, 330 B.C.–A.D. 400* (Leiden: Brill, 1997), and Heinrich Lausberg, *Handbook of Literary Rhetoric* (Leiden: Brill, 1998).

[67] See Barbara Johnstone, *Discourse Analysis* (Oxford: Blackwell, 2002), and Stanley Porter and D. A. Carson, *Discourse Analysis and Other Topics in Biblical Greek* (JNTSS 113; Sheffield: Sheffield Academic Press, 1995).

[68] Nils Dahl, "Paul and the Church at Corinth according to 1 Cor 1:10–4:21," *Christian History and Interpretation: Studies Presented to John Knox* (ed. W. R. Farmer et al.; London: Cambridge University Press, 1967): 329. See C. J. Bjerkelund, *PARAKALO: Form, Funktion und Sinn der parakalo-Sätze in den paulinischen Briefen* (Oslo: Universitetsforlaget, 1967), 141–6, and Gerhard Friedrich, "Christus, Einheit und Norm der Christen. Das Grundmotiv des 1. Korintherbriefs," *Kerygma und Dogma* 9 (1963): 235–58, on christocentrism of the letter.

In the various positions Paul is taking concerning the situation in Corinth, there is indeed a unified theological position that emerges: the theology of the cross. The existence of Christians is determined by the fact that their Lord revealed himself at the cross, in lowliness rather than in glory.

The definition of "wisdom" as "Jesus Christ" in 1:18–3:22 underscores Paul's premise that Christian existence is to be defined in terms of Christ. In chapter 4, then, Paul appeals for the diverse readers in Corinth to hear him out in terms of his Christological focus.[70] Certainly the problems regarding immorality in 5–7 are resolved by appeals to Christological understanding and reliance (5:7; 6:11, 15; 7:22, 40).[71]

The second area in which some Corinthians are exercising Christian freedom involves eating meat sacrificed to idols in 8:1–11:1. Some understand that because pagan idols amount to nothing and cannot defile anyone, it is permissible for Christians to participate in meals held in pagan temples (8:10). Paul's response is based upon his argument in 8:6 that there is but one God and one Lord, Jesus Christ. Christian liberty is not unlimited, but should be exercised in terms of Christian fellowship. Failure to conduct themselves in terms of Christ could well lead to disastrous consequences, such as those among the ancient Jews.

At 11:2 Paul shifts his attention to matters of corporate worship that continues through 14:40.[72] Problems involve covering the head in worship (11:2–16), abuses at the Lord's Supper (11:17–34), and exercising spiritual "gifts" in worship (12:1–14:40). In each instance, Paul's Christological perspective (11:11, 27; 12:3, 12, 27) provides underpinning for his deliberative arguments and appeals to consider the corporate

---

[69] Hans Conzelmann and A. Lindemann, *Interpreting the New Testament* (trans. S. Schatzmann; Peabody, Mass.; Hendrickson, 1988), 181.

[70] Margaret Mitchell, *Paul and the Rhetoric of Reconciliation: An Exegetical Investigation of the Language and Composition of 1 Corinthians* (Louisville: Westminster/John Knox, 1991), 5, n. 12, understands correctly that Paul's theological perspective is foundational to his deliberative argument for the elimination of factionalism. Note also L. L. Welborn, "Discord in Corinth: First Corinthians 1–4 and Ancient Politics," *Politics and Rhetoric in the Corinthian Epistles* (Macon, Ga: Mercer University Press, 1997), 1–42.

[71] See, among others, Brian Rosner, *Paul, Scripture, & Ethics: A Study of 1 Corinthians 5–7* (Grand Rapids: Baker, 1994), esp. 179.

[72] See H.-F. Richter, "Anstößige Freiheit in Korinth: Zur Literarkritik der Korintherbriefe (1 Kor 8,1–13 und 11,2–16)," *The Corinthian Correspondence* (BETL 125; ed. R. Bieringer; Leuven: Leuven University Press, 1996), 561–75, on the literary connection between the openings of the sections 8:1–11:1 and 11:2–14:40.

solidarity of the church rather than merely individual inclination (11:11; 27–34; 12:27–31; 14:26, 33).[73]

Continuing his emphasis upon Corinthian maturity, Paul's deliberative argument in 1 Cor 15:1–57 is that the resurrection is the goal (τέλος) that should govern all Christian decision-making.[74] Controversy on this topic was yet another aspect of Corinthian division, and Paul calls for a return to the unity of the church based upon Jesus' own resurrection.[75] Mitchell[76] concludes correctly that the whole argument in 15:1–57 serves to culminate Paul's appeal throughout 1 Corinthians. In the peroratio in 15:58, Paul did not recapitulate the specific advice he gave in the deliberative proofs on each point of Corinthian disagreement (sexual immorality, court battles, marriage, status, idol meats, hairstyles, the Lord's Supper, spiritual gifts, and the resurrection of the dead), but concludes with an appeal to unity based upon the building metaphor. The epistle concludes with various epistolary topics that are not unrelated to the principal argument for concord "in Christ."

b. *The Context of 1 Cor 8:1–11:1*. Most agree that περὶ δέ begins a new topic in 8:1 that concludes in 11:1, but the coherence of chapters 8–10 is variously understood. Following partition theories, Héring[77] divides 1 Corinthians into two letters (8 and 10:23–11:1; 9 and 10:1–22); however, Hurd[78] concludes that, based upon internal evidence, partition theories are incapable of proof. Mitchell,[79] along with most, accepts the unity of 8:1–11:1, but explains the apparent lack of coherence in terms of a main problem (sacrificial meat in 8:1–13; [10:1–13], 10:23–11:1), a side issue (idol food eaten in a temple is forbidden as idolatrous in 10:14–22), and an excursus (Paul's example in chapter 9). Alternatively, Fee[80] views the main issue as eating sacrificial food in pagan temples in 10:1-22, and the

---

[73] See Eriksson, *Traditions as Rhetorical Proof: Pauline Argumentation in 1 Corinthians*, 174–231.

[74] See W. Stenger, "Beobachtungen zur Argumentationsstruktur von 1 Kor 15," *LB* 45 (1979): 71–128.

[75] See Christopher M. Tuckett, "The Corinthians Who Say 'There is no Resurrection of the Dead' (1 Cor 15,12)," *The Corinthian Correspondence*, 247–75; and J. Holleman, "Jesus' Resurrection as the Beginning of the Eschatological Resurrection (1 Cor 15:20)," *The Corinthian Correspondence*, 653–60.

[76] Mitchell, *Paul and the Rhetoric of Reconciliation*, 291.

[77] Jean Héring, *The First Epistle of Saint Paul to the Corinthians* (trans. A. Heathcote and P. Allcock; London: Epworth, 1962), xiii–xiv.

[78] John Hurd, Jr., *The Origin of 1 Corinthians* (London: SPCK, 1965), 131–42.

[79] Mitchell, *Paul and the Rhetoric of Reconciliation*, 237–59.

[80] Gordon D. Fee, *The First Epistle to the Corinthians* (Grand Rapids: Eerdmans, 1987), 357–63.

side issue as the problem of idol meat sold in the market place in 10:23–11:1; however, Fee himself recognizes an inherent problem in his interpretation, especially of 8:10, which is basic to his theory. It is not at all certain that reading chapter 8 in terms of chapter 10 is correct. In view of this imbroglio, Delobel[81] suggests that attempts to distinguish between "main" and "side" issues may actually be *Hineininterpretierung*.

That scholars detect some incoherence in 8:1–11:1 cannot be avoided, yet if it is a literary unit, one would expect some unifying element throughout. Delobel[82] proposes correctly that the unifying element occurs at the outset, περὶ δὲ τῶν εἰδωλοθύτων in 8:1. Εἰδωλόθυτα are at the forefront of the discussion in 8:1–13 and 10:23–11:1, and are referred to in 10:19 and alluded to in 9:22. Εἰδωλόθυτον means "food offered to an idol,"[83] and Paul's argument is that there is nothing inherently wrong with this meat *per se*, since idols amount to nothing. However, when confronted with idol meat, Christians would encounter several ethical and/or religious problems.[84] Delobel's suggestion is that the variety of situations in which Christians may have to deal with sacrificial food is not capable of a simple answer. Therefore, Paul argues consistently that idol food is neutral in principle, but that it can have several meanings according to cultural and cultic contexts.

In 8:1–6, then, Paul argues that in principle idol meat is neutral and can be eaten by Christians, agreeing with "the strong." In vv. 7–13, he treats the risk of scandal involved if the strong exercise their right to eat idol meat. Oster[85] observes,

> While there was no thought of having 'non-religious' meals in pagan temples, it must be remembered that temple dining halls were also used for ceremonies other than the official *cultus* of the deity. Accordingly it is not difficult to imagine Christian attendance . . . which would not necessarily involve idolatry.

---

[81] Delobel, "Coherence and Relevance of 1 Cor 8–10," *The Corinthian Correspondence*, 180.

[82] Ibid., 182–86.

[83] So B. N. Fisk, "Eating Meat Offered to Idols: Corinthian Behavior and Pauline Response," *TrinJ* 10 (1989): 55–58.

[84] See discussion in Michael D. Goulder, *Paul and the Competing Mission in Corinth* (Peabody, Mass.: Hendrickson, 2001), 152–76.

[85] Richard Oster, Jr., "Use, Misuse and Neglect of Archaeological Evidence in Some Modern Works on 1 Corinthians (1 Cor 7,1–5; 8,10; 11,2–16; 12,14–16)," *ZNW* 83 (1992): 52–73, esp. 66, is cited by Delobel, "Coherence," *The Corinthian Correspondence*, 183.

Meals in temples with family or friends would be merely social matters for Christians,[86] but ritual meals are prohibited as idolatrous. In fact, Paul says (v. 10), exercising one's freedom to eat social meals in temples could impact negatively a "weaker" brother, which would actually be a sin against Christ (vv. 11–12). Paul concludes in v. 13, in his first appeal to the readers, that he prefers not to exercise Christian freedom in such cases, and avoids eating idol meat as a Christological matter.

In chapter 9, Paul illustrates the difference between principle and practice in terms of his own apostolic freedom, choosing not to exercise ἐξουσία to do something in order to adapt meaningfully to different types of people (9:19–23; his second appeal to the readers).[87] Just as the Corinthians should not be "stumbling blocks" to others (8:9), Paul himself does not wish to become an "obstacle" (9:12), again as a Christological matter. He concludes in 9:24–27 with a strong appeal to exercise self-control in this regard.

In 10:1–22, Paul argues that when one eats a cultic meal in the temple as worship, idol meat is not neutral but definitely associated with demons, and that the wandering Israelites serve as a serious reminder of the consequences of association with idolatry. His advice to avoid all association with idols (v. 14) is based upon his Christological stance that one cannot be involved in the Lord's Supper and the table of demons.

On the other hand, in 10:23–11:1 buying and eating of food in the market place is neutral, and it is preferable not to inquire about its origin.[88] Once it the food is known to be idol food, however, the possibility of scandal arises and the same restriction is stated as in chapter eight.[89] So, Paul advises the readers to imitate him as he imitates Christ (11:1). The entire section 8:1–11:1 involves a strong Christological argument as a response to the Corinthian problem of idol food.

c. *The Context of 1 Cor 10–13.* Illustrating the appeal for the readers to use self-control if they are to gain the prize (9:24–27),[90] Paul inserts a

---

[86] See Wendell Willis, *Idol Meat in Corinth. The Pauline Argument in I Corinthians 8 and 10* (SBLDS 68; Chico, CA: Scholars Press, 1985), 266.

[87] Alex Cheung, *Idol Food in Corinth: Jewish Background and Pauline Legacy* (JSNTSupp 176; Sheffield: Sheffield Academic Press, 1999), 137–43.

[88] David Horrell, *The Social Ethos of the Corinthian Correspondence* (Edinburgh: T&T Clark, 1996), 146–50.

[89] See Duane F. Watson, "1 Corinthians 10:23–11:1 in the Light of Greco-Roman Rhetoric: The Role of Rhetorical Questions," *JBL* 108 (1989): 301–18, esp. 312, that Paul is summarizing here the points he began to make in 8:1.

[90] Craig Blomberg, *The NIV Application Commentary on First Corinthians* (Grand Rapids: Zondervan, 1994), 191.

midrashic comment upon the lack of self-control by the ancient Israelites as a warning example for the Corinthians (10:14–22). In 10:1–5, Paul draws a parallel between the Christian sacraments and their counterparts in the ancient wilderness in which, even with their own "baptism" and "Lord's Supper" as it were, the Israelites' idolatry led to catastrophic judgment.[91] Paul interprets the OT Christologically, believing that Christ was pre-existent in OT times and assisting the Israelites.[92] This is why he wrote in v. 4, "the rock was Christ."[93] It is precisely because the two situations are analogous that what happened then is relevant for Corinthian conduct. Then, in 10:6–10, he applies this directly to the Corinthians, using four illustrations from the Exodus to appeal to the readers not to "become idolaters" (v. 7), "indulge in sexual immorality" (v. 8), "put Christ to the test" (v. 9), nor "complain" (v. 10).[94] In vv. 11–13, Paul stresses these as "warning examples," especially for those who think themselves to be "strong" and beyond temptation (9:27). Fee[95] suggests rightly that for ordinary trials God's provisions are sufficient, but that no such provisions exist for deliberate rebellion against God. Regarding eating idol food, Cheung[96] posits,

> to refuse to eat idol food presented at such meals would mark one as anti-social and invite misunderstanding and hostility . . . one would risk being ostracized for refusing to eat idol food with friends, relatives, business associates or other people of importance . . . But to those who take their stand against the idolatrous practice, the promise in 10:13 would have been necessary.

Concluding this part of his argument, Paul confronts the Corinthians with their precarious situation. Malina[97] notes correctly,

> the whole point of the rabbinic Scriptural proof in 10,1–11 is to point up the *kelal* principle in v. 12 ("Therefore let the one who thinks he stands fast watch out lest he fall"), which is a variant of the same idea expressed in 9,27—which is what Paul set out to prove in the first place.

---

[91] Eriksson, *Traditions as Rhetorical Proof: Pauline Argumentation in 1 Corinthians*, 167.
[92] Ben Witherington, *Conflict in Community in Corinth: A Socio-Rhetorical Commentary on 1 and 2 Corinthians* (Grand Rapids: Eerdmans, 1995), 218.
[93] Martin McNamara, *Palestinian Judaism and the New Testament* (Wilmington, Del.: Glazier, 1983), 241–44.
[94] See Tjitze Baarda, "1 Corinthe 10,1–13: Een schets," *GthT* 76 (1975): 1–14.
[95] Fee, *First Epistle to the Corinthians*, 442–43.
[96] Cheung, *Idol Food in Corinth*, 146.
[97] Bruce Malina, *The Palestinian Manna Tradition* (Leiden: Brill, 1968), 96.

As earlier, to sin against other Christians is to sin against Christ himself (v. 12), because one would be violating God's new creation of which Christ is the agent.[98] In 10:13, Paul removes all excuse for compromise regarding idol food, setting the stage for the directive to "avoid all idolatry" (10:14) for which chapters 8–10 have been arguing.[99] This leads directly into 10:14–22, the conclusion of the argument that began in 8:1.[100]

Regarding 10:9, Fee[101] concludes correctly, "that 'Christ,' not 'Lord,' is the word used in the original text is almost certain. That means that Paul once again, as in v. 4, is purposely tying the situations of Israel and Corinth together Christologically." As Israel tested Christ in the desert, the Corinthians test Christ by eating idol food,[102] and the warning is that they face similar catastrophic consequences.[103] Epiphanius, as with most writers whose Greek texts read κύριον, understands Paul to refer to Christ. Whether Χριστόν or κύριον, Christ is appropriate to the context, not only in terms of the immediate context but also of the Christological bases of the various replies to problems and to Paul's own Christology.

Ehrman, however, takes κύριον in v. 9 to refer to God. His only contextual argument is that κύριον in v. 9 must be taken as God in v. 5, rather than Christ in v. 4, because v. 5 is closer to v. 9 than is v. 4. Ehrman admits that Christ is pre-existent, but asserts that he is not actually the administrator of divine justice in the desert. Certainly, God was angered and destroyed the Israelites (v. 5), e.g., in v. 9 by "snakes" and in v. 10 by "the Destroyer. That is the reason Ehrman seeks to establish an orthodox corruption in v. 5. The relationship of v. 9 to the preceding involves lack of control regarding idolatry, and *testing* Him in Corinth by eating idol meat is parallel to the *testing* of Him in the desert and would, as then, surely result in catastrophic judgment.

One must remember that plausible intrinsic probability is stronger than non-existent external evidence. Rather than pursue intrinsic considerations, Ehrman turns instead to transcriptional probability to make his case that Χριστόν was inserted into v. 9 by orthodox scribes.

---

[98] Victor Furnish, *The Theology of the First Letter to the Corinthians* (Cambridge: Cambridge University Press, 1999), 72.

[99] Ben Witherington, III, *Conflict and Community in Corinth: A Socio-Rhetorical Commentary on 1 and 2 Corinthians* (Grand Rapids: Eerdmans, 1995), 224.

[100] Ericksson, *Traditions as Rhetorical Proof: Pauline Argumentation in 1 Corinthians*, 166–73.

[101] Fee, *First Epistle to the Corinthians*, 457.

[102] See Joop F.M. Smit, *"About the Idol Offerings": Rhetoric, Social Context and Theology of Paul's Discourse in First Corinthians 8:1–11:1* (Louven: Peeters, 2000), 125.

[103] Richard Hays, *First Corinthians* (Louisville: John Knox, 1997), 166.

3. Transcriptional Probability.

Given the strength and diversity of the external attestation for Χριστόν, the improbability of a Marcionite alteration and the intrinsic probability favoring Χριστόν as original, it remains to be asked when, by whom and for what reasons κύριον was introduced into the text. The variation could have been merely accidental.

It is possible, of course, that a scribe simply misread XN as KN, a mistake of the eye common in both uncial and minuscule MSS, or that Paul's use of κύριος in 1 Corinthians to mean Χριστός led to an exchange of terms without any theological motivation. It is also possible that a deliberate but non-theological change could have been made by a perceptive scribe who recognized Paul's allusion to Dt 6:16 (οὐκ ἐκπειράσεις κύριον τὸν θεόν) and wrote κύριον in v. 9 to bring the text in line with that passage.

If κύριον arose as a theologically-motivated alteration, there is reason to view it as an attempt to reduce the importance of 1 Cor 10:9 in Christological discussion. Origen, for instance, was unaware of any text that read other than Χριστόν in v. 9. A fragment of book four of his lost *Stromateis* is preserved in the margin of 1739[104] at 10:9 and reads:

> Perhaps some ingenious explanation will be produced by those who do not desire that Christ should have engaged in these experiences about the apparent allegory of the rock, but what will they say to this text? For some people did tempt him, that is, none but Christ, and therefore they were destroyed by serpents.

The force of Origen's argument is based upon Χριστόν being a firm reading in the text. Having thus touted 10:9 as an *anguis in herba* for his opponents, Origen issued an overt challenge for them to provide an alternate explanation of that verse, if indeed they could. "That rock was Christ" (v. 4) was very much part of the discussion, not capable of being altered to remove it from discussion but certainly capable of being allegorized away with some ingenious explanation as "spiritual" and dismissed, as Origen indicates. However, Origen argued that the opponents cannot similarly dismiss Χριστόν allegorically in v. 9 and must admit the indisputable fact that, "some people did tempt him, that is, none but (the pre-existent) Christ." Origen's challenge could hardly be ignored.

---

[104] Eduard von der Goltz, *Eine textkritische Arbeit des zehnten bezw. sechsten Jahrhunderts* (Leipzig: Hinrichs, 1899), 66.

Not long after, several prominent bishops met at Antioch to counter the views of Paul of Samosata. In the *Hymenaeusbriefe*, the bishops used 10:9 with the reading κύριον as evidence against his view regarding the pre-existence of Christ:

> Before the incarnation in the divine scriptures, Christ was known as "Christ." For . . . the fathers all drank the same spiritual drink for they drank from the spiritual rock that followed, and the rock was Christ. And again, neither let us tempt the Lord, as some of them tempted and were destroyed by the serpents.

Certainly κύριον, if indeed it is the original reading of the text of 1 Cor 10:9 cited in this letter, is understood by the bishops with reference to Christ rather than to God.

In view of Origen's use of 10:9 to make Christological points and his overt challenge to his opponents on the reading of this text, it is possible that a scribe introduced κύριον into the text precisely to remove the verse from theological discussion. Too late to affect $\mathfrak{P}^{46}$, it was a part of the manuscript tradition by the time of *Hymenaeusbriefe* and B-ℵ, but even then had only limited acceptance.

Ehrman's theory of orthodox corruption assumes that scribes knew theological debates and were greatly influenced by them. Assuming that orthodox scribes needed Χριστόν in the text in order to refute the adoptionists, he then explains 10:1–13 in terms of v. 5, that *God* was not well pleased with the Israelites. He posits instead that since the subject of v. 5 is unambiguous, the Israelites were destroyed after putting *God*, not "Christ," to the test (p. 90), and that it was God who destroyed, not Christ. To prove his point, Ehrman posits that the omission of ὁ θεός in 81 Clement and Irenaeus is an orthodox corruption making Christ the executioner. In fact, 81 reads ὁ θεός and NA^{27} should be corrected. Also, in Irenaeus (*Adv. haer.* 4.36.6), the "omission" of ὁ θεός occurs at the end of the citation of v. 5 and is therefore inadmissible as evidence, especially since Irenaeus himself then interprets the text in terms of God, not Christ. A similar situation exists in Clement (*Stromata* 16.104.4), where the "omission" of ὁ θεός occurs at the end and is likewise inadmissible as evidence. One cannot establish that his text omitted ὁ θεός. There is no evidence to support an orthodox corruption in v. 5.

Ehrman says that κύριον "is best attested among the *opponents* of adoptionism, (e.g., Epiphanius) and precisely in Alexandria (MSS ℵ B C 33)" (p. 116). Epiphanius, however, did not need Χριστόν in the text in order to make anti-adoptionist arguments. Just after saying, "In place of 'Lord,' Marcion put 'Christ'," Epiphanius says, "But 'Lord' and 'Christ' are the same even if Marcion disagrees, since Christ's name has already been used at the words, 'The rock was Christ'" (v. 4). Actual Epiphanian usage outweighs Ehrman's hypothetical "proto-orthodox scribe," as does the Christological reference to κύριον in *Hymenaeusbriefe*.

In asserting that 1739^mg and the *Hymenaeusbriefe* present a "(modified) form of 1 Corinthians 10:9," Ehrman reads these texts through the sole lens of "orthodox corruption," leading him to assume his conclusion. Re-interpreting these patristic texts through the lens of "orthodox corruption," Ehrman must posit the corruption of something that cannot be conclusively demonstrated to exist earlier, thus assuming his conclusion. As Fee says,[105]

> If Ehrman's case for "christological corruption" so clearly fails in our one *certain* piece of evidence for deliberate variation, then one might rightly question the degree of deliberation in a large number of other variations as well, which seem to have equally good, if not better, explanations of other kinds for their existence.

Transcriptional probability for a heterodox corruption based upon actual patristic usage certainly outweighs an orthodox corruption based upon a hypothetical "proto-orthodox scribe," who even *prior to Marcion* inserted Χριστόν (!). However, transcriptional probability is inconclusive in this instance.

4. CONCLUSION.

As Metzger says, "The reading that best explains the origin of the others is Χριστόν . . . Paul's reference to Christ here is analogous to that in ver. 4."[106] Ehrman anticipates that colleagues will disagree with many of his conclusions,[107] as Fee does in 1 Cor 10:9, noting that, "Unfortunately, Ehrman too often turns mere *possibility* into *probability*, and probability into *certainty*."[108]

External evidence and intrinsic probability both favor Χριστόν as original, and transcriptional probability is simply inconclusive in this

---

[105] Gordon D. Fee, review of Ehrman, *Orthodox Corruption of Scripture*, *Critical Review* 8 (1995): 203–06, esp. 205.

[106] Metzger, *A Textual Commentary on the Greek New Testament*. 494.

[107] Ehrman, *Orthodox Corruption of Scripture*, 275.

[108] Fee, review of *Orthodox Corruption of Scripture*, *Critical Review* (1995): 204. Note also Virginia Burrus, review of Ehrman, *Orthodox Corruption* in *Theology Today* 51 (1995): 618, "Ehrman's account of pre-Nicene doctrine is often disappointingly conventional, following a traditional pattern that minimizes differences across place and time and projects an all-too-homogenous Nicene/Chalcedonian doctrinal orthodoxy onto even the pre-Nicene period."

instance. The data indicate clearly that κύριον arose most probably during the late third and early fourth century Christological controversies in the eastern Mediterranean in which 1 Cor 10:9 with the reading Χριστόν played an important role. The reading Χριστόν constitutes yet another example of the Later Egyptian type of text used by Epiphanius in the Pauline Epistles.

CHAPTER 7

CONCLUSION

The intent of this study has been to establish the textual affinities of Acts and the Epistles in the carefully selected quotations of Epiphanius of Salamis. The results of the statistical and profile analyses of these citations in comparison with MSS selected as representative of the various types of text are summarized as follows.

1. THE TEXT OF ACTS IN EPIPHANIUS

Epiphanius has significant affinity with the Late Egyptian type of text in Acts, but no significant agreement with Family 1739 in chapters 1–12. In chapters 13–28, however, the reverse is true: Epiphanius has particular affinity with Family 1739 and somewhat less with the Late Egyptians. It is clear, however, that Epiphanius has substantially more agreement with the Late Egyptian tradition in Acts than with the Old Egyptian, "Western" or Byzantine textual traditions. So, Epiphanius' text of Acts is Late Egyptian in character, and specifically with Family 1739 in the last half of the book.

2. THE TEXT OF THE CATHOLIC EPISTLES IN EPIPHANIUS

The close relationship of Epiphanius' text to Family 1739 in Acts certainly does not carry over to the Catholic Epistles, as Epiphanius' citations of the Catholic Epistles apparently have primary affinity with the Byzantine text. A separation of 31.6 % between the Byzantine text and the Egyptian text leaves little to the imagination. The "Western" text does not exist in the Catholic Epistles. Although the thirteen readings in these citations are only slight evidence, they suggest Epiphanius' text of the Catholic Epistles was very likely Byzantine in character.

3. THE TEXT OF THE PAULINE EPISTLES IN EPIPHANIUS

Statistical data indicate that Epiphanius' text of the Pauline Epistles is solidly Egyptian, and specifically Late Egyptian in character, with little significant Byzantine and practically no "Western" agreement. There is no substantial agreement with the Old Egyptian tradition. This is affirmed by the quantitative profile analysis, and by instances in which Epiphanius comments upon variant readings known to him.

4. THE IMPORTANCE OF EPIPHANIUS' CITATIONS FOR THE EARLY HISTORY OF THE TEXT

The transmission of the NT text during the first four centuries of the Christian era is fascinating, yet the understanding of the history of the developing textual traditions during that period is far from complete. Epiphanius informs us of the nature of the text(s) he used on Cyprus, and possibly earlier in Palestine and Egypt. In view of his interaction with leading figures throughout the Mediterranean during the fourth-century Christological controversies, his citation of scripture was aimed more at castigating heretics than at simple biblical exegesis. Verbal imprecision in his citations may give the impression that he cites mostly from memory, and that he does so poorly. While Epiphanius sometimes cites texts verbatim, he often gives verbal precision to those portions of text that are vital to his point but merely the gist of the remainder. He adapts texts freely to his arguments. By following criteria designed to separate what is arguably his text from what is merely patristicism, one is able to reconstruct several portions of the biblical text of this important fourth-century Father.

Epiphanius used a text of Acts that is Egyptian, and specifically Late Egyptian (A C 81 1175), and in chapters 13-28 has significant affinity with Family 1739. The text of Acts in Roman Palestine was primarily Egyptian in nature.[1] Lake[2] thought that 1739 might represent the Origenian-Caesarean text of the epistles, and posited that one might presume the same to be true of Acts. Haenchen[3] followed Lake's lead and thought 1739 might evidence a Caesarean text-form in Acts, but did not actually pursue this line of thinking in his commentary. However, Geer[4] concluded that 1739 reflects an Egyptian text-form in Acts, specifically Late Alexandrian. Apparently a specific type of text of Acts did not exist in Roman Palestine, and 1739, while related to the region, should be viewed as Late Egyptian in character rather than as a

---

[1] Roderic Mullen, *The New Testament Text of Cyril of Jerusalem* (SBLNTGF 7; Atlanta: Scholars Press, 1997), 347–49, demonstrates Cyril's textual affinity in Acts to be primarily Egyptian, and specifically with 1739, and cites Origen and Eusebius as well. See James Hardy Ropes, "The Text of Acts," *The Beginnings of Christianity, Part I, The Acts of the Apostles* (ed. F.J. Foakes-Jackson and Kirsopp Lake; London: Macmillan, 1926), clxxxix, ccxci.

[2] Kirsopp Lake, J. de Zwaan and Morton S. Enslin, eds., "Codex 1739," *Six Collations of New Testament Manuscripts* (HTS 17; Cambridge: Harvard University Press, 1932): 145.

[3] Ernst Haenchen, "Zum Text der Apostelgeschichte," *ZTK* 54 (1957): 54–55.

[4] Thomas C. Geer, Jr., "Codex 1739 in Acts and Its Relationship to Manuscripts 945 and 1891," *Bib* 69 (1988): 31, 41–42.

"Caesarean" text. Epiphanius' citations of Acts reflect this Late Egyptian text-form.

Curiously, Epiphanius reflects a Byzantine text of the Catholic Epistles in the meager evidence available. Suggs[5] posited Eusebius' text of the Catholic Epistles to show relationship with Family 2412, without claiming that 2412 represented a type of text used in Palestine. Carder[6] proposed that 1243 does, in fact, represent a Caesarean type of text in the Catholic Epistles, to which Aland[7] responded that one can only term a text "Caesarean" if both Origen and Eusebius confirm its presence in Caesarea. Richards[8] found both 2412 and 1243 to be Alexandrian, rather than Caesarean. No special text-type has been found in the Catholic Epistles with reference to Palestine. If Brooks[9] is correct that the Byzantine text-form did not originate in Palestine but in Asia Minor, Epiphanius' Catholic Epistles quite possibly came from a different textual tradition than did his MSS of Acts and the Pauline Epistles.

It is important to note that the statement in Aland and Aland,[10] that Epiphanius' NT text "represents an early stage of the Koine text type," requires revision, as his text of Acts and the Pauline Epistles is decidedly Late Egyptian (A C P 33 81 104) and not at all Byzantine. Zuntz[11] found that 1739 has close affinity with the Egyptian text reflected in Origin and thought the so-called "Caesarean" MSS to be a sub-group of the Egyptian text. Murphy[12] concluded that Eusebius reflects an Egyptian text in Romans and 1 Corinthians. So, of the MSS used to support a Caesarean text-type for the Pauline Epistles, only 1739 has a clear link to the region. The textual affinities of the Pauline corpus used in Roman

---

[5] M. Jack Suggs, "The New Testament Text of Eusebius" (Ph.D. dissertation, Duke University 1954), 149, 235–88.

[6] Muriel Carder, "A Caesarean Text in the Catholic Epistles," NTS 16 (1969): 252-70.

[7] Kurt Aland, "Bemerkungen zu den gegenwärtigen möglichkeiten textkritischer Arbeit aus Anlass einer Untersuchung zum Cäesarea-Text der Katholischen Briefe," NTS 17 (1970): 4.

[8] W. Larry Richards, *The Classification of the Greek Manuscripts of the Johannine Epistles* (SGLDS 35; Missoula, Mont: Scholars Press, 1977), 68–69, 195–98.

[9] James Brooks, *The New Testament Text of Gregory of Nyssa* (SBLNTGF 2; Atlanta: Scholars Press, 1991), 264–66.

[10] Kurt Aland and Barbara Aland, *The Text of the New Testament* (2nd ed.; trans. E. Rhodes; Grand Rapids: Eerdmans, 1989), 178.

[11] Günther Zuntz, *The Text of the Pauline Epistles* (London: Oxford University Press, 1953), 66, 80, 153–55.

[12] Harold Murphy, "Eusebius' New Testament Text in the *Demonstratio Evangelica*," JBL 78 (1954): 162–68.

Palestine are Egyptian in character.[13] Epiphanius supports the view that the principal text of the Pauline Epistles in use in the Eastern Mediterranean in his time was Egyptian in character. Brooks thesis of an Asia Minor origin for the Byzantine textual tradition rather than Roman Palestine is not altered by Epiphanius.

That the "Western" text does not figure in Epiphanius' citations of the Apostolos underscores the fact that the so-called "Western" text was not widely used among Greek writers, including Didymus, Origen and Cyril of Jerusalem, as well as Epiphanius.[14] Further, as the Byzantine text came into existence in the fourth century, the appearance of a few exclusively Byzantine readings in Epiphanius' citations of the Apostolos is not altogether unexpected. A few readings from the Byzantine text emerging in Asia Minor found their way into his text, but his text has a great number of readings that are clearly not Byzantine. The presence of these few Byzantine readings indicates only that forces that later would produce the Byzantine text were already at work in Epiphanius' time. The Late Egyptian text with which Epiphanius agrees in Acts and the Pauline Epistles was probably not an edited recension of the Old Egyptian text, but simply an Egyptian text-form that was altered by other readings.

Epiphanius' Apostolos, which he considered to be the "true text," was actually a Late Egyptian text in Acts and the Pauline Epistles and apparently Byzantine in the Catholic Epistles. It was on the basis of this altered text that Epiphanius argued, accused, and fought for Nicean orthodoxy.

---

[13] Mullen, *NT Text of Cyril of Jerusalem*, 398-400; and Darrell Hannah, *The Text of 1 Corinthians in the Writings of Origen* (SBLNTGF 4; Scholars Press, 1997), 291–93.

[14] Contra Hermann von Soden, *Die Schriften des Neuen Testaments in ihrer ältesten erreichbaren Textgestalt* (Göttingen: Vandenhoeck und Ruprecht, 1911), 1.2.1759, who erroneously thought Epiphanius and Cyril of Jerusalem to reflect "Western" influence.

APPENDIX I

EPIPHANIUS IN THE APPARATUS OF NA²⁷

The following lists indicate 1) places in the critical apparatus of NA²⁷ in which Epiphanius' witness should be corrected, 2) places where citing Epiphanius' in support of a reading could enhance the apparatus, and 3) places where Epiphanius is cited correctly. Following the reading of Epiphanius, indication is made whether Epiphanius' reading is that of the NA²⁷ text (*txt*) or that of a variant reading (*v.l.*).

I. CORRECTIONS TO NA²⁷.

Rom 8:11   Epiph: καὶ τὰ θνητὰ σώματα (*v.l.*)[1]

1 Cor 1:20   Epiph: τούτου (*v.l.*)[2]

1 Cor 3:20   Epiph: ἀνθρώπων (*v.l.*)[3]

1 Cor 5:5   Epiph: τοῦ κυρίου (*txt*)[4]

1 Cor 7:34   Epiph: *om* καί before τῷ σώματι (*v.l.*)[5]

1 Cor 10:3   Epiph: τὸ αὐτὸ πνευματικὸν βρῶμα (*txt*)[6]

---

[1] NA²⁷ lists Epiphanius as omitting καί in some MSS, but this occurs in two inexact quotations. Actually, Epiphanius includes καί in the one exact citation of 8:11 in *Pan* 57.7.6, and he should rather be included in support of this reading in NA²⁷.

[2] Τούτου occurs in one quotation, but is omitted at the end of the other. As the variation occurs at the end of the reference, it is not possible to determine whether τούτου was omitted, and Epiphanius should be deleted from the apparatus at this point.

[3] In the one clear citation of this verse, Epiphanius does not read ἀνθρώπων, but σοφῶν, which is the reading in the NA²⁷ text.

[4] Epiphanius should be omitted as support for this reading since what would be the added words would have occurred at the end of his quotation.

[5] In Epiphanius' lone reference to this verse, a reminiscence involving a conflation with v. 32, one cannot be certain of Epiphanius' omission of καί before τῷ σώματι and thus Epiphanius should be removed from the apparatus for this reading.

[6] NA²⁷ lists Epiphanius as reading τὸ αὐτὸ πνευματικὸν βρῶμα, but Epiphanius does not cite v. 3. The citation upon which this note is based (*Pan* 42.11.8) is actually Epiphanius' citation of Marcion's text of 1 Cor 10:1-9, 11. In *Pan* 42.11.7, Epiphanius prefaces his citations from Marcion (ET from Frank Williams, *The Panarion of Epiphanius of Salamis* [Leiden: Brill, 1987], 287),

I. CORRECTIONS TO NA²⁷, cont.

1 Cor 14:15	Epiph:	ψαλῶ καὶ τῷ νοΐ (v.l.)[7]
1 Cor 14:34	Epiph:	ὑποτασσέσθωσαν (txt)[8]
2 Cor 1:20	Epiph:	διὸ καὶ δι' αὐτοῦ (txt)[9]

> I further attach the following citations against the heresiarch to this stock that I have laboriously accumulated against him. Again, I discovered in his works, in a sort of would-be semblance of the apostle Paul's epistles—not all the epistles, some of them, and these mutilated as usual by Marcion's rascality.

In *Pan* 42.11.8, Epiphanius cites 1 Cor 10:1-9, 11, from Marcion's text. Epiphanius concludes in *Pan* 42.11.9, saying,

> This is Marcion's corrupt compilation, containing a type and form of the Gospel of Luke, and an incomplete one of the apostle Paul. . . . And (I found) that this compilation had been tampered with throughout, and had supplemental material added in certain passages—not of any value, but in the form of second-rate, harmful heresies against the sound faith, creations of Marcion's insane mind.

Then, prior to beginning his vigorous refutation of Marcion's text in *Pan* 42.12.3 *elenchus* 17, Epiphanius cites Marcion's text of 1 Cor 10:1-9, 11, in *scholion* 17. In his refutation, Epiphanius discusses 1 Cor 10:3, but gives no indiction whether his biblical exemplar includes αὐτό in 10:3 or not.

That this reference is to Marcion rather than Epiphanius was noted correctly in Tischendorf's 8th edition: Marcion^epiph. Marcion should be cited in support of αὐτό, but Epiphanius should be deleted.

[7] Epiphanius reads ψαλῶ δὲ καὶ τῷ νοΐ in one of the two accurate citations with introductions, but omits δέ in the other. He either needs to be cited for both readings or omitted from the apparatus at this point.

[8] NA²⁷ cites Epiphanius for this reading. However, in the only places in Epiphanius where 1 Cor 14:34 occurs, each time it is the scholion (*Pan* 42.11.8; *Pan* 42.12.3) in which he gives Marcion's text, not his own elenchus. In the following discussion in the elenchus (*Pan* 42.12.3), the only part of 14:34 Epiphanius quotes from his own text is καθὼς καὶ ὁ νόμος λέγει, which does not have a variant reading. The only other reference to this verse in *Pan* 79.3.6 is an allusion to it and 1 Tim 2:12, in a discussion concerning the place of women in the church. Therefore, Epiphanius should not be cited in the apparatus for this variant; however, "Marcion^epiph" would be accurate.

APPENDIX I

I. CORRECTIONS TO NA²⁷, cont.

2 Cor 4:6	Epiph: λέμψει (*txt*)[10]
Gal 4:25	Epiph: γάρ (*v.l.*)[11]
Eph 3:15	Epiph: ἐν οὐρανῷ (*v.l.*)[12]
Col 2:11	Epiph: τοῦ σώματος τῶν ἁμαρτιῶν (*v.l.*)[13]
2 Thess 2:2	Epiph: τοῦ κυρίου (*txt*)[14]
1 Tim 1:17	Epiph: μόνῳ σοφῷ (*v.l.*)[15]
Heb 11:4	Epiph: ἔτι λαλεῖ (*txt*)[16]
Heb 11:32	Epiph: Σαμψών (*txt*)[17]

---

[9] NA²⁷ cites Epiphanius for the reading of the text; however, in *Pan* 42.11.8 and *Pan* 42.12.3 he merely cites Marcion's text and does not cite the text again in the discussion in the elenchus "Epiph" should be replaced with "Marcion^epiph."

[10] In all three places in *Pan* 42.12.3 (both *scholia* and the one *elenchus*), Epiphanius is merely citing Marcion's text and therefore cannot be cited as having λάμψει rather than λάμψαι in his text. Epiphanius should be removed from the apparatus of NA²⁷ at this point.

[11] NA²⁷ cites Epiphanius for this reading; however, he merely gives the gist in *Pan* 66.74.6 and does not have sufficient verbal accuracy to enable one to know whether his exemplar had this reading. So, Epiphanius should be removed from the apparatus at Gal 4:25.

[12] NA²⁷ lists "Epiph^pt." Since the only quotation reading the plural is *Pan* 74.8.3 (copied from *Anc* 71 3), which appears to be due to lack of care when copying that section into the *Pan*, and the other three citations are in the singular and are verbally precise, the NA²⁷ apparatus should be changed to read simply "Epiph."

[13] Epiphanius reads τῶν ἁμαρτιῶν, but it is a substitution for τῆς σαρκός rather than an addition to the text, as NA²⁷ indicates.

[14] As Epiphanius' only reference to this verse is a loose reminiscence, he cannot be listed supporting the reading in the NA²⁷ text and should be removed.

[15] From Epiphanius' brief and imprecise reminiscence of this verse, one cannot be certain that his biblical exemplar had this reading and he should not be included in the NA²⁷ as supporting this reading.

[16] Epiphanius' quotation is too imprecise to include him in the apparatus at this point.

[17] In the quotation that includes Heb 11:32, Epiphanius gives the gist of 11:32, 37 and 38, and lacks the necessary verbal precision to include him for the NA²⁷ text at this variant.

II. USEFUL ADDITIONS OF EPIPHANIUS TO NA[27].

Acts 2:36	Epiph: ὁ θεὸς ἐποίησε (v.l.)
Acts 5:3	Epiph: ἐπλήρωσεν (txt)[18]
Acts 9:6	Epiph: τί (v.l.)
Acts 10:38	Epiph: ὃν ἔχρισεν (v.l.)[19]
Acts 11:9	Epiph: ἀπεκρίθη δὲ μοι ἐκ δευτέρου φωνὴ ἐκ τοῦ οὐρανοῦ (v.l.)
Acts 13:4	Epiph: αὐτοὶ (txt)
Acts 15:28	Epiph: τῶν ἐπάναγκες (v.l.)
Acts 15:29	Epiph: καὶ πνικτοῦ (v.l.)
Acts 16:6	Epiph: διῆλθον (txt)
Acts 16:31	Epiph: κύριον Ἰησοῦν (om Χριστὸν; txt)
Acts 16:32	Epiph: κυρίου (txt)
Acts 20:28	Epiph: θεοῦ (txt)
Acts 24:12	Epiph: ἐπίστασιν (txt)
James 1:27	Epiph: θρησκεία δὲ (v.l.)
James 1:27	Epiph: τῷ θεῷ (txt)
James 3:8	Epiph: ἀκατάσχετον (v.l.)
James 3:9	Epiph: θεὸν (v.l.)
1 Peter 3:18	Epiph: om μὲν (v.l.)[20]

---

[18] In the two most precise quotations (*Anc* 69.8; *Pan* 74.6.8) Epiphanius has this reading.

[19] The citation in *Pan* 74.6.6 is brief, but accurate, and includes an introduction.

[20] The quotations might be too brief for certainty, but none of the six precise ones has it.

APPENDIX I

II. USEFUL ADDITIONS OF EPIPHANIUS TO NA²⁷, cont.

1 Peter 4:1	Epiph: παθόντος ὑπὲρ ἡμῶν σαρκί	(v.l.)
2 Peter 2:19	Epiph: τούτῳ καὶ	(v.l.)
1 John 2:18	Epiph: ὅτι	(txt)
1 John 2:19	Epiph: ἦσαν ἐξ ἡμῶν	(v.l.)
Rom 1:4	Epiph: προορισθέντος	(v.l)
Rom 3:8	Epiph: ἔλθη ἐφ' ἡμᾶς	(v.l.)
Rom 5:1	Epiph: ἔχομεν	(txt)
Rom 8:11	Epiph: Χριστὸν ἐκ νεκρῶν	(txt)
Rom 8:11	Epiph: τοῦ ἐνοικοῦντος αυτοῦ πνεύματος	(txt)
Rom 8:26	Epiph: υπερεντυγχάνει ὑπὲρ ἡμῶν	(v.l.)
Rom 8:34	Epiph: ὅς ἐστιν	(v.l.)
Rom 9:20	Epiph: μενοῦν γε	(txt)
Rom 14:3	Epiph: καί ὁ	(v.l.)
1 Cor 1:23	Epiph: Ἕλλησι	(v.l.)
1 Cor 1:24	Epiph: Χριστὸς θεοῦ δύναμις καὶ θεοῦ σοφία	(v.l.)
1 Cor 2:9	Epiph: ἃ	(txt)
1 Cor 2:13	Epiph: πνεύματος ἁγίου	(v.l.)
1 Cor 2:14	Epiph: om τοῦ θεοῦ	(v.l.)
1 Cor 9:7	Epiph ἐκ τοῦ καρποῦ	(v.l.)
1 Cor 9:9	Epiph: ἐν γὰρ τῷ νόμῳ γέγραπται	(v.l.)
1 Cor 10:9	Epiph: κύριον	(v.l.)
1 Cor 10:10	Epiph: γογγύζετε	(txt)

II. USEFUL ADDITIONS OF EPIPHANIUS TO NA²⁷, cont.

1 Cor 10:10	Epiph: καθάπερ (*txt*)
1 Cor 10:19	Epiph: *om* ἢ ὅτι εἴδωλόν τί ἐστιν (*v.l.*)
1 Cor 10:20	Epiph: θύουσι^pr (*txt*)
1 Cor 12:11	Epiph: *om* ἰδίᾳ (*v.l.*)
1 Cor 15:24	Epiph: παραδιδῷ (*txt*)
1 Cor 15:27	Epiph: ὅτι (*txt*)
1 Cor 15:28	Epiph: τὰ πάντα ἐν πᾶσιν (*txt*)
1 Cor 15:49	Epiph: φορέσωμεν (*v.l.*)
1 Cor 15:55	Epiph: κέντρον; ποῦ σου, ᾅδη, τὸ νῖκος; (*v.l.*)
2 Cor 3:6	Epiph: ἀποκτένει (*txt*)[21]
2 Cor 11:3	Epiph: καὶ τῆς ἁγνότητος (*txt*)[22]
Gal 2:9	Epiph: Ἰάκωβος καὶ Κηφᾶς (*txt*)[23]
Eph 5:31	Epiph: καὶ κολληθήσεται τῇ γυναικὶ αὐτοῦ (*v.l.*)
Phil 2:11	Epiph: ἐξομολογήσεται (*v.l.*)
1 Tim 4:1	Epiph: πλάνης (*v.l.*)
Tit 2:10	Epiph: *om* τὴν (*v.l.*)
Tit 2:11	Epiph: σωτῆρος (*v.l.*)

---

[21] NA²⁷ does not have an accent on the variant reading. If the variant reading is the future ἀποκτενεῖ, Epiphanius' citation as accented in Holl's edition, *Anc* 22.5, has the present active indicative third person singular of the verb with an acceptable variation in spelling.

[22] If included, Epiphanius should be cited as "(Epiph)" since he inverts the order of the two phrases ἀπὸ τῆς ἁγνότητος καὶ τῆς ἁπλότητος with D* E it^d.e.

[23] If included, Epiphanius should be cited for the reading in the text as "(Epiph)" since he transposes Κηφᾶς to the last position, but the quotation has enough precision that it is likely that it represents his biblical exemplar.

APPENDIX I

III. CORRECT INCLUSIONS OF EPIPHANIUS IN NA²⁷.

Rom 5:6	Epiph: ἔτι (*txt*)	
Rom 15:8	Epiph: γεγενῆσθαι (*txt*)	
1 Cor 2:10	Epiph: δέ (*txt*)	
1 Cor 2:10	Epiph: διὰ τοῦ πνεύματος αὐτοῦ (*v.l.*)	
1 Cor 2:16	Epiph: Χριστοῦ (*txt*)	
1 Cor 3:12	Epiph: τοῦτον (*v.l.*)	
1 Cor 3:16	Epiph: οἰκεῖ ἐν ὑμῖν (*txt*)	
1 Cor 5:7	Epiph: τὸ πάσχα ἡμῶν (*txt*)	
1 Cor 6:11	Epiph: τοῦ κυρίου ἡμῶν (*v.l.*)	
1 Cor 7:5	Epiph: τῇ προσευχῇ (*txt*)	
1 Cor 7:10	Epiph: μὴ χωρισθῆναι (*txt*)	
1 Cor 7:39	Epiph: δέδεται νόμῳ (*v.l.*)	
1 Cor 7:39	Epiph: ἀποθάνη (*v.l.*)	
1 Cor 9:9	Epiph: φιμώσεις (*v.l.*)	
1 Cor 10:11	Epiph: ταῦτα δέ (*txt*)	
1 Cor 10:11	Epiph: τυπικῶς συνέβαινεν (*txt*)	
1 Cor 10:20	Epiph: θύουσι καὶ οὐ θεῷ (*v.l.*)	
1 Cor 12:6	Epiph: ὁ δὲ αὐτός (*txt*)	
1 Cor 12:6	Epiph: θεὸς ὁ ἐνεργῶν (*txt*)	
1 Cor 12:27	Epiph: μέλους (*v.l.*)	
1 Cor 15:14	Epiph: ἄρα καί (*txt*)	
1 Cor 15:14	Epiph: πίστις ἡμῶν (*v.l.*)	

III. CORRECT INCLUSIONS OF EPIPHANIUS IN NA²⁷, cont.

1 Cor 15:25	Epiph: τοὺς ἐχθροὺς αὐτοῦ	(v.l.)
1 Cor 15:28	Epiph: τότε καὶ αὐτός	(txt)
1 Cor 15:29	Epiph: ὑπὲρ αὐτῶν	(txt)
2 Cor 3:7	Epiph: λίθοις	(txt)
2 Cor 3:17	Epiph: ἐκεῖ	(v.l.)
2 Cor 4:4	Epiph: καταυγάσαι	(v.l.)
2 Cor 4:4	Epiph: om αὐτοῖς post αὐγάσαι	(txt)
2 Cor 6:16	Epiph: ἔσονταί μοι	(v.l.)
2 Cor 11:3	Epiph: εἰς τὸν Χριστόν	(txt)
2 Cor 13:3	Epiph: εἰ δοκιμήν	(v.l.)
Gal 1:15	Epiph: εὐδόκησεν	(v.l.)
Eph 2:15	Epiph: ἐν ἑαυτῷ	(v.l.)
Eph 5:32	Epiph: τὴν ἐκκλησίαν	(v.l.)
Col 3:5	Epiph: τὰ μέλη	(txt)
1 Tim 1:12	Epiph: χάριν	(txt)
1 Tim 3:16	Epiph: ὃς ἐφανερώθη	(txt)
1 Tim 4:2	Epiph: κεκαυτηριασμένων	(v.l.)
2 Tim 2:7	Epiph: νόει ὃ λέγω	(txt)
2 Tim 2:7	Epiph: δώσει	(txt)
2 Tim 4:10	Epiph: Γαλλίαν	(v.l.)
Titus 2:13	Epiph: σωτῆρος ἡμῶν Ἰησοῦ Χριστοῦ	(txt)
Heb 7:6	Epiph: τὸν Ἀβραάμ	(v.l.)

III. CORRECT INCLUSIONS OF EPIPHANIUS IN NA²⁷, cont.

Heb 11:6   Epiph: θεῷ (*v.l.*)

Heb 13:5   Epiph: ἐγκαταλίπω (*txt*)

APPENDIX II

EPIPHANIUS IN THE APPARATUS OF UBS⁴

The following list indicates places in the critical apparatus of UBS⁴ in which Epiphanius' witness should be cited or changed, based upon the data included in this study. Only those readings are included for which the edition already provides an apparatus. Following the reading of Epiphanius, indication is made whether Epiphanius' reading is that of UBS⁴ text (*txt*) or that of a variant reading (*v.l.*).

I. CORRECTIONS TO UBS⁴.

Acts 2:24	Epiph: Ἅδου (*v.l.*)[1]
Acts 5:3	Epiph: ἐπλήρωσεν (*txt*$^{2/4}$); ἐπείρασεν (*v.l.*$^{2/4}$)[2]
Acts 16:7	Epiph: τὸ πνεῦμα (*om* Ἰησοῦ; *v.l.*)[3]
Acts 27:37	Epiph: ὡς ἑβδομήκοντα ἕξ (*v.l.*)[4]
Rom 4:19	Epiph: ἤδη (*txt*)[5]
Rom 8:26	Epiph: ὑπερεντυγχάνει (*txt*)[6]

---

[1] As Epiphanius has this word at the end of the verse as a substitution for αὐτοῦ, he does not read it as a substitution for θανάτου and should be removed from the apparatus as support for this reading.

[2] Epiphanius' two verbally precise citations read ἐπλήρωσεν and he should be included as only supporting this text in the apparatus.

[3] UBS⁴ lists Epiphanius as omitting Ἰησοῦ, but the omission occurs at the end of the quotation and it cannot be known whether Ἰησοῦ was in his exemplar. Certainly Epiphanius should not be cited in support of the omission of Ἰησοῦ.

[4] Epiphanius is listed in UBS⁴ as reading "ὡς ἑβδομήκοντα ἕξ Epiphanius$^{1/2}$ (Epiphanius$^{1/2}$ om ἕξ)." This is misleading. In one quotation, Epiphanius reads ὡς ἑβδομήκοντα, but in the other ὡς ὀγδοήκοντα. So, Epiphanius reads "70" or "80" souls, but in neither reference does he read ὡς ἑβδομήκοντα ἕξ, as UBS⁴ indicates.

[5] UBS⁴ cites "Epiphanius^{vid}." but the quotation is a loose reminiscence, which means he cannot be cited as reading ἤδη and should be removed.

[6] UBS⁴ lists Epiphanius as omitting ὑπὲρ ἡμῶν in 1/4 instances. However, in *Pan* 55.5.3, Tischendorf followed the faulty edition of Petavius and erroneously cited Epiphanius in support of the omission in this text. Epiphanius includes ὑπὲρ ἡμῶν in all of his quotations of 8:26 and should be listed in the *v.l.* as supporting the longer text.

I. CORRECTIONS TO UBS⁴, cont.

Rom 9:4	Epiph: αἱ διαθῆκαι (*txt*)[7]
1 Cor 2:4	Epiph: πειθοῖ σοφίας λόγων (*v.l.*)[8]
1 Cor 5:5	Epiph: κυρίου (*txt*)[9]
1 Cor 15:47	Epiph: ἄνθρωπος (*txt*)[10]
Gal 4:25	Epiph: γάρ Σινᾶ (*v.l.*)[11]
1 Thess 4:11	Epiph: ἰδίαις (*txt*)[12]
2 Thess 2:3	Epiph: ἀνομίας (*txt*)[13]
Rev 1:8	Epiph: ῏Ω (*txt*)[14]

---

[7] As Epiphanius' only reference to this verse is a brief gist leading into 9:5, he should not be included as supporting this reading.

[8] UBS⁴ cites "(Epiphanius)" for this reading. However, the text in *Anc* 70.8 reads "πειθοῖ σοφίας λόγοις" and is a reminiscence that conflates 2:4 and 13, giving an imprecise rendering of 2:12. Epiphanius gives only the gist of the context, making it uncertain which reading was in his exemplar. Epiphanius should be removed from the apparatus for this reading.

[9] Epiphanius should be omitted as support for this reading since what would be the added words would have occurred at the end of his quotation.

[10] UBS⁴ has parentheses around Epiphanius, but his text does not have ἄνθρωπος here, or any of the other variant readings; therefore, he should be removed from the apparatus at this point.

[11] UBS⁴ cites "(Epiphanius)." However, since in this quotation Epiphanius only gives the gist of portions of vv. 24 and 25, there is not sufficient verbal accuracy to enable one to be certain of the reading of his exemplar, and he should be removed from the UBS apparatus here.

[12] UBS⁴ cites Epiphanius for this reading. However, in none of Epiphanius' writings does he ever cite the text of 1 Thessalonians 4:11 (cf. J. Allenbach, et. al. *Biblia Patristica* [Paris: Centre National de la Recherche Scientifique, 1987] 4:313), and he should be removed from the UBS apparatus here.

[13] In accordance with stated criteria for usable data, the quotation is too imprecise and Epiphanius should be removed from the apparatus.

[14] As the words in question, ἀρχὴ καὶ τέλος, occur at the end of Epiphanius' quotation of 1:8, it cannot be known whether his exemplar omitted these words or whether Epiphanius simply stopped short of them. So Epiphanius should not be cited in support of the shorter text.

II. USEFUL ADDITIONS OF EPIPHANIUS TO UBS⁴.

Acts 15:29	Epiph: καὶ πνικτοῦ	(v.l.)
Rom 5:6	Epiph: ἔτι γάρ...ἔτι	(txt)
1 Cor 10:11	Epiph: ταῦτα δέ	(txt)
Phil 2:11	Epiph: ἐξομολογήσεται	(v.l.)

III. CORRECT INCLUSIONS OF EPIPHANIUS IN UBS⁴.

Acts 1:11	Epiph εἰς τὸν οὐρανόν	(txt)
Acts 16:32	Epiph: τοῦ κυρίου	(txt)
Acts 20:28	Epiph: θεοῦ	(txt)
James 3:8	Epiph: ἀκατάσχετον	(v.l.)
James 3:9	Epiph: θεόν	(v.l.)
1 Peter 4:1	Epiph: παθόντος ὑπὲρ ἡμῶν	(v.l.)
1 John 2:18	Epiph: ὅτι	(txt)
Jude 8	Epiph: κυριότητα	(txt)
Rom 5:1	Epiph: ἔχομεν	(txt)
Rom 7:22	Epiph: τοῦ θεοῦ	(txt)
Rom 8:11	Epiph τοῦ ἐνοικοῦντος αὐτοῦ πνεύματος	(txt)
1 Cor 2:10	Epiph: δέ	(txt)
1 Cor 2:16	Epiph: Χριστοῦ	(txt)
1 Cor 3:2	Epiph: ἔτι	(txt)
1 Cor 6:11	Epiph ἡμῶν Ἰησοῦ Χριστοῦ	(v.l.)
1 Cor 7:5	Epiph: τῇ προσευχῇ	(txt)

III. CORRECT INCLUSIONS OF EPIPHANIUS IN UBS⁴, cont.

1 Cor 10:9	Epiph: κύριον (*v.l.*)
1 Cor 10:20	Epiph: ἅ θύουσι δαιμονίοις θύουσι καὶ οὐ θεῷ (*v.l.*)
1 Cor 15:14	Epiph: ἡμῶν (*v.l.*)
1 Cor 15:49	Epiph: φορέσωμεν (*v.l.*)
1 Cor 15:55	Epiph: κέντρον; ποῦ σου, ᾅδη, τὸ νῖκος; (*v.l.*)
2 Cor 11:3	Epiph: ἀπὸ τῆς ἁγνότητος καὶ τῆς ἁπλότητος (*v.l.*)
Gal 1:15	Epiph: εὐδόκησεν (*v.l.*)
Gal 2:5	Epiph: οἷς οὐδέ (*txt*)
Eph 5:14	Epiph: ἐπιφαύσει σοι ὁ Χριστός (*txt*)
Phil 2:9	Epiph: ὄνομα (*v.l.*)
Phil 2:11	Epiph: κύριος Ἰησοῦς Χριστός (*txt*)
1 Thess 5:4	Epiph: κλέπτης (*txt*)
1 Tim 3:16	Epiph: ὅς (*txt*)
2 Tim 4:10	Epiph: Γαλλίαν (*v.l.*)
Rev 2:20	Epiph: γυναῖκα (*txt*)

BIBLIOGRAPHY

I. EDITIONS OF THE TEXT OF EPIPHANIUS

Amidon, Philip R. *The Panarion of St. Epiphanius, Bishop of Salamis: Selected Passages*. Oxford: Oxford University Press, 1990.
Dean, J. E. *Epiphanius' Treatise on Weights and Measures: The Syriac Version*. Studies in Ancient Oriental Civilizations 11. Chicago: University of Chicago Press, 1935.
Holl, Karl. "Die Handschriftliche Überlieferung des Epiphanius." Pages 1–98 in *Texte und Untersuchungen* 36. Leipzig: J. C. Hinrichs, 1910.
———. "Die Schriften des Epiphanius gegen die Bilderverehrung." Pages 360–63 in *Gesammelte Aufsätze zur Kirchengeschichte II*. Tübingen: J. C. B. Mohr, 1928.
———. "Ein Bruchstück aus einem bisher unbekannten Brief des Epiphanius." Pages 204–24 in *Gesammelte Aufsätze zur Kirchengeschichte II*. Tübingen: J. C. B. Mohr, 1928
———. *Epiphanius*. Die griechischen christlichen Schriftsteller der ersten drei Jahrhunderte 25. Leipzig: J. C. Hinrichs, 1915.
———. *Epiphanius*. Die griechischen christlichen Schriftsteller der ersten drei Jahrhunderte 31. 2nd ed. Edited by J. Dummer. Berlin: Akademie-Verlag, 1980.
———. *Epiphanius*. Die griechischen christlichen Schriftsteller der ersten drei Jahrhunderte 37. 2nd ed. Edited by J. Dummer. Berlin: Akademie-Verlag, 1985.
Koch, Glenn Alan. "A Critical Investigation of Epiphanius' Knowledge of the Ebionites: A Translation and Critical Discussion of *Panarion* 30." Ph.D. Dissertation at the University of Pennsylvania, 1976.
Maas, Paul. "Die ikonoklastische Episode des Epiphanios an Johannes." *Biblische Zeitschrift* 30 (1929-30): 279-86.
Patrologia graeca. Edited by J.-P. Migne. Vol. 43. Paris, 1863.

II. BIBLICAL TEXTS

Aland, Kurt. "Neue neutestamentliche Papyri." *New Testament Studies* 3 (1957): 266-78.
———, et al., eds. *The Greek New Testament*. 3d corr. ed. New York: United Bible Societies, 1983.
———, et al., eds. *Novum Testamentum Graece*. 27th ed. Stuttgart: Deutsche Bibelgesellschaft, 1993.
Bilabel, Friedrich. *Veröffentlichungen aus den badischen Papyrus-Sammlungen*. Heidelberg: im Selbstverlag des Verfassers, 1924.

II. BIBLICAL TEXTS, cont.

Blass, F. *Acta Apostolorum sive Lucae ad Theophilum liber alter*. Leipzig: Teubner, 1896.
Bover, Joseph, ed. *Novi Testamenti: Biblia Graece et Latina*. 5th ed. Madrid: Gráficas Cóndor, 1968.
Greenlee, J. Harold. *Nine Uncial Palimpsests of the Greek New Testament*. Studies and Documents 39. Salt Lake City: University of Utah Press, 1968.
Kenyon, Frederic G. *The Chester Beatty Biblical Papyri: Pauline Epistles: Text*. London: Emery Walker, 1936.
―――. *The Chester Beatty Biblical Papyri: Pauline Epistles: Plates*. London: Emery Walker, 1937.
―――. *The Codex Alexandrinus in Reduced Photographic Facsimile: New Testament and the Clementine Epistles*. London: British Museum, 1909.
Lake, Kirsopp, and Helen Lake. *Codex Sinaiticus Petropolitanus*. Oxford: Clarendon, 1911.
Lyon, Robert. "A Re-Examination of Codex Ephraemi Rescriptus." Ph.D. Dissertation at the University of St. Andrews, 1959.
Matthaei, Christiano F. *Epistolarum Pauli Codex Graecus cum versione Latina veteri vulgo Antehieronymiana olim Boernerianus*. Misenae: Erbstein, 1791.
Merk, Augustinus, ed. *Novum Testamentum: Graece et Latine*. 9th ed. Rome: Pontifical Biblical Institute, 1964.
Rahlfs, Alfred, ed. *Septuaginta*. 8th ed. Stuttgart: Württembergische Bibelanstalt, 1965.
Reichardt, Alexander. *Der Codex Boernerianus*. Leipzig: K. W. Hiersemann, 1909.
Sanders, Henry A. *A Third-Century Papyrus Codex of the Epistles of Paul*. Ann Arbor: University of Michigan Press, 1935.
Soden, Hermann von. *Die Schriften des Neuen Testaments in ihrer ältesten erreichbaren Textgestalt*. Göttingen: Vandenhoeck & Ruprecht, 1913.
The Textus Receptus. Edited by Lloyd. Oxford: 1873.
Tischendorf, Constantin. *Codex Claromontanus*. Leipzig: Brockhaus, 1852.
―――, ed. *Epistulae Pauli et Catholicae: fere integrae ex Libro Porphyrii Episcopi Palimpsesto*. Leipzig: J. C. Hinrichs, 1865.
―――, ed. *Novum Testamentum*. 8th ed. Leipzig: Giesecke & Devrient, 1872.
Tregelles, S. P. *The Greek New Testament*. London: Bagster, 1857-1879.
Westcott, B. F., and F. J. A. Hort, *The New Testament in the Original Greek*. Cambridge: Macmillan, 1881, 1882.

III. BOOKS AND ARTICLES

Aland, Kurt. "Bemerkungen zu den gegenwärtigen Möglichkeiten textkritischer Arbeit aus Anlass einer Untersuchung zum Cäsarea-Text der katholischen Briefe." *New Testament Studies* 17 (1970): 1-9.
―――. *Kurzgefasste Liste der griechischen Handschriften des Neuen Testaments*. Arbeiten zur neutestamentlichen Textforschung 1. Berlin: W. de Gruyter, 1963.

III. BOOKS AND ARTICLES, cont.

Aland, Kurt. "The Significance of the Papyri for N. T. Research." Pages 325–46 in *The Bible in Modern Scholarship*. Edited by J. P. Hyatt. London: Carey Kingsgate, 1966.

———. *Text und Textwert der griechischen Handschriften des Neuen Testaments. I: Die Katholischen Briefe*. Arbeiten zur neutestamentlichen Textforschung 9-11. Berlin: W. de Gruyter, 1987.

———. *Text und Textwert der griechischen Handschriften des Neuen Testaments. III: Die Apostelgeschichte*. Arbeiten zur neutestamentlichen Textforschung 20. Berlin: W. de Gruyter, 1993.

———, and Barbara Aland. *The Text of the New Testament*. 2d ed. Translated by E. Rhodes. Grand Rapids: Eerdmans, 1989.

Altaner, Berthold. *Patrologie*. 6th ed. Freiburg: Herder, 1960.

Amantos, Constantine. *Prolegomena to the History of the Byzantine Empire*. Translated by K. Johnstone. Amsterdam: A. Hakkert, 1969.

Amphoux, C.-B. "Le Texte des épîtres catholiques. Essais de classement des états de texte, préparatoires à une histoire du texte de ces épîtres." Ph.D. Dissertation at Paris-Sorbonne, 1981.

Aune, David. *The New Testament in Its Literary Environment*. Philadelphia: Westminster, 1987.

Bardy, Gustav. "Le texte de l'epître aux Romains dans le commentaire d'Origène-Rufin." *Revue biblique* 29 (1920): 229–241.

Bauer, Walter. *Orthodoxy and Heresy in Earliest Christianity*. Translated by R. Kraft and G. Krodel. London: SCM, 1971.

Bebb, J. M. "The Evidence of the Early Versions and Patristic Quotations on the Text of the Books of the New Testament." Pages 195–213 in *Studia Biblica et Ecclesiastica: Essays Chiefly in Biblical and Patristic Criticism*. Oxford: Clarendon, 1890.

Bennett, C. G. "The Cults of the Ancient Greek Cypriotes." Ph.D. Dissertation at the University of Pennsylvania, 1980.

Benoit, Père. "Réflexions sur l'Histoire du Texte Paulinien." *Revue biblique* 59 (1952): 5–22.

Betz, Hans Dieter. "Orthodoxy and Heresy in Primitive Christianity." *Interpretation* 19 (1965): 299-311.

Black, Matthew. "The Syriac New Testament in Early Patristic Tradition." Pages 263–78 in *La Bible et les Pères*. Edited by A. Benoit and P. Prigent. Paris: Presses Universitaires de France, 1971.

———. "The Syriac Versional Tradition." Pages 120–59 in Arbeiten zur neutestamentlichen Textforschung 5. Edited by K. Aland. Berlin: W. de Gruyter, 1972.

Blakely, Wayne. "Manuscript Relationships as Indicated by the Epistles of Jude and II Peter." Ph.D. Dissertation at Emory University, 1964.

Boismard, M.-E. "Critique textuelle et citations patristiques." *Revue biblique* 55 (1948): 5–34.

III. BOOKS AND ARTICLES, cont.

Boismard M.-E., and A. Lamouille. *Le texte occidentale des Actes des Apôtres: Reconstruction et réhabilitation.* Paris: Éditions recherche sur les civilisations, 1984.

Bauer, W., et al. *Greek-English Lexicon of the New Testament and Other Early Christian Literature.* 3d ed. Chicago: University of Chicago Press, 1999.

Brooks, James. *The New Testament Text of Gregory of Nyssa.* Society of Biblical Literature The New Testament in the Greek Fathers 2. Atlanta: Scholars Press, 1991.

Cameron, Averil. *The Mediterranean World in Late Antiquity (A.D. 395-600).* London: Routledge, 1993.

Carder, Muriel. "A Caesarean Text in the Catholic Epistles." *New Testament Studies* 16 (1970): 252–70.

Chadwick, Henry. *The Church in Ancient Society.* Oxford: Oxford University Press, 2001.

———. *The Early Church.* Revised edition. London: Penguin, 1993.

Cheung, Alex. *Idol Food in Corinth: Jewish Background and Pauline Legacy.* Journal for the Study of the New Testament: Supplement Series 176. Sheffield: Sheffield Academic Press, 1999.

Christ, Wilhelm von. *Geschichte der griechischen Litteratur.* 6th ed. Edited by W. Schmid and O. Stählin. Munich: C. H. Beck, 1924.

Clark, A. C. *The Acts of the Apostles.* Oxford: Clarendon, 1933.

Clark, Kenneth. "The Effect of Recent Textual Criticism upon New Testament Studies." Pages 27-50 in *The Background of the New Testament and its Eschatology.* Edited by W. D. Davies and D. Daube. Cambridge: Cambridge University Press, 1956.

Colwell, E. C. "Method in Locating a Newly-Discovered Manuscript Within the Manuscript Tradition of the Greek New Testament." Pages 26–44 in *Studies in Methodology in Textual Criticism of the New Testament.* New Testament Tools and Studies 9. Leiden: E. J. Brill, 1969.

———. "The Significance of Grouping of New Testament Manuscripts." *New Testament Studies* 4 (1958): 90.

———, and Ernest W. Tune, "The Quantitative Relationships Between MS Text-Types." Pages 25–32 in *Biblical and Patristic Studies in Memory of Robert Pierce Casey.* Edited by J. N. Birdsall and R. W. Thomson. Freiburg: Herder, 1963.

———, and Ernest W. Tune. "Variant Readings: Classification and Use." *Journal of Biblical Literature* 83 (1964): 253–61.

Dechow, Jon F. *Dogma and Mysticism in Early Christianity: Epiphanius of Cyprus and the Legacy of Origen.* North American Patristic Society, Patristic Monograph Series 13. Macon, Ga.: Mercer University Press, 1988.

Delebecque, E. "Les deux prologues des Actes des Apôtres." *Revue thomiste* 80 (1980): 628-34.

Downey, Glanville. *A History of Antioch in Syria: from Seleucus to the Arab Conquest.* Princeton: Princeton University Press, 1961.

III. BOOKS AND ARTICLES, cont.

Dummer, Jürgen. "Die Sprachkenntnisse des Epiphanius." Pages 434-35 in *Die Araber in der alten Welt*. Edited by F. Altheim and R. Stiehl. Berlin: W. de Gruyter, 1968.

Dunn, Marilyn. *The Emergence of Monasticism*. Oxford: Blackwell, 2000.

Duplacy, Jean. "Citations patristiques et critique textuelle du Nouveau Testament." *Recherches de science religieuse* 47 (1959): 391-400.

———. "Classification des états d'un texte, mathématiques et informatique: repères historiques et recherches méthodologiques." *Revue de l'histoire des religions* 5 (1975): 249-309.

———. *Études du critique textuelle du Nouveau Testament*. Bobliotheca ephemeridum theologicarum lovaniensium 78. Leuven: Leuven University Press, 1987.

———. "Histoire des manuscrits et histoire du texte du Nouveau Testament." *New Testament Studies* 12 (1965): 124–39.

Duplacy, Jean. "Le Texte 'occidental' des épîtres catholiques." *New Testament Studies* 16 (1969): 397–99.

Duruy, Victor. *History of the Middle Ages*. New York: Holt, 1891.

Ehrman, Bart D. *Didymus the Blind and the Text of the Gospels*. Society of Biblical Literature The New Testament in the Greek Fathers 1. Atlanta: Scholars Press, 1986.

———. "Methodological Developments in the Analysis and Classification of New Testament Documentary Evidence." *Novum Testamentum* 29 (1987): 22–45.

———. *The Orthodox Corruption of Scripture: The Effect of Early Christological Controversies on the Text of the New Testament*. Oxford: Oxford University Press, 1993.

———. "A Problem of Textual Circularity: The Alands on the Classification of New Testament Manuscripts." *Biblica* 70 (1989): 377–88.

———. "The Use of Group Profiles for the Classification of New Testament Documentary Evidence." *Journal of Biblical Literature* 106 (1987): 465–86.

Eldridge, Lawrence A. *The Gospel Text of Epiphanius of Salamis*. Studies and Documents 41 Salt Lake City: University of Utah Press, 1969.

Elliott, J. Keith. *The Principles and Practice of New Testament Textual Criticism: Collected Essays of G. D. Kilpatrick*. Bibliotheca ephemeridum theologicarum lovaniensium 96. Louvain: Louvain University Press, 1990.

———. "Thoroughgoing Eclecticism in New Testament Textual Criticism." Pages 321-335 in *The Text of the New Testament in Contemporary Research: A Volume in Honor of Bruce M. Metzger*. Edited by B. Ehrman and M. Holmes. Grand Rapids: Eerdmans, 1995

Elliott, W. J. "The Need for an Accurate and Comprehensive Collation of all Known Greek NT Manuscripts." Pages 137–43 in *Studies in New Testament Language and Text*. Novum Testamentum Supplement 44. Edited by J. K. Elliott. Leiden: Brill, 1976.

III. BOOKS AND ARTICLES, cont.

Epp, Eldon J. "The Claremont Profile-Method for Grouping New Testament Minuscule Manuscripts." Pages 27–38 in *Studies in the History and Text of the New Testament*. Edited by B. Daniels and M. J. Suggs. Studies and Documents 29. Salt Lake City: University of Utah Press, 1967.

———. "The Eclectic Method in New Testament Textual Criticism: Solution or Symptom?" Pages 141-173 in *Studies in the Theory and Method of New Testament Textual Criticism*. Edited by G. Fee and E. Epp. Grand Rapids: Eerdmans, 1993.

———. "New Testament Textual Criticism, Past, Present, and Future." *Harvard Theological Review* 82 (1989): 213-29.

———. "Toward the Clarification of the Term 'Textual Variant.'" Pages 153–73 in *Studies in New Testament Text and Language: Essays in Honour of George D. Kilpatrick*. Edited by J. K. Elliott. Leiden: Brill, 1976.

——— and G. W. MacRae, eds. *The New Testament and Its Modern Interpreters*. Atlanta: Scholars Press, 1989.

Ericksson, Anders. *Traditions as Rhetorical Proof: Pauline Argumentation in 1 Corinthians*. Coniectanea biblica: New Testament Series 29. Stockholm: Almqvist & Wiksesll, 1998.

Fee, Gordon D. "Codex Sinaiticus in the Gospel of John: A Contribution to Methodology in Establishing Textual Relationships." *New Testament Studies* 15 (1968): 23–44.

———. *The First Epistle to the Corinthians*. Grand Rapids: Eerdmans, 1987.

———. "On the Types, Classification, and Presentation in Textual Variation." Pages 62–79 in *Studies in the Theory and Method of New Testament Textual Criticism*. Edited by E. Epp and G. Fee. Studies and Documents 45. Grand Rapids: Eerdmans, 1993.

———. *Papyrus Bodmer II ($\mathfrak{P}^{66}$): Its Textual Relationships and Scribal Characteristics*. Studies and Documents 34. Salt Lake City: University of Utah Press, 1968.

———. "$\mathfrak{P}^{75}$, $\mathfrak{P}^{66}$ and Origen: The Myth of Early Textual Recension in Alexandria." Pages 19–45 in *New Dimensions in New Testament Study*. Edited by R. Longenecker and M. Tenney. Grand Rapids: Zondervan, 1974.

———. Review of Lawrence Eldridge, *The Gospel Text of Epiphanius of Salamis*. *Journal of Biblical Literature* 90 (1971): 368-370.

———. "The Text of John in *The Jerusalem Bible*: A Critique of the Use of Patristic Citations in New Testament Textual Criticism." *Journal of Biblical Literature* 90 (1971): 169.

———. "The Text of John in Origen and Cyril of Alexandria: A Contribution to Methodology in the Recovery and Analysis of Patristic Citations." *Biblica* 52 (1971): 357-94.

———. "The Use of Greek Patristic Citations in New Testament Textual Criticism." Pages 344-359 in *Studies in the Theory and Method of New Testament Textual Criticism*. Studies and Documents 45. Edited by G. Fee and E. Epp. Grand Rapids: Eerdmans, 1993.

III. BOOKS AND ARTICLES, cont.

Fee, Gordon D. "The Use of the Greek Fathers for New Testament Textual Criticism." Pages 191-207 in *The Text of the New Testament in Contemporary Research*. Studies and Documents 46. Edited by B. Ehrman and M. Holmes. Grand Rapids: Eerdmans, 1995.

Frede, Hermann J. "Bibelzitate bei Kirchenvätern." Pages 79–96 in *La Bible et les Pères*. Paris: Presses Universitaires de France, 1971.

Gallagher, J. Tim. "A Study of von Soden's H-Text in the Catholic Epistles." *Andrews University Seminary Studies* 8 (1970): 97-119

Geer, Thomas C., Jr. "An Investigation of a Select Group of So-called Western Cursives in Acts." Ph.D Dissertation at Boston University, 1985.

———. "Codex 1739 in Acts and Its Relationship to Manuscripts 945 and 1891." *Biblica* 69 (1988): 31-42.

———. *Family 1739 in Acts*. Society of Biblical Literature Monograph Series 48. Atlanta: Scholars Press, 1994.

———. "The Presence and Significance of Lucanisms in the 'Western' Text of Acts." *Journal for the Study of the New Testament* 39 (1990): 59-76.

———. "The Text of Acts in Epiphanius of Salamis." M.Th. Thesis, Harding Graduate School of Religion, 1980.

———. "The Two Faces of Codex 33 in Acts." *Novum Testamentum* 31 (1989): 39-47.

Grant, Robert M. "The Citation of Patristic Evidence in an Apparatus Criticus." Pages 117-24 in *New Testament Manuscript Studies*. Edited by M. Parvis and A. Wikgren. Chicago: University of Chicago Press, 1950.

Greenlee, J. Harold. *Introduction to New Testament Textual Criticism*. 2d ed. Grand Rapids: Eerdmans, 1964.

Gregory, Caspar R. *Vorschläge für eine kritische Ausgabe des griechischen Neuen Testament*. Leipzig: J. C. Hinrichs, 1911.

Griggs, C. W. *Early Egyptian Christianity from its Origins to 451 C.E.* Coptic Studies 2. Leiden: Brill, 1990.

Haenchen, Ernst. *The Acts of the Apostles*. Philadelphia: Westminster, 1971.

———. "Zum Text der Apostelgeschichte." *Zeitschrift für Theologie und Kirche* 54 (1957): 54-55.

Hall, Stuart. *Doctrine and Practice in the Early Church*. London: SPCK, 1991.

Hannah, Darrell. *The Text of 1 Corinthians in the Writings of Origen*. Society of Biblical Literature The New Testament in the Greek Fathers 4. Atlanta: Scholars Press, 1997.

Harnack, Adolf von. *Marcion: Das Evangelium vom fremden Gott*. Texte und Untersuchungen 45. Leipzig: Hinrichs, 1921.

Harvey, W. W. *Sancti Irenaei*. Cambridge: Cambridge University Press, 1857.

Hatch, W. H. P. "On the Relationship of Codex Augiensis and Codex Boernerianus of the Pauline Epistles." *Harvard Studies in Classical Philology* 60 (1951): 187-99.

Holl, Karl. *Gesammelte Aufsätze zur Kirchengeschichte II*. Tübingen: J. C. B Mohr, 1928.

III. BOOKS AND ARTICLES, cont.

Holmes, Michael. "Reasoned Eclecticism in New Testament Textual Criticism." Pages 336-360 in *The Text of the New Testament in Contemporary Research*. Studies and Documents 46. Edited by B. Ehrman and M. Holmes. Grand Rapids: Eerdmans, 1995.

Hönnecke, Gustav. *Das Judenchristentum in Ersten und Zweiten Jahrhundert*. Berlin: Twowitzsch , 1908.

Horrell, David. *The Social Ethos of the Corinthian Correspondence*. Edinburgh: T&T Clark, 1996.

Hurtado, Larry. *Text-Critical Methodology and the Pre-Caesarean Text*. Grand Rapids: Eerdmans, 1981.

Hutton, E. A. *An Atlas of Textual Criticism*. Cambridge: Cambridge University Press, 1911.

Jaubert, Annie. *The Date of the Last Supper: The Biblical Calendar and Christian Liturgy*. Staten Island, NY: Alba House, 1965.

Johnstone, Barbara. *Discourse Analysis*. Oxford: Blackwell, 2002.

Jones, A. H. M. *The Later Roman Empire, 284–602: A Social, Economic and Administrative Survey*. Oxford: Blackwell, 1964.

Karlin-Hayter, P. "Activity of the Bishop of Constantinople Outside his *Paroikia* Between 381 and 451." Pages 179-88 in *ΚΑΘΗΓΗΤΡΙΑ: Essays presented to Joan Hussey*. Edited by J. Chrysostomides. Camberley, Surrey: Porphyrogenitus, 1988.

Kenyon, F. G. *Handbook to the Textual Criticism of the New Testament*. London: Macmillan, 1901.

Klijn, A. F. J. "In Search of the Original Text of Acts." Pages 103-10 in *Studies in Luke-Acts: Essays Presented in Honor of Paul Schubert*. Edited by L. Keck and J. L. Martyn. Nashville: Abingdon, 1966.

Klostermann, August. *Probleme im Aposteltexte neu erörtert*. Gotha: Friedrich Undreas Berthes, 1883.

Kubo, Sakae. "A Comparative Study of $\mathfrak{P}^{74}$ and Codex Vaticanus." Ph.D. Dissertation at the University of Chicago, 1964.

———. *$\mathfrak{P}^{72}$ and Codex Vaticanus*. Studies and Documents 27. Salt Lake City: University of Utah Press, 1965.

Kvalheim, O. M. "A Data-Analytical Examination of the Claremont Profile Method for Classifying and Evaluating Manuscript Evidence." *Symbolae Osloenses* 63 (1988): 133-44.

Lagrange, M.-J. *Introduction a l'etude du nouveau testament, 2. critique textuelle*. 2d ed. Paris: Librairie Lecoffre, 1935.

Layton, Bentley. "The Riddle of the Thunder." Pages 37-54 in *Nag Hammadi, Gnosticism, and Early Christianity*. Edited by C. Hedrick and R. Hodgson. Peabody, Mass.: Hendrickson, 1986.

Lietzmann, Hans. *Die Briefe des Apostels Paulus*. Handbuch zum Neuen Testament 3.1. Tübingen: J. C. B. Mohr, 1910.

Louth, A. *The Origins of the Christian Mystical Tradition: From Plato to Denys*. Oxford: Oxford University Press, 1981.

III. BOOKS AND ARTICLES, cont.

Loofs, Friedrich. *Paulus von Samosata.* Texte und Untersuchungen 24.5. Leipzig: J. C. Hinrichs, 1924.
Malina, Bruce. *The Palestinian Manna Tradition.* Leiden: Brill, 1968.
Mango, Cyril. *Byzantium: The Empire of New Rome.* New York: C. Scribner's Sons, 1980.
Martini, Carlo. "Is There a Late Alexandrian Text of the Gospels?" *New Testament Studies* 24 (1978): 285–96.
Mees, Michael. *Die Zitate aus dem Neuen Testament bei Clemens von Alexandrien.* Rome: Istituto de Letteratura Cristiana Antica dell' Universita Bari, 1970.
Metzger, Bruce M. "The Caesarean Text of the Gospels." Pages 42-72 in *Chapters in the History of New Testament Textual Study.* New Testament Tools and Studies 4. Grand Rapids: Eerdmans, 1963.
———. "Explicit References in the Works of Origen to Variant Readings in New Testament Manuscripts." Pages 78-95 in *Biblical and Patristic Studies in Memory of Robert Pierce Casey.* Edited by J. N. Birdsall and R. W. Thompson. Freiburg: Herder, 1963.
———. "Patristic Evidence and the Textual Tradition of the New Testment." *New Testament Studies* 18 (1972): 398–99.
———. *Studies in Methodology in Textual Criticism of the New Testament.* New Testament Tools and Studies 9. Leiden: Brill, 1969.
———. "The Practice of Textual Criticism Among the Church Fathers," *Studia Patristica XII.* Pages 340-49 in Texte und Untersuchungen 115. Berlin: Akademie Verlag, 1975.
———. *The Text of the New Testament: Its Transmission, Corruption, and Restoration.* 3d ed. Oxford: Oxford University Press, 1992.
———. *A Textual Commentary on the Greek New Testament.* 2d edition. New York: United Bible Societies, 1994.
Meyendorff, John. *Byzantine Theology: Historical Trends and Doctrinal Themes.* New York: Fordham University Press, 1974.
Mitford, T. B. "Some New Inscriptions from Early Christian Cyprus," *Byzantion* 20 (1950): 105-75.
Morrill, Bruce. "The Classification of the Greek Manuscripts of 1 Corinthians." M.A. Thesis, Harding Graduate School of Religion, 1981.
Moutsoulas, E. "La tradition manuscrite de l'oeuvre d'Epiphane de Salamine *De mensuris et ponderibus.*" Pages 429–40 in *Texte und Textkritik.* Edited by J. Dummer. Berlin: Akademie-Verlag, 1987.
Mullen, Roderic L. *The New Testament Text of Cyril of Jerusalem.* Society of Biblical Literature The New Testament in the Greek Fathers 7. Atlanta: Scholars Press, 1997.
Munro, J. A. R., and H. A. Tubbs. "Excavations in Cyprus, 1890: The Third Season's Work. Salamis." *Journal of Hellenic Studies* 12 (1891): 59–198.
Murphy, Harold. "'Eusebius' New Testament Text in the *Demonstratio Evangelica.*" *Journal of Biblical Literature* 78 (1954): 152–68.
Nautin, Pierre. "Épiphane de Salamine." *Dictionnaire d'histoire et de géographie* 15 (1963): 617–31.

III. BOOKS AND ARTICLES, cont.

Nestle, Eberhard. *Einführung in das griechische Neue Testament*. Göttingen: Vandenhoeck und Ruprecht, 1899.

Norwich, John Julius. *Byzantium: The Early Centuries*. New York: A. Knopf, 1989.

Osburn, Carroll D. "The Text of 1 Corinthians 10:9." Pages 201–12 in *New Testament Textual Criticism: Essays in Honour of Bruce M. Metzger*. Edited by E. Epp & G. Fee. Oxford: Clarendon, 1981.

———. "The Text of the Pauline Epistles in Epiphanius of Salamis." Ph.D. Dissertation at the University of St. Andrews, 1974.

———. "The Text of the Pauline Epistles in Hippolytus of Rome." *Second Century* 2 (1982): 97–124.

Paulsen, H. "Schisma und Häresie, Untersuchungen zu 1 Kor. 11, 18.19." *Zeitschrift für Theologie und Kirche* 79 (1982): 180–83.

Pitra, J. B. *Analecta sacra spicilegio solesmensi parata*. Paris: Roger et Chernowitz, 1852-58.

Porter, Stanley, ed. *Handbook of Classical Rhetoric in the Hellenistic Period, 330 B.C.– A.D. 400*. Leiden: Brill, 1997.

Pourkier, Aline. *L'hérésiologie chez Épiphane de Salamine*. Convivium assisiense 4. Paris: Beauchesne, 1992.

Quasten, Johannes. *Patrology*. Utrecht: Spectrum, 1966.

Richards, W. Larry. *The Classification of the Greek Manuscripts of the Johannine Epistles*. Society of Biblical Literature Dissertation Series 35. Missoula, Mont.: Scholars Press, 1977.

———. "Gregory 1175: Alexandrian or Byzantine in the Catholic Epistles?" *Andrews University Seminar Studies* 21 (1983): 155-68.

Rolando, Giovanni, and Tyndarus Caragliano. "Ricostruzione Teologico-Critica del Testo Latino del Vangelo di S. Luca Usato da S. Ambrogio." *Biblica* 26 (1945): 238–276.

———. "Ricostruzione Teologico-Critica del Testo Latino del Vangelo di S. Luca Usato da S. Ambrogio." *Biblica* 27 (1946): 3–17, 30-64, 210–240.

Ropes, James Hardy. "The Text of Acts." *The Beginnings of Christianity. Part I. The Acts of the Apostles*. Edited by F. Foakes Jackson and K. Lake. London: Macmillan, 1926.

Routh, M. J. *Reliquiae Sacrae*. 2d ed. Oxford: Oxford University Press, 1846.

Sanday, W., and C. H. Turner. *Nouum Testamentum S. Irenaei*. Oxford: Oxford University Press, 1923.

Schmidtke, A. *Neue Fragmente und Untersuchungen zu den Judenchristlichen Evangelien: Ein Beitrag zur Literatur und Geschichte des Judenchristen*. Texte und Untersuchungen 37.1. Leipzig: J. C. Hinrichs, 1911.

Schneemelcher, W. "Epiphanius von Salamis." *Reallexikon für Antike und Christentum* 5 (1962): 909-27.

Schwartz, Eduard. *Eine fingierte Korrespondenz mit Paulus dem Samosatener*. München: Bayerische Akademie der Wissenschaften, 1927.

———. *Eusebius Werke*. Leipzig: J. C. Hinrichs, 1903.

III. BOOKS AND ARTICLES, cont

Scrivener, F. H. A. *A Plain Introduction to the Criticism of the New Testament*. 3d ed. Cambridge: Deighton, Bell, 1883.

Stowers, Stanley. *Letter Writing in Greco-Roman Antiquity*. Philadelphia: Westminster, 1986.

Strange, W. A. *The Problem of the Text of Acts*. Society for New Testament Studies Monograph Series 71. Cambridge: Cambridge University Press, 1992.

Sturz, Harry A. *The Byzantine Text-Type and New Testament Textual Criticism*. Nashville: T. Nelson, 1984.

Suggs, M. Jack. "The New Testament Text of Eusebius of Caesarea." Ph.D. Dissertation at Duke University. 1954.

———. "The Use of Patristic Evidence in the Search for a Primitive New Testament Text." *New Testament Studies* 4 (1958): 139-47.

Thomas, Joseph. *Le Mouvement Baptiste en Palestine et Syrie (150 av. J.-C. -300 ap. J.-C.)*. Gembloux: J. Duculot, 1935.

Vaganay, Leon. *An Introduction to New Testament Textual Criticism*. 2d ed. Revised by C.-B. Amphoux. Translated by J. Heimerdinger. Cambridge: Cambridge University Press, 1982.

Wachtel, Klaus. *Der Byzantinische Text der Katholischen Briefe*. Arbeiten zur neutestamentlichen Textforschung 24. Berlin: W. de Gruyter, 1995.

Weischer, B. M. "Die ursprüngliche nikänische Form des ersten Glaubenssymbols im *Ancyrotos* des Epiphanios von Salamis." *Theologie und Philosophie* 53 (1978): 407–14.

White, H.G. Evelyn. *The Monasteries of the Wâdi'n Natrun, 2: The History of the Monasteries of Nitria and of Scetis*. Edited by W. Hanser. New York: Metropolitan Museum of Art, 1932.

Willard, L. Charles. "A Critical Study of the Euthalian Apparatus." Ph.D. Dissertation at Yale University, 1970.

Wisse, Frederik. *The Profile Method for Classification and Evaluation of Manuscript Evidence*. Studies and Documents 44. Grand Rapids: Eerdmans, 1982.

Witherington III, Ben. *Conflict in Community in Corinth: A Socio-Rhetorical Commentary on 1 and 2 Corinthians*. Grand Rapids: Eerdmans, 1995.

Zahn, Theodor. "Eine neue Quelle für die Textgeschichte des Neuen Testaments." *Theologisches Literaturblatt* (1899): 180.

Zuntz, Günther. *The Text of the Epistles: A Disquisition Upon the Corpus Paulinum*. London: Oxford University Press, 1953.

www.ingramcontent.com/pod-product-compliance
Lightning Source LLC
Chambersburg PA
CBHW031707230426
43668CB00006B/140